Spiritual Democracy

Spiritual Democracy

The Wisdom of Early American
Visionaries for the Journey Forward

STEVEN B. HERRMANN

Foreword by John Beebe

North Atlantic Books
Berkeley, California

North Atlantic Books
P.O. Box 12327
Berkeley, California 94712

Cover art: *Our Banner in the Sky* by Frederic Edwin Church (1861), oil on paper,
    by permission of Fine Arts Museums of San Francisco
Cover and book design by Mary Ann Casler

Printed in the United States of America

Spiritual Democracy: The Wisdom of Early American Visionaries for the Journey Forward is sponsored and published by the Society for the Study of Native Arts and Sciences (dba North Atlantic Books), an educational nonprofit based in Berkeley, California, that collaborates with partners to develop cross-cultural perspectives, nurture holistic views of art, science, the humanities, and healing, and seed personal and global transformation by publishing work on the relationship of body, spirit, and nature.

North Atlantic Books' publications are available through most bookstores. For further information, visit our website at www.northatlanticbooks.com or call 800–733–3000.

Library of Congress Cataloging-in-Publication Data
Herrmann, Steven B., author.
  Spiritual democracy : the wisdom of early American visionaries for the journey forward /
Steven B. Herrmann ; foreword by John Beebe.
        pages cm.— (Sacred activism)
ISBN 978–1–58394–833–0 (paperback)
  1. American poetry—19th century—History and criticism. 2. Vision in literature.
3. Whitman, Walt, 1819–1892—Criticism and interpretation. 4. Melville, Herman,
1819–1891—Criticism and interpretation. 5. Dickinson, Emily, 1830–1886—Criticism
and interpretation. 6. Forecasting in literature. 7. Psychology and literature. I. Title.
PS310.V57H47 2014
811'.309—dc23   2014007227

1 2 3 4 5 6 7 8 9 SHERIDAN 18 17 16 15 14

Printed on recycled paper

ACKNOWLEDGMENTS

The seeds for this book were planted when I was invited to submit a review, "Murray Stein: The Transformative Image," to the *San Francisco Jung Institute Library Journal* in 1998. Stein's books helped me see a miraculous interconnection between transformations of the self in individuals and deep structural change in political and social collectivities. By that time, I had written a lengthy manuscript on the poetry of Emily Dickinson and Walt Whitman, and I knew that Spiritual Democracy is at the center and heart of Whitman's vision of global transformation. I subsequently embarked upon a four-year sea voyage, with Herman Melville's collected writings in my attaché case and completed a four hundred-page manuscript on his works by the time I came back to the main shore. In terms of the antecedents of my research into the field of American literary studies, it all began with my conversations with William Everson and Donald Sandner on the subject of shamanism in American poetry in 1991 and moved from there to my writing on Dickinson in 1995, and then Whitman in 1996, and Melville between 1998 and 2002. Then, by happenstance, I had a casual conversation with Stein at a Jungian conference in 2002, about what I was seeing in Melville's *Moby Dick* as an example of the kinds of large metamorphoses of the self that were beginning to happen all around, in individuals and collectivities, transnationally in post-9/11 America and the world. Stein, the International Association for Analytical Psychology president at that time, graciously asked me to write up my thoughts in a paper, so he could post them on the IAAP website. Naturally, this led to the penning of the 2003 essay, "Melville's Vision of

Evil," which appeared in expanded form at iaap.org in 2005 and is still available online as a download under "articles." My 2003 Melville essay was then picked up by Thomas Singer and this led to our coteaching a workshop together in 2004 at San Francisco Jung Institute's Extended Education program, entitled "Melville's Moby Dick/Islam and the West." In the same year, I wrote my paper, "The Cultural Complex in Walt Whitman," and I was asked to present it at the C. G. Jung Institute of Chicago, in 2005, which happened to be the one hundred fiftieth anniversary of the publication of the first edition of *Leaves of Grass.*

In the summer of 2008, I gave a talk at the IAAP-International Association for Jungian Scholars (IAJS) Conference held at the ETH, Zurich, Switzerland. This paper was later published by Murray Stein, under the title "The Emergence of Moby Dick in the Dreams of a Five-Year-Old Boy." It was rapidly becoming apparent to me that the field of analytical psychology was focusing increasingly on political issues, and from the responses I was getting to my work on American poetry, it was self-evident that the myths Whitman and Melville created nearly one hundred fifty years ago were speaking directly to depth-psychotherapists and scholars of a Jungian persuasion, who were all engaged together on a common search for ways to teach Jung that might be relevant not only to individual analysis, but to international politics, religious studies, and economics in our "global village."

Following the inner line of these developments, in 2010, I published my first book, *William Everson: The Shaman's Call.* Not long after my book's release, I received a glowing letter of congratulations from Anglican priest, Matthew Fox, which began a four-year friendship and regular lunch meetings at Whole Foods, in Oakland, and where we discussed everything under the sun. At this juncture, I got right to work on my second book, published in 2011, *Walt Whitman: Shamanism, Spiritual Democracy, and the World Soul.*

It became apparent to me that the idea of Spiritual Democracy was capturing people's attention, and I began presenting papers in various places of interest, such as to the Washington Friends of Walt Whitman at the home of my comrade, Neil Richardson; the Unitarian-Universalist Church of Kensington, with discussant Matthew Fox; and at International House (I-House) at UC Berkeley. What better place to promote my first book on Spiritual Democracy than at a Unitarian Church, followed by a UC Campus! By the time I spoke at UCB, on February 10, the Arab Spring was in full swing. There seemed to be a line of evolution linking all of these events together in time.

The central idea for this book, however, and the actual process of releasing the nuclear core of energy from Whitman's big notion really began with my delving deeply into the vistas of Alexander von Humboldt's volume of *Cosmos*, to see the star of my own Muse and her destiny more clearly than ever before. Matthew Fox was a big support at this time, and I was having monthly coffee chats, at my home, with my first English professor and longtime friend, Clark McKowen. I decided to write this book as I became aware that Spiritual Democracy can inspire and motivate people to think about ways to take concrete action in the world through writing. I saw that the American poets of the nineteenth century were ahead of their times by over one hundred fifty years, and their visions of Spiritual Democracy are antecedents to the sweeping cultural changes we are seeing at an international level, since 9/11/01 and the Arab Spring. People are asking for religious liberty, they are asking for equality, they are asking for democracy. Democracy was being called for in Middle East, LGBT people were asking for equal marriage rights, and people from many nations of the world were beginning to insist on change everywhere. It seemed common sense that religious equality may be the next step in the movement toward global peace. We have Walt Whitman to thank for being the first to clearly articulate this, along with his contemporaries, Herman Melville and Emily Dickinson.

I want to especially thank my old friend and mentor William Everson for awakening me to the calling to vocation. I worked as Bill's teaching assistant at UCSC from 1980 to 1981, and I am eternally grateful to him for transmitting to me a felt sense of the importance of vocation in the life of a modern California poet. In fact, so many people supported my ideas over the past two decades that I fear I might omit to mention them here, so I want take a moment to heartily thank Alan Campo, Sam Kimbles, Thomas Singer, Dyane Sherwood, Dennis Turner, Steven Joseph, Neil Kostick, Jean Kirsch, and Thomas Kirsch for their confidence in my vocation as a Jungian. I want to mention the support of my son, Immanuel, and my wife, Lori, for her careful reading of my manuscript, for her helpful editorial feedback and comments, and undivided love and support.

With regards to the book's focus on gender politics, same-sex marriage, integrity, and the role of the trickster in American literature, however, and for his superb editorial assistance over the last nineteen years, I want say a big tribute of thanks to John Beebe, without whom this book never could have been born. John has been behind my work since 1995, and has never wavered for a moment in his belief in me. It is for such reasons and more that I asked him to write a foreword for this volume.

Finally, there is developmental editor Cindy Collins-Taylor, to thank for her great work on this manuscript and equal gratitude and warmth to all the people at North Atlantic Books, Doug Reil, Emily Boyd, and Louis Swaim for their guidance and suggestions throughout the publication process, Elizabeth Kennedy for her final copyediting, and Mary Ann Casler for her fabulous design. I really want to acknowledge and heartily thank project editor Louis Swaim, moreover, for his inspiration during the final stages of the manuscript's writing. In a letter exchange, Louis asked me if I had considered Whitman's seven-page poem "To The Sayers of Words," which he rightly saw as being central to the method of "Vocalism" and therefore the practice of Spiritual Democracy. Upon reading this poem, I immediately recognized its centrality, and these reflections now form a sort of nucleus of Walt's big idea.

I am dedicating this book to Matthew Fox. It was my talks with Matthew before and after the emergence of the Arab Revolution (and my talks with my wife Lori) that led me to write this book. Matthew provided the spark of inspiration to chart out my own vision of Western spirituality and relate it to American poetry and Jungian psychology. And of course, this series' visionary and teacher of sacred activism, Andrew Harvey, deserves to be heartily thanked. I am honored to have been invited to be a part, with many of the authors who are contributing to his vision, in this group effort. I am grateful, Andrew, for your leadership in this call to action.

CONTENTS

PART 3

FOREWORD

Everyone who so much as turns the pages of *Leaves of Grass* realizes that Walt Whitman had a crush on America. That fact no longer embarrasses those who continue to read him. We realize, in our psychological time, that immature emotional material has often been the springboard for a far-diving poetic imagination. Nevertheless, these days, readers who have civilized themselves through cinema more often gravitate toward *Moby Dick*, grateful that Whitman's compatriot and close contemporary Herman Melville had the noir vision in the midst of the same nineteenth century, to home in on a whaling ship as the mise-en-scène for his more ambivalent survey of American ambition. What most readers of both of these classic American authors ignore, however, is the degree to which Whitman's idealism and Melville's irony shared prophetic concern for the prospects of America itself.

America, from its first days as a new nation, had held the promise of a New Jerusalem in which Jewish, Christian, and Muslim interpretations of monotheism could inform freedom of religion with the sense of a shared spirit. But as this uniting spirit was progressively tested throughout the nineteenth century with the lingering problem of slavery, the looming longing for women's emancipation, and the near-phantomatic presence of what the author of the present book calls "bi-erotic libido" (the homoerotic side of which is so modernly manifest in the self-revealing narratives of Whitman and Melville), it became evident that an abstract image of America as a "land of freedom" was not enough to satisfy the longings of actual Americans. They wanted to be able to exercise their birthright in ways unanticipated by America's Founding Fathers. The kind of self-determination Americans began to demand in the nineteenth century required something else. That something was a common acceptance of the spiritual side of democracy. This is the value that unites Whitman and Melville, as Steven Herrmann brilliantly argues in this book.

Understanding exactly what they proposed to a world audience ready to embrace the potential of America, but short on the particulars of what that might consist of, is made easier for the reader by the poise of Herrmann's prose, which always manages to balance the load of the information he imparts. A poet himself, he knows that poets do not take the philosophies they argue lightly and that we cannot understand their meanings if we ignore their content and concentrate only on their styles. In like manner, we have to understand Spiritual Democracy in order to appreciate Whitman's and Melville's passion for the incomplete psychological project they witnessed in antebellum America.

Spiritual Democracy, in Herrmann's considered view, is not just a transcendentalist addendum to the American Constitution, any more than the oeuvres of Whitman and Melville are footnotes providing the background to Lincoln's Gettysburg Address. It was an American attempt, led by poets, here as always the "unacknowledged legislators of the world," to establish a political and moral philosophy that could inform the new Cosmos that Humboldt had revealed to the world through his explorations of all the Americas. It was the psychological equivalent of the spatial freedom that Lewis and Clark had verified as the new country's manifest destiny. Spiritual Democracy was not only Jeffersonian in its continent-embracing sweep, it was Jacksonian in its populist appeal to those who would like to inhabit and enjoy the spread of ideas that the New Jerusalem had become.

Both Whitman and Melville dreamed of a sexually and geographically liberated continent where authoritarian quests to impose Ahab-like solutions were doomed to fail. In our present, pluralistic age, this vision is both close yet maddeningly far. If, as Jung argued, one task of responsible living is to take up the uncompleted projects of the dead, this book can help us to see that the template for what we need has already been prepared for us by two poets whose legacy we have yet to unpack. Their vision of a shared freedom of the psyche, though first published on American soil, is one the whole world would be wise to examine anew. It would be a pity if those of us into whose hands this book has fortunately fallen did not avail ourselves of the opportunity to study that vision in detail, when it has been so painstakingly illuminated for us in the pages that follow.

John Beebe, author of *Integrity in Depth*

INTRODUCTION

This is a book about literary innovator Walt Whitman's vision: worldwide Spiritual Democracy. The principles of Spiritual Democracy are not necessarily unique to America, although the vision's uniqueness is American in the sense that it took an evolution of ideas to bring it to birth in a nation of many nations that refused to adhere to any one religion in its proclamation of a new notion of God.[1]

We as individuals and as humanity suffer from a lack of connection to other people, religious and political strife, alienation from nature and its rhythms, militarism, and corporate hegemony, resulting in environmental destruction; the decimation of many species of wildlife, forests, and wildflowers; the poisoning of our rivers, seas, and air; and climate change, to the point where our very survival as a species is in question. Adopting the big idea of Spiritual Democracy, the realization of the oneness of humanity with the universe and all its forces, can help people feel joy, peace, and interconnectedness on an individual basis. It can also inspire us to undertake sacred activism, the channeling of such forces into callings that are compassionating, just, and of equitable heart and conscience, and give us some tools to start solving some of these grave global problems, while uniting people on the planet.

The equality of the whole human race, without any special privileges given to one religion, nation, or ethnicity over another, and vouchsafed with equal freedoms and liberties to every member of the global community regardless of color, gender, or sexual orientation, can be realized by anyone through an experience of oneness with nature and its miraculous energies. The miracle of divinity in nature is a foundation stone of all religions, and its origins are cosmic. The marvel of human consciousness reaches the farthest depths of inner and outer space and emerges through the ground of being, and highest spiritual vistas inside each individual, as a vocation to live by.[2] The ability to tap into this vitalizing source of equalizing, vocational energy and transmit a sense of profound purpose and peace, when natural changes in consciousness have set in and are channeled effectively through sacred actions via the speech center, is a primary human need for mirroring and understanding through verbal communication. This book offers to meet a basic need: a psychological and literary view of some practical methodologies. These methods may be of pragmatic use to bring about global transformation and holy work through language experiments that can be undertaken by anyone, anywhere, during any time in history. Like no other function of the human being, language makes sacred work instantaneously possible. A study into the origins of our national poetry can offer tips, therefore, for applying Whitman's powerful notion, through a study of the roots of American English that gave his notion agency. Whitman latched onto the newest developments in science, literature, philosophy, and modern astronomy to make his notion of religious equality clear for us; yet, his primary calling to sacred activism was mythopoetic.[3]

In the mid-nineteenth century, the vehicle of poetry became a primary catalyst for a new revelation of the sacred and an impetus to put an end, once and for all, to the long march of theological wars, dictatorships, and oppressive regimes that had plagued the world for centuries. A blend of new ideas about science, nature, and religion were most clearly articulated in poetic form through America's greatest literary giants in the era spanning 1844 to 1885. Writers such as Walt Whitman, Emily Dickinson, and Herman Melville believed that a new unity and equality among mankind could be accomplished in part by putting people in harmony with the rhythms of nature.

At this time, American writers' focus on these restorative properties of nature, as well as the transcendent power of the human soul and the majesty of the natural forms in the universe, intertwined with the blossoming democracy of a young, raucous country. The age's accompanying burst of scientific knowledge, exemplified by the earth-shaking publication of books including Charles Darwin's masterwork *On the Origin of Species* and Prussian naturalist and geographer Alexander von Humboldt's five-volume *Cosmos: A Sketch of the Physical Description of the Universe*, melded and merged, particularly in the mind of Whitman, who also brought a strong spirituality into the mix.

The three poets—Whitman, Dickinson, and Melville—all came to separate realizations that the time had arrived for the world to develop a transnational spiritual outlook. Religious equality thus became the key.

Taking this empirical vision forward, Whitman conceived his Big Idea—the future of religion as a movement to bring about a truly democratic spirituality. Spiritual synthesis, which became known as the "Science of God," is contained in his notion of a *Deus Quadriune*—the combination of all religions in a one-world brotherhood and sisterhood of cosmic relatedness that exists in each of us. This idea of the unity of the human race is expressed most clearly by the founding forefathers in the term e pluribus unum, "out of many, one."[4] A quintessential American, Whitman felt it was his vocation to answer this call for a new religion in America. He called his universal vision *Spiritual Democracy*.

Whitman's passion, Spiritual Democracy, can be viewed as a dynamic action or effect of the cosmos and psyche, operating through American poetry and the world soul. This numinous factor—the self as a collective archetypal reality of unity and totality coursing through the unconscious—gripped Walt Whitman, and he became its seminal poet.[5]

Spiritual Democracy embraces a notion of God in Nature, a simple way of saying that we all come from God. Thus, Spiritual Democracy is the simple recognition of God in each person's nature—a truly democratic notion. As we all come from nature, we are all carriers of divinity. Therefore, Spiritual Democracy is the science of a God that must by necessity begin and end with nature—and this means our *inner* nature as well as our *outer* nature.

A contemplation of the psyche based on empirical knowledge rests upon the facts registered by science. God, in all of its rich variety, is known through direct experience. This includes those who are not sure whether there is a God, but can nevertheless connect with an experience of something meaningful or sacred in her own life. It took a mind like that of Walt Whitman to treat the creeds or various schools of religion as manifestations of God. To the question *What religion is the most universal?*, Whitman answered: all are equals.

Through his work, Whitman spoke equally to all religions across the globe. Such a unitary vision of God has its roots in Native American shamanism. It is out of this foundation that a nascent form of Spiritual Democracy was first transmitted to Benjamin Franklin and the founding fathers by way of a transcendent notion, *Kaianerekowa*, the Great Law of Peace, which bound the nations of the Iroquois Confederacy together in a form of participatory democracy.[6] No national God-images are present in the writing of the U.S. Constitution. There is one reference in the Declaration of Independence that reflects the transnational notion of God that Thomas Jefferson preserved from his discussions with the founding fathers. They referred to it as *Nature's God*.[7]

In formulating his new religion, Whitman drew upon the principles of the U.S. Constitution. At its foreground are ideas of equal rights for everyone, justice, happiness for the collectivity, and, especially, religious liberty—spiritual freedom for all. The idea of Spiritual Democracy that forms the backbone of his religious vision was latent, he believed, in the U.S. Constitution and the debates by the founding fathers, who insisted on the firm separation of church and state, an argument that had been going on since the beginning of the Republic.

Whitman's grand idea is intrinsically bound with the greatest ideals of the young nation. If all men (and, ultimately, all women) truly are created equal, then an American spiritual vision must incorporate an "isness"—a state of elemental existence that excludes no one. It must *equalize* religion.

Whitman expressed this concept succinctly in his famous poem, "Song of Myself": *In the faces of men and women I see God, and in my own face in the glass.*[8] As humans, we all face daunting global challenges, but Whitman gave us one of the best ideas America—or the world, for that matter—has ever produced. For this, he can be widely celebrated today. It is more evident than ever that Spiritual Democracy, as a science of God, is an idea whose time has come.[9]

Thus, Whitman is not a fossil-poet of the nineteenth century. He is alive in the present, for he is a poetic forebear of change and transformation whose vision has inspired many throughout the world, and continues to do so today. Spiritual Democracy, as he envisioned it, is long overdue.

With the recent fall of the dictatorships in the Middle East, beginning with Afghanistan and Iraq, and followed by Tunisia, Egypt, and Libya, it is clear that people are taking to the streets in an effort to confront and topple evil political and economic regimes with the aim of creating democratic governments that are fairer to everyone. They are calling for democratic solutions to problems of dictatorships that have their roots in archaic laws and religious history. In recent years we have seen other upheavals, protests, and economic battles on the national and international level, from the congressional stalemates over debt ceilings and budgets to the collapse of the Greek economy. We witnessed the mass movement in many cities throughout the United States that began with the Occupy Wall Street rally, and which signaled a widespread feeling of general unrest in the American economy, and spread rapidly to hundreds of cities throughout the country and then to many European nations.

Of course we must place such developments, stirring as they are, in their proper context, which is the need not just for new governments, but for a new spirit that can inform effective government in the world today.[10] This need has long been evident to some of the authors whose views are discussed in this book.

What the people of the world appear to be calling for through civil unrest, speaking up, and even outright war against arcane forms of government is true Spiritual Democracy: political, economic, and religious *equality* for all.

This worthy goal isn't as remote as it once seemed. For the first time, the people of the world have a real chance to communicate and organize quickly en masse through the Internet, which played a key part in the uprising during the Arab Spring. The Internet contributes to the equalizing of power from hierarchical and archaic forms of government to the people. Indeed, it is becoming a worldwide vehicle for the vocalism that Whitman championed.

If the reader can grasp that the notion of Spiritual Democracy is meant to bring about global change by bringing peace in one's own mind and soul, she will understand the main point of this book. Its aim is to stimulate vocations in readers, callings to speak out, to challenge, and to expose the evils of religious fundamentalism as illnesses in the human heart. In discussing Spiritual Democracy, we have to talk about the shadow and we have to talk about evil, as well as good and light. And, if we start with ourselves, then we might begin to bring it about in the collectivity.

As Whitman showed, the core of the idea of religious relativism or equality is not found in conventional religion, creeds, Sunday schools, sermons, or Bibles, but rather in an overarching "consciousness," a spiritual *conscience that is unitary,* latent in every person, "a thought that rises, independent, lifted out from all else, calm, like the stars, shining eternal. This is the thought of identity— yours for you, whoever you are, as mine for me," as Whitman wrote in *Democratic Vistas.* "Miracle of miracles,"[11] Whitman said of its discovery, meaning the miracle of reflecting consciousness that perceives Spiritual Democracy shining at the summit of democracy's most advanced stage: the star of human destiny.

Each of us, it seems, is guided by such a star and it varies in its fixed orbits, in different fields of sacred action, in every person's life. A central existential task is to discover what that star is and to make its light, the inner fire of human love, burn brightly against the darkness, as a calling to live by. Readers interested in vocation as a practical path to healing problems that are currently plaguing our nation and world will find inspiration in these pages.[12] In this book we'll take a mythopoetic journey to the foundational ideas in American art-speech that have given birth to a new myth for our times and discover how this myth relates to the core notion of this series: what Andrew Harvey calls "sacred activism." Sacred activism is a spiritual practice for bringing about planetary changes through a receptivity to, and response to, experiences of a mysterious energy, force, or power, which move through the human body, psyche, and entire cosmos in an effort to bring about alterations in consciousness, cultural transformation, and ultimately: world peace.

The last section of this book offers ten practical ways to bring this task into daily living in such a way that the basic principles contained in Whitman's idea can come alive for the reader and be applied pragmatically for personal and cultural change.

Spiritual Democracy, as Whitman originally envisioned it, is an ideal—but an ideal we can make happen. It will never come about through inaction, and it can only be striven toward through right feeling[13] and thinking, applied practically to solving the world's problems as a form of holy work. In short, change must begin with you and me.

Part One

I

COSMOS

In 1844, the same year Alexander von Humboldt's *Cosmos* was published in Germany, the famous American essayist and transcendentalist poet Ralph Waldo Emerson wrote his seminal essay "The Poet," in which he announced from a stately and rationally empirical perspective:

> I look in vain for the poet who I describe. . . . Time and nature yields us many gifts, but not yet the timely man, the new religion, the reconciler, whom all things await. . . . We have yet had no genius in America, with tyrannous eye. . . . Yet America is a poem in our eyes; its ample geography dazzles the imagination, and it will not wait long for meters.[1]

It is out of this evolution of religious ideas in Emerson's work coinciding with the publication of *Cosmos* that Whitman's calling as a poet was born in a burst of unprecedented creativity.[2] Whitman took into account the "higher point of view" of the idea of the Cosmos that was made possible by the famous world traveler, geologist, and explorer Alexander von Humboldt in *Cosmos: A Sketch of the Physical Description of the Universe*.[3] Humboldt spent four years exploring vast regions throughout South and Central America and Mexico before visiting Thomas Jefferson at the White House. Humboldt's "rational empiricism," which Whitman embraced, concerned "facts registered by science."[4] Whitman's poetry is a celebration of what Humboldt called "an image of infinity revealed on every side, whether we look upward to the starry vault of heaven, scan the far-stretching plain before us, or seek to trace the dim horizon across the vast expanse of ocean,"[5] and this image was made clear to Humboldt from Quito and

3

Chimborazo in Ecuador. Chimborazo and Quito were to become emblems for Spiritual Democracy in America, as they appear also in the substantive writings of Emerson, Melville, and Dickinson. Whitman's ideas on Spiritual Democracy, however, are unique. He was a true American original, seeing even further into the depths of the collective soul. This enabled him to envision and articulate what the world needed in order to advance toward higher vistas of consciousness in an age of Spiritual Democracy.

Seeking a language that could democratize God, Whitman and the American poets turned their attention outward—to Judea, Europe, Africa, India, Polynesia, and the Middle East—in their search for a metaphorical language that could do away with the absolutism of religious creeds. In doing so, they embraced the conception of "the cosmos"—the harmoniously ordered whole—as the chief source for Nature's God. This breakthrough came through the spectacular new vision provided by astronomy and the "new science," which was articulated brilliantly by von Humboldt.

In *Cosmos,* Humboldt provided a remarkable view of Nature as a *unity within diversity*—a concord of all human races, all languages, all nations, and all families of the Earth, plant as well as animal, in an effervescent variety of a single species, life itself, vouchsafed with equal enjoyments and pleasures on a planet, itself a living entity, spinning in space. Ascending in his sketch of the "phenomena of organization" from "the simplest cell—the first manifestation of life—progressively to higher structures," he created a portrait so vast as to stagger the mind with a completely new vision of divinity: a "presentiment of the order and harmony pervading the whole universe."[6]

What Humboldt offered to American poetry was a "science of the cosmos" based on a foundation of rational empiricism, a feeling of "communion" contemplating all created things in their unity. Such a unitary notion is one that inextricably links together and forms "one *whole,* animated by internal forces."[7] Humboldt's view of science limited itself to an investigation of facts within the sphere of empirical ideas and left out all metaphysical speculations, yet, to Humboldt's great credit, his vision in all of its complexity repels the "depressing assumption of superior and inferior races of men." Rejecting the common prejudice of the time, Humboldt wrote: "All are in like degree designed for freedom."[8]

Indeed, without Humboldt, Whitman's masterly collection of equality-exalting poems, *Leaves of Grass,* could never have been written. Whitman brought Humboldt's vision of science down into the American body and soul. He applied it to the needs of all through a vehicle of speech by which everyone's passion (religious, erotic, political) could be heard. He called this diverse, bois-terous expression of opinion and appetite "vocalism."

Whitman expressed his embrace of this chorus of multitudes in the poem "I Hear America Singing":

I hear America singing, the varied carols I hear . . .
Each singing what belongs to him or her and to none else[9]

While embracing democracy and individual worth, Whitman did not exclude evil from his religious vision. Evil—in the form of the U.S. Civil War—shaped him, made him into its instrument, and subordinated his ego to the archetype of war. The bloody Union versus Confederacy battles opened Whitman's mind to the grim realities present in Spiritual Democracy and the long shadow war cast on human history. As a national poet, he spoke out against the abuses and hor-rors of slavery. As a healer of many nations, he spoke as a promoter of world peace through this paradoxical solution: the transformation of God into the individual's own deity, divinity, or form of worship.

Later, the prominent Swiss psychotherapist and psychiatrist Carl Jung fur-ther articulated this universal idea and cautioned his readers of dire consequences if humanity is not successful in advancing toward a unitary and quaternary con-ception of God. As with Whitman's Deus Quadriune, Jung's idea includes both masculine and feminine, good and evil, and a psychological understanding of the opposites in divinity as they are playing themselves out in human history. He warned that ignoring the duality of the opposites in a unitary notion such as Spiritual Democracy might result in a "universal genocide" as a consequence of our inability to relate more responsibly to the cosmos. Jung gets right to the point about the importance of the integration of the shadow and evil in "The Philosophical Tree":

Filling the conscious mind with ideal conceptions is a characteristic of Western theosophy, but not the confrontation with the shadow and the world of darkness. One does not become enlightened by imagining fig-ures of light, but by making the darkness conscious.[10]

Whitman's famous contemporary, Herman Melville, had a finely tuned eye for evil, and his ability to stare it down is uncanny. Melville did not hesitate to say what others in his generation did not want to hear about the atrocities of slavery, Indian hating, Islamophobia, homophobia, greed in America and the world, and the slaughter of countless wild species of animals. His vision of evil often sounds shocking to modern ears, but reading his work can be redemp-tive because he illuminates the darkness of human nature in such a way that the shadow of Spiritual Democracy, religious fundamentalism, dictatorships, homophobia, and war, is illuminated brightly. Melville fed on what is still largely indigestible to most humans, and he digested the *reality* of evil through a radical deconstruction of the Judeo-Christian-Islamic mythos, creating a new myth to complement and complete it.[11] We'll explore that myth in part 2 of this book.

Melville shows us that we have to do away with all of the false talk of Jewish, Christian, and Islamic brotherhood and sisterhood—talk that is unaware of its own evil. We can't have a God that is based solely on love, compassion, and light. It is just not going to happen. Two thousand years of the repression of the shadow in Europe and the Americas, the extermination of countless indigenous tribes, overpopulation and deforestation across the globe, jihads, holy wars, and crusades have shown the world that man's religion is good *and* evil. Spiritual Democracy has to make plenty of space for visions of evil; otherwise it is all New Age superficiality and triteness, and will die out as a hopeful global phenomenon.

Spiritual Democracy needs a vision of the dark to counterbalance its brightness, for without a vision of evil the science of God would be unscientific, and without a notion of evil we are doomed. There Melville made his contribution. Whitman gets full credit for the conception of the term Spiritual Democracy,[12] but Melville completes it by illuminating the darkness leaping out of the light, as in Ahab's famous statements in *Moby Dick,* or in the symbol of that novel's famous White Whale, which is perhaps the most potent symbol for Nature's God in nineteenth-century world literature.

A complete idea of Spiritual Democracy—if it is equalizing and ends theological disputes about whose God is better than whose—must also give equal value to Satan, the devil, and evil. If we do not assimilate our own evil by recognizing the harm we are inflicting onto the environment, we will ultimately be excoriated when human hubris is finally humbled by increasing climate change.

When Whitman declared that he had inaugurated a new religion, he meant that the same is possible for the reader, as religion is a subjective understanding that can only come about through the individual. He was speaking about the discovery of one's personal myth, a method, and a vision that needs to be developed in each reader. Like Emerson and the American writer Henry James, he teaches us to value the real thing: *spiritual experience.*

Whitman also believed, as did Melville and Dickinson, that if the world religions could learn to adapt to the variety and richness that each one has to offer, we would all get along much better on the planet. What more relevant message could be heard in times of global religious strife?

Jung was one of the first thinkers in the twentieth century to see that the world is on the verge of a spiritual rebirth. Such a time had been foreseen by Walt Whitman in his 1871 essay, "Democratic Vistas," in which he laid the groundwork for his plan for a transformation of values in the New World.

In 1934 Jung mused, "I have become convinced that *the psychological problem of today is a spiritual problem, a religious problem*. . . . [i]t does not seem beyond the range of possibility to believe that we stand on the threshold of a new spiritual epoch; and that from the depths of man's own psychic life new spiritual forms will be born."[13] Today, this prediction seems not far-fetched or vague, or in as much danger of being misapplied to reactionary currents. We would be wise, therefore, to adopt a view of cosmos into our understanding of modern psychology.

In volume 1 of *Cosmos,* which Whitman had on his writing desk while he was composing the first forty-four-page folio of *Leaves of Grass,* Alexander von Humboldt had traced the word *kosmos* (Whitman maintained the Greek and German spelling) to the Homeric ages. According to accounts of the ancient philosophers, Pythagoras coined it for the "order observed in the movements of the heavenly bodies, to the whole universe, and then finally, to the world in which this harmony was reflected."[14] In an attempt to provide his physical sketch of the universe, Humboldt filled the celestial section of *Cosmos,* volume 1, with a marvelous description not only of night stars and planets, but also meteors, meteorites, cosmic clouds, the physics of zodiacal light, and the very "veil of the Milky Way."[15]

However, alongside those frequent feelings of celebration for the exalted grandeur of the "works of creation,"[16] which Humboldt sought to illustrate, he stayed away from the heavily charged political and religious polemics of his day, wisely refusing as a scientist to mention the word "God." Using the word "kosmos" from 1855 onward, Whitman filled in the blanks by celebrating the God he *knows* as "a kelson of creation," a keelson, or keel that "is love."[17]

Humboldt went on, in volume 2 of *Cosmos,* in an ambitious attempt to create "one sole picture of the universe" by considering impressions of the Cosmos "reflected by the external senses on the feelings, and on the poetic imagination of mankind."[18] He declares: "In order to depict nature in its exalted sublimity, we must not dwell exclusively on its external manifestations, but we must trace its image, reflected in the mind of man."[19]

Turning his scientific eye to the Greeks (where as we have just seen, the term kosmos first appeared in Pythagoras), Humboldt proceeded to look through the eyes of poets who "almost unconsciously to himself takes Nature" as a subject of "imagination" through "skillfully artistical versification."[20]

Here, the scientist-explorer zeroed in on "The great poem of nature, which Lucretius [in *De Rerum Natura*] has so richly decked with the charms of his poetic genius," as a work that "embraces the whole Cosmos."[21] Extending Lucretius's vision in *De Rerum Natura* to a point of apotheosis far surpassing anything that had been previously conceived about the existence and experience of cosmic unity—a high point of Greek poetry and a volume Whitman read after he entered the attorney general's department[22] in 1866—Humboldt proceeded to illustrate the veneration and praise for Nature that is revealed as early as in the Sanskrit hymns of the *Rig-Veda,* and later in the Persian Zend Avesta and the mystical poetry of Rumi, Hafiz, and Saadi. Yet, Hebrew poetry may have moved Humboldt to celebration most, for "besides all its innate exalted sublimity," he wrote, it "presents the nations of the West with the special attraction of being interwoven with numerous reminiscences connected with the local seat of religion professed by the followers of the three most widely-diffused forms of belief, Judaism, Christianity, and Mohammedanism."[23] Humboldt writes in particular: "It might be almost said that one single psalm (104) represents the image of the whole Cosmos."[24]

Goethe, Schiller, Dante, and Camoens are all included in Humboldt's list of poets who attempted to objectify an image of the Cosmos through their powers of versification. A remarkable quote from Gregory of Nyssa, the brother of Basil the Great, stands out, furthermore, as a shining example from Christian poetry: "He who contemplates them [who feels the harmony of the wondrous powers pervading all things] with the eye of the soul, feels the littleness of man amid the greatness of the universe."[25] From this objective view, derived from the Hebrew dispensation and modern science, Humboldt continued with his magnificent thesis: "Christianity has materially contributed to call forth the idea of the unity of the human race, and has thus tended to exercise a favorable influence on the *humanization* of nations in their morals, manners, and institutions."[26]

After a long tribute to the discoverers of the New World, especially the Genoese for opening up the European mind to the remarkable diversity of native peoples who had been occupying the North American continent for millennia, and opening up a vista to the Southern sky as well, Humboldt then proceeded to amplify his theme by hailing: "The periods of the greatest discoveries in space over the surface of our planet" as having been "immediately succeeded by the revelations of the telescope, through which man may be said to have taken possession of a considerable portion of the heavens." More: "The application of a newly-created organ—an instrument possessed of power of piercing the depths of space—calls forth a new world of ideas. Now began a brilliant age of

astronomy and mathematics; and in the latter, the long series of profound inqui-
ries" that led to the brilliant discoveries of the "seventeenth century, the age of
Kepler, Galileo, and Bacon, of Tycho Brahe, Descartes, Huygens, of Fermat,
Newton, and Leibniz."[27]

Taking these insights into his own self-proclaimed field of American poetry,
Whitman advanced the idea that we are each called to live in accord with the all.
He writes: "A vast similitude interlocks all."[28] By similitude, he means likeness,
equality, equivalence: a vast Spiritual Democracy interlocking everything in the
entire universe, a great chain of destiny, interlocked as a stupendous miracle of
being and non-being, self and no-self. Similitude extends throughout the entire
cosmos through an equality of everything in a constantly evolving cycle of the
miraculous.

Whitman's Spiritual Democracy welcomes all world faiths, rejecting none,
even the most orthodox. He is not opposed to faith, and says paradoxically that
he has the greatest faith and the least of faiths, because he has gone beyond them
to claim his own vision of the "science of God." He has, in this sense, left God
for the infinite cosmos, which subsumes all religions. For Whitman the self is
a living "mirror" of the universe: "O daring joy, but safe!" he exclaims while
sailing in imagination on a ship in "Passage to India," "are they not all the seas
of God?"[29]

In a centennial poem called "Eidólons," moreover, written in 1876, Whitman takes such meanings further. Nature and cosmos, he says, are patterned by
images; indeed, space and time are all images too. "All space, all time, / (The
stars, the terrible perturbations of the suns, / Swelling, collapsing, ending, serving
their longer, shorter use,) / Fill'd with eidólons only."[30] "Eidólons" puts science
and astrophysics and soul (or psyche) on a similar, if not same, footing; they are
at least interconnected and interrelated. The complementarity between Whitman
and Jung, moreover, is provided for through Whitman's mythopoetic use of active
visioning. In "Eidólons," vocalism is elucidated as a visionary verse method in
the opening line: "I met a seer." This spiritual seer (the democratic One who *sees*
democratic spirituality everywhere he looks in the universe) tells him to put certain things into his chants, and Whitman does as he is instructed. "Eidólons" is
Whitman's *key* to the marriage between soul and cosmos, psyche and universe.
In Whitman's view, soul and matter coexist in the great *similitude*. Thus, in
"Eidólons," he taps into self-images by vocalizing them out of his emotional center: "The old, old urge, / Based on the ancient pinnacles, lo, newer, higher pinnacles, / From science and the modern still impell'd, / The old, old urge, eidólons."[31]

Spiritual Democracy is only possible through an expansion of consciousness made possible, in Whitman's view, by the union of "high" and "low," as a *quality* of consciousness of all creation inflected in the soul's body and breath. How does von Humboldt's science compare with Whitman's *imaginative launch* to the "vast Rondure, swimming in space"?[32] In "Passage to India," Whitman writes further: "Athwart the shapeless vastness of space, / How should I think, how breathe a single breath, how speak, if, / out of myself, / I could not launch, to those, superior universes?"[33] In another poem, he adds: "You tides with ceaseless swell! you power that does this work! / You unseen force, centripetal, centrifugal, through space's spread, / . . . Holding the universe with all its parts as one—as sailing in a ship?"[34]

In psychological terms, Whitman's launch is provided through vocalism or free verse; it is essential for his life and meaning to give shape to divine words. In section forty-eight of "Song of Myself" he says: "Let your soul stand cool and composed before a million universes."[35] A million universes! And this, before the Hubble spacecraft peered into the Deep Field in 1996. Astrophysics revealed then a cosmos hitherto unimaginable, seen by the Hubble in a relatively small portion of space, containing 1,500 galaxies—a launch that opened our eyes to a fathomless universe without apparent end. Of course, Whitman had Humboldt's *Cosmos* on his writing desk, as a reference book, when he penned these lines. But we still have to marvel at his courage and audacity to take such words into sacred action.

What Whitman means by *superior universes* cannot be captured in speech, for his vocation is to heal the division between Nature and man, science and art, politics and religion through "vocalism." This is a process that is never fully perfected in a human lifetime.

Spiritual Democracy reaches, therefore, the rondure of infinite space and is also present in a spider, as well as in a single spear of grass: "I believe a leaf of grass is no less than the journey-work of the stars."[36] The aim here is to connect us with the cosmic whole.

How to achieve universal religious equality for all people, in a way that is open to all faiths, is the central mystery of this chapter. To convey the ability of such ideas to impress the psyche of someone still only reaching to understand them, prior to my reading of Alexander von Humboldt's work, I'll provide a brief personal example. While I was preparing to give a talk at the International House (I-House) at the University of California at Berkeley in February of 2011, I had a powerful dream of a blue spiral-galaxy woman—a vision of a luminous female form that had apparently descended down from the furthest nebula of the universe to sit in quiet contemplation with me in my home office where I do my writing. She had the body of a woman and her head was shaped in a spiral of stars: a spiral galaxy. We sat together in a sea of silence.

I had this dream before my reading of Humboldt. Several days after the dream, I wrote in my journal: "She was not the World Soul, but the Soul of a Galaxy. She was personal and impersonal, human and inhuman. Her consciousness was cosmic, and I was in communion with her, in silence. She was communicating with me through her spiral-eyes, myriads of them. I realized she wanted something from me, something objective and divine, and that her divinity is our divinity, and we are made of the same cosmic stuff, with the same interconnectedness and the same Spiritual Democracy." I offer the following personal meditation on my dream to illustrate how reading this book can be applied practically to our lives as a spiritual path, for its way is visionary, cosmic, and dream-centered.

This inner dream-woman communed with me through her star-eyes in an eloquent way, yet not one word was spoken. "Had the same type of visitor from outer and inner space—that had come to visit and energize me—come close to Walt Whitman when he started to feel the gravitational pull of Humboldt's big idea of one indissoluble chain that binds together all nature?" What might Humboldt's image of the cosmos, which galvanized so many in the nineteenth century, have to do with Walt Whitman's global vistas of Spiritual Democracy, and why was it important that I grasp the energy field of this image of the divine feminine in the early stages of writing this book? If approaching the idea of Spiritual Democracy for a lecture could bring to my dreaming consciousness a visitor from far outside the earth's atmosphere, with the stupendous attraction of an entire galaxy, couldn't the idea itself reflect a cosmic legacy?

For several weeks, I lived in a kind of intuitive insight into the play of obscure scientific forces that have always led to American poetry. The dream pressed me to look deeper than I previously had into Whitman's writings on astronomy, for this was an area I had left virtually unexplored across the full span of his writings. That Whitman had been strongly attracted to astronomy before he wrote *Leaves of Grass* had been evident to me long ago, when I read his 1855 "Preface," and particularly section forty-four of "Song of Myself," yet, I had not fully grasped the immensity of Whitman, how vast his insight really was, until I examined his celestial statements side by side. I'd seen references to stars scattered throughout his poetry and prose before, but I had not looked systematically at them to gain the gestalt of his total cosmology. Fifteen years earlier, I had discovered a footnote in Whitman's 1847 *Notebook* by the editor Edward F. Grier. This caught my eye:

When did WW develop his sense of cosmic unity? On the evidence of the present notebook, one would say 1847.[37]

I'd been struck by these words "cosmic unity" for years, but had never imagined there was a scientific source for them until I began to read Humboldt, the Prussian ancestor that had led Whitman himself to the organizing notion of kosmos as the deeper part of his identity. It was not until after my dream of the spiral-galaxy woman that I happened to discover that Whitman had published an editorial on astronomy on March of 1847 while serving as editor of the *Brooklyn Daily Eagle*. In this editorial he supports the construction of astronomical observatories to promote this science in the United States. But we also must see in this ambition an expansion of the American vista he was already celebrating into the universe itself. It was around the same time that he penned his 1847 poem "Fierce Wrestler!" After my own dream of the blue woman who was also a galaxy, it began to make sense to me that for Whitman, astronomy and sexuality belonged together. As we've seen, moreover, Whitman took the term for his self-definition as a kosmos from Humboldt, even preserving the German spelling.

Following my dream I lived in a kind of hazy state of mind, as if my consciousness were shrouded behind the vapory veil of a galaxy as seen from afar. Finally, upon studying Humboldt to see if by reading him I might gain a more specific understanding of the scientific insights that had informed Whitman's vision, I experienced a revelation. It was as if I had stepped from behind the sentimental mist to see the cosmic perspective for what it could offer. Humboldt wrote:

> Nature considered rationally that is to say, submitted to the process of thought, is a unity in diversity of phenomena; a harmony blending together all created things, however dissimilar in form and attributes; one great whole . . . animated by the breath of life.[38]

Passages like these led me to see how much Whitman had chosen Humboldt's empirical observations of the unity of the cosmos as his own point of departure for his shamanistic flight into the oneness that links all of us. When Whitman writes in 1847 "I dilate you with tremendous breath—,"[39] he is offering the reader a chance to experience the same expansion. Whitman captures the idea of sexual, religious, and spiritual harmony beautifully in the word *equality*.

Equality is at the center of everything we do in our attempts to bring about peace in human relationships; it is one of the main meanings of the life-urge. Without equality, Spiritual Democracy could not exist, and for these reasons among others I believe we must help humanity usher it in, each in our own unique ways.

Whether they are a gay couple wanting to marry in California or women in Saudi Arabia who want to be able to drive cars, all people want equality. Liberty is the way of the future. As more and more people demand religious freedom, it will, in time, come about. Religious freedom is like women's rights. When enough women spoke up, the vote happened. It is the same with the black vote, followed by the civil rights movement.

As I make clear in my chapters on *Moby Dick,* mirrored events in Melville's novel are in fact real. Many people of the Middle East are making it clear that they, too, are ready to embrace a different way forward. The Arab Spring may have signaled the moment of the archetype's coming-into-consciousness from the cosmic realm with its signature of universal relatedness among nations and diverse peoples of this beautiful green-blue globe spinning in the cosmos. Like von Humboldt and Whitman, Melville grasped the essential connectedness that exists among all people, all animals, all nature. In the figure of Ishmael we find a peacemaker, a bringer of peace between nations, a healer of divisions between all world religions, a lover of light, consciousness, and pure joy. Ishmael is a true practitioner of Spiritual Democracy. Call us all Ishmael.[40]

2

SPIRITUAL DEMOCRACY
AS A SCIENCE OF GOD

We've explored the influence of Alexander von Humboldt's five-volume book set *Cosmos: A Sketch of the Physical Description of the Universe* on the genesis of Walt Whitman's big idea. The books were a bit shocking by the standards of their time because they made "no mention of God."[1] Such an omission, however, presented no difficulty for the unconventional Whitman. Taking Humboldt's empirical vision forward, Whitman conceived of the future direction of religion into a truly Democratic Spirituality, as the "science of God."

Whatever Spiritual Democracy is—science, religion, or something else— it's clear that it's a dynamic effect of the cosmos and psyche, operating through American poetry and the world soul. We're conditioned to see science and religion as opposites, but such contradictions melt away when every person's experience of God is viewed as valid.

To be sure, there's a difference between the way Whitman wrote about Spiritual Democracy and the way Swiss psychotherapist Carl Jung wrote about the "Self" in his scientific writings. Whereas Whitman saw himself as the inaugurator of a new world religion, Jung never claimed such a calling. Responding to such a question, Jung said modestly, during his seventh trip to the United States, in 1937: "People sometimes call me a religious leader. I am not that. I have no message, no mission; I attempt only to understand."[2] Jung was always an empirical scientist, first and foremost. Whitman was influenced by science too, but he also felt free to go beyond it—which he often did.

To better understand the "science of God" as contemporary readers, we'll look at what Whitman actually said about it, with various amplifications:

utterances from other American poets, Herman Melville and Emily Dickinson, who were Whitman's contemporaries and equals; the philosophy of Ralph Waldo Emerson; the pragmatism of William James; and what has become a touchstone for present-day people—Carl Jung's vision of analytical psychology, a vision of the self that is grounded in a truly global collective unconscious, and which has become, like Whitman's Spiritual Democracy, perennially inspiring to an American audience.[3]

Jung's analytical psychology is central to an understanding of Whitman's vision because of his reflections on the dark side of the psychological God-image. Yet Jung's focus on evil was, at times, excessive. Despite all of the atrocities Whitman saw on the battlefields of the U.S. Civil War, his vision of Spiritual Democracy is far lighter than Jung's.

Religious fundamentalism is a very real problem in all world religions, and Jung takes this issue head on, from a standpoint rooted in science. Many religious people today want to make a universal deity out of their own particular God-images. But to deify evil as an equivalent principle with good is problematic. What can come about, if we make Spiritual Democracy a pragmatic reality in our own lives, is a general recognition that we are all carriers of a goal that is divinely inspired by principles of right action. Right feeling and thinking lead to a path with a heart—and an appreciation that we are all sisters and brothers. This is the essence of what Whitman teaches.[4]

While visions of Spiritual Democracy are clearly present in the intuitions of Hebraic and German mysticism, Native American shamanism, Hinduism and Sufism, in the work of Emerson and James, and in Jung's understanding of Meister Eckhart's God-concept[5]—where the self is postulated as the common psychological bedrock of all religious experience—the first full elucidation of the idea appeared in Walt Whitman's post–Civil War prose essay "Democratic Vistas," published in 1871.

Whitman shares a relativistic faith with German mysticism and science, the Hindu and Sufi poets, Ralph Waldo Emerson, William James, Carl Jung, as well as with his American compatriots Herman Melville and Emily Dickinson. Religious equality, as Whitman conceived it, is at the base of American Democracy, and in order for it to become alive and active in the reader as a realizable ideal, a radical change in attitudes must happen at a personal and international level to light the way to global transformation and world peace. Whitman puts it this way:

> One main contrast of the ideas behind every page of my verses, compared with establish'd poems, is their different relative attitude towards
> God, towards the objective universe, and still more (by reflection,

confession, assumption, &c.) the quite changed attitude of the ego, the one chanting or talking, towards himself and towards his fellow humanity.[6]

This different relative attitude toward God and changed attitude of the ego toward the objective universe is at the center of Spiritual Democracy. It offers a practical path to healing problems that are currently plaguing us as a nation and a world, and is a blueprint for what Whitman calls the "radical foundation of the new religion."[7] His vision is indeed radical because it departs from all previous religions and looks forward to the establishment of a new "relativistic attitude" in the present and future. Spiritual Democracy, as Whitman imagined it, was still in its "embryo condition" in 1871. As a word, Whitman wrote, democracy "still sleeps, quite unawaken'd."[8] It was, nevertheless, awakened in him and he was inspired to help rouse his readers, one person at a time.

Riding on waves of the Hindu, Sufi, and Germanic intuitions, Emerson's breakthrough synthesis, and his own scintillating inspirations in the first editions of *Leaves of Grass*, Whitman hypothesized that there are three basic strata of American Democracy:

1. The political stratum: putting down on record the basic principles of American democracy in Congress, including the statutes and amendments of the Constitution;

2. The material stratum: accruing the wealth and infrastructure to make a nation prosperous, which, during Whitman's lifetime, was foregrounded through land grants; the advance of science, technology, and industry; the completion of the Transcontinental Railroad; and the development of electricity and the telegraph. The enormous outgrowth of material riches and prosperity that exploded during the California Gold Rush also boosted the fortunes of a young United States and created an atmosphere in which democracy could thrive;

3. The religious or spiritual stratum: adopting a "new religion," or "new relativistic attitude toward God," where all spiritual traditions of the world might be valued equally in a common celebration of coming into cosmic selfhood. By 1871, Whitman felt his own "seed" of personality had evolved in his published poetry to the point that he could hail the birth of Spiritual Democracy.[9]

Although some fundamentalists today might argue that the purpose of the framers of the U.S. Constitution was to make the United States a Christian country, the nation could not, thankfully, become a Christian-only nation, because that would violate its basic idea of equality. It has to remain a nation of many nations, free of any one specific religious myth, if it is to become a global leader that welcomes world faiths, and unites them in one central union of a nondiscriminatory democracy. Equality is at the foundation of Spiritual Democracy, and it is at the foundation of democracy at all three levels.

Thus, in the first five editions of *Leaves of Grass*, Whitman presented a new idea to the world, which is the idea of "one-self," "Myself," or "Yourself" as the supreme principle of democratic spirituality latent in the universe—namely, human incarnation. This religious idea, which grew out of the Protestant Reformation and paved the way for believers to seek a personal relationship with God, is similar in many respects with the psychological idea of the self, which Carl Jung championed as the foundation stone for analytical psychology. Whitman extends this effort in the West and provides an idea for what a real Spiritual Democracy might look like in America, as a "science of God."

Most of us have read at least some of Whitman's rhapsodic outbursts of feeling. Yet, Whitman did not think Spiritual Democracy was like a fine perfume one might put on occasionally. He meant to accent the body in reverential and spiritual ways and to equalize the body's place in deification, making it coequal with the soul. He delights in the body in such ways that he leaves Emerson behind, and sails out for deeper waters across the seas of God: "Accepting the rough deific sketches to fill out better in myself, bestowing them freely on each man and woman I see."[10] This is classic Whitman. He does not get intoxicated on religion, but rather is a spiritual democrat through and through, who values the body equally with the soul.

Jungian and post-Jungian writers have spoken about the existence of two conjunctions (or marriages) in the human psyche—for instance, one heteroerotic and the other homoerotic. Whitman's breakthrough in 1860 enables us to postulate a possible third, based on the available evidence offered at the same era by Melville and Dickinson. The archetype unites them at a higher plane of order—the bi-erotic. This third is structured by a uniting symbol, which takes a unique form in Melville's, Whitman's, and Dickinson's poetry. While Jung advanced the theory of spiritual marriage in his various writings on alchemy, he could find no convincing evidence for bi-erotic conjunction possibilities in European poetry. In American poetry, however, we can hypothesize two conjunctions—the heteroerotic and the homoerotic—that, united together, may constitute a bi-erotic structure of human wholeness in the world soul that is inclusive of "lower" and "higher" copulation imagery.[11]

In this regard, Whitman is akin to Emily Dickinson, who writes of her vision of a "Republic of Delight," where "each is Citizen."[12] This is a republic of the body as well as the soul. Like Dickinson, Whitman celebrates the body in its bi-erotic unity, and with this new realization he salutes the world. Jung expresses this idea in psychological terms in his 1921 essay on Meister Eckhart, where he says that to turn God into an inner possession, so one has God within oneself as an inner object, God then becomes, in Eckhart's words, "the world."[13]

This is precisely what Whitman means by Spiritual Democracy: *Spiritual Democracy is becoming the world.* This notion is not an intellectual concept either; it is an empirically embodied experience made explicit by Whitman in his *Leaves of Grass.* Herman Melville arrives at the same basic experience in his third novel, *Mardi,* which in early Arabic means imply "my world." To become the world is to be a citizen of the world, a citizen of the psyche, for at bottom psyche and cosmos are inseparable.

This experience of the unity of the soul and world (or psyche and cosmos) is expressed most clearly by Whitman in a poem by that name: "Salut au Monde!" The poem is essentially Whitman's salutation to the nations, his greeting from the self, as a global symbol awakened democratically in the New World. Whitman used the French phrase *monde,* or world, to speak of the seed of "becoming" in the human collectivity. "Each of us here as divinely as any is here,"[14] he says. It is significant to note, moreover, that this *salut* is addressed to the world in a poem that aimed to marry all nations of the globe to Spiritual Democracy as a healing notion, as a cure for what was ill in the religious domain of Europe's spiritual attitudes. He did this by calling forth the French Revolution–era motto of "liberty, equality, and fraternity." In retrospect, this was indeed a vision with integrity, for France has followed Britain as one of the most recent European nations to legalize same-sex marriage, a decision Walt Whitman would have applauded.

When such victories occur, they express the "spinal meaning" of democracy, which is located in the spinal axis of the personality. Everyone has a latent seed of identity through "the formation of a typical personality of character."[15] Whitman's aim is to bring life to this seed, or potential, in the collective soul of humanity through the reading of *Leaves of Grass,* in hope of transforming the consciousness of the globe.

As much as American democracy helped to lift the masses up during the industrial age, both prior to and after the Civil War, Whitman excoriated the material underbelly of democracy for failing to produce anything of lasting religious, moral, literary, or aesthetic value for the world, leaving the nation with "little or no soul."[16] To Whitman, the soul was "literature,"[17] and in order for it to breathe new life into the world, a method was needed to forge the way ahead. He sought a technique that might help to endow American "literature with grand archetypal models . . . to achieve spiritual meanings, and suggest the future—these, and these only, satisfy the soul."[18] Translated into a contemporary language this means finding that source of satisfaction that comes from writing as a practical path in any vocation.

From the standpoint of an awakened consciousness of character—at the third strata of democracy—Whitman looked out from a spiritual vista toward a "spinal" meaning in American civilization, and he criticized our great cities from that view. Whitman did not subscribe to what today might be called American exceptionalism, but rather he said the United States in 1871 reeked of "robbery" and "scoundrelism." He complained, moreover, that the aim of the "all-devouring word business" is pecuniary gain[19] and feared that the economic strata would eat away at the American soul, until the evil hiding behind the Christian mask of charity and civility would become rampant.

Whitman expressed fear of such developments in biblical-sounding words, hearkening back to the book of Job: "Unwieldy and immense, who shall hold in behemoth? who bridle leviathan? Flaunt it as we choose, athwart and over the roads of our progress loom huge uncertainty, and dreadful, threatening gloom."[20] He then writes: "We sail a dangerous sea of seething currents, cross and undercurrents, vortices—all so dark, untried—and whither shall we turn?"[21]

Despite such doubts about the second strata of democracy, Whitman never gave up hope in the American future. He maintained his wish that Spiritual Democracy would prove victorious throughout the world in the future. Such a viewpoint resonates today in our efforts to become increasingly global in our spiritual visioning. Whitman's role as a poet in helping to spread Spiritual Democracy as a universal medicine might help us alleviate at least some of our suffering during a time of political, economic, and religious upheaval. His vision of religious equality for women and men is a living "seed" of "becoming" in the general populace that we would be wise to cultivate into a new myth for our times.

It is here, in the domain of Whitman's hope in humanity and vision of the future, that his image of the self and Jung's hypothesis of the self part company and proceed along separate but complementary paths. If Spiritual Democracy as Whitman envisioned is truly to "become the world," then the peace at the center of such a vision must radiate outward to speed up the process of bringing it about through sacred actions, day by day, minute by minute, by each of us and all of us. For ultimately, everything we do in time is patterned by peace, friendship, and brotherhood in Whitman's vision, and it can be realized by anyone in the perpetual now.

3

FROM HUMBOLDT
TO JUNG

The unity of the human race is realized in the idea of Spiritual Democracy, a notion whose roots run deep. Its origins stems not from one person, but from a plurality of men and woman of genius equipped with a gift for an international language. Their work proved to be mutually influential on the genesis of Whitman's central notion.

One can follow a thread of genius toward higher forms of conceptual organization that culminate in Whitman's writings on Spiritual Democracy. It begins with the discoveries in science made possible by Alexander von Humboldt in Central and South America, and it extends to Thomas Jefferson and James Madison in the newly created United States, to Johann Wolfgang von Goethe and Friedrich Schiller in Germany, to Ralph Waldo Emerson, Walt Whitman, Emily Dickinson, Herman Melville, and William James in mid–nineteenth century America, and to the empirical psychology of Carl Jung in Switzerland.

Alexander von Humboldt plays an early and key role in the shaping of the American mind, a process that eventually produced the genius idea known as Spiritual Democracy. Born in Berlin in 1769, Humboldt was seven years old when the Declaration of Independence was drafted. In 1794, he was introduced to Goethe and Schiller in Jena, Germany, by his elder brother William von Humboldt, and the men formed a strong friendship. From his brother, Alexander von Humboldt received the notion of the unity of all human languages. Humboldt maintained a lifelong love for the principles of American democracy, and in 1804 he began a correspondence with Thomas Jefferson after he visited the United States following a five-year trek to South America. In addition to

Jefferson, Humboldt met with James Madison and other prominent Americans. These dignitaries were reportedly delighted to meet Humboldt, in part because he was a man of science who could give them important information about Mexico and other lands south of the United States. Ralph Waldo Emerson, who, like Jung and Freud, modeled himself after Goethe, introduced Humboldt to Henry David Thoreau, and later to Whitman.

When Humboldt's masterwork *Cosmos* was first translated into English in 1845, the American literary intelligentsia was duly impressed with the integrative quality of Humboldt's mind, his simultaneous regard for all branches of the natural sciences, and the meditative tone of his book. Humboldt described awe-inspiring moments of communion with nature, such as his breathtaking trek scaling Mount Chimborazo in Ecuador (which at the time was believed to be the highest peak in the world), as well as stargazing in the Southern Hemisphere, where he reported on the miraculous spectacle of our own spiral galaxy, the Milky Way. Humboldt was remarkable in his ability to see the unity of all created forms. *Unity within diversity* is really where the notion of Spiritual Democracy stems from, and German poetry played a pivotal part in its discovery.

What Humboldt brings to our awareness of Whitman's notion and its influences is the immense variety in nature and human culture. For instance, in plant life, which far exceeds the variety of animal life on the planet, he sees endless forms of social uniformity covering vast extents of land.[1] Internal unity within diversity also finds its way into Humboldt's reflections on the unity of different languages and races. The most important questions of civilization and "destinies of nations" are connected, Humboldt judges, with the very "ideas of races."[2]

Humboldt believed in the universal equality of the "human race"[3] as a whole and rejected the widespread belief in white racial superiority. Not only did he not share the ethnocentric assumptions of some of his European contemporaries, he unequivocally disavowed them, even against a tide of criticism.[4] The idea of white, and specifically Aryan, exceptionalism, which later plagued his very own nation of Germany through its xenophobic use by the Nazis, was excluded from the start of his career by the integrity of his vision in Quinto, Ecuador. From his home in Quinto, in the heart of volcano country, the geologist-explorer would look out and gain a glimpse of the vast cordilleras of the Andes, a vision that filled him with great equanimity and peace. Anti-Semitism, or any other kind of racial qualification of the full status of all humans' birthright to participate in the life of the cosmos, was an idea that Humboldt would have abhorred. In Quito, Humboldt was able to gain a vision of vast diversity—ethnic, cultural, linguistic, religious, and cosmic—and this vision would open Whitman's mind to the unmistakable and essential *equality* that exists between all human beings regardless of economic rank, color, or religion.

In fact, Humboldt found in our American democracy a terrible contradiction: while the opening of the Declaration of Independence clearly states that all men are created equal, Humboldt saw that slavery was an evil affront to this ideal of the U.S. Republic, and he spoke out vociferously against it. Humboldt had also seen the damage and suffering the Spanish inflicted on the indigenous peoples of Central and South America, wiping out untold numbers of Aztecs, Mayans, and Incas, along with their languages, cultures, civilizations, art, and religions. Such a perspective led him to lament and then sharply criticize North America's policies toward slavery. The plague of violence and cultural destruction appeared in our nation with its treatment of the native North American peoples, and these atrocities became part of Humboldt's ongoing discussions with Jefferson.

As U.S. democracy shaped Humboldt's thinking, the American system was in turn shaped by the thinking of Humboldt. In this trajectory, Humboldt undoubtedly had an enormous impact on the American mind, but literary history has yet to integrate the degree to which Humboldt's research helped to shape American poetry. Emerson became the main spokesperson for Humboldt's science in America, and he even went so far as to laud the mid-nineteenth century as the "Age of Humboldt." But the impact of Humboldt on Whitman, Melville, and Dickinson, for instance, is largely unsung.

Let us reach for the connections then, starting with the very basis of what became a new poetic praxis on the American continent—language itself. Based on a sampling of 200 languages that Humboldt brought back to Germany in his notebook sketches from ethnographic studies of South American tribes, Alexander von Humboldt's older brother William put together a book on the variety of languages. Together the two brothers traced the roots of spiritual life to a common source: cosmos. Alexander von Humboldt quotes his brother William in the last pages of *Cosmos*, volume 1, where he says that their aim was to strive to establish "our common humanity" and "treat all mankind, without reference to religion, nation, or color, as one fraternity, one great community, fitted for the attainment of one object, the unrestrained development of the physical powers."[5] This vision of the equality of all races made possible through a universal language, more than any other attribute, "binds together the whole human race."[6] Indeed, Whitman was an informed reader of William von Humboldt, as well as of his more famous brother.

The Humboldt brothers' equalizing revelation of a common human inheritance so enlarged Whitman's mind as to subsume the globe into a unifying vision that found its way into his 1855 edition of *Leaves of Grass* and his 1856 poem "Salut au Monde," which contemplates the brotherhood and sisterhood of all humanity. Alexander von Humboldt's vision of science united with William von Humboldt's vision of language led Walt Whitman to assert that all religions are essentially equivalent, that all languages are formed by a common poetic or literary archetype, and that to put any one religion above another would be to go against the basic principles of our Constitution.

The same was true where the subject matter of a properly American poetry was concerned. Just as Humboldt was highly influenced by the principles of our Constitution, so too was Whitman influenced by Humboldt's vision of science, to the point where he universalized religion. "Variety within diversity" is an idea, moreover, that also spoke to William James, the young and future father of American psychology. James went on the expedition to South America with Humboldt's team to see for himself some of the rich diversity of culture before it was too late. He brought back with him a foundational intuition for what would later become *The Varieties of Religious Experience.*

James, like many of his contemporaries, had read Whitman and saw that his poetry is a celebration of the diversity of religions contained in a unique American idiom. To this, Whitman adds a concept of his very own: the validity and desirability of taking one's very own personal religion, one's personal spiritual image, one's individual truth, as an alternate, visionary path. While it had planted the seeds for such an integrated view, Humboldt's science of the cosmos was not clear enough to show how this utopia might be embraced by the hearts of average human beings. This opened the door for Walt Whitman to emerge with largesse onto the world stage as a poet chanting his own hymns to show just how this could happen.

In America, this notion that democracy could apply equally to the individual soul, as well as to the body politic, though attractive to Whitman, actually begins with Emerson. Emerson is the great fountainhead, the wellspring of creativity from which the rivers of the American transcendentalist mind flowed forth to nourish the native visionary experience of a religious nation in quest of a new guiding myth. Transcendentalism also carried forth deism, the belief that reason, coupled with observation of nature, is enough to determine the existence of God. In a more psychological way, transcendentalism was based on continuing revelation in the individual, and therefore reflected the American ideal of "self reliance." How Emerson came upon his ideas regarding the equality of religions to pave the way for America's poets, who then took the insights of the transcendentalists to new levels of spiritual realization, is no small miracle.

It was during Emerson's readings of the Bhagavad Gita in 1831 and the Zoroastrian bible, or Zend Avesta, in 1832 that the ancient Hindu and Persian religions first began to enter his thoughts. The lengthy dialogues between Krishna and Arjuna in the Gita were of particular interest to him at the time, as were the interactions of the twin brothers, Ahriman and Ormuzd, in the Zend Avesta (they were the hostile brothers that so interested Herman Melville, Friedrich Nietzsche, and Carl Jung). From 1832 until the end of his lifetime, Emerson placed the Gita on an equal standing with the Christian gospels.[7] In 1844, Emerson revived his interest in Zoroastrianism and began to read deeply into the wisdom traditions of the medieval poets of Persia, particularly Saadi, Jami, Rumi, and especially Hafiz. He also read the religious Hindu text known as the *Vishnu Purana*, from which he drew deep insights for his poem "Brahma."[8]

Unlike Emerson, who was a Unitarian minister, Whitman never affiliated himself with a church, congregation, or religious institution. His church was the cosmos itself. To be sure, this idea can be traced, in part, to one of Emerson's early lecture series called "The Philosophy of History." In it, Emerson drew on the Hindu concept of the "universal mind," of which each person is a potential embodiment. In this concept the mind becomes a state of pure receptive consciousness, of transparent seeing that beholds the objective reality of the cosmos, and of the individual's part in it as a recipient of the Holy Spirit. In another lecture, called "The Individual," Emerson writes: "*religion* is the emotion of reverence which the conscious presence and activity of the Universal Mind inspires."[9]

Melville's criticism of Emerson shows us precisely where he stood on the conundrum that William James was the first to identify: the problem of the integration of evil. Melville wrote about Emerson: "Nay I do not oscillate in Emerson's rainbow. . . . I could readily see in Mr. Emerson, notwithstanding his merit, a gaping flaw."[10]

What was Emerson's flaw, in Melville's opinion, and how can it help us understand why a chapter on *Moby Dick* is so important in this book on Spiritual Democracy? In Emerson's view, "all nature is the rapid efflux of goodness executing and organizing itself."[11] Emerson was attempting to throw off eighteen centuries of Christian theology when he wrote this comment. But, he couldn't get into his good-natured head that in order to return us to a vision of "Nature's God"—that is neither good nor evil but transcendence of both—the Bible would have to be radically deconstructed with a goodness-destroying symbol.

In essence, *Moby Dick* is Melville's solution to the problem of the splitting of good and evil in the three Abrahamic monotheisms. He presents us with a symbol of "Nature's God"—the White Whale—to solve this. Evil, slavery, Indian-hating, homophobia, Islamophobia, white prejudice and cruelty against dark races, mass slaughter of whales, and general destruction of the environment are not part of "the good" in Melville's view. How can any of these be good? In his view, good and evil stand together, side by side. Where Emerson wrote in *The Conduct of Life* "the first lesson of history is the good of evil," Melville argued against that view in his marginalia to his copy of that book: "He still bethinks himself of his optimism—he must make that good against the eternal hell itself. . . . Another species of Mr. Emerson's errors, or rather, blindness, proceeds from a defect in the region of the heart."[12] Moreover, in Melville's annotations of Emerson's *Essays*, he writes perceptively, "A perfectly Good being therefore would see no evil.—But what did Christ see? He saw what made him weep. . . . To annihilate all this nonsense read the Sermon on the Mount, and consider what it implies."[13] As we will see, Melville exposed the psychological mechanism by which evil executes and organizes itself in human nature, namely, the problem of projecting the human shadow.

VARIETIES OF RELIGIOUS EXPERIENCE

At the turn of the twentieth century, William James, the father of American pragmatism, would locate the science of religion in the domain of exceptional mental states, and especially in the "varieties of religious experience." This trend in modern psychology, to focus on the spiritual aspect of the human psyche, would later be followed by Carl Jung's work in what he called "the archetypal cores of the complexes," which he made the subject of his analytical psychology. Through empirical psychology, the new science of religion made possible an analysis of the archetypes of culture, which were invariably religiously toned, and this opened the way for every individual to chart the seas of spiritual seeing and visioning toward God in a spiritual *unus mundus*—a sort of unified reality underlying existence. And Jung's psychological vision was fully anticipated by Whitman in his poetry.[14]

The democratizing potential inherent in the foundation of every religion of the world had been realized at an early age and carried to the West by the twenty-nine year old Indian national Hindu spiritual teacher, Narendra Nath Datta (1863–1902). Narendra Datta took the name Swami Vivekananda shortly before he left Bombay, India, for Chicago in commemoration of the World's Columbian Exposition in 1893. His relevance to the notion of Spiritual Democracy and how it bears on Whitman's great idea, and the cross-pollination that we're uncovering here, is made self-evident in his opening remarks spoken at the World's Parliament of Religions, Sept. 11, 1893. "Sisters and Brothers of America," Vivekananda began. With this warm greeting, the Swami was applauded by a thunderous audience of seven thousand strong for spreading his message of religious unity to a mostly American and Christian audience. The address was widely covered by American newspapers, and amongst those who read about it was the young William James. In the opening speech at the Parliament, the Swami said eloquently: "I am proud to belong to a religion which has taught the world both tolerance and universal acceptance. We believe not only in universal toleration, but we accept all religions as true . . . It was reserved for America to proclaim to all quarters of the globe that the Lord is in every religion . . . Hail, Columbia, motherland of liberty!" (TCWSV 1: 3-20).[15]

From the psychological angle, after Emerson, Humboldt, Whitman, and Melville, the idea of Spiritual Democracy in America reached a point of scholastic brilliance in the pioneering efforts of William James in 1902. It is with James that the intuition of Spiritual Democracy first entered the field of American academic psychology. In his views, we see a sketch of a subjective religion of Spiritual Democracy, based solely on experience. In *The Varieties of Religious Experience*, James's idea of religion based on personal experience, is central to our extension of religious democracy. In this book, which was based on his Gifford Lectures on natural religion at the University of Edinburgh in 1902 and 1903, James, like Jung, viewed the subconscious self as the gateway to all spiritual realization.

James brought a pluralistic, pragmatic, and empirical attitude into academic psychology that surveyed American poetry (Whitman primarily) and attempted to give examples from many of the world religions. His views had a direct impact on the psychology of Carl Jung, particularly following Jung's meeting of James at Clark University in Massachusetts in 1909. James illuminates something important for our extension of Whitman's views on Spiritual Democracy, and that is his inspection of the world religions as a whole. His ideas are expressed perhaps most clearly in a simple letter written to a friend in Edinburgh:

> The problem I have set myself is a hard one: first, to defend . . . "experience" against "philosophy" as being the real backbone of the world's religious life . . . and second, to make the hearer or reader believe, what I myself invincibly do believe, that, although all the special manifestations of religions may have been absurd (I mean its creeds and theories), yet the life of it as a whole is mankind's most important function.[16]

Although James never uses the specific term "Spiritual Democracy," he does describe the notion clearly in his references on religion. This is a precise definition of what James means by Spiritual Democracy: *the backbone of the world's religions as a whole, is humanity's most important function*. "Function" here means a spiritual purpose present in everyone.

Perhaps James's greatest contribution to the history of religious thought is his insistence that the type of religion he calls "healthy-mindedness"—a religion based on a perpetual state of happiness and good cheer that he traces directly to Walt Whitman—"deliberately excluded evil from its field of vision."[17] Deliberately minimizing evil could become a form of blindness and insensitivity to the darker aspects of the objective reality of things, and is, in James' view, therefore quite dangerous.

I emphasize this exclusionary principle here because Jung's project to rehabilitate world religion in the direction of a Spiritual Democracy ultimately argues for the inclusion of evil as well as good into our *Weltanschauung*, our own philosophy of life. This is a view William James shares with Whitman, Melville, Dickinson, and his brother, Henry James. It is also my belief that if we as a world cannot grasp this fact of religion's dark side, we are endangered as a species and may be headed for extinction. William James, like Jung, brings a vision of evil into his psychological discussions on religion in a way Whitman couldn't—or wouldn't—fully grasp. He helps us see that evil is as much a function of God as good is.

James asks us to consider: "How *can* religion on the whole be the most important of all human functions?" His thesis is that it "will have to be our final contention."[18] For ultimately, we are all dependent upon the universe, he says, and the "subconscious self" is the real seat of religious experiences.[19] By religious function, moreover, James means *feeling*. He asserts: "I do believe that feeling is the deeper source of religion, and that philosophic and theological formulas are secondary products, like translations of a text into another tongue."[20]

In *The Varieties of Religious Experience*, James discredits the intellectualism of dogmatic theologies or philosophies and advances pragmatism as a solution, or what he calls the "science of religions."[21] In this case "science" is an empirical view toward religious experiences as facts that prove the divine is actually present, as a *"plus, a thisness*, which feeling alone can answer for."[22] He adds, in this context: "the science of religions would depend for its original material on facts of personal experience, and would have to square itself with personal experience through all its critical reconstructions."[23]

In putting forth the hypothesis of a science of religion, James does not mean that we should all espouse the empirical investigation of natural religion as a religion in its own right, for science will never be "an equivalent for living religion."[24] In his conclusions, James sums up his main points about religious experience:

1. It evokes our individual or "private destiny";
2. It rehabilitates the feeling element in religion and subordinates its intellectual parts;[25]
3. It leads to the *"fact that the conscious person is continuous with a wider self through which saving experiences come"*;[26] and,
4. The pragmatic way of taking religion is the "deeper way" because it gives the "body as well as soul" some "characteristic realm of fact as its very own."[27]

James's contributions can add something of the lived experience that is so important for Spiritual Democracy. As we will see, the last criterion on the list—taking the empirical facts of body as well as soul as subjectively and objectively real, and as the basis of a "higher synthesis" of religion—is the only way forward toward a saner and more democratic future,[28] where the presumption of the absolute nature of fundamentalist beliefs will hopefully be replaced by a greater global tolerance for variety.

JUNG IN AMERICA

Carl Jung had a strong admiration for James's astuteness. Recalling memories of his trip to Clark University with Sigmund Freud and Hungarian neurologist Salvador Ferenczi in 1909, Jung wrote fondly to an inquirer about his reminiscences of James: "I spent two delightful evenings with William James alone and I was tremendously impressed by the clearness of his mind and the complete absence of intellectual prejudices."[29] In another letter he adds that James also tackled the Old Testament problem of Job's doubts that an all-good God could have designed the world.[30] "No!" James exclaimed in Lecture XVIII of his Gifford Lectures, "the book of Job went over this whole matter once for all and definitively."[31] In one of Jung's seminars on Nietzsche's *Zarathustra* he pointed moreover to another chapter from James's celebrated lectures and said to his audience, "Read William James."[32]

It is not often recognized that Carl Jung began his quest for a new guiding myth for the advancement of modern culture while writing a lengthy exegesis of the poetic fantasies of an American woman. Jung's amplifications included an extended analysis of a nineteenth-century American poet's own development of Native American myth, Henry Wadsworth Longfellow's epic poem "The Song of Hiawatha," which had influenced some of the woman's fantasies. The lengthy narrative poem, long a staple of student education on both sides of the Atlantic, was published the same year Whitman launched *Leaves of Grass*, in 1855.

The young woman who provided the fantasies discussed a half century later by Jung in his groundbreaking *Transformations and Symbols of the Libido* (published in America in 1916 and translated into English by Beatrice Hinkle as *Psychology of the Unconscious*) happens to have been a poet herself, writing under the pseudonym "Miss Frank Miller." Théodore Flournoy, a trusted personal friend of William James and a mentor of Jung's, first made Miss Miller's fantasies available to the public in 1906 through the *Archives de Psychologie* (Geneva), which Jung read. Frederick Myers, who founded England's Society for Psychical Research in 1882, another important figure in the developing psychology of the unconscious, spoke of the mind's "mythopoetic function" and its "unconscious tendency to weave fantasies."[33] The content of Miss Miller's semihypnotic reveries illustrated this tendency, and Jung, too, developed his own technique of fantasy weaving in his dialogues and in his depictions of his adventures with his own soul in the *Red Book*. Later, Jung admitted he had been projecting his soul-image (expelling a subjective content of his soul, a mythopoetic image) onto Miss Miller, who served as a muse to open the door for him to an experience of the collective unconscious.

It has not been often enough noted in the history of analytical psychology that his discovery of a doorway to the objective psyche came, therefore, through an American cultural lens, given the influence of Longfellow's poem on Miss Miller, which Jung did not fail to note and discuss at length. American poetry must be realized, then, as a leading source of Jung's vision of a world soul. This becomes even clearer when we compare Jung's visions to that of Longfellow's three major contemporaries, Melville, Whitman, and Dickinson, who, in the views of many literary critics, were the progenitors of a new world poetry. Longfellow, of course, has receded into the background as a slight figure in the history of verse. Nevertheless, at the turn of the twentieth century, when Jung read Longfellow in 1911, the poet still garnered considerable influence for poems like "Hiawatha," which Jung felt able to discuss at length before an educated audience. Despite "the certainty of Longfellow's minor stature,"[34] "Hiawatha" was a mythopoetic work, implying the possibility of a new source of imagination for poets beyond the Roman, Celtic, Judeo-Christian, and Germanic works that had previously dominated Western poetic explorations. For that reason we need to consider what Jung found in American literature to advance his notion of a collective unconscious that went beyond typical ethnic and ethnographic boundaries of cultural diffusion.

In the 1950 foreword to the fourth (Swiss) edition of *Wandlüngen und Symbole der Libido,* or *Symbols of Transformation* in the English versions, Jung recalls that while writing the book in 1911 he asked himself, "What is the myth you are living?" This is a question to which he could find no clear answer. Hardly had Jung finished the book when he took it upon himself to come to know the nature of the myth ordering his own life. In treating patients, of course, Jung had long sensed that he must make due allowance for the "personal factor," or "personal equation," so necessary for arriving at the full knowledge of another human being. But there the "task of tasks," to "get to know" one's own individual myth took him well beyond what was necessary for clinical objectivity. He had begun to recognize a task for all individuals: to find a way to relate responsibly to the transpersonal and transcultural psyche within the context of one's own national mythos. This was precisely the American poet Longfellow's standpoint, fifty years earlier. It was while making liberal use of Longfellow's "Hiawatha" that Jung began to recognize his own need to learn what "preconscious myth was forming" him. This, as he put it, would be the "rhizome" from which the plant of his individuation sprang.[35] Still unaware of what his personal myth was, Jung, in his notion of the collective unconscious, had intuited the archetype of Spiritual Democracy as a superordinate notion of a transnational self with power to unite modern psychology and the world's religions with the "civilizing" tendency we might call "globalization" today. This archetype can be found in all world mythologies, not just as a rationalization for the spread of capitalism but as the friend of men and women useful in the efforts to become more human.

By analyzing the dream-visions of Miss Miller, Jung was seeking to discover a universal language that could prove the existence of a structure of the unconscious that is everywhere the same and functions the same in every individual. At the center of Jung's search for his personal myth are the first clear articulations of his notion of an empirical God-image that transcends cultural definitions of what God is. In addition to looking at the major world religions, he also drew upon images and symbols of the archaic mind, which pattern the mythologies of all peoples, all races, all ages. Hence, he was searching to find a master concept that could answer a question about the foundation of the human mind. In doing so he arrived at the notion of national complexes, echoing Jacob Burckhardt's reflections on Goethe's *Faust,* in which Burckhardt proposed that each nation creates a "genuine myth, i.e., a great primordial image, in which every man has to discover his own being and destiny in his own way . . ." Jung refined the notion. "There must, then, be typical myths," he writes, "which serve to work out our racial and national complexes."[36] Jung is suggesting that our great national myths can help us sort out our complexes and lead us to discover our personal destinies by way of certain resonances that speak to us rhythmically and metaphorically.

Jung makes it clear that his hypotheses were never meant to be absolute, and his science of the human psyche was meant to remain open to further empirical investigations. He admits how "hazardous" the comparisons between Longfellow's poem and Miss Miller's dream-visions seemed, even to him, yet he insists: "Miss Miller named her sources herself."[37] Jung then asserts that since "the basic structure of the human psyche is everywhere more or less the same, it is possible to compare what look like individual dream-motifs with mythologems of whatever origin. So I have no hesitation in making comparisons between American Indian myth and the modern American psyche."[38]

Although we in the twenty-first century can agree with Jung that many aspects of the human psyche are the same everywhere in everyone, the myths of various nations that help large groups of people work out their national complexes are importantly diverse and significantly varied in color and content, so that the typical motifs that are emphasized vary from country to country. They show striking contrasts that can lead to rival hypotheses about certain psychological questions, such as the nature of the libido and its transformations.[39] Thus, we have to inquire whether Jung's reflections on American poetry need to be adjusted to accommodate what we actually read in the poems. Moreover, we must ask ourselves today what Jung asked one hundred years ago: what is the myth we are living?

First we owe to Jung an intuition that there is an archetype in Longfellow's "Hiawatha" that forms a core variable of a national myth to offer en route to the discovery of our own collective mythology: the transnational mythos of Spiritual Democracy. Jung begins his astute analysis of "Hiawatha" by quoting the first canto of Longfellow's "Evangelium," where Gitche Manito—the "master of life"—says: "I will send a Prophet to you, / A Deliverer of the nations."[40] This concise saying by Gitche Manito is a reference to Hiawatha as the peacemaker among different peoples. Moreover, the reference to a "Deliverer of nations" borders a prototype of Spiritual Democracy: one who is a unifier of diverse cultures, politics, and religions. While the historical figure Hiawatha was understandably not exactly that transnationally situated in his spiritual outlook because he lacked a vision of modernity, he nevertheless represents a movement in this direction.

Jung's 1912 book, *Wandlüngen und Symbole der Libido*, contains a literary and psychological analysis of "Hiawatha" that amplifies Miss Miller's fantasies in a brilliant way. After discussing Gitche Manito in Longfellow's poem as a "creator of nations," a kind of "Original Man (Anthropos)" shown standing erect on "the great Red Pipestone quarry," Jung recounts that from the footsteps of this mighty figure flowed forth a river that "Gleamed like Ishkoohah, the comet."[41] Interestingly, Jung then cites the dance step of the Pueblo Indians, the dancing dervishes, and even makes reference to Humboldt's *Cosmos*, a text that informed Emerson and Whitman. Jung writes, "The comparison of water flowing from Gitche Manito's footprints with a comet means that it is a light or libido-symbol for the fertilizing moisture (sperma). According to a note in *Cosmos*, certain native South American tribes call meteors 'piss of the stars.'"[42] This is an important leap on Jung's part, because he is grounding his intuition about the transformation of the libido in the Hiawatha myth in the best scientific text his grandparent's generation had to offer. (In fact, Jung's grandfather was acquainted with Humboldt, who had gone on to personally recommend the elder Jung to the University of Basel, where this first Carl Gustav Jung ultimately became a doctor and a professor of medicine, a rector of the university, and the grandmaster and head of the Swiss society of Freemasons.) Thus, "Hiawatha" and *Cosmos* helped Jung arrive at a place of intersection with Whitman's project, and from that point they seem to be traveling down a similar road, which Jung would later name the unus mundus and Whitman earlier called Spiritual Democracy.

The notion of the founding of American Democracy as the basis for advancing a new world spirit coincides with the early writings of Benjamin Franklin, who was also a Freemason. Franklin's discussions with Native American nations during the many treaty councils he attended and published from his own printing press in Philadelphia, prior to the American Revolution, led to the establishment of a government based not on a declaration of war, but on *Kaianerekowa*. This iconic law was handed down through oral tradition from Hiawatha to the Iroquois League of Five Nations, originally comprising the Senecas, Ondondagas, Oneidas, Mohawks, and Cayugas. Iroquoian sources suggest the League was formed somewhere between 1000 and 1400 AD. In 1714, a sixth nation, the Tuscaroras, joined the League. According to Iroquois legend, the idea of a federal union to make peace between the warring tribes came through the dream of a Huron man, who chose Hiawatha to realize his vision.

Benjamin Franklin raised the principles of the Great Treaty of Peace during discussions with the authors of the Constitution. As Bruce E. Johansen writes in *Forgotten Founders: How the American Indian Helped Shape Democracy:* "The American Indians' theory and practice affected Franklin's observations on the need for appreciation of diverse cultures and religions, public opinion as the basis for polity, the nature of liberty and happiness, and the social role of property."[43] The rest of the founding fathers were also well aware of the six-nation treaty. Significantly, one of its central principles is freedom of religion.[44] After attending several treaty councils, Franklin put forth the following definition of federalism, according to Johansen: "Independence of each other, and separate interests, tho' among a people united by common manners, language, and, I may say, religion." Religious "self-righteousness and pomposity," Johansen adds, "was a favorite target of Franklin's pen, and he often used Indians to illustrate the religious relativism that was basic to his own Deistic faith."[45]

Several historians have noted that, in addition to Franklin, the founding fathers James Madison, Thomas Jefferson, and John Adams all integrated notions of the Great Law of Peace into U.S. policies. Much later these ideas were carried forward into the passage of Resolution 76, introduced in the U.S. Congress in 1987, when a debt of thanks was finally repaid to the Iroquois Confederacy and other Indian Nations by the Republic of the United States on the occasion of the two hundredth anniversary of the signing of the U.S. Constitution. This event was preceded by a 1977 presentation of a document called "Basic Call to Consciousness" by a Seneca elder, John Mohawk, to a United Nations conference in Geneva, Switzerland—Jung's home base.[46] Mohawk and other representatives of the Six Nation Iroquois called for developed nations to implement basic changes in their policies and to stop environmental destruction.

Thus, Miss Miller helped Jung make a link to a myth that is at the very foundation not only of the writing of the U.S. Constitution, but is also one of the central principles of the United Nations Education, Scientific, and Cultural Organization, UNESCO. The organization's purpose is to contribute to peace through promoting international collaboration among nations. Likewise, Spiritual Democracy aims to deliver the nations of the world from tyranny, treachery, and religious fundamentalism of all kinds, and above all, from the world-threatening horrors of war. Jung was likely unaware of the role the Iroquois played in the development of his own spiritual attitude since he first encountered "Hiawatha" in the American Miss Miller's fantasies, but it is evident as late as his brief to the United Nations in 1948, when he outlined to UNESCO his specific thoughts and recommendations on what is required to avert wars in an essay entitled "Techniques of Attitude Change Conducive to World Peace."[47]

Jung does tell us in his English Seminars, which he conducted in Zürich in 1925, that he realized he had been projecting his own soul—*anima* in Latin—onto Miss Miller in 1911, and this projectile helped connect him to the mythopoetic ground of the collective unconscious. While Jung was writing *Symbols of Transformation*, Miller served as a sort of mediator to his inferior function of sensation, which is an elementary function that subjectively perceives external and internal phenomena and connects one to the reality of psychic and physical facts. "I had to realize then," Jung recounts "that in Miss Miller I was analyzing my own fantasy function."[48] Fantasy thinking enabled Jung to observe an objective picture of the mythopoetic function while he was constructing his *Red Book*. Jung's anima was strongly heterosexual, and in retrospect this may have slanted his theory of the libido too sharply toward the side of heterosexuality.

Jung saw in 1925 that *Symbols of Transformation* "seemed to forecast the future."[49] He realized that Miss Miller had taken over his "fantasy and became stage director to it. . . . In other words, she became an anima figure, a carrier of an inferior function of which I was little conscious."[50] Jung recalls, "I assimilated the Miller side of myself, which did me much good. To speak figuratively, I found a lump of clay, turned it to gold and put it in my pocket. I got Miller into myself and strengthened my fantasy power by the mythological material."[51] Thus, Miller provided Jung with some of the spiritual gold he was looking for: her evocations of American poetic vision.

In "Concerning Two Kinds of Thinking" Jung supports the intuition that he had found a nugget of pure mythopoetic gold, an international language of rhythmic speech patterns in the collective psyche: "How are fantasies created?" he asks. "From poets," he says, "we learn much about it; from science we learn little."[52] This view would of course change in his later years when he was writing out his scientific theory of synchronicity, but until then Jung needed to relax his scientific mind, for his real interests as a child and as a young man had been theology, philosophy, and perhaps especially, poetry. Jung, though well versed in German poetry, was not a systematic student of comparative literature, but had he turned to Whitman, Melville, and Dickinson to advance his systematic model of the structure of the unconscious, rather than turning to Longfellow, we might have been able to understand the American psyche better than what *Symbols* teaches.

Part of the problem may have been that, as we've seen, Jung's understanding of the anima was almost exclusively heterosexual, and he maintained an aversion to homosexuality as a path to the development of the soul. We can learn a lot from Jung's manuscript about the spiritualization of the heterosexual libido as it is depicted in Goethe and Nietzsche, but that leaves us with a riddle to solve about Whitman, Dickinson, and Melville: Why were their libido analogies, gradients, or transformers *contra* Jung, bi-erotic? What does this say about the structure and dynamics of the American soul and the national complexes we have been trying to work out and resolve through the living out of our personal destinies?[53] What can their texts teach us about same-sex marriage, and why is it so important as a political and religious issue across so many nations of the world today?

Such an important set of questions notwithstanding, poets such as Longfellow (as well as Goethe and Schiller, Nietzsche, and Hölderlein) taught Jung to value Spiritual Democracy, which would later become the prime material for his life's work in the notion of a collective unconscious promoting a unus mundus (one united world) as the goal of psychological and religious development. Jung learned from such poets and his first American muse,[54] Miss Frank Miller, how to access the mythopoetic unconscious. To advance his scientific theories, Jung learned how to switch off his directed thinking and let fantasy thinking have its way with him. Poetry became a key.

In his amplifications on the meaning of the American mythos, Jung was trying to get at the roots of what is behind the hero myth, to the place beyond the hero motif, where the hero/heroine is forced to sacrifice his or her personal will to the universal will of the self. In Longfellow's poem, Hiawatha wrestles with Mondamin ("Rise, O youth, and wrestle with me!")[55] Here Hiawatha finds the much-needed strength within himself to do battle with the West Wind, and he himself becomes thereby a prophet of the wisdom of the West. In this myth, what Hiawatha is really wrestling with is himself, the source of his own creativity, his true genius, and as Jung emphasizes further: "Whoever succeeds in this has triumphed indeed."[56]

Whatever the indigenous forces are that have shaped American poetry (whatever the "soil," influences that affect any era's patterns of speech, dreams, religion, appearance, sexuality, and spirituality), the American poet-shamans (Whitman, Melville, Dickinson)[57] were aware of them, often to a marked degree. Jung, too, recognized the effect of Native American traditions on Europeans who had settled in America. He saw, as had Burckhardt, that every nation that creates a national mythology through which large groups can work out their national and racial complexes and through which each citizen can realize their individual destiny, in his own way; each person who is called to develop methods of attitude change conducive to global transformation would be wise to ask what the nature of the national complex is.

Based upon the work of Whitman, Melville, and Dickinson, the nuclear core of this complex appears to be a primordial image of Spiritual Democracy in America and the world. Whitman was clearly channeling this archetype when he wrote in his 1847 Notebook:

> I am the poet of women as well as men.
> The woman is not less than the man
> But she is never the same,
> (the Peacemaker)[58]

This is the same image of the peacemaker that we find in the Hiawatha myth, for "Peacemaker" is another name for the fifteenth-century Algonquin hero, and another name for the self, regardless of its gender, ethnicity, religion, or sex, in any nation.

4

JUNG ON SPIRITUAL
DEMOCRACY

Carl Jung's way of viewing religious experience in the unus mundus sheds light on the work of Walt Whitman, Herman Melville, and Emily Dickinson, and on their conscious efforts to unite their readers in a new world of spiritual experience sharable by everyone.

Jung, who had read Alexander von Humboldt's work by 1912, appears to have been riding on the intellectual thought currents issuing forth from the efforts of the influential Prussian botanist, explorer, and philosopher who did so much to create a unitary view of our lives in the cosmos. These currents were already eddying through Jung's dreams when one in particular, about a glowing, circular, giant type of protozoa known as a radiolarian, galvanized the pastor's son to take up natural sciences at the University of Basel. Jung's vocation to science was clarified through further dreams and the sort of coincidences he later called synchronistic events. They eventually led him into what was then a poor outpost of science, psychiatry. Jung set out to explore, in the psyches of deeply split individuals, the microcosm of the human soul as its own cosmos. And, despite the fact that he was not as fond of American democracy as Humboldt was, he ultimately ended up with as fully a democratic vision of how each individual might realize cosmos in his or her own "symbolic life."

In a reply to an inquiry made during a California seminar in 1954, Jung revealed his views regarding the obliteration of religious experience by the anonymous and highest ruling authorities of our lives—the state. Jung warned that if we are not steadfast in our relationship to the inner voice of the divine, then government might assume hegemony over our individual conscience, whether the system be communist, fascist, or democratic. Jung cites communism, in particular, as the ultimate realization of this unfortunate situation. He adds, "Unfortunately our democracy has nothing to offer in the way of different ideals; it also believes in the concrete power of the state. There is no spiritual authority comparable to that of the state anywhere." Jung concludes his reply, "We are badly in need of a spiritual counterbalance,"[1] meaning "a re-establishment of Man as the microcosm, i.e., man's cosmic relatedness."[2] Our relatedness to the cosmos must be reestablished by a psychological process of individuation, he says, and *"Individuation is the life in God."*[3] Hence, "cosmic relatedness" is life in God, Jung's solution to the problem of the state and the first two levels of democracy (political and economic) that Whitman outlined for us.

Indeed, Whitman's idea of Spiritual Democracy anticipated Jung's. Jung, following a Swiss Protestant tradition, offered his individual confession of faith as a solution to what he felt was missing in organized religion, which turned out to be grounded in a way of relating to the cosmos that he discovered outside European Christianity. Whitman feels authorized to give more than a subjective confession of faith because he is a poet and not a scientist. In fact, he provides a new metaphysical assertion, emphasizing, with an extroverted flourish, the magnitude of the individual and of the cosmos too. "I swear I begin to see the meaning of these things," Whitman says. "It is not the earth, it is not America [the democratic State] who is great, / It is I who am great or to be great, it is You up there [Cosmos], or any one [each self/Self]."[4]

In Whitman's view, individuals are coequal with the cosmos, and our aim on this beautiful, miraculous planet is to reestablish our cosmic connectedness to all things. The most important center within the cosmos in Whitman's view is "You" with a capital Y—Yourself, Your own separate Person. You are, in Whitman's understanding, the most important event in the universe, and nothing surpasses the individual's coming into cosmic selfhood, not even God. "I will make cities and civilizations defer to me, / This is what I have learnt from America—it is the amount, and I teach it again."[5] Practically speaking Whitman means that we are made of the same cosmic stuff as planets and atoms, and our vocations are vehicles of the same cosmic energy. This electrically charged and potentially violent energy needs to be channeled into our callings to help heal the earth, the air, and the seas, and move us all in the direction of increasing compassion for one another and of embracing peaceful nonviolence.

For Whitman, the democratic ideal most worth striving for was the one he named: Spiritual Democracy. As this concept leaps beyond Whitman's works and legacy like a rocket to present us with a new view of the Earth, it will encompass similar visions achieved by Melville, Dickinson, and Jung. According to Whitman, who launched, but never wished to "own" the idea, Spiritual Democracy is neither Christian nor Hindu, Protestant nor Catholic, Jewish nor Islamic. It imitates no religious founder; it identifies with none; it will have none of this. The individual realization of self resists imitation in this vision. In Whitman's view the self destroys all religious teachers, including himself. The self proclaims only what is most democratic, cosmic, and new. Paradoxically, it destroys and celebrates all previous God-images in history by asserting the rights of Nature's God as coequal to all other symbols of divinity. To be spiritually democratic, in Whitman's view, therefore, means that one is able to celebrate the self uninhibitedly. It means that we are all vehicles of cosmic awareness.

Thrilling as this vision is, it does not allow us to be naive about what Spiritual Democracy can achieve. We can't assume, uncritically, that in the revelations of Whitman or other visionaries that peace can maintain itself without conflict, that is, without fighting and war. World peace must be maintained through consistent and continuous negotiations between nations, and in order to play a part in the whole, one must first become a carrier of the calling from the self, that is, someone whose vocation springs from the seed of destiny and is illuminated by love for what is right. In the United States, this means claiming one's own birthright by standing up for the highest principles of religious liberty—a battle perennially worth waging. The shadow, whether in political, sexual, or religious form, has to be included in the holistic effort to unite the world, and nothing that this entails is omitted in Jung's and Whitman's visions, not even war.

In a letter, written to James Redpath, in October 1863, Whitman wrote unequivocally:

> I never questioned the decision that led me into the war; whatever the years have brought—whatever sickness, what not—I have accepted the result as inevitable and right. This is the very center, circumference, umbilicus, of my whole career. . . . It was a religion with me. A religion? Well, every man has a religion; has something in heaven or earth which he will give up everything else for—something which absorbs him, possesses itself of him, makes him over in its image—something. It may be something regarded by others as being very paltry, inadequate, useless, yet it is his dream; it is his lodestar; it is his master. That, whatever it is, seized upon me, made me its servant, slave; induced me to set aside other ambitions—a trail of glory in the heavens, which I followed, followed with a full heart.[6]

As we've seen, Whitman, like Jung, did not exclude evil from his religious vision. The evil in the Civil War, and its root cause, slavery, persisted in a country that insisted it was already a democracy. As we shall see, the battle for abolition of slavery was his lodestar. For Whitman, his dual vocation as a poet and nurse in the hospital wards of Washington during the Civil War was his religion: it opened his mind to the grim realities of Spiritual Democracy and the long shadow cast by private property, which had inevitably led to a collision between types of "freedom." Whitman included in his metaphysical vision of war an ethic that could set things right in a religious attitude based on equality. This was an ethic of justice, right judgment, right feeling, and right vocation. At both the center and the circumference of his calling was the power of the American dream: not Manifest Destiny, but the destiny of the American Republic to lead the human race, individually and collectively, in Spiritual Democracy. That "great Idea" made him its "servant, slave," as he tended to the sick and dying during the war. After the bloody and divisive conflict, a vision of a phantom of all the past poets of wars accosted him with a stern visage and moved him to chant an extended *"song of the throes of Democracy."*[7]

This calling, as bard intoning the brutal implications of the Civil War, conjures the problem of evil. Whitman, like Jung, realized that a vision of the shadow enables democracy to advance, and he knew why such a psychological achievement is so vital and necessary for the maintenance of peace in all nations of the globe. Jung, too, formulated many great passages about this. In "The Philosophical Tree," he writes: "One does not become enlightened by imagining figures of light, but by making the darkness conscious."[8] In *Jung and the Problem of Evil*, published in 1958 when Jung was still alive, the author H. L. Phillip features a long correspondence between Jung and himself, in the form of questions and answers. Here Jung's views on religious belief are made clear. Jung is quoted as saying:

> Christ has shown how everyone will be crucified upon his destiny, i.e., upon his self, as he was. . . . We are threatened with universal genocide if we cannot work out the way of salvation by a symbolic death.[9]

In these two passages Jung is cautioning readers that humanity must perform crucial tasks: it must make the darkness and evil of the unconscious conscious, and it must undergo the necessary sacrifice of self-idealizing notions. If humanity doesn't assume the individual moral responsibility for the integration of the opposites of good and evil in divinity, our collective failure to raise our awareness to a deeper, vaster, and more spiritually inclusive way of relating to the cosmos will lead to final Armageddon. Such an outcome will be made all but inevitable by the pursuit of such splitting notions as the forces of good and the forces of evil that every world nation had managed to take into actual warfare with its fantasy of finally killing the demonized "other." This means, above all, that we must first as individuals, and then as nations, learn to be modest in our outlooks on life. Jung teaches us to see the ego's limitations "before the One who dwells within him, whose form has no knowable boundaries, who encompasses him on all sides, fathomless as the abysms of the earth and vast as the sky."[10] Such modesty is essential if Spiritual Democracy is to come about in the world as a force of peace that can effect change at all levels of culture.

Ultimately, in Jung's cosmic/microcosmic view of life we must sacrifice our ego on the cross of destiny—the cross of vocation—that we are called to carry throughout life, each in our own way. Thus, each of us must accept, therefore, the reality of our calling from the "inner voice," which includes the integration of our own evil. And only then can nations do the same.

In a 1948 memorandum to the United Nations Educational, Scientific and Cultural Organization (UNESCO), Jung outlined his specific thoughts and recommendations on what is required to avert wars in an essay entitled "Techniques of Attitude Change Conducive to World Peace." In this seminal document, written in fluent English, Jung made it clear that "an attitude is governed and sustained by a dominant conscious idea accompanied by a so-called 'feeling-tone,' i.e., an *emotional* value, which accounts for the efficacy of the idea. The mere idea has no practical or moral effect whatever if it is not supported by an emotional quality having as a rule an *ethical* value."[11] Here Jung is talking about vocation—how we are called to act—which in his view must include the knowledge of one's potential for violence through a careful observation of one's dreams and fantasies, if the result is to be truly peaceful action.

Whitman, a century earlier, knew the potential for violence within himself. He knew how to understand and accept his own evil. He knew in his heart that only through the complete and final abolishment of slavery in America could the dominant idea of Spiritual Democracy be fully ratified. What Whitman was fighting for through spiritual violence (the explosive power of his great, electrically charged idea) was the principle of individuation inherent in all people. In this way he lived what Jung called, using an empirical term, the "hypothesis" of his truly experimental life. If we are to fulfill our destiny, Jung says, we must live our hypothesis. Jung again refers to the Christ-image as an exemplar for this: "We all must do what Christ did. We must make our experiment. We must make mistakes. We must live out our vision of life."[12] As with the prophet Isaiah, the path of Jesus was not the way of war and physical violence, it was a path of the sacred heart, and the same path, in fact, that Whitman and Melville and Dickinson and Jung were all following: the path of the Peacemaker.[13]

After the end of World War II, Jung addressed the United Nations (then developing its headquarters in the United States) with words that Melville or Whitman might have written: "A man whose heart is not changed will not change any others."[14] Those who have tried to advance Spiritual Democracy have always known that change must occur at the level of the heart, for that is the center or beating drum of the cosmos, which our shaman-poets have always heard. In his brief to the United Nations, Jung advanced this drumbeat by insisting that a change of attitude conducive to world peace would require any would-be leader or teacher to "be absolutely convinced that his personal attitude is in need of revision, even of actual change." For Jung, it was only from this conviction—which accepts the truth that there will be error, darkness, and mistakes—that one may arrive, hopefully, at the following "conclusion: the world is wrong and therefore I am wrong too. To pronounce such words is easy, but to feel their truth in the marrow of one's bones is a very different proposition, yet it is the sine qua non of the true teacher."[15] During his last trip to the United States in 1937, Jung went to the very city, New York, that Whitman regarded as the center of the world. There, he addressed the question: "Is analytical psychology a religion?" Jung was clear in his response:

> Many people have asked me, and doubtless asked you too, whether analytical psychology is not a religion. . . . We must all do what Christ did. We must make our experiment. . . . This sounds like a religion, but it is not. I am speaking just as a philosopher. People sometimes call me a religious leader. I am not that. I have no message, no mission; I attempt only to understand. We are philosophers in the old sense of the word, lovers of wisdom.[16]

What did Jung mean when he said that we must all do what Christ did? How can this statement be applied to the world by starting with each reader? How can Spiritual Democracy play a role in helping to realize this experiment in our own lives in a practical way? After Jung traveled from New York to Yale University in New Haven, Connecticut, where he paid a tribute to William James in his opening address at the Terry Lectures, he defined religion as a particular "attitude peculiar to a consciousness which has been changed by experience of the numinosum."[17] By numinosum—a term coined by Rudolph Otto in his book The Idea of the Holy—Jung intended to invoke a "dynamic agency or effect not caused by an arbitrary act of will. On the contrary, it seizes and controls the human subject, who is always rather its victim than its creator."[18] The idea of being changed is crucial here. If we are not changed, Jung says, nothing happens. Spiritual Democracy begins, then, with a change in you and me. It is a passionate fire that rises up through inward meditation, prayer, visioning, and ritual. No change results in no advance in consciousness.

As Jung pointed out at Yale, any new psychology of religion cannot be based on a creed, only on a peculiar attitude of mind toward an experience of something that adjusts us in the area of our religiousness, in the area of our hearts, and can create a changed religious attitude. And concomitant with such an adjustment is the Greek term written as "πίστις, that is to say, trust or loyalty, faith and confidence in a certain experience of a numinous nature and the change of consciousness that ensues."[19] Jung said the same thing in 1937 as he did later, in his epistle to the United Nations, regarding attitudinal changes conducive to world peace: "A change of attitude [or consciousness] never starts with a group but only with an individual."[20]

Jung is not often seen as modest, any more than Whitman and Melville, but his modesty shines through here. His recommendation is cautious, circumspect, and wise, even though the effort to put forth a new psychological attitude toward the religions that have always called us to action is promoted potentially in the light of the right conscience in that it promises to be conducive to world peace. Significantly, this change in attitude toward religion does not call itself a new religion, rather it is a new religious attitude grounded in the findings of modern psychology, so that we may all be better informed as to the nature of the individual soul through which, individually and privately, religion works in each of us, for better or for worse. The "psychologist, if he takes up a scientific attitude, has to disregard the claims of every creed to be the unique and eternal truth,"[21] Jung asserts.

This was not the first time Jung's views on religion as an individual experiment in radical democratic spiritual conscience had been presented to an audience in the United States. In 1916, when Jung's ideas on religion became available to a U.S. readership as *Psychology of the Unconscious*, Beatrice Hinkle's translation of *Wandlüngen und Symbole der Libido*, Jung had cited Humboldt, the European who had first brought the idea of cosmos to American shores and linked the concept, inevitably, to the New World vision of democracy. One of the most important passages in Jung's American-published book is a discussion on the meaning of religious symbols, a view Jung says that "is in no way allied to transcendentalism, either in positive or negative relation."[22] This exclusion makes it explicit that Jung, who knew Ralph Waldo Emerson's work, did not align himself, or his psychology, with Emersonian idealism. The passage is inserted as a footnote during Jung's in-depth discussion of Longfellow's poem "Hiawatha."

From the beginning of his career, then, Jung was actively addressing American audiences, and throughout it, it would be his destiny to teach the receptive U.S. public to value a democratic ideal regarding questions of religion. He emphasized the importance of sacrificing one's individual will, or egotism, for the good of the community, the people, and the interests of a common, scientifically verifiable truth. Analytic work, both Freudian and Jungian, has taught us that if we want relatedness and world peace we need to sacrifice our *"delusion through belief in the religious symbols,"* as Jung put it in *Psychology of the Unconscious.* This is what he means by the symbolic death of old religious forms, and old forms of religious attitudes. For an attitude toward religion to emerge that is spiritually democratic (or relativistic), each of us must find a way to submit to the self to realize the vocation calling us to participate in a new global community of fellow sufferers whose hearts have all been broken by the evil that we are collectively doing to our Mother Earth and the air we breathe.

Jung is interested only in what he will later term "facts of the heart" after his meeting with the Hopi elder known as Mountain Lake, at the Taos Pueblo in New Mexico, in the winter of 1925. Years earlier, in 1916, he wrote, "I think *belief should be replaced by understanding;* then we would keep the beauty of the symbol, but still remain free from the depressing results of submission to belief."[23] To believe in Christ and his death on the cross is one thing, in Jung's view, yet to carry the burden of one's own cross and to be crucified on one's destiny is another matter altogether, for it means that we will all have to suffer together as a species in the face of possible genocide. The difference between the sign of the cross in the life of Jesus and the symbol of the cross as a living thing, on which we all must be crucified, is the difference between faith and understanding. Belief and disbelief limit the individual from seeing and feeling the vast expanse and beauty of the cosmos and humanity's part in it. "Understanding is never the handmaiden of faith—on the contrary, faith completes understanding."[24]

Jung, Whitman, Melville, and Dickinson emphasize the original religious revelation and the changes of consciousness that ensue from such deep experiences, including our confrontation with evil. Jung is writing a myth of Spiritual Democracy within the cultural metaphor of divinity that was given to him at birth, and his work is to doctor what he diagnosed as sickness in Western religion. This means that many of the metaphors that he uses are Christian in derivation, as are, to some extent, Whitman's, Melville's and Dickinson's. But as we will see, all of these carriers of a vision of a new religious attitude place "Nature's God" at the center of even the Christian myth, and all agree that the Christian idea most worth carrying forward is not creed but rather recognition that change starts with individuals.

Jung, in his brief to the United Nations, insisted, *"If the whole is to change the individual must change himself. . . . Only with the individual can anything be done."*[25] He knew that it is in the nature of any collective to resist change, but he argued that this resistance stems from *"direct and indirect egotism,* i.e., unconsciousness of the ultimate equality of our fellow men."[26] Hence, the need for crucifixion in our earthly society, the sacrifice of excessive egotism on the cross of our vocation, the quaternity (Whitman calls the new God-image a Deus Quadriune), and the maternal. In Jung's words: all men and all women are *equal,* hence "the ultimate equality" of our fellow humans. Although Jung concludes, a bit pietistically, that we must all "become brothers of Christ,"[27] what he means is clearly a Spiritual Democracy of men and women beyond any creed or confession except one individually natural and organic—meaning no traditional "conversion to Christianity" is required.

When he was in the United States, Jung in fact analyzed the phenomenon of *collective religious feeling* as a symptom of an emerging psychic epidemic in the state. Jung's modesty on the part of his vocation required him, at times, to be a prophet, although he did not assume he was being a religious leader or a world teacher. Rather, he saw himself as a physician of the soul who recognized his sense of service to the generality:

> I hope, therefore, that a psychiatrist, who in the course of a long life has devoted himself to the causes and consequences of psychic disorders, may be permitted to express his opinion, in all the modesty enjoined upon him as an individual, about the questions raised by the world situation today. I am neither spurred on by excessive optimism nor in love with high ideals, but am merely concerned with the fate of the individual human being—that infinitesimal unit on whom a world depends, and in whom, if I read the meaning of the Christian message aright, even God seeks his goal.[28]

While Jung judged collective movements negatively, he also saw the incredible potential of human love, symbolized in his own religious tradition by Christ, as a spiritual counterbalance to the state.

The idea of being gripped by such an archetype is a psychological phenomenon that was clarified by Jung through his use of the German word

Ergriffenheit—a state of being seized or possessed. Whitman undoubtedly experienced this state, as did President Lincoln during the Civil War. "The term postulates not only an *Ergriffener* (one who is seized) but also an *Ergriefer* (one who seizes)."[29] The god that seizes us may be good or evil, and therefore Jung's refrain that he is "neither spurred on by excessive optimism nor in love with high ideals" is sobering. In his 1936 essay "Wotan," Jung notes that the *furor teutonicus* that possessed Germans in the 1930s and whipped them into a state of "fury" had so infected a whole nation and moved it toward a state of insanity that "everything is set in motion and has started rolling on its course toward perdition."[30]

On a more positive note, Jung spoke optimistically about the medieval theologian Meister Eckhart[31] as a German mystic who was also an Ergriffener. Jung suggests that a spiritual movement can captivate and arouse the best minds of its age, if it is not suppressed by oppressive creedal authorities, such as Eckhart was at the beginning of the fourteenth century, when Pope John XXII issued a papal bull, or a charter, that deemed dozens of Eckhart's articles either heretical, sacrilegious, or "suspect of heresy." The Ergreifer, the one who takes possession of the soul of such a person or religious group, Jung says, is always "God."[32] In spite of the suppression of his work, the example of Eckhart shows that, while it is certainly possible for a people to fall en masse into the grip of evil, it is equally possible that a large group, nation, or the world could be gripped by the powers of good, such as India under the leadership of Mahatma Gandhi.

A holistic feeling for religious relativism is at the center of Eckhart's mystical path, just as it is in the visions of Whitman and Jung. As we have seen, Emerson, Melville, Whitman, and William James all fought to keep the factor of religious experiences alive in a time of spiritual atrophy. As Jung put it, "Religious thought keeps alive the archaic state of mind even today in a time bereft of gods."[33] Indeed, religious thought is something that offers a model for how we might live our lives today, during a time of war. To arrive at a dominant conscious idea attended by what we have seen Jung call a strong "feeling-tone," he suggests it would need to be supported by an emotional quality having an ethical value. To carry such a value forward as he and Whitman did, one needs moral courage. Without courage there is no way to celebrate our equality with the divine.

Three years before Jung's death at the age of eighty-four, he summed up his ideas about religious belief in seven basic principles. These simple notions are fully in accord with Whitman's views on Spiritual Democracy, though there is no evidence the poet's writings had been directly received by Jung.[34] Each principle applies to Whitman's grand notion:

1. The average person identifies religion with a creed—Judaism, Christianity, Islam, Hinduism, Buddhism, Daoism, Yoga, and so on. Today, the New Age might include shamanism, pantheism, and paganism in this equation. To put the individual experience of a religious factor, the self or the numinosum, above life in any creed, or religious community, however, is largely considered irreligious, heretical, or even insane today. Community is considered to be the place of religious experience, not solitude, dreams, or the individual psyche. Hence, we are becoming less and less religious by the day, and less cosmically related, as few value the subjective truth of individual religious experience anymore. Moreover, the social function of being a vehicle of God's voice is today being shunned: "To be God's voice is not a social function anymore."[35] Thus, vocation is Jung's solution.

2. In a psychological age, we are all vehicles for the divine voice. Jung is clear that analytical psychology is not a religion. It is a way that promotes a calling to the divine whereby we are all spiritually attuned, through our vocations, to the power of the cosmos and nature.

3. When a person succeeds in projecting the self onto the God-image of a creed, government, or community, one might, if one is lucky, begin to wake the self up within. Then, things could, theoretically and practically, begin to happen. For God's voice to occur in one, Jung says an "act of *introjection* is needed, i.e., the realization that the self lives in you and not in the external figure separated and different from yourself."[36] This is known as *psychological relativity*, a development in Western religion Jung traces to Meister Eckhart.

4. No one creed possesses the absolute truth above all other religions. All religions possess part of the truth. Jung admits: "I cannot see why one creed should possess the unique and perfect truth. Each creed claims this prerogative, hence the general disagreement! This is not very helpful. Something must be wrong."[37] To help matters out, Jung looks within himself to see what is wrong, even and especially at his own attitude—as we all must do today in a Spiritual Democracy. Spiritual Democracy is religious experience, and it's not based on any particular creed.

5. If the founding fathers of the United States had made our states parts of one Christian nation, they would have placed at the religious foundation of our Constitution the archetypal image of Christ. Instead, they saw, correctly, as did Jung and Whitman, that the self rules religious

experience, not God-concepts or religious figures such as Yahweh, Jesus, Allah, Buddha, or Confucius, which are all only *images* of the self. The religious foundation, Spiritual Democracy, the self, will always remain democratic. All images of divinity can be found in the collective foundation of the world soul. On this point Jung is empirically relativistic in his spiritual outlook. "Christ," he says "belongs to the (collective) foundations of the psyche. I identify him therefore with what I call the self. The self rules the whole of the psyche."[38] Jung is careful to write *foundations* in the pluralistic sense here. Through the continuing incarnation of the Holy Spirit (the third person of the Trinity) in humanity and by the inclusion of a "fourth," feminine principle of relatedness and evil, expanded to include such diverse elements of the divine as the Goddess and the pantheism of the entire cosmos, the self can truly be said to rule the whole of the psyche for the post-Christian Jung. There are many foundations of the psyche—in fact, there are as many as there are human beings on the planet. Each of us exists in a cultural milieu that is based on a religious foundation, which in turn is often national in character. To get at the image of the self, any national foundation might lead the way, yet the self, in Whitman's, Melville's, and Dickinson's views, is multireligious, multicultural, and democratic, which leads to a different kind of mythos. It is less Christian, and also more connected to the indigenous base—to the instinctive roots of the impulse toward Spiritual Democracy.

6. With the foundation provided for by analytical psychology, all God-images of the world's revealed religions will have to change, as every living religion, in Jung's view, must *change with the times.* (If Whitman's intuition is correct, moreover, all creeds must become democratic if they are to continue to survive in modernity.) The many myths of the world need new interpretations, and the Christian myth, Jung insists, "needs to be retold in a new spiritual language."[39] Jung goes on to admit "that I mean the self in dealing with the idea of Christ, and since I do not know anything beyond the self I cling to his archetype."[40] The Christ symbol, in Jung's view, is not only an external image to be believed in outwardly, or identified with, but is an archetype alive with its own mythic vision of the cosmic mystery in our own selfhood, our own spiritual reality, and our own essential being.

7. Like Emerson, Whitman, Melville, and Dickinson, all of whom were well read in the religions of the East, Jung was mindful of being inclusive,

and said: "I actually prefer the term 'self' because I am talking to Hindus as well as Christians, and I do not want to divide but unite."[41] For Jung, Spiritual Democracy is not arrogant but modest (a Chinese virtue most dear to the philosopher Laozi) about the validity of the name-giving one assigns to the divine. The equality of the God-images, and their many foundations, is relative to one's "personal myth" waiting to be discovered inside every individual. For this reason Jung says, "I am unable to envisage anything beyond the self, since it is—by definition—a borderline concept designating the unknown totality of man: there are no known limits to the unconscious. There is no reason why you should or should not call the beyond-self Christ or Buddha or Purusha or Dao or Khidr or Tefereth. All these terms are recognizable formulations of what I call the 'self.' Moreover I dislike the insistence upon a special name, since my brethren are as good and as valid as I am. Why should their name-giving be less valid than mine?"[42] Call God what we will, it will always remain, as Laozi said, nameless. The quote raises moral and ethical questions about one's religious attitude. Jung, in his scientific modesty, could not call the base of the psyche love, because he experienced it as paradoxical: love and hate, compassion and violence, peace and war. Only when these opposites have been integrated can one become a true promoter of world peace.

Jung started searching for answers to moral questions in his early medical-school fraternity Zofingia lectures, but he grappled with the moral problem with full personal intensity in his pre–World War II *Red Book*. In that work, his search for a solution to the problem of integrating good and evil led him to experience the birth of a new God-image, a living symbol transcendent of ethical polarities. The German philosopher Friedrich Nietzsche said: "Zarathustra committed the most portentous error, morality."[43] For Jung, morality as taught in the sacred texts of the Zoroastrian religion, the Zend Avesta, was not an error; rather, he viewed it as he did Old Testament Mosaic Law, as part of the divine drama of evolution during the continuing enfoldment of the God-image in human history that, for better or for worse, is playing itself out in world history.

Each person, Jung believed, is called by an inner voice to wrestle with the problem of good and evil and its synthesis in the self. This is a central problem Jung outlines for us in his psychology of individuation. All other issues in analytical psychology pale in comparison to this moral question. It is the alpha and omega of all religious problems, whether in the East, Middle East, or the West. Healing the split between good and evil in as many people and nations as possible will hopefully lead us to see that morality and ethics, centered on cosmic relatedness, are necessary for the transformation of God. Bringing the opposites of good and evil together into a unity of personality during this miraculous age inevitably leads to love for oneself, one's neighbors, the world's nations, and all religions, for the ultimate aim of integration is love, by which is meant the fullest possible appreciation of each other in this cosmos, that is, the planet humans share. It is the way Whitman calls Spiritual Democracy, or what Jung calls "The Way of What Is to Come." This new way, Jung says *"leads to mutual love in community."*[44] "Love" in this case means affection and understanding among groups in a global community—a love that may radiate outward toward a larger relatedness of all.

In recent times, the Arab Spring prodemocracy uprisings in the Middle East and North Africa spotlighted the moral issues facing the world, including many matters of equality between the governed and the governors, such as equal rights for women even in traditional "patriarchal" cultures. Additionally, racial, ethnic, and sexual minorities within contemporary nations and their individual states and provinces are posing a direct challenge: everyone must integrate with each other. Whitman gives us the poetic energy to rise to the challenge. As he would say, we must keep its light burning bright.

Saudi Arabia, for instance, perhaps one of the most repressive regimes in the world but a nation long supported by the United States, has only recently granted women the right to vote—a move that was deeply unpopular with many of the nation's religious and cultural leaders, the imams. Women there still cannot drive cars nor leave their homes without a veil. The oppressive and misogynistic conditions will not end unless a new religious vision supersedes this draconian interpretation of Islamic law.

Jung learned essential tenets of Islam from a Somali friend on his trip to Africa in 1925, a religious man who belonged to a Mohammedan sect. When Jung asked his friend about Khidr, "the green prophet" who is a most sacred figure to Islam, this Somali man picked up a blade of grass and said: "he [Khidr] may appear like this."[45] From this statement it is easy to recognize Khidr in the irony of Whitman's lines in the final section of "Song of Myself": "I bequeath myself to the dirt to grow from the grass I love, / If you want me again look for me under your boot-soles."[46]

The American poets were steeped in Islamic mysticism of the Persian Sufi poets, and Jung, too, appears to have been influenced by Sufism when he said: "we have a funny idea of Islam through bad education. It is represented by our theologians as dry and empty, but there is tremendous life in it, particularly in

Islamic mysticism, which is the secret backbone of Islam."[47] Thus, in his view, the spine of Islam is to be found in Sufism, as well as in chapter 18 of the Koran, where Khidr appears. Jung spoke about the importance of bringing the two strong imprints, the Islamic and the Christian streams, together for the development of the personality. Although he felt that the apparently irreconcilable nature of the two religions needed to be reconciled in us, he was unable to model this consciously through directed thinking. Instead, he tells a story of a famous judge, where we can hear "the trickster" speaking within him: "One man made a speech, and he said, 'Yes, you are right,' then another man said exactly the opposite, and he said 'Yes, you also are right.'"[48] Now this is Spiritual Democracy: all religious truths are right in their own way. Jung continues, in this same context, with even greater specificity when he points to the benefits of Islamic submission, "To arrive again at a primordial religious phenomenon, man must return to a condition where that functioning is absolutely unprejudiced, where one cannot say that it is good or that it is evil, where one has to give up all bias as to the nature of religion; for as long as there is any kind of bias, there is no submission. . . . God can appear in any form he chooses."[49]

The prophet Muhammad, the founder of Islam, preached the urgent need for people to return to the true *(hanif)* religion of Abraham. Readers of the holy book, the Koran, are invited to submit to this creed and embrace monotheism by worshipping Allah. If Jews and Christians and Muslims are all what the Koran refers to as "people of the book"—those who recognize the God of Abraham as the one and only God—the question remains: what about the rest of the world religions and people who cannot believe in any of the monotheisms? Clearly there is an unconscious trickster in all of the early attempts to represent Spiritual Democracy in the world's religions.

The sanctity of the spirit that calls each Muslim to prayer every day led Jung to praise the transcendent splendor of Islam. His positive feelings for the creed reveal his efforts to put forth a myth of the democratic meaning of religion, as revealed to him by his Somali friend. Jung gives his views on Islam in an unprejudiced way that reflects some of the critical thinking we find in his later judgments of the Hebrew Bible and in revelations in Jung's 1952 book *Answer to Job*. Jung's wisdom is thinking based on strong feelings for the oneness of religious experience, and this feeling for the numinous element common to all of them (displayed, for example, in the Somali man's lifting of a blade of grass) has the added benefit of a consciousness that can unite the opposites.

Allah, who, the Koran says, "sent His Messenger with the guidance and the true religion, in order to make it triumph over every religion," (Sûrah 9:33)[50] is at first glance not the supreme meaning Jung conveys in his simple story of the Somali friend. For, what does triumph mean in Islam, and why should any religion triumph over all others? In fact, it is not the triumph of one religion or even three that matters, but the triumph of the monotheistic notion. Like the Hebraic and the Christian religions, Islam is concerned with the victory of the concept of truth over falsehood (Sûrah 2: 42).[51] We find the same absolutism in Mosaic Law and in the Christian precepts with regards to "the One." Unity-in-variety is what Spiritual Democracy means to Whitman and Melville and Jung, and monotheism reflects this unity.

As we have seen, Spiritual Democracy provides an answer to the short-sightedness pervasive in all the world religions, because its aim is to grasp the evolutionary significance of human vision within religion as a whole. It exists outside any one particular faith and encompasses a pluralistic view that does not fail to recognize God's totality, but no longer restricts the God-image to a particular cultural reception of it that is then transmitted as dogma. Jung calls this totality "the self," meaning that part of God that can be realized by human beings in their individual lives.

Though he believed in staying rooted in one's own tradition, Jung saw that becoming mired in only one religious revelation or dispensation that splits or confines the real range of possibilities tends to limit a larger vision of wholeness. Thus, in his writings he urged and modeled an education in the comparative study of religions, using the personal tool of psychology to witness and experience the deep, archetypal connectedness in the different faiths. Starting with the individual search for meaning in soul experiences, he eventually embraced the idea of a "World Soul," the anima mundi of the Neoplatonists, which provided the basis for the Spiritual Democracy that could contain William James's *The Varieties of Religious Experience*. The corollary, of course, is that no religion can represent the whole truth about the nature of God and its relativity in any one dispensation. (The Austrian-born Israeli philosopher Martin Buber was only one of the thinkers that recognized that this was Jung's meaning, and he resented the implication.)

Jung himself, though a lifelong Christian, gave thanks, near the end of his life, for his early reading of the discourses of the Buddha for providing insights that could lead him to build the foundation for analytical psychology.[52] Over the entranceway to Jung's front door to his house in Kusnacht, Switzerland, moreover, is written the clearest psychological expression of his submission to a God who is not summoned by dogma: *Vocatus atque non vocatus, dues aderit* ("Whether called upon or not, God will be present").

Vocation was the main goal for Jung, as it was also for Whitman, Melville, and Dickinson; theirs was a vocation that they felt linked them to other seekers of spirit. All were originally Christian, and each was crucified on the cross of their destinies. They expected others to suffer as well, each in her own way. In January of 1922, Jung had a dialogue with his "soul," who appears in the Red Book in the form of his anima, Salome. She tells him: "above all your calling comes first."[53] Jung asks, "But what is my calling?" She replies: "The new religion and its proclamation." He immediately responds to her, "Oh God, how should I do this?"[54]

We need to ask, did Jung literally believe it was his calling to proclaim a new religion? Despite what some of his readers have preferred to believe, Jung did not consider analytical psychology to be a new religion. Ultimately, he did not allow himself to become a new religious teacher, like Moses, Jesus, Muhammad, Buddha, Laozi, Confucius, or even Whitman. He was, of course, sometimes willing to act as a prophet who could interpret what the psyche meant by the "Way of What Is to Come," which he came to call the "Christification of the many."[55] This involved replacing the personal, separate ego with a self capable of participating in an unus mundus of embodied spiritual understanding. This was his view of the religious potential of individuation, glimpsed through analytic work with individual souls. Jung therefore placed insistence on the powers of one's own consciousness, and on its single self-reliant dependence upon some living image of God toward which one has established a psychological experience.

Doubtless, Jung felt he was approaching a new religious dispensation during his imaginations of 1913 to 1916, recorded in the present edition of the *Red Book*, which was unpublished in his lifetime. These dreams make clear that he felt he had to separate his individual standpoint from his still somewhat Christian "soul," or anima figure: an inner feminine companion that was not as evolved as his modern, spiritually democratic and scientifically grounded ego consciousness. The old wine of Judeo-Christian religion had to be poured in a new scientifically designed bottle, concomitant with the spirit of the times in a post-Humboldtian Age. This changed attitude toward religion is reflected in some unpublished notes from the hand of his patient Cary Fink (later Baynes), who discussed portions of *Liber Novus* with Jung in 1924 and 1925. In annotations from January 1924, Fink jotted down precisely what Jung told her: "You were sure that this latter [Philemon] was the same who inspired Buddha, Mani, Christ, Mahomet—all of those who may be said to have communed with God. But the others had identified with him. You absolutely refused to. It could not be for you, you said, you had to remain the psychologist—the person who understood the process."[56]

By this time in Jung's spiritual journey he realized that his religious vision was no longer entirely Christian, while, on the other hand, it still was. Such a paradoxical realization came to him shortly after finishing *Symbols of Transformation*. "I had written a book about the hero, I had explained the myths of past peoples, but what about my own myth? I had to admit I had none; I knew theirs but none of my own, nor did anyone else have one today."[57] In *Memories, Dreams, Reflections*, he asked himself after writing *Wandlüngen*: "But in what myth does man live nowadays? In the Christian myth, the answer might be. 'Do you *live* in it?' I asked myself. To be honest the answer was no. . . . 'But then what is your myth—the myth in which you do live?' At this point the dialogue with myself became uncomfortable, and I stopped thinking. I had reached a dead end."[58] Jung wrote: "Hardly had I finished the manuscript when it struck me what it means to live with a myth, and what it means to live without one."[59]

Jung's realization of his own "mythlessness" then marked the beginning of his discovery of a new scientific way of psychic objectivity that closes the door to the specialized status of any religion in the domain of theology and metaphysical reality and makes room for all myths and religions to be empirically valid. Psychological relativity, of course, is not uniquely Jungian. Jung himself traced it to Meister Eckhart, the greatest thinker of his time, the post-Christian era of the mystics in the fourteenth century. Yet what is original and new is Jung's scientific stamp on religion and his broad range of knowledge from all world mythologies, which he considered drafts of a psychology yet to be completed. All religions of the world have in common the basic psychological factor of vocation, which Jung interpreted in post-Christian terms as the cross that we each—and not just our forerunner Christ—must bear. It is the archetype of destiny.

Jung, therefore, was the bearer of a new religious revelation for humankind, a new God-image, or a new myth, after he traveled to the Muslim city of Tunis, Tunisia. By this time, he had completed a section on "The Relativity of the God-Concept in Meister Eckhart" in *Psychological Types*, which would soon be published. Jung had by then begun to take Mother religions, Hinduism, Buddhism, Judaism, Christianity, Zoroastrianism, Mithraicism, Mesopotamian, Egyptian, and Greek religions into account as antecedents for his psychology of the self-realization of the unconscious, the process he called individuation. Additionally, Jung was reflecting on Islam prior to the outbreak of World War II. In a lecture Jung gave in 1934, he told students:

It [the Greek Orthodox Church] makes you feel like Christ when he drove all those money-changers from the temple. Islam is a decent religion in comparison. We get the wrong side of it [Islam] because only theologians are interested in religions, and they are of course against religions other than their own, so they paint them black. I was amazed to find Islam so much more spiritual than Eastern Christianity, which is only a degenerate remnant of Christian Gnosticism.[60]

Here Jung is referring to what he saw in his visits to Tunisia in 1920 and Egypt in 1925. Jung himself was of Catholic ancestry, but his paternal grandfather had been baptized a Swiss Reform Protestant by Schleiermacher, one of the founders of the school of hermeneutics, or text interpretation, that would ultimately open many Christians to the possibilities of all religions as purveyors of experiences of a deeper self. Jung's insistently contradictory and paradoxical stance toward religion is akin to Whitman's call for his Spiritual Democracy.

Jung's version of that idea can be found in his *Red Book*, where the self takes the central role as the shaper of his destiny-pattern. There, he speaks of the birth of a new God in the "Opening of the Egg." Jung engages in a dialogue with a Christian, "The Anchorite," probably St. Anthony, though he bears the name Ammonius in Jung's vision, a man who holds in his hands a Greek gospel with beautiful black handwriting from the Libyan Desert. "I read the gospels and seek their meaning which is yet to come," Ammonius says. He adds words Whitman would have celebrated: "It is erroneous to believe that religions differ in their innermost essence. Every subsequent form of religion is the meaning of the antecedent."[61]

Jung's efforts to put forth a new scientific myth of the self go further than identification with any religious archetype. Analytical psychology aims not at the meaning of individual religious antecedents, but rather, at unveiling the "supreme meaning" of all religions. Jung provides us with four principles to keep in mind as practical guides for the maintenance of sacred action:

1. The new religion "expresses itself only in the transformation of human relations";
2. "The way is symbolic,"[62] and all paths point the way to the self, or Spiritual Democracy, as "The Way of What Is to Come";
3. "God is an image, and those who worship him must worship him in the images of the supreme meaning,"[63] by which Jung means an individual meaning given to each of us through a calling to live by;
4. "The spirit of the depths has seized mankind and forces self-sacrifice

upon it."[64] Jung wrote this passage right before the outbreak of World War I. Thus, psychological and spiritual work that is holy must include the acknowledgment of our own evil. Self-sacrifice, as we have seen, means a higher understanding of the mystery of crucifixion than ever before. We will all, as Jung said above, have to be crucified upon the cross of our individual destiny if we are to survive the possibility of universal extinction as a species. Only if we can do this, each in our own way, with a light and passion that emanates from the heart, will world peace truly come about.

Today, we are either going to arrive collectively at a similar view that would permit a religious world peace, or we will risk extermination in the aftermath of a new crusade, jihad, and holocaust. If we are to arrive at the equality of all people, all tribes, in one family across the globe, human interdependence and cosmic relatedness are needed. This is not psychologically impossible. As Jung optimistically says: "The self is relatedness. Only when the self mirrors itself in so many mirrors does it really exist—then it has roots. . . . The self only exists inasmuch as you appear. Not that you are, but that you do is the self. The self appears in your deeds, and deeds always mean relationship."[65]

Thus, to follow the way of the heart is to take action in ways that are just and promote religious equality for everything on the planet. It means practicing a reverence for trees, lakes, forests, and the air we breathe. It means that we must listen to the voice of God in the stillness of inward meditation and the beauty of nature.

5

HEALING THE
NATIONAL COMPLEX

While it is widely recognized that Walt Whitman is the founding father of American poetry, it's less widely known that his fight for the abolition of slavery was at the root of his vision of a multicultural Spiritual Democracy.[1] Whitman's heartfelt desire to "merge" with peoples of all races, colors, and nationalities was never expressed more absolutely and convincingly than in his stated sympathy for black slaves. He saw slavery as the central illness of his culture and his times.

Whitman's sympathy for suffering slaves led him to a deeper sort of humanitarianism than anyone might have imagined—an almost shamanic sympathy that allowed Whitman to "leave" his own body and experience an imaginative and emotional merge with another person. Such ability transgressed the racial and sexual divide of white and black, gay and heterosexual, Christian and Hindu, Muslim and Jew.

By confronting the sources of bigotry in America, Whitman became a healer of the political psyche of the nation, exposing the infections of slavery and slave labor in which the body politic festered. In 1855, Whitman could write in *Leaves of Grass:* "I only am he who places over you no master, owner, better, God, beyond what waits intrinsically in yourself."[2] Whitman's remarkable egalitarianism toward blacks as an element of his progressive spiritual vision was part and parcel of his agenda as a political poet of American democracy and as an inaugurator of a new religion.

In the mid-nineteenth century the antislavery movement was an emergent phenomenon arising in the psyches of large groups and of nations throughout the western hemisphere. It shaped perceptions and on both sides of the slavery issue, exacerbating tensions and widening a divide in the nation—a split that needed desperately to be resolved. Addressing this need, Whitman offered us a new world myth to live by: Spiritual Democracy. Its origins were violent and bloody, but its end is filled with a burning fire of love, peace, and religious passion that rose to the highest vistas of oratory in the magnificent words of Martin Luther King Jr. during the civil rights marches, a century after the Civil War.

The arc of history from slavery to the rise of Martin Luther King Jr. was filled with violence and upheaval. Starting in the colonial era, agitation in the nation's transplanted African community manifested itself through a number of significant slave rebellions. In New York in 1712, for example, twenty-five black slaves armed themselves with guns and clubs and set fire to houses on the northern edge of New York City, killing the first nine whites who arrived on the scene. Another significant uprising occurred in South Carolina in 1739, and that revolt left twenty-one whites dead. The most famous of the slave uprisings, Nat Turner's 1831 rebellion in Southampton County, Virginia, left sixty whites dead before it was finally suppressed.

Interestingly, in the three major slave uprisings in the nineteenth century, which took place between 1800 and 1831 and included the Nat Turner revolt, the biblical story of the Israelites escaping Egyptian bondage, the language of Thomas Paine's influential book the *Rights of Man*, and the Declaration of Independence were used to justify the rebellions. Clearly religion, philosophy, law, and politics all played a significant role in the emergence of a new consciousness and movement in the direction of a more just and equitable vision of the true meaning of democracy. Thus, Spiritual Democracy often begins with revolution—a call to action—but its highest spiritual aims are nonviolent.

From a psychological angle, such movements emerged out of a growing conviction in the African American cultural group that slavery and bondage were against the Bible. In the case of slave-preacher Nat Turner—a mystic who saw visions of black and white angels fighting in the sky and the heavens turning red with blood—we can see the role of his calling to vocation at play in his belief that he had been chosen by God to lead his people to freedom. For when Turner was asked shortly after he was apprehended if he regretted what he had done, his last words were "Was not Christ crucified?" Here we can see the constellation, arising out of the tension of opposites in American politics and spiritual life, of a new God-image being born on American soil: the image of a black fellow sufferer with Christ.

Tracing the split in the national complex of slavery and freedom to the God-concept of the Old and New Testaments can help us see better why Whitman's new myth of Spiritual Democracy was so necessary. Turner's visions reflect the general agitation in the world soul over the institution of slavery as a cultural epidemic in the western hemisphere, a sickness in the political and religious and legal conscience of Europe and America which needed desperately to be healed. It is out of this tremendous need in the collective psyche that Whitman emerged as America's fiercest Civil War poet. The fact of slavery in the American republic struck at the core of the ethical and religious attitudes in the Puritan mentality and created an irreconcilable paradox, a conflict of opposites, which would only be resolved through the teleological anticipation of Turner's apocalyptic visions in American history. Whitman's resounding answer to the contradiction is laudatory.

Jungian theory presupposes an "attitude" or cultural attitudes through which archetypes and complexes may be assimilated, whether in individuals, groups, or nations. It is implicit in Jung's theory of individuation that there is an answer to the problem of the dissociability of the psyche—its tendency to split into separate personalities—and that answer is the realization of the self, which he hypothesized as an incarnation of the wholeness of humanity at large in a single consciousness. It is the individual's life task and moral responsibility to make the self and its precious gift of reflective consciousness available to others. The attitude required on the part of the subject to reflect such a consciousness is what Jung called "assimilation."

Jungian analyst Joseph Henderson identified five basic attitude types through which assimilation of an archetype or complex can occur: the aesthetic, the philosophical, the social, the religious, and the psychological.[3] To fully formulate the elements of Whitman's poetry, five additional cultural attitudes can be added: environmental, political, economic, scientific, and—Whitman's version of a quintessential attitude linking the others—ethical. Henderson himself saw the scientific attitude as a branch of the philosophic orientation and would doubtless have seen the political attitude as a subspecies of the social attitude. Yet these attitudes can also be seen as distinct from the others, despite their historical derivations, because they help solve the riddle about Whitman's views on slavery and race.[4]

In Whitman's own early writings his cultural attitudes toward slavery and race appear to have split along all of these ten demarcations (which at times overlap). He took up quite contradictory points of view when addressing these two profound issues, as did most of his contemporaries. Yet, when it comes to his religious vision of Spiritual Democracy, no trace of a contradiction may be found.

While there is some evidence to suggest that George Washington was caught in the same world of racial superiority as Thomas Jefferson (who was admired by both Whitman and his father), a recent book by Henry Wiencek suggests that Washington was clearly no racist, for he never believed slaves were inherently inferior as a people. Washington, in Wiencek's view, helped create the new world, yet, he did allow an infection to proliferate: slavery. Upon discovering his moral system was wrong—he struggled with the moral guilt of having gained "advantages" for the sale of his "Negroes"—Washington is purported to have dreamed of a "great light," and a barely visible figure of an "angel" that emerged out of it. This new light led him to a moral epiphany: in his final will and testament Washington asserted that after the death of his wife, Martha, his 123 slaves were to be set free, that they were to be supported and educated by his heirs, and that his requests were to be "religiously fulfilled." Where Washington had experienced a moral defeat in his political career over the issue of slavery, he now set a high ethical standard for the rest of the world to follow. Wiencek writes:

> To this day, scholars disagree over the origins of the fundamental nature of slavery, particularly over the question of which came first, racial prejudice or race-based slavery. Did racial prejudice lead to the enslavement of Africans, with resulting economic benefits that perpetuated slavery? Or did desire for wealth lead to enslavement, which created and perpetuated racial prejudice? Did whites despise slaves because they were black, or on a class basis, because they were slaves?[5]

It was left to Whitman to attempt a synthesis of these ten cultural attitudes. Undoubtedly cultural attitudes can be one-sided, and such opinions can become rigidly fixed into belief systems and moral absolutes that petrify as fundamentalism. Spiritual Democracy is an antidote. Such spiritual equality was also expressed by Abraham Lincoln, who wrote: "There is no reason in the world why the negro is not entitled to all the natural rights enumerated in the Declaration of Independence, the right to life, liberty, and the pursuit of happiness. I hold that he is as much entitled to these as the white man. . . . He is my equal . . . and the equal of every living man."[6]

Even before Lincoln's presidential term, however, Whitman intuited a possible American "answer" to the slavery problem that was bedeviling the country. In his 1855 preface to *Leaves of Grass*, Whitman embraced the abolitionist movement in ecstatic tones, foreseeing that "slavery" would be overcome by "the tremendous spreading of hands" that would emerge to sternly oppose it. He further predicts that political opposition "shall never cease until it [slavery] ceases."[7] Such sentiments correspond roughly to the ideas of George Washington, who famously said: "I can clearly foresee that nothing but the rooting out of slavery can perpetuate the existence of our union."[8] But Whitman's vision was far grander because he knew he was confronting a social, economic, and political problem that had plagued humanity since time immemorial, and that this thorny problem had religious and ethical roots.

Bursting the seams of his bardic identity as a white American, Whitman began to speak for the ethical conscience of the whole world by espousing a moral tolerance for the opposites—black and white, inner and outer, light and dark. This hope for humanity to rise above its divisions is made evident in his new image of a self (he calls it simply "Myself"), transcendent of racial description, bearing all the colors of the earth. Something about the presence of the African American slave figure in the depths of the American psyche spoke to Whitman and propelled him forward toward his creative destiny in the New World. In the poem "The Sleepers," for example, the name "Black Lucifer" is used as representative for the so-called "shadow" of the "civilized" world. The image became a powerful nucleus around which all of his mental and physical energies could pour, and a sustaining symbol for his integrity and his ethical and spiritual wholeness.

The name "Black Lucifer" first appears in Whitman's notebooks and comes to poetic maturity in *Leaves of Grass*, in 1855. Whitman uses this national complex to personify a nuclear dynamic with the American self that was about to discharge and finally explode into a full-blown Civil War. In the following passage, Whitman's ego complex merges with this nuclear dynamism in the nation to show his profound sympathies with black suffrage, referring to and even identifying momentarily with this angry, destructive, and hateful figure—even employing the personal pronoun "I":

> *Now Lucifer was not dead—or if he was I am his sorrowful terrible heir;*
> *I have been wronged—I am oppressed—I hate him that oppresses me,*
> *I will either destroy him, or he shall release me.*[9]

As Whitman begins to produce what a Jungian would call "self-symbolism" in his work, it becomes clear that Whitman's vision of this Americanized self is not dualistic (a conscience rendered in two by opposites); rather, it is shockingly monotheistic, African American, and Native American, an emergent symbol of insistent wholeness. The Hebrew-Christian quality of his image of the self is exemplified by the lineage of pacifists in his family of origin and can be traced to both his personal relationship to his mother as well as to the pacifist streak in his ancestry. Whitman's father, Walter Whitman, was a descendent of English Puritan farmers, and his mother, Louisa Van Velsor, was of Dutch descent. The family practiced the Quaker faith. Significantly, the first proponents of the antislavery movement in the western hemisphere were Quakers—John Woolman (1720–72) and Anthony Benezet (1713–84) in the English colonies on the American mainland, and Richard Baxter (1615–1691) in Great Britain. Whitman appears to have absorbed Quaker values during his childhood and later had them "switched on" through evocation at the age of ten when he heard the Quaker spiritualist Elias Hicks deliver a rousing sermon. American Whitman biographer Justin Kaplan tells us that Hicks "looked like a cross between an Indian and a black, 'without a drop of white blood in his veins.' Whitman recalled that Hicks did not speak of doctrinal disputes, but only of the 'light within,' the single guiding principle, as it impressed itself on the boy, of man's 'religious conscience' and 'moral nature.'"[10]

Realizing this evocation of an image of the American self in Whitman's boyhood helps us understand Whitman's need, not so different from Jung's several decades later, to establish an image of wholeness that links human and divine experience within a complex unitary structure contained within the body and soul of America. Whitman himself intended his image of cultural wholeness expressed through the panoply of the world's divinities, while setting Manito, the nature god of the Algonquin Indians, in his "portfolio"[11] to act as a metaphor for cultural transformation in all peoples and nations of the world. The foundation of this structure of the self is ethical and religious at its roots, because it traces the source of this image to indigenous America as the palimpsest for Spiritual Democracy. Whitman's vision of Spiritual Democracy is a prophetic answer to our national call for a deliverer and peacemaker. What is most striking about Whitman's symbols of Spiritual Democracy (and what most anticipates the emergence of Jung) is his inclusion not only of Black Lucifer and Manito, but of Satan and the feminine spirit, Santa Spirita, as personalities that all belong within the godhead.

Not unlike Jung in his alchemical writings, Whitman recognizes the importance of including the body and the soul that must transform the divine energies into life. Two of the title lines he originally considered for "Chanting the Square Deific"—"Quadriune" and "Deus Quadriune" (which appear on his notes for the contents page of *Leaves of Grass*)[12]—make clear that he had in mind a new

God image for Spiritual Democracy that would be more inclusive than anything previously conceived of in history. This kind of theological musing and urging of a movement beyond the traditional conception of trinity toward quaternary models of the godhead, while familiar to readers of Jung's writings in the twentieth century, was quite undoubtedly revolutionary for a poet in 1860. Keeping this in mind can also help us see why the symbol of the Deus Quadriune helped Whitman resolve the splits that were active in the American psyche through the ten salient cultural attitudes identified in Whitman's work. To hold these ten attitudes in consciousness on such important issues as slavery and race was truly a heroic attempt on Whitman's part, for it was his project to bridge the gap between science and poetry, through a psychological and spiritual solution, before modern psychology had emerged.

The motto of Whitman's political strategy during this time is conveyed in the original title of another poem, which he refers to in his notes as "E Pluribus Unum," the "Poem of Many in One."[13] This poem was later titled "By Blue Ontario's Shore." In it, Whitman gives birth to an even more organic, living image of the self, one he makes us feel is emerging out of the world soul to find subjective resonance for Whitman's contemporaries in the seal of the American Republic. Through this image of unity in diversity, beginning with Black Lucifer and Manito, two streams of the incipient national complex are integrated into one unitary channel by means of his new emerging myth of Spiritual Democracy.

The great seal of the United States, with its famous motto, "e pluribus unum," was meant by Whitman to be an image of unity within diversity in which the various nationalities, politics, races, trades, economies, and religions of the world were to be spiritually unified in a new formulation of the meaning of the word democracy. The Deus Quadriune, and the specifically American words "e pluribus unum" were offered up by Whitman to the world as a geopolitical answer to its cultural and national splits. At the base of these international complexes infecting the world soul, not least of which were slavery and racism, was the moral and ethical splitting in the God-complex beneath.

Whitman used an aesthetic and religious strategy to include all people as his sisters and brothers in thought, body, and soul, within the circle of humanity's thoughts and dramas, creating a "single unitary being," a self-aware American citizen, who attempts in his embodied experience to assimilate the transnational selfhood consisting of "every hue and trade and rank."[14] This was a transcendent image in which Whitman clothed his subjective body, the sexualized body he celebrates in so many of his mature poems, because it carries a potential for realization of a selfhood greater than his own.

Whitman, not surprisingly, attempts to resolve the narrow splits in the ten cultural attitudes by becoming "commensurate with a people,"[15] that is commensurate with the unum—the Deus Quadriune—he has birthed out of himself, and out of his belief in what an American can be. Following the Civil War, Whitman hailed the "absolute extirpation and erasure of slavery from the States" as "the greatest revolutionary step in the history of the United States, (perhaps the greatest of the world, our century)."[16]

The contradiction in Whitman's personality over the issues of slavery and race was not untypical of the state of the American self during the years surrounding the Civil War. Of the ten cultural attitudes mentioned as shaping a superordinate transnational consciousness, five—the religious, aesthetic, environmental, ethical, and psychological—at times appear to have been at odds with the other five—the economic, social, scientific, philosophic, and political attitudes. It was the splitting of the potential wholeness implied by this full complement of ten attitudes that created the contradiction in the American character, which meant, for many whites, an American self that could actually embrace slavery and racism on one hand and freedom and equality for all people on the other. This is the illness that Whitman's poetry intended to heal.

As a man of his time, Whitman occasionally engaged in the dualistic and horizontal thinking of his age, but it isn't hard to see that the greater personality was always the poet's. It was through Whitman that the religious attitude of Spiritual Democracy could hold all ten cultural attitudes in a unitary way while channeling the American self, and it was through this breakthrough that the poet emerged with all his cultural attitudes intact to fully embrace the world as a keeper of the psychic integrity of the global community. What preserved him throughout his language experiments in poetry and prose were his religious attitudes, which embraced the equality of all people around the globe and celebrated the planets, trees, animals, and stars. Whitman's vision of America as "Liberty's nation"[17] was clearly an image of the multiethnic, multicultural, and transnational self, emerging in the world-consciousness of all nations—a counterbalance to the complex-ridden states usually associated with nations and their limiting notions of personhood.

Whitman sought to heal the national complex of slavery and race by melding opposites. Whitman scholar Ed Folsom points out: "Whitman resolves irreconcilable opposites by marrying them, by constructing a unity that is large enough to embody both."[18] Marriage symbolism is evident in Whitman's reflections on his days gone by as editor at the *New Orleans Crescent* newspaper. In his poetry he presented a laudable, transcendent vision of the unity of all people, including African Americans and Native Americans, and Whitman's time in New Orleans expanded his sense of inclusivity to encompass an appreciation for racial intermarriage. During his three-month 1848 stay in "The Crescent City" Whitman saw in the biracial Creole people a model for the future civilization of one-world humanity. Speaking to his friend and biographer Horace Traubel, Whitman said: "I have considered the problem from all sides. It is wonderful the readiness with which the French and Negro, or Spanish and Negro, will marry—interlock—and the results are always good."[19]

In this prose passage the marriage symbolism shines through clearly as the archetype of love that unites us all. Whitman appears to have arrived at a transcendent attitude representative of his noble notion of Spiritual Democracy through the creation of a transnational marriage symbol that integrates all ten cultural attitudes.

In 1848, the population of New Orleans comprised a mixture of African American, Native American, French, and Hispanic people. Whitman's stint at the *Crescent* (which advertised daily the sale of slaves) was the occasion for a fabled story about a "New Orleans romance" with a so-called Creole woman of higher social class with whom Whitman, in a letter to John Addington Symonds, admitted to having fathered six illegitimate children. Today scholars see through this assertion as a cover for Whitman's homosexuality, yet it is also a basis for his vision of the intermarriage of different races and nationalities in his notion of Spiritual Democracy.

New Orleans provides a contemporary example of the timeless nature of the strife and successes inherent in the story of the African American struggle for racial equality and full participation in U.S. society. The devastation caused by Hurricane Katrina in 2005—and the lack of governmental response—had a sharp impact on the American public, which once again found itself engaged with the issue of black suffering. Just a few years after much of New Orleans was left in ruins, the United States elected Barack Obama, the country's first African American president. As we struggle with the same issues that met Whitman and his contemporaries, then, let us remember the integrity of the poet's attempt to arrive at a transnational vision through which he hoped to bring about healing in all ten of the cultural attitudes.

Whitman's views on worldwide Spiritual Democracy do not support the average American presumption of his day that the United States could be credited with having discovered an entirely "new" democratic "idea." For Whitman, "Real Democracy" meant "a world democracy,"[20] not only an American democracy. World democracy, when it is not wielded in the empire of any one nation, but rather is fostered as a universal notion and is embraced by many nations, all with equal rights, can truly become libertarian in the broadest sense of the word through the solidarity of the races of the entire globe. This is the view put forth by Whitman when he says to Horace Traubel, "No man is a democrat, a true democrat, who forgets that he is interested in the welfare of the race. Who asks only, what is best for America? Instead of what is best for man— the whole of man? . . . A man is no democrat if he takes the narrow in preference to the broad view."[21]

It was the poet's calling from the start to enclose such a broad view for the future of the world. Whitman strove to encircle the globe, to engird it with his vision—not to close America off to its future international role as one of many world leaders, or to obscure the illustrious past of the history of the race, but to pay back a debt owed to humanity thought across all ages, even the most archaic, ancient, or antique. For the "seed stuff of our American liberty" can be found, Whitman asserts, in the language of the "Elizabethan period of England" and in "Greek and Roman sources."[22] The idea of enclosing ancient and modern forms of worship in a one-world democracy is captured by his noble international intention to include the whole of man in this expansive vision: "Something that presents the sentiment of the Druid walking in the woods . . . of the Indian pow-wow . . . of the Sacramental supper . . . of the Grecian religious rites."[23]

Here, we can see the beginnings of Whitman's notion of vast unity within diversity, of all humanity united with the cosmos, wedded and interlinked, and all races contained in union through the symbol of intermarriage. Whitman's claim to nonoriginality is his way of sloughing off American egotism, for his internationalism is universal, ethical, religious, and just. In borrowing from the spiritual democrats of the past, his aim is to pay all back by unselfishly claiming nothing original for himself. "Do you ever think," he asks Traubel, "what infernal plagiarists the big fellows are—big lawyers, big preachers, big writers— even Shakespeare, Longfellow; how much they borrow and never pay back?"[24]

For Whitman, democracy, if it is to truly reach the world at the third international stage he envisions, will have to be revolutionized by science. By "science" he means Humboldtian science, Darwinian science, and also a science that did not yet exist, for he recognized that "All the real problems, the fundamentals, are yet ahead of us."[25] Such a scientific attitude in the future is something Whitman strongly believed in, and he longed for the unity of humankind made possible through the upcoming science of God. "I have great faith in science— real science: the science that is the science of the soul as well as the science of the body (you know, many men of half sciences seem to forget the soul)."[26] Whitman never forgot the soul.

The idea of world democracy is part and parcel of a great universal spiritual design. It belongs to no one, and therefore it is not original with Whitman, but is rather a science of the soul that emerges in his poem "Years of the Modern." Such a science of the soul was foreseen by the poet in an emergent, empirical attitude.

Whitman was first and foremost a healer and a medicine man by vocation. The shaman-poet often suffers from the infections of his or her race, prior to offering a universal remedy. His medicine is a universal religion—Spiritual Democracy—symbolized best by racial intermarriage in Whitman's time and same-sex marriage in our own time.

The one-world religious democracy Whitman believed in is a religion, therefore, that seeks to offer curing through uniting the ten cultural attitudes and healing the contradictions that disunite them. If Whitman had maintained a Humboldtian vision of science, he might have transcended his racism from the start, and there would have been no reason for remorse. The same scientific attitude (Humboldt's) that eventually gripped Whitman can also heal the world, "not only by Liberty's nation but other nations preparing," by "tremendous entrances and exits, new combinations, the solidarity of the races," as Whitman put forth this vision in "Years of the Modern." Such a unification of the nations of the world were "advancing with irresistible power on the world's stage," with "Freedom, completely arm'd and victorious" and with "Law on one side and Peace on the other." In the same poem, Whitman asked: "Are all nations communing? is there going to be one heart to the globe? / Is humanity forming en-masse? for tyrants tremble, crowns grow dim, / The earth, restive, confronts a new era, perhaps a general divine war."[27]

Thus, religious equality itself turns out to be part of a "general divine war" that was first envisioned by Nat Turner in his dreams of black and white angels fighting in the sky, shortly after Whitman's birth. For Whitman, this new war might be fought for the stage of religious evolution he names for us: Spiritual Democracy.

6

WHITMAN'S "NEW BIBLE"
The Foundation of a Religious Vision

If America is going live up to its promise of freedom of religion and truly be free from allegiance to a particular church and a de facto establishment of a national creed, it will have to endorse an international, interfaith, and intersexual definition of God's identity. Walt Whitman's specific commitment was to fill in the blanks of the Deist notion of religion sanctioned by the founding fathers of America[1]—a view that spurned a belief in religious orthodoxy and enabled the founders to champion the separation of church and state and advocate for the oneness of humanity. Whitman's own espoused starting point for the new religious attitude he was trying to advance was the founding of an American Republic. For this new religion, Whitman even inaugurated a post-Christian calendar year beginning with Independence Day, July 4, 1776, and he dated the 1860 edition of *Leaves of Grass* "Year 85 of the States," thereby diminishing the significance of Christ's birth to one among many births of divinity across the globe.[2]

How was the acceptance of his new Spiritual Democracy to occur? By speaking up for it, Whitman answered. By 1857, Whitman had become preoccupied with a "spinal idea" for a lecture: "*Founding a new American religion* (? No Religion)."[3] The question mark after "*religion*" represents Whitman's ambivalence about whether his spiritual vision could be called a religion at all, even though he repeats the word "religion" seven times in capital letters in "Prot-Leaf." Whether what Whitman puts forth in his book was a new American religion or not has been the subject of debate. Whitman himself was unsure at first, but later concluded his achievement was indeed a religion, as underscored by song and the new attitude of science "—the entire revolution made by science in the poetic method."⁴ In June of 1857, Whitman wrote further: "*The Great Construction* of the *New Bible*," the "main life work—the Three Hundred & Sixty five—(it ought to be ready in 1859.—(June '57)."⁵ Whitman goes beyond just speaking up and commits his own poetic voice to the project of convincing his contemporaries on the eve of the Civil War that a new relativism is necessary, for which he would write the "New Bible." Here, Whitman's project is made translucent: It is religious at its core and international and scientific in scope.

Recent scholarship has shed new light on Whitman's religious mission in a way that can help us clarify what he actually means by an "internationality of the concept of God." In a prose piece, "The Bible as Poetry," Whitman celebrated the Bible and sang its praises:

> Translated into all languages, how it has united this diverse world! . . . And except for which this America of ours, with its polity and essentials, could not now be existing. No true bard will ever contravene the Bible.⁶

Whitman does not contravene the Bible, yet he nevertheless makes an important contribution to the history of the Judeo-Christian-Islamic myth and its development by suggesting that those who read the Bible or the Koran need to give them new life by writing their own extensions of them. In section forty-nine of "Song of Myself," the speaker says: "I hear your whispering there O stars of heaven, / O suns—O grass of graves—O perpetual transfers and promotions, / If you do not say anything how can I say anything?"⁷ This anticipates what Carl Jung was to tell to some of his patients a half century later in Switzerland, namely that they would be wise to each write their own "New Book."⁸

Whitman, however, was even more syncretic and amalgamative than Jung, because he had, as a poet, so wide a world literary tradition in which to articulate his spiritual breadth. In 1888's "A Backward Glance O'er Travel'd Roads" Whitman wrote, shortly before his seventieth birthday, that among his early major literary influences prior to the writing of *Leaves of Grass* were the poetry of Walter Scott, the Bible, Shakespeare, Homer, Ossian, Aeschylus, Sophocles, Dante, the German Nibelungen, and the ancient Hindu poems. He tells us, moreover, that he read these texts at intervals, during summers and falls, for weeks at a stretch, in the New York countryside, or on Long Island's shores—on the peninsula of Orient, on the northeast end of Paumanok in a sheltered hollow of rocks and sand, with the sea on each side—"in the full presence of Nature, under the sun, with the far-spreading landscape and vistas, or the sea rolling in."[9] What he does not tell us is that he was also reading Alexander von Humboldt's *Cosmos,* known as *Kosmos* in its original German, a word that appears not only in the 1855 preface to *Leaves of Grass* but also as the title of a poem in the "New Bible," simply called "Kosmos."[10]

By Spiritual Democracy, then, Whitman does not mean a new Abrahamic religion; he means a global vision, international in scope, bringing worldwide solidarity and a unification of all religions of the globe into a transnational One World spirituality—a vista that sees all people and all things in the cosmos as divine. As he writes in section thirteen of "Salut au Monde!":

> My spirit has pass'd in compassion and determination around
> the whole earth,
> I have looked for equals and lovers and found them ready for me
> in all lands,
> I think some divine rapport has equalized me with them.[11]

Here is the idea of spiritual equality again, which for Whitman transcended any one nation or religion. This equality was based on kindred spirits—a community of lovers like himself. Whitman had no intention to contravene any of the world's great religions. He hears them all, sees them all from a vista, and celebrates them all. He embraces each he comes into contact with and merges with, and then confidently, biding his time, he moves beyond them, because he has science in his view and sees that all agree that love is the greatest thing the cosmos can confer on humans. In "Passage to India," he writes: "Greater than stars or suns, Bounding O soul thou journeyest forth; / What love than thine and ours could wider amplify?"[12]

That the Vedic and Buddhist scriptures were an essential part of Whitman's experience of the oneness of all religions shows that he followed the transcendentalists, who were highly inspired by these Asian texts, as can be seen, for example, in Emerson's poem "Brahma." But Whitman went further in appropriating Indian spiritual classics. He related to one of his key disciples, Edward Carpenter, that he knew sections of the great Hindu epic the *Ramayana,*[13] and he also makes it clear in his essay "The Bible as Poetry" that he had read the *Mahabharata.*[14] Even so, it was not the cosmology of ancient India as put forth in the Vedas that gave him his own cosmic consciousness; it was nineteenth-century science. Science, and particularly astronomy, gave him the transport to see all religions as reaching toward a unitary reality.

As we have seen, the nucleus for Whitman's ideas about Religious Democracy can be found in his poem "Salut au Monde!" and it is promulgated further in his 1860 volume, "Chants Native American and Democratic," in which he writes:

> O you teeming cities! . . . .
> O race of the future! O women!
> O fathers! O you men of passion and the storm!
> O native power only! O beauty!
> O yourself! O God! O divine average! . . . .
> O poets to come, I depend upon you![15]

Here is another Whitman breakthrough: "divine average"—an American native vocalism affirming the speech of the democratic individual on all continents, devoid of religious orthodoxy and sourced on realism. It was evident to Whitman that the "poets to come" would be an international breed from all nations and lands. America as a "nation of nations" was for him merely a symbol for the new city of friendship that was destined to emerge in the future. In section one of the 1860 "Chants," he writes:

> A NATION announcing itself, (many in one,)
> I myself make the only growth by which I can be appreciated,
> I reject none, accept all, reproduce all in my own forms.
>
> . . . .
> O days of the future, I believe in you!
>
> . . . .
> The whole theory of the universe is directed to one single individual—
>   namely to You.[16]

Here we have it: Religion is directed, not to men and women in general, but to You! You, in your own subjective experiencing, Whitman is saying, are the most important spiritual event in the whole history of the universe, regardless of your race, sexual orientation, religion, or nationality. "To sing the Song of that law of average Identity, and of Yourself, consistently with the divine law of the universal, is the main intention of those 'Leaves.'"[17] No wonder readers in every possible variation of these considerations have felt Whitman speaks to them. The important thing is to realize the equality of all religions in oneself. This is what he says he *knows:* "It is useless to protest, I know all and expose it."[18] "Here is not merely a nation, but a teeming nation of nations, . . . here the crowds, equality, diversity, the Soul loves."[19] These lines from the 1855 preface have their inception in his 1847 *albot Wilson* notebook, where we find the aim of his poetic enterprise expressed even further: "Vast and tremendous is the scheme! It involves no less than constructing a nation of nations."[20]

Whitman strove to unite people in his vision. It is at this time that he first begins to speak of gathering a group of "young men" around him who would be his "disciples that new superior churches and politics shall come."[21] The true meaning of the United States of America lies hidden sometime in the world's future, when the "Third" stage of Spiritual Democracy will be awakened in all of us. As Whitman sees it the only way to bring this about is to realize it in one-self first: "The Many in One—what is it finally except myself? / These States—what are they except myself?"[22] Whitman's dialectic of cultural individuation is exquisite in envisioning an end to the alienation of the individual in society. It looks forward, in fact, to William James's pragmatism and Jung's theory of individuation.

Whitman's extensive dialogues in *Leaves of Grass* are between the I, which he refers to as "Myself," and his soul, a world-embracing spiritual largeness that is male and female, masculine and feminine, heterosexual and homosexual, black and white. Like Jung, he attempts to internationalize his subjective experience into a composite self that reaches across all cultures. And, as in Jung's writings, when the opposites are united, they speak to all nations. Whitman tells us "Happiness not in another place, but this place . . . not for another hour, but this hour."[23] The word happiness was not capitalized in the 1855 volume, but in the later 1860 edition "HAPPINESS" appears in capitalized type. The poet is not in a hypomanic state here. He has full command of his art. He intends for his happiness to circumnavigate the globe. "For I am mad with devouring ecstasy to make joyous hymns for the whole earth!"[24]

There are no accidents, no causal connections concerning human fate and human destiny, Whitman concluded, that are not intended to be experienced as miracles:

> I believe in the flesh and the appetites,
> Seeing hearing and feeling are miracles, and each part and tag of me
>   is a miracle.
> Divine am I inside and out, and I make holy whatever I touch
>   or am touched from;
> The scent of these arm-pits is aroma finer than prayer,
> This head is more than churches or bibles or creeds.
> If I worship any particular thing it shall be some of the spread
>   of my body.[25]

No one in human history had ever publicly expressed that conviction before in such a nonchalant, down-to-earth way, and with such forthrightness. We have to take Whitman's homespun metaphors for what they connote in the overarching transnational reach of his spiritual vision of democracy, and for their richness in psychological depth. "For I say," he wrote in "Democratic Vistas": "At the core of democracy, finally, is the religious element,"[26] and this religious element is not separate from the body. In fact, the body is holy and sacred, Whitman would say, in all of its parts. If democracy is to be globalized, it will have to include all forms of worship, even those that include the rude delights of the body at which Protestant Christianity, particularly, had turned up its nose. Whitman adds later: "It is my dream to devote the rest of my life . . . to the study and promulgation of the new religion."[27] In his book *Worshiping Walt*, Michael Robertson shows how Whitman realized this dream yet also stayed true to his original vision. He wanted no "school" founded after him, for he stood for no "isms." Whitman said, "It is queer how the whole world is crazy with the notion that one book, one ism . . . is to save things."[28] With uncharacteristic modesty, he had his doubts that any spiritual text, *Leaves of Grass* included, could save the world.

Whitman in fact charges us to find our own freedom in this regard. Whitman's teaching is a technique, no less than Emily Dickinson's and that of all shamanic poets (cf. Rumi & Hafiz), a method for experiencing ecstasy and the most ecstatic secret of the universe, which is love. In number fifteen of the "Chants Democratic," he exclaims: "And who has been happiest? O I think it is I! I think no one was ever happier than I."[29] In Whitman's view such a religion is here and now, in the eternal moment, as he says in his 1856 meditation: "—realize where you are at present located,—the point you stand, that is now to you the center of all.—"[30] This is shamanism and also astronomy. The origins of religion in science and the end of religion in science are made one in Whitman; he has viewed the globe and found the one in its vista of spiritual transcendence: "Sail, sail thy best, ship of Democracy."[31]

When Whitman says his head is greater than churches or bibles or creeds, he means that his mind can imagine all the archetypes of all religions, putting him on equally good terms with Jehovah and Allah and Buddha. Science is his new monotheism-and-atheism-in-one, which he experiences as an energized illuminating perspective that is as natural as the sun. In his 1872 preface, Whitman writes, "Science, which now, like a new sunrise, ascending, begins to illuminate all."[32]

Whitman's "attempt at an utterance, of New World songs and an epic of Democracy" was of importance to the world's spiritual evolution not just because it heralded progress in democracy's ongoing march. We hear that part, of course: "To me, the United States are important because in this colossal drama they are unquestionably designated for the leading parts, for many a century to come. In them history and humanity seem to culminate . . ."[33] But driving all of his poems is the even larger "religious purpose,"[34] one that will eventually be made clear by "science": "And on these areas of ours, as on a stage, sooner or later, something like an *éclaircissement* of all the past civilizations of Europe and Asia is to probably to be evolved."[35] Democracy and universal spirituality are ministers of the supreme and final science of God.

To Whitman, the "science of God" implies that each person is the vehicle of his or her own God-concept. It's clear in his collected poetry and prose works that Whitman was attempting the empirical verification of the divinity within human beings. He found evidence for this in his own character, through dreams, ecstasies, visions, poetry, and songs. Through singing, in particular, Whitman found justification for his belief of the existence of God in all of us. By existence, he means *experience:* his experience of God, and your experience of God. Together they form a democratic unity in the self, or what Whitman calls "Myself" and "Yourself." If we take the religions of the world in a true spirit of democracy, we come to the experience of divinity in all people, the glory and wonder of the self in all races, all cultures, all sexual orientations, and ethnicities of the globe. "In thee, America, the soul, its destinies, / Thou globe of globes! . . . / thou New, indeed new, Spiritual World!"[36] In "Salut au Monde!" Whitman is clearly seeking to include everyone. Globalizing democracy through commonality of spiritual aspiration is at the same time a scientific recognition of what it means to be human.

When each person undertakes the spiritual work to pursue what Whitman calls the science of God, the world's people may then begin to arrive at a new vista of transnationalism where misleading separation will be disavowed because it constitutes a misreading of the brotherhood of man. Women, too, are included in Whitman's vision, for he speaks of "my brothers and sisters."[37]

Whitman encourages us to move in our spiritual evolution from religious one-sidedness to internationalism and then to what might be called a "cosmic seeing" where even God passes away.

> Let contradictions prevail! Let one thing contradict another!
> and let one line of my poems contradict another!
> . . . .
> Let the earth desert God, nor let there ever henceforth be
> mentioned the name of God!
> Let there be no God![38]

By becoming poet first of the globe, and then of the cosmos, and finally of a transcreational self, Whitman radically democratizes religion. In fact, he makes democracy and religion one and the same. If everything is divine, then the goal of human evolution is to realize that within and to eschew any ethnocentrism or prejudiced discrimination. For everything tends in time toward the realization of the sacred miracle of being itself: "I say the whole earth, and all the stars in the sky, are for Religion's sake. / . . . None has begun to think how divine he himself is, or how certain the future is."[39]

Whitman seems to know that the God-images not only operate across cultures, nations, and races from residues of collective memory, but that they all connote the coming of a world soul. The remarkable thing is that he gets above the God-images of history to envision a new Spiritual Democracy that makes room, on the model of the American government, for equality and religious liberty and freedom for all peoples in all lands.[40]

Spiritual Democracy cancels out religious superiority by recovering the sacred in everyday values, occupations, and, above all, sex and the enjoyments of the human body. Placing no God above the divinity of the physical nature of each woman or man, he formulates a new metaphor of love that includes everyone's most private ecstasy. Religious democracy needs a divine voice that is not afraid of the bodies of others. For Whitman, the bodily vehicle for this is the human voice. *Vocalism*, "the divine power to speak words,"[41] he writes, is waiting to be released in any person, in any nation. Whitman asks his reader: why not find it in yourself?

Whitman doesn't neglect the dark side inherent in all of us. No discussion of Spiritual Democracy would be complete without mentioning that it "includes Satan, the genius of revolt, dissatisfaction, discord, in his conception of divinity."[42] This way of handling Milton's idea of a counter to the Christian God concept is perhaps Whitman's most controversial assertion. He not only makes room for what Jung in the twentieth century would call "the shadow" and "absolute evil," but he anticipates Jung's decision to make Satan part of the godhead itself.

How might this realization have arisen in Whitman's time? One factor was that the evil of slavery was not self-evident to everyone, with some Americans even believing that it was part of the divine order. Prior to the Civil War, religious denominations including Methodists, Baptists, and Presbyterians had split over the issue of slavery in the north and south, and the priests of Whitman's day used Old and New Testament passages as rationale for their disaffections. Although Whitman took issue with literal interpretations of religious texts, he could not fail to see in such readings the glimmer of the dark truth that what the divine plan revealed in the Bible was not exclusively good. Thus he painted an archetypal portrait of Satan as an aspect of God—a facet of the deity that carried a religious charge. Whitman used it himself as a spiritualizing principle to infuse his poetry with a power to bless the outrageous. If God did not sing the glory of women, slaves, and homosexuals in the Old and New Testaments or the Koran, then Satan did. It was vitally important that Whitman challenge God's notions of the good self to answer the call for the promotion of the universal, equalizing identity in each and every "You." By this he meant everyone: "I sing the songs of the glory of none, not God, sooner than I sing the songs of the glory of you."[43] "I only am he," Whitman says after he declares he has unashamedly loved many women and men, and "places over you no master, owner, better, God, beyond what waits intrinsically in yourself."[44]

In "To You," he paints a portrait of God with a "nimbus of gold-colored light" around "myriads of heads," the light that emphasizes God's divinity flowing "from the brain of every man and woman."[45] For Whitman personally this religious element had been evoked by his homosexual experience of comradeship. This became, of course, universalized, a world-healing spiritual vision all poets may take up:

> Comradeship, uniting closer and closer not only the American States, but all nations, and all humanity. That, O poets! is that not a theme worth chanting, striving for? Why not fix your verses henceforth to the gauge of the round globe? the whole race? Perhaps the most illustrious culmination of the modern may thus prove to be a single growth of joyous, more exalted bards of adhesiveness, identically one in soul, but contributed by every nation, each after its distinctive kind.[46]

7

WALT WHITMAN'S
GLOBAL VISION

While Whitman's global visions of Spiritual Democracy cannot be attributed to any belief, school, or organized religion, the American transcendentalism that made his dream possible began as a reform movement in the Unitarian Church and culminated in Ralph Waldo Emerson's 1938 "Divinity School Address," in which he radically repudiated the church's emphasis on religious forms and favored direct experience of God as the way of the future. It is out of this big breakthrough that Whitman emerged with his own unique view, and it is not surprising that he has been warmly embraced by Unitarian-Universalists congregations throughout North America like in no other spiritual institution.[1]

The first of seven principles of the Unitarian Universalist Association, or UUA, is respect for "The Inherent Worth and Dignity of All People." No American poet expresses this transnational value better than Walt Whitman, for he believed in the inherent divinity of all people as a cornerstone of his worldview.

We can see Whitman's compatibility with the UUA in that organization's other major stated principles, namely:

- Justice, equity, and compassion in human relations;
- Acceptance of one another and encouragement to spiritual growth in UUA congregations;
- A free and responsible search for truth and meaning;
- The goal of world community with peace, liberty, and justice for all;

- The right of conscience and the use of the democratic process within UUA congregations and society at large; and
- Respect for the interdependent web of all existence of which we are a part.

All seven of the UUA principles—and many more—are subsumed under Whitman's great idea of Spiritual Democracy.

To grasp the wondrous simplicity of Whitman's mind, it might be best to start at the beginning and work outward from there. In his 1847 Notebook, Whitman stated the intention of his vast poetic project in these simple terms: "Bring all the art and science of the world, and baffle and humble it with one spear of grass."[2] Today, after a century and a half of false starts, half-kept promises, and numerous disappointments, we have to ask: How could one spear of grass launch an international movement toward change? But in the same notebook, Whitman confidently writes: "I am the Poet of Equality."[3] Thus, Spiritual Democracy is religious equality, plain and simple.

In 1847, at the age of twenty-eight, Walt Whitman wrote: "Not all the traditions can put vitality in churches / They are not alive, they are cold mortar and brick, / I can easily build as good, and so can you."[4] The "churches of men and women"[5] that he had in mind are far removed from anything anyone might have imagined for someone born in the nineteenth century. Whitman's father was a house builder, so when the poet says he can build, he's tapping into his father function as the keystone of American poetry. This was no mere poet of a single nation but one of a teeming nation of nations for whom only an international church—which many traditionalists would say is no church at all—would satisfy his soul. Churches, for him, were merely mediums for a new global vision made possible by the advances in science and particularly astronomy, advanced by the brilliant breakthrough of Alexander von Humboldt in *Cosmos*.

Whitman says this himself in a note he penned for a lecture on religion called "God Abdicates":

> I say to you that all forms of religion, without excepting one, any age, any land, are but mediums, temporary yet necessary, fitted to the lower mass-ranges of perception of the race—part of the infant school—and that the developed soul passes through one or all of them, to the clear homogeneous atmosphere above them—There all meet—previous distinctions are lost—Jew meets Hindu, and Persian Greek and Asiatic and European and American are joined—and any one religion is just as good as another.[6]

This is a concise definition of Spiritual Democracy indeed, as Whitman saw it: *In the homogeneous atmosphere above, where all religious are joined, any one religion is just as good as another.* In other words, our individual religions don't make us better, confirm that we are an elect of the enlightened, or the saved, because we are already and forever all equal. To call the great religions of the world "infant schools" might sound dismissive, but Whitman had another aim. He teaches us to go beyond teachings of traditional religious faiths to a more mature and, to his mind, scientific view of God, existing in an elevated "homogeneous atmosphere" from where all religions of the world can be viewed. Here is another passage from section forty-three of "Song of Myself":

> I do not despise you priests, all time, the world over,
> My faith is the greatest of faiths and the least of faiths,
> Enclosing worship ancient and modern and all between
>   ancient and modern,
>
> . . . .
>
>   beating the serpent-skin drum . . .[7]

The serpent-skin drum, in essence, is shamanism: Whitman beats the serpent-skin drum for Spiritual Democracy. In the centennial anniversary year of the birth of the United States, 1876, Whitman writes:

> Without being a scientist, I have thoroughly adopted the conclusions of the great Savans and great Experimentalists of our time, and of the last hundred years, and they have interiorly tinged the chyle of my verse for purposes beyond.[8]

What is the inspiration that gave him the wings to transcend all nations in the name of the new science of progress? Like Emerson and Thoreau, Whitman's mind caught the zeitgeist of Europe: the "Age of Humboldt." But a newer science, rising just as he was writing, likely led him to take Humboldt further: psychology, of the kind being pioneered by Arthur Schopenhauer, Friedrich Nietzsche, and, in our own country, William James—men who developed and initiated the pragmatic study of the soul. Whitman appears to have arrived at his vision of the equality of all religions by reaching a psychological vista situated "above all creeds and schools" in what he called the "supreme and final science."[9] By "above," moreover, Whitman does not mean "better than"; he means "supreme" or "just as good." In other words, Whitman is saying: "Don't judge!" Thus, American science, clarified by James as "pragmatism," made possible the vision to behold the unity of all religions for the first time in human history, from an astronomical altitude outside religious factionalism.

The idea of getting a compilation of the major world religions into a series of volumes had been on the minds of James's godfather, Ralph Waldo Emerson, as well as Margaret Fuller and other transcendentalists for at least six years before Whitman emerged onto the world stage as a spiritual liberator. As Thoreau wrote in 1849, "It would be worthy of the age to print together the scriptures or sacred writings of the several nations, the Chinese, the Hindoos, the Persians, the Hebrews, and others, as the Scripture of Mankind. . . . This would be the Bible, or Book of Books."[10] Yet, none of the transcendentalists imagined that an American-born poet would be so bold to attempt to write a new transnational scripture of humankind in which all the world's religions could be equalized at a higher spiritual plane of psychological understanding, and where all may be made one in the relativity of science. While Whitman had no intentions to destroy sacred institutions, he was nevertheless not very fond of the priests of his day. As he wrote in some famous lines in his 1855 Preface:

> There will soon be no more priests: their work is done . . .
> A new order shall arise and they shall be the priests of man,
> And every man shall be his own priest.[11]

He would probably have been a lot happier with the new age of spirituality that is fostered by figures as disparate in their training as the Dalai Lama and Matthew Fox, Ram Dass and the Wicca women, emerging in the United States and the world today. This egalitarian spirit is exemplified by the UUA and Creation Spirituality.[12] Yet Whitman was always ahead of his times as a visionary seer, and despite his most egalitarian moments of religious modesty in the early 1860s he wrote:

> Really, what has America to do with all this mummery of prayer and rituals and the rant of exhorters and priests? We are not at all deceived by this great show that confronts us of churches, priests and rituals—for piercing beneath, we find there is no life, no faith, no reality of belief, but that all is essentially a pretense, a sham. I say that there is today little perhaps no religion—it is a matter of dress only.[13]

One may wonder: "If one religion is really just as good as another and we are all equal, then why is Walt Whitman so damned hard on churches and priests?" Whitman has the best answer for this: "Do I contradict myself?" he asks in section fifty-one of "Song of Myself," "Very well then I contradict myself, / (I am large, I contain multitudes.)"[14]

Whitman certainly pulled no punches when it came to criticism of organized religion, particularly the Christian Church's attempts to make itself the

central institution in nineteenth-century America—something the Deist founding fathers would have abhorred. It should be understood that for Whitman,
religion needs to be experienced firsthand as an ever-recurring miracle that is
forever evolving. The ministers of his day had little, if anything, positive to say
about sex, especially passion between men, the love that was considered beneath
naming. When Whitman uses the words "piercing beneath" he is speaking about
getting to the real life that is hidden below the surface. As a word crafter, he
chooses his metaphors very carefully. So we have to analyze his words through
the method of linguistic amplification and trace them to their psychological
roots. To have one's sexual experience completely ignored by Puritan ministers
of his day must have felt like a terrible insult to Whitman. No wonder he saw
the church as a "sham." He actually felt ashamed of religion in America, and he
wanted to make it better by broadening its scope and opening it up to a more
natural and cosmic view of God. In his notebook entry "Poem Incarnating the
Mind," Whitman wrote, "One grand faculty we want,—and that is the power to
pierce fine clothing and thick coated shams, and settle for sure what the reality of
the thing clothed and disguised is."[15]

The true "sham" was the illness of sexual repression and, not least, homophobia hidden behind Puritan clothing. This was the pretense that Whitman wanted
to uncover in his violent criticisms of the church, priests, and religious rituals.
Like the UUA, which has been fighting a valiant fight against homophobia for
more than four decades, Whitman's adversarial life force in defense of bonded
same-sex love is still alive. It was present in spirit at the brawl of the famous
gay uprising against a police raid at the Stonewall Inn tavern in the Greenwich
Village neighborhood of New York in 1969. His is still a powerful presence at
the forefront of the fight for same-sex marriage today. In a famous photo of
Whitman and the New York street-car driver Peter Doyle, the men sit as proudly
as any nineteenth-century couple having their picture taken in a traditional wedding pose, one hundred years prior to the Stonewall riots that ignited the gay
liberation movement in America. (More recently, there has been a restoration of
a series of same-sex portraits depicting Whitman with four different men, seated
in a traditional "marriage" pose, which makes his affirmation of homosexuality
even more obvious.)[16]

The year 1969 marks a major turning point for the stance of all organized
religions on homosexuality. Whitman, again, is a model for such solidarity with
other freedom movements. He never wavered on abolition and women's rights,
and from 1847 onward he was one of the fiercest opponents to forced servitude
of all kinds. Disputes over slavery were present among the Methodists, Baptists,

and Presbyterians, and it is not remarkable, though it is sad, that many Puritans were caught in national splits that plagued the United States during the Civil War. As we've seen, justifications for and against slavery were argued on both sides of the national debate, based at least partly on biblical interpretations of what God is alleged to have said about slavery in the Old and New Testaments. Many Southern churches believed God sanctioned slavery in the Bible, so they justified their arguments with scriptural references as political ammunition against the abolitionists. For the past one hundred fifty years, the religious right has used the same types of biblical arguments, based on one-sided scriptural interpretations, in justification for the war against equal rights in the domain of sex, gender, and marriage equality. Whitman, while denying all churches, synagogues, and mosques elite status in his Spiritual Democracy, would certainly celebrate the political conscience of those institutions that have endorsed same-sex marriage.

The open support by some enlightened religious organizations for Lesbian-Gay-Bisexual-Transgender (LGBT) issues is influenced by unconscious factors in the national psyche of America, as well as other nations. Whitman was influenced by the same factors. An example of his remarkable egalitarianism can be seen in a quote from his poem "Song of the Open Road":

> Camerado, I give you my hand!
> I give you my love more precious than money,
> I give you myself before preaching or law;
> Will you give me yourself? will you come travel with me?
> Shall we stick by each other as long as we live?[17]

Whitman coined the term *camerado*, which is linguistically derived from the Spanish word *camarada* and translates literally as "bedmate." It has often been debated among academic scholars what Whitman meant by the "Calamus" poems, a cluster of forty-five songs inserted into the 1860 edition of *Leaves of Grass* that he referred to in a notebook as part of his "New Bible." It's evident from this edition and from his 1847 notebook that a decisive sexual experience and his reading of Humboldt transformed this average newspaper editor and poetaster into the cosmic "I" of "Song of Myself," and that experience, and perhaps others like it, was undoubtedly homosexual.[18] Today it's clear that Whitman's call to the Spanish-speaking world and beyond is being answered, as countries including Spain and Argentina, as well as Canada, Iceland, Belgium, France, Portugal, the Netherlands, Norway, Sweden, South Africa, and New Zealand have already institutionalized same-sex marriage. Whitman's call for religious equality in "Salut au Monde!" reverberates through the ages and is being answered by these nations, which have given equal rights to LGBT people. The United States, sadly, is lagging behind this trend. Until recently, many states were passing legislation opposing same-sex unions, but with President Obama's endorsement of LGBT rights and the recent legalization of gay marriage in several states, including recently California, it seems the movement toward Spiritual Democracy is as realizable as ever.

When a discussion took place in Philadelphia in the spring of 1890 about the meaning of "comradeship" in Whitman's works, the poet himself replied:

> I like it much—it is to me, for my intentions, indispensable—the sun revolves about it, it is the timbre of the ship—not there alone in that one series of poems, but in all, belonging to all.[19]

Whitman's specific way of loving his comrades opened him to the possibility of love more personally, as an eros at the heart of his call for Spiritual Democracy, which would hear of no barriers to love of man or God on the basis of a particular dogma. What he means by "all" is that his poetic epic entire, *Leaves of Grass*, could be said to revolve around his single religious, phallic, flexible symbol, namely the one spear of grass with which he intended, by asserting it, to baffle and humble us all with all the science and art of being compassionate and caring in the world.

A passage Whitman wrote in his prose essay "Democratic Vistas" gives an impression of just how far seeing he really was and continues to be today:

> Democracy, in silence, biding its time, ponders its own ideals, not in literature and art only—not of men only, but of women. The idea of the women of America, (extricated from this daze, this fossil and unhealthy air which hangs about the word lady), develop'd, raised to become the robust equals, workers, and, it may be, even practical and political deciders with the men—greater than man, we may admit, through their divine maternity, as always their towering, emblematical attribute—but great, at any rate, as man, in all departments.[20]

Whitman's own sense of vocation, that is, of having been called to realize the democratic vision of the equality of the divinity as a destiny contained in images in everyone, men and women alike, led him to embrace the conviction that he had a duty to call others to experience the "vast Divinity spanning all" as well. In his poem "Eidólons," a Greek word that means "phantom," or "images," he repeats the word "eidólons" after each sequence of twenty-one verses, building in harmonic cadences toward a crescendo, where the word is intoned in repetition three times, to connote the three strata of Spiritual Democracy: "Eidólons,

eidólons, eidólons."[21] He taps into primordial images by vocalizing them with religious reverence out of his emotional center: the self.

> The old, old urge,
> Based on the ancient pinnacles, lo, newer, higher pinnacles,
> From science and the modern still impell'd,
> The old, old urge, eidólons.[22]

Spiritual Democracy is only possible through an expansion of consciousness made possible, in his view, by a union of "high" and "low," as a quality of cosmic light inflected in the soul's body and breath. Whitman accepts his vocation, in other words, by enacting it lyrically via images, in the specific activity in a poem whose very title names it: "Vocalism." The chant-like act of repetition— "the divine power to speak words"—thrice repeated in "Vocalism," acts as a driving stimulus, a downward steady beat, as in a drum's rhythm, which is attuned to the rhythms of his human body. Vocalism is essentially a shamanic technique,[23] a method of trance-induction, whereby the reader may be potentially transported—if he or she is open to it—into "cosmic consciousness."[24]

Salut au Monde!

By 1855, when the first edition of *Leaves of Grass* was published, Whitman had one purpose, and that was to spread Spiritual Democracy around the globe.[25] Spiritual Democracy is the "axis" upon which *Leaves of Grass* turns, just as the Civil War is;[26] the two exist together side by side. By Spiritual Democracy, Whitman means a new international religious attitude that he felt was essential for America to foster. His aim is an idea that may be of particular interest to readers who are involved in a similar project today. Whitman's clearest statement of his dream to inaugurate an "internationality of poems and poets" came during the publication of the first Russian translation of his poetry, wherein he sent his love and "hearty comradeship" to "all nations of the earth" during his first contact with what he called the "great Russian peoples."[27]

Prior to the Civil War, Whitman was interested in infusing into the churches of his day a new vitality, a new energy, a new electricity of the living God, beyond all creeds, beyond all denominations, beyond any one organized religion. Whitman used the terms "religion" and "spirituality" interchangeably. Such a cosmic vision was made possible by the new advances in modern science, in archaeology, geology, astronomy, and the nautical sciences, which were emerging in the mid-nineteenth century and would culminate in the publication, in

1859, of Charles Darwin's *The Origin of Species*. In Whitman's view, every religion is a necessary and temporary medium through which the developed soul passes in its spiritual journey through life to a point of transcendence, where it is possible to gain a glimpse of the earth from a point of view above all religions, where all religions of the globe meet and are joined in a homogeneous atmosphere of equality.[28] Thus, Spiritual Democracy is religious correspondence, plain and simple, an individual path with a one-world heart.

That's not to say that Whitman thought, because spirituality could evolve in different ways, that he considered all religions of equal value. In Whitman's view, any change in the world must begin with the individual. All changes in attitude are changes of the heart, otherwise there is no change. Thus, if a poem is to reach the world, it must speak with the language of the heart—the universal, the language of the cosmos—for cosmic understanding is ultimately all we have to sustain us: an understanding that we are all really the same. We are equals, regardless of our class, ethnicity, education, religion, gender, sexual orientation; we are all people of the earth, and love is what we must teach and offer the world through our leadership. When Whitman says, "I can easily build as good, and so can you,"[29] he means each individual, from each religious faith and each nationality, can help with the co-construction of sacred scriptures.

This is not St. Francis of Assisi being called by the holy crucifix of San Damiano again to rebuild the church for the nation of Italy or the nations of Europe, or Martin Luther insisting on ethical reform that required paring the European Christian church back to its bare essentials to release a contemporary ethic; it's a call for a widening of latitude and longitude across all continents of the globe reaching out to all nationalities, north and south, east and west, to the very axis-ends upon which the earth turns. The "churches of men and women"[30] Whitman had in mind were merely the medium, he said, for a new global vision made possible by the transit of railroads and electric telegraphs spreading across all lands and ships circumnavigating the globe. Whitman sought to open the churches up to a new vision of an international spirit appearing on the horizon of the future at a democratic vista that is unprecedented in human history.

The new religion Whitman refers to might, in fact, be an extension of Christ's teachings, for he says that he accepts the gospels, "knowing assuredly that he [Christ] is divine"[31] and, then again, it might be an extension of the monotheism of Islam, for he says he equally respects the Koran.[32] It could also be extensions of the teachings of Judaism, yoga, Daoism, Buddhism, Hinduism, Sufism, the religions of the Polynesian islanders or Native Americans, or the animism of Africa. Whatever the new Spiritual Democracy of the future might be, Whitman says, he has faith that he will have his part to play—major or minor—in helping to usher it in for the benefit of the world soul. His work may in fact help augment the teachings of any one religious dispensation toward an achievement of greater cross-cultural relativity in the current "Age of Wholeness."

Under this religion, science is a point of view in what Carl Jung called an experience of "objective cognition" that makes "the real *coniunctio* possible,"[33] or the psyche reflecting on itself through detached empirical observation. By Spiritual Democracy, Whitman means that every religion has a threshold—a portal, an opening, or aperture, like the top of a teepee through which the smoke may pass, or the central point of the ceilings of the beautiful mandalas of the great synagogues, churches, or mosques of the world, through which the developed soul may travel to attain a democratic vista, above all faiths, where each religion meets and is joined together in celebration of the divine life of all things animate and inanimate, co-eternal with the universal God, whether Brahman, Christ, Great Spirit, Allah, Sophia, Mary, Isis, or whatever words one may use to define the deity.[34]

In his prose "Preface," Whitman extols the achievements of "Exact Science" and adds that "There shall be love between the poet and the man of demonstrable science."[35] The emergence of practical demonstrations of the benefits of science in the century is what made the birth of *Leaves of Grass* possible. By the emergence of "an internationality of poems, and poets, binding the lands of the earth closer than all treaties and diplomacy,"[36] moreover, he means the "solidarity of the world."[37] Such solidarity can only be made possible by the findings of modern science.

We may not know what new international religion is emerging on the horizon of the future, but Whitman says we can each build on it in our own ways. Science is the "fatherstuff" of the "sinewy race of bards"[38] he says and:

Each of us is inevitable,
Each of us limitless—each of us with his or her right upon the earth,
Each of us allow'd the eternal purports of the earth,
Each of us here as divinely as any is here.[39]

Whitman is one of the intellectual giants who built on the New Church, New Synagogue, New Mosque, New Temple, New Ashram, New Hogan, or New Teepee of the world. His vision is not only international but transnational, for transnationality is finally where the religions of the world meet at the place of holy worship in the world soul. We are finally joined there at the apex of human consciousness by the poets of the modern and the postmodern, with Emily Dickinson being a supreme example of this. Today, of course, we would also call it "globalization." But the word "transnational" applies because Whitman's aim was to call for an internationality of poems and poets across all nations of the world, and his point of spiritual reference from 1855 onward was from a view situated in cosmic awareness, above the countries of the world, at an altitude high above the various God-images of all nations whence they could be objectified and made relative by our own subjective myths. In section three of "A Song for Occupations," Whitman comments on the Bible in a very seminal way when he says, superseding scripture:

> We consider bibles and religions divine—I do not say they are
>   not divine,
> I say they have grown out of you, and may grow out of you
>   still,
> It is not they who give the life, it is you who give the life.[40]

It is clear to many Whitman scholars today that Whitman's intent was not to found a new church in America. His aim was to plant the seeds for an international religion that had never existed before on the face of the earth, one that would be celebrated, he hoped, throughout the entire world. In his vision, it would not end with science, but rather be crowned by the poet: "After the noble inventors, after the scientists, after the chemist, the geologist, / Finally shall come the poet worthy that name, / The true son of God shall come singing his songs."[41]

What is the transport that gave Whitman the wings to believe he could transcend all nations? It may indeed have been America's enthusiasm for its potential to release spiritual progress—starting with the quest for religious liberty that brought the Pilgrims to Native American land seeking equality and freedom from the churches of Europe. This quest for religious freedom was carried forward by the New England transcendentalists prior to Whitman's emergence onto the world stage, the chief architect being Ralph Waldo Emerson and his followers, Henry David Thoreau and Margaret Fuller. It was out of this spiritual current and its tremendous energy stream that Whitman was enabled to pass into a state of transnationalism above the world's religions where he could view them from a psychological angle, situated in what he called the "supreme" science of "God":

> With science, the old theology of the East, long in its dotage, begins
> evidently to die and disappear. But (to my mind) science—and maybe

such will prove its principal service—as evidently prepares the way for One indescribably grander—Time's young but perfect offspring—the new theology—heir of the West—lusty and loving, and wondrous beautiful. For America, and for today, just the same as any day, the supreme and final science is the science of God—what we call science being only its minister—as Democracy is, or shall be also.[42]

Science made possible the vision of the unity of all religions, not just from a philosophical bird's-eye view but from a scientifically discovered "astronomical" altitude outside religious nationalism. In order to gain such a vista, Whitman needed shoulders to stand on to take wing like a bird of passage to the four corners of the earth. His winged migrations were provided for by the strong and stable spine of his master, Emerson, from whose shoulders he soared to greet the world.

Emerson, who had graduated from Harvard University at the age of eighteen, left his Unitarian church pulpit in Boston in 1832, because he could no longer subscribe to the tenets of Christianity. Emerson wrote his great manifesto "Nature" in 1836, and he later returned to Harvard in 1838 to deliver the famous Phi Beta Kappa Divinity School Address, which resulted in his expulsion from this Unitarian-based group. What had begun as an initial dissatisfaction with Unitarianism soon ran in the direction of a radical repudiation of the entire established religious order of his times. In a series of essays from 1841 to 1844, Emerson literally transformed the field of American letters with a mind on fire, set ablaze by his reading of Goethe, the Sufi poets, Hafiz, Saadhi, the sacred spiritual texts of India, and the rational empiricism of von Humboldt's scientific masterpiece, *Cosmos*. In "The American Scholar," Emerson went so far as to situate the scholar above the priest, and he replaced the myth of the God in Jesus with an image of God in the "Oversoul" present in all nature.

Whereas Emerson provided a philosophical basis for spiritual individuation, Whitman gave ecstatic inspiration to the body. In his 1844 essay "The Poet," Emerson confessed his sense of failure in not having lived up to the ideals he envisioned for himself as an international bard. He then called for a new "Language-maker," an American poet, to rise up and take transcendentalism and its principles (which he attempted to versify in his poem "Brahma") further. While Emerson did not develop a new international religion of his own, he nevertheless paved the way for the emergence of Whitman, who would take the works of his master to a new altitude altogether. As Emerson wrote to Whitman, in what is one of the most famous letters in the annals of American poetry:

DEAR SIR, I am not blind to the worth of the wonderful gift of "LEAVES OF GRASS." I find it the most extraordinary piece of wit and wisdom that America has yet contributed. I am very happy in reading it. . . .

I give you joy of your free and brave thought. I have great joy in it. I find incomparable things said incomparably well, as they must be. I find the courage of treatment which so delights us, and which large perception only can inspire.

I greet you at the beginning of a great career, which yet must have had a long foreground somewhere, for such a start. I rubbed my eyes a little, so to see if this sunbeam were no illusion; but the solid sense of the book is a sober certainty.[43]

If Emerson's congratulatory words "I greet you at the beginning of a great career" were not enough to convince Whitman that he had answered his call for a new international bard to rise up and take America forward, then he was likely persuaded by Thoreau, who was equally dazzled:

I do not believe that all the sermons, so-called, that have been preached in this land put together are equal to it for preaching. We ought to rejoice greatly in him . . . He is Democracy.[44]

Some of Whitman's most perceptive readers, Thoreau among them, were moved by him in a way they had never been by any preacher before. In Thoreau's words, Whitman had not only dipped his hat into the river of religious democracy: he was democracy, and he spoke from the river mouth. Thoreau replied with the best word he could, the religious word: "rejoice."

Whitman, as a staunch supporter of abolition, advocated and even agitated for the Civil War, even though he was to meet the agonizing effects of war first-hand in the suffering of countless wounded soldiers. As early as 1847, he recognized the paradox of fighting for good, when he said "I am the poet of sin, / For I do not believe in sin."[45] In section seven of "Starting From Paumanok," he said that he espoused evil and added that he was just as much evil as good, as was his nation:

Omnes! Omnes! let others ignore what they may,
I make the poem of evil also, I commemorate that part also,
I am myself just as much evil as good, and my nation is—[46]

The word *omnes* with an exclamation mark refers to the state of being all-comprehensive, to allness, or universality, which Whitman brings into his Deus Quadriune, or Quaternary God-image, in 1865. It's a new symbol for human completeness that his "New Bible" is meant to announce. Whitman said that there are really three greatnesses: "The greatness of Love and Democracy, and the greatness of Religion."[47] He held the tension of opposites by expressing his love to the injured and dying men in the hospital wards of Washington during his stint as a nurse during the bloody Succession War and by espousing both love and violence, good and evil in his poetry.

While other nations of the globe had founded their national identities on the basis of certain religious creeds and ideologies in the past, Whitman came along as a transnational transformer and equalized religious arguments by getting to the root source of Greek Dionysianism (well before Friedrich Nietzsche) in "The Birth of Tragedy." In "Song of Myself" Whitman rhapsodizes, "Dancing yet through the streets in a phallic procession, rapt, / . . . beating the serpent-skin drum."[48] He doesn't mean this literally, but symbolically; beating the serpent-skin drum, he sounds his call for Spiritual Democracy. Here Whitman thinks philosophically from the rhythms of the earth—from the green stuff of the world, his thoughts are rhythmically woven out of the soul's body's beat and the primal heartbeat of the drum. "I see the battlefields of the earth, grass grows on them and blossoms and corn."[49] In a notebook entry written during the 1860s called "A Spinal Thought," Whitman wrote:

> The whole scene shifts.—The relative positions change.—Man comes forward, inherent, superb,—the soul, the judge, the common average man advances,—ascends to place.—God disappears.[50]

The idea of God's disappearance comes forth most clearly in section forty-four of "Song of Myself" where he transports himself to the far reaches of outer and inner space and sees the huge first "Nothing" out of which he and the cosmos were born.[51] He says, "Before I was born out of my mother generations guided me, / My embryo has never been torpid. / Cycles ferried my cradle, rowing and rowing like cheerful boatmen."[52] The cycles that ferried his cradle like cheering, rowing boatmen suggests that his remembrance of his identity is made possible through his remembrance of his evolutionary history, and it does not end with a return to the mother alone; his regression goes back deeper to the father: the "fatherstuff" of science that "sent the seed of the conception of it."[53]

It is in his 1856 poem "Salut au Monde!" that Whitman "internationalizes" this vision of the science of evolution to a point of transcendence where all religions meet, and this poem is the axis upon which all of his major poems turn. His meaning is evident in the poem's title: the French word salut means "hello," a gesture of greeting or respect; *au* means "to"; and *monde* means "world." Salut, moreover, comes from the Latin root *salus,* meaning "health." So "Salut au Monde!" is Whitman's poem of greeting to the world: "health to you!" he says. "Good will to you all, from me and America sent!"[54] The theme of the poem is the extension of the democratic ideal of human brotherhood and sisterhood to all nations of the globe in the form of a new world religion in which all the gods and goddesses of the earth are valued as equals in an all-comprehensive scientific God-image that is inclusive of such heretical notions, for the nineteenth century, as the values of the feminine principle, homosexuality, and evil. In his prose essay "Democratic Vistas" published in 1871, Whitman defined two grand stages of preparation strata for American Democracy that the nation was passing through at that time, and he intuited that the United States was showing unmistakable signs of its readiness to reach an unprecedented third stage of what Whitman called Spiritual Democracy that his poem "Salut au Monde!" promulgates. The stages are:

1. Political: "Planning and putting on record the political foundation rights of immense masses of people—indeed all people," i.e., the Declaration of Independence, its amendments, the federal Constitution, etc.;

2. Economic: "Material prosperity," and the "organization of great cities;" and

3. Religious: "Spiritual Democracy" that Whitman will make "illustrious"; it will reconstruct and "democratize society."[55]

Whitman believed the people of America had been "listening enough" to the poets of other nations, and it was time to move beyond them toward a new vision of world solidarity. He called for new American poetry to "soar above others" in "its original styles in literature and art" and supply its own "intellectual and esthetic masterpieces, archetypal, and consistent with itself."[56]

As we have seen, such a vista of psychological potential for spiritual development was also glimpsed by the Swiss psychiatrist Carl Jung who called it the "transcendent function" in a 1916 essay by that name. The transcendent function Jung refers to is the "God-function" in the psyche, as he made clear in his 1921 essay on Meister Eckhart. Jung maintains that there is a religious function in the psyche of every person that can be accessed through the development of various psychological or spiritual techniques. This opens the door to a spiritual relativity that Whitman speaks out for in many of his finest poems in *Leaves of Grass,* where he gets outside the religions of the earth and objectifies them through the method he created, namely free verse, suggesting the right of the individual to voice his or her own reality.

Spiritual Democracy, as Whitman sees it, begins with the political. Inscribed in the U.S. Constitution and Bill of Rights is the first principle of the founding fathers: the freedom of religion. In an 1847 notebook, Whitman writes, "If I walk with Jah [God] in Heaven and he assumes to be intrinsically greater than I, it offends me; and I shall certainly withdraw from Heaven,—for the soul prefers freedom in the prairie and the untrodden woods."[57] His pantheism is transparent here. Whitman is more of a pantheist poet par excellence, a post-Buddhist poet,[58] and animist than most academic scholars have acknowledged.

The basic principles of the American Constitution—equality for all people, basic human rights, the pursuit of happiness, and religious liberty—are all transformed in Whitman's works and synthesized into a new scientifically informed monotheism, whereby he sees all religions on the same plane; he levels them all out and makes them all equivalents. Beating his serpent-skin drum, Whitman goes to the source—shamanism—and returns us thereby to our spiritual foundations on the earth.

Whitman then turns, with a penetrating gaze, toward you and me. He declares that if he is to worship anything it will be some spread of his own body, that nothing is more divine than You, including God! Not only does he personalize God in his celebration of life, he divinizes your personhood and sacralizes your body and soul by celebrating the self and no-self, the Atman and Anatman, Christ and the Godhead, Jah and the Goddess, in You.

One wonders if the idea of Spiritual Democracy could have existed for Whitman without the image of Christ, and whether, for that matter, Christ might be the best and final symbol for it in Whitman's work. Again, Whitman evolved his notion of religious equality from his reading of Alexander von Humboldt, who wrote, in *Cosmos II:*

> [T]he feeling of the unity and common condition of the whole human race, and of the equal rights of all men, has a nobler origin, and is based on the internal promptings of the spirit and of the force of religious convictions. Christianity has materially contributed to call forth this idea of the unity of the human race, and thus has tended to exercise a favorable influence on the humanization of nations in their morals, manners, and institutions.[59]

As we have seen, Humboldt was deeply inspired by the principles of the U.S. Constitution, and, taking his vision of unity within diversity across all nations toward a more moral foundation for what he found in the United States, wrote: "The principle of individual and political freedom is implanted in the ineradicable conviction of the equal rights of one sole human race." It is, above all, the moral element, however, that "elevates and animates cosmical life." And in Humboldt's magisterial delineation of the "great epoch of the history of the universe," he concludes, the "religion of Christ enlarged these views of mankind" so that it forever altered our "general, intellectual, moral, and social development."[60]

It can't be denied that the Christ-symbol figures prominently in Walt Whitman's vision, and it's to the credit of von Humboldt that he was able to achieve such objectivity. In section thirty-three of "Song of Myself," for instance, Whitman writes: "Walking the old hills of Judea with the beautiful gentle God by my side."[61] He does not place himself above Christ in this poem, he walks with him at his side, and he is not inferior or subordinate to Christ; he is his equal, no more, no less. To the extent that Whitman universalizes Christ in relationship to all other God-images across the nations, he universalizes love— brotherhood and sisterhood—and human compassion. Yet, as we all know, love and compassion are also found in Judaism, Islam, Hinduism, Greek Eros, Sufism, Buddhism, and in African spirituality, in the Goddess religions, and in all other faiths, and Whitman understood this. He had intimate knowledge of other belief traditions from anthropology studies, travel books, and archeological discoveries. Moreover, Whitman did not merely have faith or belief in the equality of all religions. He had more than book knowledge—he had direct spiritual experience: he knew. He had objective cognition. He wasn't interested in universalizing the Christ image so much as he was in the transnationalizing of human compassion and love to all world cultures, including New Guinea, Madagascar, Polynesian islands, China, Japan, and Egypt.

Whitman turned to Christ, however, for his model of what he liked to call "the new religion of personalism." For him, Christ, who appeared in the moral-spiritual field as an embodiment of the absolute soul and divine brother of everyone, emerged in time so that each person might see that there is something in the human body and soul of each person, a conscience: "something so transcendent, so incapable of gradations, (like life,) that, to that extent, it places all beings on a common level, utterly regardless of the distinctions of intellect, virtue, station, or any height or lowliness whatever—."[62] This is the cornerstone of Whitman's new religion. By "new religion" Whitman means a new experimental point of view, a post-Humboltian rational empiricism that might best be called pragmatic or psychological, and is based on the sound principles of a science of myth.

While the Hebrew-Christian Bible helped to make the idea of religious equality possible in Whitman (Isa. 28:16; Matt 21: 42; Mark 12:10; 1 Pet. 2:6), it would be incorrect to reduce his vision to the spiritual benefit of Isaiah, or Christ alone. For who before Whitman brought sin into his God-image? Whitman received his equalizing vision from many religions, from his Quaker ancestry, from the oratory he heard at the age of ten from the mouth of the spiritualist Elias Hicks, and even earlier than that: from the solitary voice of the he-bird, the mockingbird, the lone brother who chanted to him in his lyrical masterpiece "Out of the Cradle Endlessly Rocking," long before he'd heard of Emerson, or read *Cosmos*. Additionally, the Vedas; Upanishads; Chinese texts; and Persian, Egyptian, Native American, and Polynesian religions all played pivotal parts in giving birth to Whitman's international vision of Spiritual Democracy in the West. In fact, without Whitman's reading of the great world religions, *Leaves of Grass* would never have been born.

It should be emphasized again that, in Whitman's view, all God-images of humanity are placed on an evolutionary footing—a footing of equality. All have mutual rights and equal rights; none are greater; none are lesser; all are divine; all are equivalents. All infighting of religions, based on inferior and superior statuses, passes away in the divine economy of human friendship and love. The brief divine sketches he paints for us in "Chanting the Square Deific" are seen in contrast to the way they are better filled out by a person who makes all the world's people divine in a new postscientific relativity in art.

In a conversation with the English architect J. W. Wallace, Whitman declared that his main object in the writing and publishing of *Leaves of Grass* was "To arouse that something in the reader we call character . . . Not to describe things outside you—creeds, or bibles, or anything else—but arouse that which is in you. It is in you."[63] By something "in you," he means spiritual character, a conscience illuminated by the new enlightenment of science, a light so strong and immortal, like billions of suns that can stand above any law that is arbitrary, including those supporting claims to final authority. As Whitman says of himself in his 1855 "Preface," as the American bard:

> He is no arguer, he is judgment.
> He judges not as the judge judges, but as the sun falling around a helpless
>   thing.
> As he sees the farthest he has the most faith.[64]

Whitman does not preach discipleship. He teaches self-reliance and the democratization of religious experience. Spiritual Democracy is not elitist; it is part of a changing world vision that includes an evolution of ethical values that are not absolute facts but facts of science that need to be scientifically tested to be deemed just and moral and right by the people.

In one of his last poems "L. of G.'s Purport," written with "shadowy Death" dogging his steps, Whitman said his aim had been not to pick out or expose evils from their formidable masses, "but to add, fuse, complete, extend—celebrate the immortal and the good" and "span vast realms of space and time, / Evolution—the cumulative—growths and generations."[65]

What he teaches must be experienced through a wrestling with the moral opposites and a spiritual transcendence of the split between good and evil that inevitably leads to the perpetuation of holy wars, crusades, and jihads. In a dialogue with his biographer Horace Traubel, shortly before his death, Whitman said:

> I claim everything for religion: after the claims of my religion are satisfied nothing is left for anything else; yet I have been called irreligious—an infidel (God help me!): as if I could have written a word of the Leaves without its religious root-ground.[66]

Now here is the problem we face today in the age of science and technology: The religions of the world, past and present, are all part and parcel of what Whitman called the "infant schools," and he means this not literally, but metaphorically. In essence he's saying that many believers have not yet grown up to realize that we are really all equals, and all the same. As the history of the world has shown and continues to show in its violent displays of force, crusades and jihads are destructive to God and the Goddess Earth herself, because she is our sister and our mother, and whatever we do to the earth; we do to the water, trees, and the air we breathe. We do it to ourselves.

Whitman believed we are on the verge of arriving at a new international myth that he, for one, disseminates. It is one that does not discriminate or hold itself up as possessing mastery over other religions, but rather is modest and immodest, humble and arrogant, loving and warlike, impulsive and wise, in a union of contradictory opposites, held in a tension of contraries by a devout and transformational consciousness. Religion, in Whitman's view, is about union, comradeship, and caring. But insofar as he included sin and evil in his Deus Quadriune, he does not want these to be gilded. As he said to Horace Traubel, "Be sure to write about me honest: whatever you do do not prettify me: include all the hells and damns."[67] This is a call for a new symbol of completeness in the human being. Hence, it's imperative to extend Walt Whitman's vision of Spiritual Democracy during a time of the United States' role in the world as an international leader. But how can one attain religious equality in a globalized world? Whitman answers: it's in yourself.

Spiritual Democracy begins with the Civil War, which was fought for freedom from slavery, the subject of the first experiments with free verse in Whitman's oeuvre. Only when slavery was abolished in the United States was Whitman's clearest articulation of the meaning of religious democracy imaginable. Then, the divine potential he dreamed about as possible within each of us was asserted. When each of us attains it first within ourselves, the world can be free. Once religious equality is realized in the masses, the world may become whole, but not until then.

As we saw in his 1847 notebook, Whitman has a simple image for this: "Bring all the art and science of the world, and baffle and humble it with one spear of grass."[68] Whitman was also one of the fiercest promoters of marriage equality, women's rights, and religious liberty across the globe, and his role as a liberator of world culture was spearheaded by a single spear of grass. This is extraordinary. What miracle is this? Whitman's answer is really quite simple. In another entry in the same Notebook he writes: "My life is a miracle and my body which lives is a miracle."[69] These trial lines eventually found their way into his 1856 poem "Miracles," where he teaches us to value the miracles of everyday life—such as a blade of grass—and depart from supernaturalism.

It's clear that some kind of a sexual experience led Whitman to the transcendent emotion of happiness that he speaks of in sections five and fifty of "Song of Myself." In the first edition of *Leaves of Grass* is the following metaphor, its experiential basis unmistakable: "Thruster holding me tight and that I hold tight! / We hurt each other as the bridegroom and the bride hurt each other."[70] Contained in this description of penetrative copulation between two men is a new image of the sacred in which homosexual and heterosexual union are placed on a level of physical and spiritual equivalence. This equivalence of meaning is captured beautifully in the image of the single spear of grass. The concern with equality is as pertinent to our sociopolitical debates today, particularly with our debates on same-sex marriage, and it demonstrates how relevant Whitman's views on equality are for LGBT people, as well as for women, for all nationalities, and for all races. As Whitman said to Horace Traubel: "Sex, sex: always immanent . . . sex, sex, the root of roots: the life below the life!"[71]

The spear of grass is a prime symbol for the libido, a God-concept that

Freud and Jung would wrestle with in their race for the prize. In the close-to-the-earthiness of the grass metaphor, however, with regards to the libido as a sexual and spiritual notion, Walt Whitman has virtually no antecedents. He is unique, self-created through and through.

> A child said What is the grass? fetching it to me with full hands;
> How could I answer the child? I do not know what it is any more
>   than he.
> I guess it must be the flag of my disposition, out of hopeful
>   green stuff woven.
> Or I guess it is the handkerchief of the Lord,
> . . . .
> Or I guess the grass is itself a child, the produced
>   babe of the vegetation.
> Or I guess it is a uniform hieroglyphic,
> . . . .
> I am the mate and companion of people, all just as immortal
>   and fathomless as myself,
> (They do not know how immortal, but I know.)[72]

His aim was astonishing: not merely to liberate all forms of sexuality from social repression (a project he shared with many in the Victorian era), but to bring it into the church with a new vigor and vitality. As Whitman said to Traubel, he felt the public had no notion of him as a "spiritualistic being," yet he also insisted that he had his "connections" and that they are "deep-rooted—that they penetrate shows, phenomena."[73] His vision is so new, in fact, that we have still, for the most part, not caught up with his egalitarian libido symbol yet. As Whitman wrote in his preface about the American poet: "High up out of reach he stands turning a concentrated light, he turns the pivot with his finger. / He baffles the swiftest runners as he stands and easily overtakes and envelops them."[74]

In a cluster of poems he wrote in 1860 addressed specifically to women, "The Children of Adam," Whitman created a way to sexual and spiritual liberation for women, and this is an excellent example of what he means by Religious Democracy. As he wrote in a letter:

> [O]nly when sex is properly treated, talked, avowed, accepted, will the
> woman be equal with the man, and pass where the man passes, and meet
> his words with her words, and his rights with her rights.[75]

Whitman's vision of national liberation is equally relevant to the current struggles against oppressive regimes, particularly those being waged in Western

Asia. And how might they speak to us today in light of the concurrent rise of religious extremist groups such as the Muslim Brotherhood?

Whitman is able to turn his own embodied experiences into transnational transport. The 1856 poem "Salut au Monde!" provides salient insight into this technique. In the first line of this poem, an international companion, friend, or comrade addresses the Poet, "O take my hand, Walt Whitman! / . . . What widens within you, Walt Whitman?" Here we have a portrait of divine lover, a male peacemaker of all nations who asks Whitman—and, by extension, us—to take his hand. This is none other than the elder hand of God as it has incarnated in all the nations of the world and in its barbarous and civilized mythologies. Whitman says: "Within me latitude widens, longitude lengthens, / Asia, Africa, Europe, are to the east—America is provided for in the west."[76] From here, he literally soars on a first-of-its-kind soul-flight to survey the interconnectedness of all objects of nature in an equal belongingness where all may experience the miraculous and participate in it.

From his aerial view above the earth, Whitman sees the divine origin of democratic human brotherhood and its extension throughout the globe when he hears the "Spanish dance with castanets," the "fierce French liberty-songs," the "chirp of the Mexican muleteer, and the bells of the mule," the "Arab muezzin calling from the top of the mosque," the "Christian priests at the altars of their churches," the "cry of the Cossack," the "wheeze of the slave-coffle as slaves march on, as husky gangs pass on by twos and threes, fasten'd together with wrist-chains and ankle chains," the "Hebrew reading his records and psalms," the recitation of the "rhythmic myths of the Greeks," and the voice of the "Hindoo teaching his favorite pupil." From listening long to the "poets who wrote three thousand years ago," he sees, during his moments of visionary transport, the Andes, the Himalayas, the mountains of China, Vesuvius and Etna, the Red Mountains of Madagascar, the gulf of New Guinea, the "site of the old empire of Assyria, and that of Persia, and that of India." He sees the "temples of the deaths of the bodies of Gods," the "old signifiers," and he sees the "Brazilian vaquero," the "Bolivian ascending mount Sorata," and the "Wacho crossing the plains."[77]

Note that in the midst of this great aerial view of a catalogue of the world's religious singers and colorful nationalities is the sound of the heavy tread of the "slave-coffle": men treading in "wrist-chains" and "ankle-chains." This metrical shuffle of the feet toward the earth in anticipation of the Civil War is a sound Whitman does not hesitate to bring forward into his cosmic vision. (In fact, within a matter of five years, Whitman became one of the fiercest promoters of the Civil War.) This magnificent poem contains the kernel of his international religious vision: the spiritual elevation leads him to experience, during vision-ary rapture, the equality of all religions at a vista made possible by the break-throughs in modern astronomy and nautical navigation and rational empiricism.

In his vision, Whitman is one with the crucified Christ and with all the dead gods and goddesses of the earth, for they have all culminated in his experience of a new international religious revelation through his passage through the "first huge Nothing": the void of the cosmos. He has attained the unification point, the axis, around which all religions are made one. He does not place himself above the religions of the world, for in this state of knowing, they are all present, and he recognizes all sentient beings as his sisters and brothers.

> I see Teheran, I see Muscat and Medina and the intervening
>   sands, I see the caravans toiling onward,
> I see Egypt and the Egyptians, I see the pyramids and obelisks,
> I look on chisell'd histories, records of conquering kings,
>   dynasties, cut in slabs of sand-stone, or on granite blocks,
> I see at Memphis mummy-pits containing mummies embalm'd,
>   swathed in linen cloth, lying there many centuries,
>
> . . . .
>
> Salut au monde!
>
> . . . .
>
> Toward you all, in America's name,
> I raise high the perpendicular hand, I make the signal . . .[78]

All the gods and goddesses are united in him because he has attained the great transcendental experience of happiness: "Do you see my brothers and sis-ters?" he says in section fifty of "Song of Myself": "It is not chaos or death—it is form, union, plan—it is eternal life—it is Happiness."[79]

It should not surprise us, then, that the great spiritual teacher of twentieth-century India, Sri Aurobindo, wrote of Whitman's transcendent achievement:

> His creation . . . draws from it a unique broadness of view, vitality of
> force and sky-wide atmosphere of greatness. . . . That which the old
> Indian seers called the mahān ātmā, the Great Self, the Great Spirit,
> which is seen through the vast strain of the cosmic thought and cosmic
> life . . . is the subject of some of his highest strains.[80]

8

THE BI-EROTIC AS
TRANSCENDENT SEXUALITY

ENFANS D'ADAM—THE EQUALITY OF WOMEN

Two poem clusters in Walt Whitman's influential work *Leaves of Grass* contain the cornerstone of his vision of Spiritual Democracy. They are the "Children of Adam" and "Calamus" groupings. The clusters stand together, side by side, in a bi-erotic portrait of gender equality that includes two types of marriage possibilities, one heterosexual, the other homosexual.

Here *bi-erotic* means that men and women alike will not be afraid to embrace the body of a same-sex person, nor fear allowing themselves to feel their erotic and affectionate feelings, and will learn to hold these emotions in consciousness in a nondefensive way. As Whitman wrote in "Salut au Monde!": "I see male and female everywhere, / . . . I mix indiscriminately, / And I salute all the inhabitants of the earth."[1]

Whitman begins the 1860 "Enfans d'Adam" ("Children of Adam") cluster by asking readers to behold his "resurrection" and he speaks of "the quivering fire that ever plays" through his limbs "for reasons most wondrous."[2] The idea of his resurrection identifies him immediately with the crucified Christ, who has returned to the earth in a new form, this time taking incarnation through mystic fire to the level of the body's ecstasy, as a sexual as well as spiritual liberator of women and men, without prejudice toward gender or sexual orientation. In chant two of "Enfans d'Adam," Whitman sings the song of the "phallus" and "procreation" issuing from "pent up rivers" deep within him. He creates a "divine list" of erotic images in a state of "mystic deliria," inviting readers—men and women alike—to join him in his experiences of sensual "delighting."[3]

As we have seen, delight, joy, bliss, and ecstasy are important emotions for Whitman, as they form the nuclear affects in his poem "I Sing the Body Electric," where he says: "I do not ask any more delight, I swim in it as in a sea."[4] Although Emily Dickinson also spoke of ecstasy in shamanic-poetic ways that affirmed the bi-erotic imagination, no one in American history had written about the delights of sex in such a candid and open way before Whitman. To think that he was doing this during the Victorian era, the year before Sigmund Freud's birth, is astonishing. It is also an achievement cognate with the transcendentalists' attempt to escape the confines of prudish Protestant attitudes of viewing the body as a distraction from the divine, for Whitman was arguing that sex is the gateway to God: "We enjoy each other, and exhaust each other"[5] he says.

> From sex—from the warp and the woof,
> . . . .
> From the long-sustained kiss on the mouth or the bosom,
> . . . .
> From what the divine husband knows—from the work of fatherhood,
> From exultation, victory, and relief—from the bedfellow's embrace
> In the night,
> . . . .
> From the bending curve and the clinch.[6]

In chant three, Whitman refers to readers as his *enfans*, his children, or divine mates, and adds that his calling is to "charge" readers with the "charge of the Soul." Taking the form of the New Adam, he asks forthrightly: "If the body were not the Soul, what were the Soul?"[7] In Whitman's view, body and soul are one. There is no division, and no higher over lower copulation imagery may be found in his poems; both are equally divine. Only the head creates dualisms, whereas the awakened body and soul yoked together in the love-grip create unions both heterosexual and homosexual, and they are equals, hence, his call to write the "New Bible"—one not bound by traditional heterosexual limits.

The symbolism basic to this cluster—the poet's identity with the New Adam—aims to transform the Hebrew-Christian views of his day, particularly the ecclesiastical view that sexuality is inherently shameful, and sinful and evil, especially onanism and homosexuality. These poems are clearly a celebration of all forms of sexuality: masturbation, heterosexuality, bisexuality, and homosexuality.

Not only are body and soul one in Whitman's works, but the Holy Spirit too is equalized in the universal ground of the Mother Goddess, Santa Spirita. In a notebook entry called "The Mother of These States," Whitman envisioned a new Goddess-image arising for humanity. He wrote: "None of the emblems of the classic goddess—nor any feudal emblems—are fit symbols for the republic." In another entry, he says further, "bring the idea of the Mother—the idea of the mother with numerous children—all, great and small, old and young, equal in her eyes—as the identity of America."[8] All the world's children are equal in her eyes. In his post-Civil War poems he will refer to her simply as the "Mother of All."[9] In a conversation, late in life with his biographer Horace Traubel, Whitman went further in pointing out the centrality of women:

> Leaves of Grass is essentially a woman's book: the women do not know it, but every now and then a woman shows that she knows it: it speaks out of the necessities, its cry is the cry of the right and wrong of the woman sex—of the woman first of all, of the facts of creation first of all—of the feminine: speaks out loud: warns, encourages, persuades, points the way.[10]

What Whitman is putting forth here is a new dispensation of the Holy Spirit, Santa Spirita, an explicitly feminine incarnating principle of divinity inherent in humanity: "Beneath thy look O Maternal."[11] As we've seen, the new image of God for the world soul can only be quaternary, in his view, a Deus Quadriune. For Whitman, as for Carl Jung, this squared deific includes the body and divine feminine. Although Whitman did not put this hypothesis forth fully until his 1865 poem "Chanting the Square Deific," the seeds for it are present in the poem "Salut au Monde!" nine years earlier. There, as we've seen, he objectivizes the God-images of all nations and sees them from a scientific viewpoint as complexities of various national identities that are all striving toward the realization that we are all one, equivalent parts of a great universal evolutionary design of fate and destiny in human history being worked out by the race as we strive toward the sacred divinity of Spiritual Democracy. In a transconscious state of international cosmic seeing, Whitman envisions a worldwide recognition of relativity of the God-notion, which can be realized across all nations only if it includes all sexual orientations in a conscious androgyny everyone may identify with and celebrate.

Women, of course, were essential to the success of such a project, as Whitman realized. In his 1856 "Poem of Remembrance," Whitman asks readers to remember the "organic compact of these States" and envision with him a new republic of poetically potent females: "Anticipate the best women!" he writes. "I say an unnumbered new race of hardy and well-defined women are to spread through all these States."[12] He sees himself in "The Children of Adam" as the "divine husband" of this new breed of American women, who are to be set spiritually free through the liberating power of the procreating urge. "This is the female form," he says. "A divine nimbus exhales from it from head to foot, / It attracts with fierce undeniable attraction."[13] Here is the nimbus image again, only this time it's not portrayed as a "gold-colored light" shining above the head only, like a Christian halo; it's a spiritual outbreath of the entire body.

Staying with his bi-erotic notion of the ecstasy involved in such spirituality, he speaks tenderly of women's "hair, bosom, hips, bend of legs" and the "love-flesh swelling and deliciously aching."[14] It is important to note that in these poems he is comfortable enough with his own sexuality in its bi-erotic totality, which has allowed him to treat the woman's body as an equal object of his desire, a temple of divinity. His aim is to return all readers to the Garden, the delights of Eden as an earthly paradise, on which the joys of the body are first and foremost innocent pleasures touched with grace. Unlike other male poets who call forth a feminine soul-image to lead their subjectivity forward, Whitman does not address only particular women or female goddesses for his creativity; rather he gives women and their bodies full recognition, as capable of similar pleasures that he himself delights in. He also gives women's bodies an independent status focusing on their liberty and their enjoyment rather than on the voluptuousness women can bring to men, including Whitman. The female body in these poems has an objective independent reality of its own and is not to be denied. Whitman celebrates women as he celebrates himself, and he celebrates women's liberation from patriarchal oppression with the same enthusiasm he has previously given to his own. The liberation of female sexuality is central to his vision of Spiritual Democracy, and this is one more way he extends himself not only far beyond his times, but far beyond the confines of his own body through his own subjective experience with women.

Whitman goes so far as to cede his own guardianship of the new spiritual freedom he is envisioning to the women he is celebrating. "Be not ashamed, women," Whitman writes. "You are the gates of the body, and you are the gates of the Soul."[15] His poetry is a *logos*, a word, of the spirit, but the spirit he is celebrating is an erotic spirit. Moreover, it is bi-erotic in the sense that it inheres to the embodied erotic experience of both women and men in both their heterosexual and homosexual iterations of it. He treats the female body as the gates of *eros* and all higher forms of human spiritual evolution emanate from the maternal ground of being: the bodies of women are embodiments of the divine feminine, just as the African American slave figure who he calls the "teeming mother of mothers"[16] is viewed as cosmic and sacred in all of her aspects. "The man's body is sacred, and the woman's body is sacred, / No matter who it is, it is sacred; / Is it a slave?"[17] he asks.

Spiritual Democracy really begins here: not only are women's bodies and men's bodies sacred, but so too are the bodies of the two African American slaves at auction. The slave's bodies are said to inflect the same "divine mystery, the same old beautiful mystery."[18] Whitman puts forth his vision of internationality for the globe here, indistinguishable of all racial divisions: "Do you not see," he asks, in the role of a Southern auctioneer, "that these are exactly the same to all, in all nations and times, all over the earth? / If anything is sacred the human body is sacred."[19]

Spiritual Democracy was for Whitman "the nucleus" of his vision, for which its ultimate symbol was the soul's marriage with nature: the "Bridegroom-night of love, working surely and softly into the prostrate dawn, / Lost in the cleave of the clasping and sweet-fleshed day."[20] The beauty of these images lies in the fact that though they are embodied; he does not tell us what gender night and dawn are. They could be either gender—expressing either sex—which is to say that they are bi-erotic, transcendent of the paradox of masculine and feminine opposites that has traditionally limited the fantasies of poets. As the "New Adam" addressing a new era of women's individuation, Whitman seeks to free his women readers up to become creative, to vocalize, to write poems of their own, and to hunt, shoot, and play sports. He envisions potent mothers, who are equals to men, even who will eventually surpass men in the spiritual domain. Yet, it's worth asking how literally he intends readers to take all this. Is he credible as the boundlessly potent and promiscuous lover of women that he claims to be in these poems, or is he engaging women's imagination simply to impregnate them with a more abstract vision of how the world might be?

As a promoter of Spiritual Democracy, Whitman says he pours the "stuff to start sons and daughters fit for These States."[21] By "stuff" he means both imaginal semen and the "fatherstuff" of exact science: "Always of their fatherstuff must be begotten the sinewy races of bards." For, "in the beauty of poems are the tuft and final applause of science."[22] From a psychological view, he appears to be preparing the way for a new civilization and culture across the globe, a new society of orators, or new international *literatus* order that will include women and eventually be led by them. It is clear that he wants to be applauded not for his sexual prowess so much as for his seminal achievements as the father of the new American poetry, and insofar as his audience includes women, he will champion their liberation: "The drops I distil upon you shall grow fierce and athletic girls, new artists, musicians, and singers."[23]

Whitman will do the same for men in "Calamus," yet the tone of that cluster is more emotionally conflicted, more intimate, and more personal, suggesting that this second grouping of poems reflects his equivalent experiences, even though he mostly leaves out explicit homosexual references. In the earlier "Children of Adam" poems, where he addresses women, rarely in the catalogue of his own emotions does he include feelings of vulnerability, hurt, rejection, loss, envy, grief, and anguish, although his sexual images are clearly in evidence. When he says he desires and loves women equally with men, he does so with a flourish of sexual bravado and tactile sensitivity, but without any possible hint of emotional injury. In fact, he turns around the traditional heterosexual role of the poet who sexualizes the soul by becoming, in addition to the male lover, a muse, a bridegroom, a husband, and a mate for all women: "I see that they understand me, and do not deny me, / I see that they are worthy of me—I will be the robust husband of these women."[24]

The paradox of this cluster appears to be resolved in "Enfans d'Adam," chant five—"Spontaneous Me," where the three logical directions of love—autoerotic, heteroerotic, and homoerotic—are revealed as belonging to the very same body: "The body of my love—the body of the woman I love—the body of the man—the body of the earth."[25] Again, the accent is on the bi-erotic. A basic principle in his Spiritual Democracy appears to be nature itself as the source of his bi-eroticism. "O to drink the mystic deliria deeper than any other man!" he exclaims in the next poem in the cluster, "O bridegroom and bride. / . . . O to return to Paradise! / . . . . O the puzzle—the thrice-tied knot— . . . O all united and illuminated!"[26]

The "thrice-tied knot" refers to his tying, and thus personally binding, the knot of bi-erotic marriage, not to a woman and a man alone, for that would indicate two marriage-types only, but a third, through himself as an avatar of an all-encompassing nature. He reveals himself as evidence that not everyone is called to wed, and sings equally for those who are lonely and unmarried. Whitman also explicitly says that masturbation is okay, nothing to be ashamed about, for it is only natural to seek erotic release: "The pulse pounding through the palms and trembling encircling fingers."[27] "O trembling!" he says a few pages later, "To ascend—to leap to the heavens of the love indicated to me! / To rise thither with my inebriate Soul!"[28] This is not only self-love but love itself: union with the beloved. Whitman's connection to his own body electrifies him with ecstasy, which frees his soul to ascend to the upper world of cosmic seeing where he can love every imagined reader.

The only sadness apparent in "Enfans d'Adam" appears in chant nine, where it is not the poet-lover who is sad, but one woman who he says tried to detain him for love, and clung passionately to him, and who he now again sees close beside him in his poetic reverie, "with silent lips, sad and tremulous."[29] Whitman, however, cannot linger long in his evolution in exclusive attachment. He ends this cluster, saying to all readers: "Be not afraid of my body."[30] Be not afraid. He is canceling out not only homophobia, but all phobic reactions to the body and sex, which he sees as natural.

Spiritual Democracy was always the ground of his vision. It was not only the foundation of his poetic calling, what he called his "religious root-ground"; it was a goal for society to achieve. We hear the call to political action in these lines:

I am the poet of slaves and the master of slaves
. . . .
I go with the slaves of the earth equally with the masters
And I will stand between the masters and the slaves,
Entering into both so that both shall understand me alike.[31]

"Ethiopia Saluting the Colors," written in 1867, carries forward Whitman's growing uncertainty about the future of America and the spread of democracy in a globalized world. The figure of "Ethiopia" in this poem is an ancient one. She is clearly from another continent, and she portends something mysterious in the world soul. This is the only poem Whitman wrote about a black woman, and though it was written three years after President Lincoln signed the Emancipation Proclamation, he is recalling a time when slaves were required to set themselves free. The woman who observes Sherman's soldiers wears Ethiopia's national colors in her turban—yellow, red, and green—an assertion of her African identity superordinate to her status as a slave.

In the poem, this woman, who is named "Ethiopia," emerges from her shanty to meet eyes with a sole white soldier among 62,000 of General Sherman's men, all marching toward the sea in Carolina. This one soldier—the poet—watches her as she "courtesies to the regiment" and salutes the stars and stripes of our American flag: the red, white, and blue. Her head in its "high-borne turban" "wags" as she "rolls her darkling eye" to the "guidons moving by."

She is an old woman, as well, a wisdom-figure. Whitman's soldier-poet asks this "hardly human" figure who she is, with her "wooly-white and turban'd head, and bare bony feet?" Puzzled, Whitman also asks: "What is it fateful woman, so blear, hardly human? / Why wag your head with turban bound, yellow, red and green? / Are the things so strange and marvelous you see or have seen?"[32] Well might Whitman have asked. The Ethiopian slave trade did not operate in the Americas; it was directed toward the Middle East and supplied Arabian countries with slaves. So, the very presence of an Ethiopian woman in the Carolinas in 1864 is puzzling.

Ethiopia answers Whitman by saying that her master, a cruel slaver, told her she was abducted from her native land over one hundred years ago when she was sundered from her parents as a little girl, and brought across the sea to America. In the poem, after emerging from the "hovel door" to meet eyes with the "soldier-poet" she singles out by the roadside, Ethiopia recounts her traumatic history of being abducted into slavery. The meeting of her eyes with the poet's is momentous.

Why did Whitman's poetic instinct put her there? However allegorically, she must have been a vision. She can be seen as an image of the world soul, or what Emily Dickinson calls "The Ethiop within."[33] "Ethiop" was a term in common usage in the mid-nineteenth century and had become more or less synonymous with "African." In the poem, Whitman refers to her as a "dusky" African American woman, whose turban signifies pride in a transnational identity. He sees her as a "fateful woman"—and he is right. The colors of her turban now appear in the Jamaica-originated Rastafarian movement as a symbol of Pan-Africanism, as close to a living embodiment of transnationalism as our time has seen. American democracy after the Civil War, Whitman said, will become either the "destin'd conqueror" or "most tremendous failure of time."[34] In "Ethiopia Saluting the Colors," Whitman envisioned what would actually come to pass.

Today the nation of Ethiopia is politically fragile. Famines ravaged the country in the 1980s, and geopolitics and civil wars and human-rights violations resulting in a catastrophic death count of about one million have seriously thrown into question the fate of Spiritual Democracy in this particular African state. Whitman's statement that Ethiopia is a "fateful" woman reminds us of the fragility of Spiritual Democracy as well. The three colors of the Ethiopian flag mirror the three colors in the American flag, revealing a mirror-symmetry inherent in Spiritual Democracy, as its scope and aim is transnational, and is meant to spread its colorful possibilities to all races of the globe.

While Whitman is well known throughout the world as a sexual liberator of both women and men, his bi-erotic poems, although central to his visions of

Spiritual Democracy, ceased to be charged with the same luminosity of a religious vision as he found previously in his calling as bard of the Civil War. From
1861, when he heard his call, to the 1871 publication of his prose essay "Democratic Vistas," Whitman was in transition toward a new metamorphosis of his
religious identity. During this time, his notion of the bi-erotic would undergo
a marked transformation. Part of this change came to him through a profound
experience of rejection in male love.

CALAMUS—THE ANDROGYNOUS IDENTITY

It's important to closely examine Whitman's evolution through the two poetic
clusters, the "Children of Adam," and "Calamus" poems, to fully understand
what he refers to as "erotic fire." Interestingly, though, the "Calamus" poems do
not contain a single concrete description of sex. In this cluster of poems, addressed
mainly to men, the homosexuality is scarcely visible. All that is left (with a few
notable exceptions), as we shall see, is homoeros and homospirit—not enough to
confirm Whitman as the prototype of a contemporary "out" gay man.

By 1855, when the sexual poems were first published, Whitman had already
realized that his erotic identity as a man who could love men was equivalent with
his identity as a lover of women. He was, in this respect, as much like women
as like most other men, and his bi-eroticism made him identical with the eternal principle of androgyny in everyone. He saw us all, erotically, as "two fishes
swimming in the sea together."[35]

When he celebrated every atom of this androgyny that belonged to himself,
he meant that birthright also belongs to us, and not only to us but to the rocks,
the oaks, the blossoms, and the mountains, as well. Our bi-erotic nature made us
all in his eyes "two predatory hawks—we soar above and look down."[36]

This identity with androgyny anticipates Jung's understanding of the self.
When Whitman announced himself as the "New Adam," in 1860, celebrating
sexuality in all its varied forms in the "Children of Adam" poems, his decision
to leave sexuality in and not omit the controversial "Prostitute" from the third
edition was a decision not to claim his rights alone, but to claim everybody's
rights to be recognized as a sexual being. The great transcendentalist Ralph
Waldo Emerson advised Whitman to take out the explicit sexual metaphors, references, and images. Emerson's words to him were "more precious than gold,"
Whitman wrote, because of the great "paradoxical lesson"[37] that he drew from
them—that he must include the sexual with all the ambiguity that would entail
in the ongoing body of his work. Whitman's absolute conviction to follow his

own individual conscience is made self-evident in his unequivocal rejection of Emerson's sage advice.

To be sure, in 1865 he got himself into a great deal of trouble with his superiors at the Interior Department in Washington, DC, where he was working as a clerk, when his poems were judged as "indecent" by Secretary of the Interior James Harlan, who'd discovered the poems in the drawers of Whitman's desk. Had Whitman listened to Emerson, he might have preserved his career and private income. But his poetry was more precious than gold, for it contained the alchemical elixir, the alexipharmic, or the new alchemy of the golden West. This domain, interestingly enough, proves to be feminine for both Emerson and Whitman, for as we have seen, Whitman told Traubel: "*Leaves of Grass* is essentially a woman's book," and justifies "the right and wrong of the woman sex," for in it "the feminine: speaks out loud: warns, encourages, persuades, points the way."[38] Whitman appears to be envisioning the future here: the emergence of feminism.

By staying true to his vision, his calling from the American self, Whitman was able to assert what Freud would only get to a half century later, the a priori existence of a transnational bi-erotic identity to which any individual ego is only the subject. Further, the paradoxical lesson Whitman learned from Emerson was the necessity of staying true to the inner voice within, which was his calling to vocalism, and, therefore, to the sexual liberation of women and emergent spirituality of women as global leaders. His embodied version of "self-reliance" is close to Jung's view of individuation, where there can be no development of the personality without adherence to vocation. Standing up for the sexual in all its forms was Whitman's "life task," although, by 1860, world religion—the subject of "Salut au Monde!"—began to take center stage.

In Jung's model of the human psyche there are "*a priori* instinct-types"[39] that are inborn with the personality and that have a certain natural light, a *lumen naturae*, that illuminates their meaning autonomously. It's up to the individual to see by this light what the goal of sexuality really is. Whitman did just this in his poetry. The lack of explicitness in key places in the "Calamus" cluster has baffled many critics, but that, too, is part of the poet's fidelity to seeing the problem of sexuality in a natural light. Our instinct-types can only be grasped "approximately," Jung writes, by the conscious mind, and never in a fully realized form; for the images of these instinctive patterns lie in the "ultra-violet part" of what he calls the "*psychoid* system," something anterior to the psyche about which nothing can be known directly.[40] What we can realize are the effects on consciousness, for example, archetypal ideas, words, and images that give

form and voice to our charismatic vocation.[41] It is through a "careful consideration" of such objective factors that the ego constructs its sexuality.

Whitman felt the worst kind of book was an expurgated book, and rather
than be persuaded to self censor the 1860 edition of *Leaves of Grass,* the poet let
all of his sexual metaphors stand intact, including "Prostitute." This decision,
of course, was challenged. The sixth printing of *Leaves,* in 1881, led the district
attorney of Boston to put his publishers, Osgood and Company, under notice
that the book violated obscenity laws. It was thus viewed as immoral by the
Society for the Suppression of Vice. This led to Whitman's withdrawing of the
1881 edition of *Leaves* from publication in Boston. Yet Whitman's attempts to
speak out of the self-centeredness of the great androgenic personality, the self
within him, for all nations of the world, was a celebration not of his separate
identity alone, but of a disobedient loyalty to the inborn law of his being, an
assertion of an "I" (which, in an interesting anticipation of Jung, he refers to as
"Myself").

It was on the basis of what he knew about this inner "Myself" that Whitman could have a role as a culture-shaper, changing what nineteenth-century
America was willing to consider about the nature of sexuality. Like his contemporaries Emily Dickinson and Herman Melville, Whitman knew in the depths
and heights of his soul that the world is bi-erotic, and more than either of his
contemporary poetic peers, he was willing to say so explicitly. Bi-eroticism is
pivotal to his vision of Spiritual Democracy if it is to be inclusive of all at the
instinctive level on which that vision's realization depends.

Present-day Jungians and post-Jungians tend to speak about the homoerotic and heteroerotic as two conjunction possibilities in the human. Whitman's poetry, however, brings forth a third postulate that contains both of these
as equivalent values. In "Proto-Leaf," Whitman reveals that he knows he is
speaking to both genders in a poem he addresses to a man:

> Aware of the buffalo, the peace-herds, the bull, strong-breasted and hairy,
> Aware of the mocking-bird of the wilds at day-break,
> Solitary, singing in the west, I strike up for a new world.
> . . . .
> What do you seek, so pensive and silent?
> What do you need, comrade?
> Mon cher! do you think it is love?[42]

To do justice to Whitman's vision, a terminology that transcends the categories of gender and sexual identity is needed. In a poem like this, a descriptor

such as "the Bi-Erotic Imagination" applies. Whitman makes room in his text for both homoerotic and heteroerotic modes of imagining spiritual fulfillment through sexual connection. His most radical assertion is that both modes of expression are needed to provide an adequate model to the American nation and the world of its potential for Spiritual Democracy. Only in the present century, with the centrality of gay marriage in our national discourse, can we begin to glimpse why Whitman found such inclusiveness necessary to democracy's wholeness.

The empirical evidence for this view rests in the fact that Whitman placed the "Children of Adam" and "Calamus" clusters side by side, as if they were meant to lie together as equal unions resting on the same seed bed. The term Bi-Erotic Imagination needs its capital letters because Whitman sees the two sexual connections—heteroerotic and homoerotic—as creating a whole that is superordinate to either. As we have seen, he called this whole "Myself." As early as 1855, when he wrote "I CELEBRATE myself, and sing myself,"[43] he was able simultaneously to claim with conviction "I contain multitudes."[44] Such largeness enables him to embrace and imagine his bi-erotic complement. Indeed, his poetry has always convinced a heterosexual readership that it is speaking to their deepest erotic strivings. This equality of his vision demonstrates his modesty.

Our culture still has to find a better way of articulating Whitman's linking vision than our present erotic categories permit. Better language might enable us to illuminate the external changes we are seeing in our nation and the world today, and we would be wise to consider that Whitman has already provided the basic elements of such a language and attitude.

In "Calamus," Whitman makes numerous references to feelings of rejection, desire, wounding, loss, agony, fulfillment, envy, hurt, rejoicing, and longing. Such contradictory feelings in the domain of same-sex eros are contained by his complementary bi-eroticism. His courage to reveal his sexual feelings for women enables him to do the same for men, although with greater circumspection and caution. In the first poem in this cluster, for instance, Whitman says he is going to publish "standards" not previously printed, in other words, made public. He says his soul and the soul of the man he speaks about—his personal example of an archetypal comrade—"feeds, rejoices only in comrades."[45] Out of this figure, in chant two, he creates what Jung calls a religious symbol. This is a construction born of love. Jung says that religious symbols "do not come from the head at all, but from some other place, perhaps the heart; certainly from a deep psychic level very little resembling consciousness. . . . They are anything rather than thought up; on the contrary, in the course of the millennia, they have developed, plant-like, as natural manifestations of the human psyche."[46] Whitman's image of the grass of the calamus plant amplifies the way the symbol of the comrade has taken root, not only in his soul, but as a psychic development that will outlive him, and the following lines provide us with a great illustration of this:

> Scented herbage of my breast,
> Leaves from you I yield, I write, to be perused afterwards,
> Tomb-leaves, body-leaves, growing up above me, above death.[47]

To grow up above the tomb, the body, and death also suggests a spiritual transcendence through rebirth of a dead love that went unfulfilled in Whitman's lifetime. The comrade has literally died to his old life, and is now reborn as a new "bridegroom." The comrade Whitman could not keep has now become the spiritual husband of all men. And the transparency of his enduring feeling for the man he has lost is palpable. "Publish my name," he says, "and hang up my picture as that of the tenderest lover, / The friend, the lover's portrait, of whom his friend, his lover was fondest."[48] This is the path of the brokenhearted, the way of the shaman in all world cultures.

Such wishes in the face of unrequited love are very human emotions, earthy and religious at the same time, and all the more intense for being literally unfulfilled. The calamus grasses, images of ramifications of the phallic fantasies that in this relationship evidently went unfulfilled, are referred to as "blossoms of my blood!" that "burn" and "throb" and "sting" Whitman with "bitterness," more bitter than he says he can bear.[49] He adds emphasis to this in a line that is itself a coming out: "Unbare this broad breast of mine—I have long enough stifled and choked."[50] "Away!" he continues:

> I will escape from the sham that was proposed to me,
> I will sound myself and comrades only—I will never again utter a call,
>   only their call,
> I will raise, with it, immortal reverberations through The States.[51]

To write such lines in a homophobic age took courage. We are reminded here of the "sham" of the churches Whitman spoke about as the limiting shells enclosing divinity that needed to be broken out of. Whitman will not let unspoken love and its eventual death "balk" his personal identity or his call for Spiritual Democracy any longer, for behind the "perennial roots" of the fantasies involved lies the "real reality"[52]: the reality of the cosmos. This is the call of divine selfhood that he is summoned to teach. What he means by this cannot be precisely defined, of course, because as a religious symbol the calamus grass is a living thing that can never be completely clarified. Its significance for Whitman rests in the way it looks forward to a new archetypal husband and comrade:

> Here to put your lips upon mine I permit you,
> With the comrade's long-dwelling kiss, or the new husband's kiss,
> For I am the new husband, and I am the comrade.[53]

Here, moreover, the partners in the reconstituted marriage couple are both male. In "The Soul and Death," Jung says: "From middle life onward, only he remains vitally alive who is ready to *die with life*."[54] If we are to imagine each unreturned attraction he must have suffered as real, by the time Whitman reached forty, he'd "died" many times through mortifying love experiences. But it was this particular lost affection that fueled his spiritual development from 1860 onward. In "To My Soul," Whitman employs what Jung terms "psychologically correct thinking," which "always retains its connection with the heart, with the depths of the psyche, the tap-root."[55] Whitman intuits and feels the experience of the death of this particular love as psychologically real. It is out of this burning passion in his body that he bequeaths to us his *Leaves*.

Something changed in Whitman in 1860; some new internationalizing impulse emerged in him and filled him with a new religious significance. The man he has loved and lost travels with him, in these poems, and, holding his hand to keep his touch sure, charges him to speak with hitherto "untold and untellable wisdom." Touch for Whitman is always the essential thing, the real reality. When he is touched through accepting the reality of the psyche by the man he loves, he says he is silent, requiring nothing further.[56] In "Calamus" chant nine, the jealousy he had previously felt toward this man, who had not adequately reciprocated his love, turns into a "long, sore, and heavy-hearted" loss, celebrated by the cries of the poet who exclaims in the face of the rejection: "I am what I am."[57] The loss is palpable and real; it fills him with torment and dejection. At night, he is startled awake by anguish. His mind is tinged with lonely thoughts about the man who rejected him.[58] He reports anguish and depression[59]—in fact a true experience of lost passion.

Emphasizing its pathos, he speaks of a "sick, sick dread, lest the one he loved might secretly be indifferent to him."[60] The poet speaks of not being "happy" when he hears his name was "received with plaudits in the capitol." Fame cannot move him. The only happiness he knew through experience was when his dear friend was "on his way coming to see me."[61] When the poet's arm lay lightly around the breast of this man one night, then, he says, he was "happy."[62] This is a far cry from the transcendent, innocent happiness of the 1855 Walt Whitman.

He has clearly gone through some kind of a major crisis as a consequence of his suffering over a love that was not returned. What it was or who it was is not certain.

By chant seventeen, he is reporting a "dream" wherein he says he heard that the man he loved day and night was "dead" and that he "searched in vain" through "burial-places" to find him and found that "every place was a burial-place."[63] Although it is doubtful the comrade who could not repay Whitman's passion actually died, or was mortally wounded as Whitman himself may have momentarily been, the imagery looks forward to his poem "The Wound Dresser," which was based on Whitman's experience tending to thousands of sick and dying Civil War soldiers. The loss involved was not only physical. Whitman here speaks further of "close companionship" between men as a "spiritual corresponding."[64] And when he reads books of the "brotherhood of lovers," he says he has to put these books down and walk away, "filled with the bitterest envy."[65]

Despite the personal rebuff and the human feelings that accompanied it, the loss itself became the source of his greatest soul-offering to the globe, his vision of the potential inherent in human evolution toward worldwide Spiritual Democracy. For this we can be grateful. But this ideal was not to be realized in his lifetime, for the world is plagued by religious wars even today, and, sadly, a great deal of intolerance for men loving men and women loving women persists in many parts of the globe, even in places generally considered progressive and enlightened, such as California. Nevertheless, aware of the healing potential of his vision of comradeship, Whitman never gave up hope, nor must we. For instance, Whitman made a promise to California—which in our time, at least until 2013, was still struggling with the idea of homosexual marriage—to "teach robust American love." He says he knows well that such love belongs among men on the "Western Sea,"[66] a reference perhaps to the same-sex marriages Melville had seen celebrated among Pacific islanders and that Whitman had read about for his review of *Typee*. Chant thirty-eight is an interesting complement to Whitman's earlier effusions in "Children of Adam." It reads, "O bride! O wife! more resistless, more enduring than I can tell, the thought of you!"— but this is written now to his dear male comrade.[67]

This is a love that fills Whitman with torment. In chant thirty-nine, he writes: "SOMETIMES with one I love, I fill myself with rage, for fear I effuse unrequited love."[68] *Leaves of Grass* "speaks out of the necessities, its cry is the cry of the right and wrong of the woman sex,"[69] yet it's also more than that. He makes it explicitly clear here: "Doubtless I could not have perceived the universe, or written one of my poems, if I had not given myself to comrades, to love."[70] For Whitman, Spiritual Democracy begins with love between men, and love of men is deepened by the vision of a lost chance to have a male lover who meant so much to him. This loss, and what he makes of the effects it stimulates in him, forms the cornerstone of his mature work. It is out of this foundation that he becomes the crowned sexual-spiritual athlete and champion of women. "Homoaffection" becomes the base of his more modest bi-erotic vision, which includes everyone.

In chant forty-one, his words again summon the archetype of what he had hoped to realize as something his readers can realize with him. "Lover and perfect equal!" he says to each reader, in a truly egalitarian way: "I meant that you should discover me so, by my faint indirections."[71] He ends his self-exploration and self-revealing in "Calamus" with some words to his "élève," making the reader his spiritual pupil. This designation is meant to be the "most baffling"[72] of all. Whitman admits he "shades down" his thoughts and does not fully bare them. "I do not expose them," he writes, "and yet they [the Calamus-leaves] expose me more than all my other poems."[73] What these poems expose is Whitman's bi-eroticism: his equal consideration of all types of love.[74]

Whitman announced on the eve of the U.S. Civil War that we are all equals in the marriage-dance of nations. Such a vision is as far seeing as it is new. And it's a political vision as much as an economically egalitarian and spiritual vision. In chant five of "Calamus" he addresses the "States!": "Were you looking to be held together by the lawyers? / By an agreement on a paper? Or by arms? / Away!" he writes. Whitman brings the loving vision of *Leaves of Grass*, "essentially a woman's book" to encourage, persuade, and point us to "the way," to all Americans "beyond all the forces of courts and arms."[75]

In his preface to the first edition of *Leaves of Grass*, Whitman wrote: "THE GREATEST POET is a seer, he is individual, he is complete in himself."[76] He then adds: "IF THE GREATNESSES are in conjunction in a man or woman it is enough, / The fact will prevail through the universe."[77] Whitman's vision of Spiritual Democracy therefore offers hope for the LGBT movement, which is searching for religious equality and an end to the projection of the shadow onto those advocates of democracy who do not suppress their homosexuality. And he is still ahead even of our time.

9

SHAMANISM AND SPIRITUAL DEMOCRACY
A Post-Humboldtian Notion of the Cosmos

DEUS QUADRIUNE

We've seen that Walt Whitman was the first poet to consciously assume the mantle of the American bard and to stimulate a potential path of revolutionary movement toward world peace. For Whitman, body, soul, and spirit were one. Spiritual Democracy, in his view, was not based upon a Trinitarian notion of God as Father, Son, and Holy Spirit. Rather it was based upon a quaternity, a Deus Quadriune, of feminine and masculine, good and evil. In his poem "Chanting the Square Deific," Whitman even assigns God a feminine name: Santa Spirita, the breather of life. Thus, Spiritual Democracy brings the Holy Spirit down into matter through the spiritual marriage, and it's to this idea in American poetry that we shall now turn.

Visionary poets such as Walt Whitman, Herman Melville, and Emily Dickinson have something unique to add to Carl Jung's reflections on the inner marriage of the opposites. According to Jung, spiritual marriage is the meaning of an archetypal phenomenon, the syzygy, or conjunction of sun and moon, that in human life can only be experienced fully in relationship to a partner. (In alchemy, the archetypal syzygy was a metaphor for coniunctio, the mysterious binding power that created chemical combinations, which had not yet been scientifically explored.) Such a union of high and low is often a threat to marriages, because it is typically experienced through projection, an unconscious process of externalizing one's fantasies rather than engaging them in a dialogue in a conscious way with an inner partner, friend, or lover. It's not easy to be wed internally, moreover, with someone one relates to every day, for it is rather extraordinary to experience spiritual marriage as an inner phenomenon. When the motif is concretized in an adulterous love affair, moreover, the results may be disastrous, and will result in anything but the uniting of personalities. As an archetype, however, the syzygy can signify an inner coming together. Even within, such a union is fallible and seems to set into motion a compensatory process the alchemists called *mortificatio,* in which the temporarily united consciousness undergoes a decadent rot through which the passing sense of fulfilled wholeness undergoes a shocking, disorienting dismemberment.

We've seen such a process of disintegration and reconstitution of the personality in Whitman's "Calamus" poem cluster in *Leaves of Grass,* where the love that he wanted underwent a decay followed by a resurrection into a new spiritual body in preparation for his expanding, scientifically informed visions of Spiritual Democracy. Some contemporary scholars, although not all, would agree that the catalyst that led Walt Whitman to his experience of Spiritual Democracy—a sense of equality and interconnectedness with all life—was his experience of the unrequited love for a man. Frustrated on the outside, Whitman's love turned inward to fuel an inner bi-erotic "marriage" that made his ultimate partner himself, especially his own capacity to love both sexes. He was then able to return this love to all the people in the world in his vision of Spiritual Democracy.

Prior to this vision's rebirth, Melville placed same-sex marriage as the principal motif of the transformation of his central character, Ishmael, in *Moby Dick.* Melville's greatest epistle of love emerged, furthermore, in a letter of appreciation to a man, his fellow novelist Nathaniel Hawthorne, to whom he dedicated his masterpiece. Similarly, Dickinson employed same-sex imagery in her poetry, which confesses that she, too, was equally drawn to loving women and men. In nineteenth-century America, a new vision passed among poets, who glimpsed a new archetype that consisted of bi-erotic marriage as a central channel for the experience of the united self. It had the ability to energize democracy in all three of its postulated stages: political/constitutional, economic/material, and religious/spiritual.

Shamanistic traditions tap into primeval ways of gaining access to what is perceived as "the spirit world." Appreciating the bi-erotic is one of the prerogatives of the shamanic healer, and it is not too much to claim such an ancient role for Whitman. In *Shaman: The Wounded Healer,* the anthropologist Joan Halifax brings to light some remarkable structural representations of the "shaman's wound" as the organizing symbol for what she call the shamanic complex.

Her remarkable book opens with an image: a carving of an Eskimo shaman wounding himself with a harpoon. Halifax comments that the act of self wounding connects this native healer with the animal world during the time of the great hunt, the Paleolithic period.[1] This archaic symbol suggests an archetype that is many thousands of years old, but the self-wounder springs to new life in the culture of pre–Civil War American poetry. Whitman, Melville, and Dickinson followed the shamanic pattern of wounding themselves to bring about a bi-erotic vision of love, or eros, for the collective. On the eve of our most disruptive and violent conflict, one in which brother turned against brother, these writers found the imagery to support spiritual comradeship as the essential energy of democracy. Their vision of union was as compelling as Lincoln's, and played nearly as great a role in ensuring the continuity of American culture.

Nobody exemplifies the shaman's wound, the mystical source of the archetype's healing power, better than the reclusive and introverted Dickinson. She illuminates the shamanic archetype[2] in American poetry, perhaps more completely than any other poet-shaman does. Dickinson achieves the spiritual marriage through bi-erotic symbolism. Not enough has been written about the influence of the "Animals of the Soul," or "Animal People" on Dickinson's development, not as a direct ethnographic or anthropological literary influence but as an unconsciously transmitted shamanistic influence via direct ecstatic experiences, most notably Snake, Frog, Robin, Bluebird, and Hummingbird. Many of her metaphors wed shamanic symbolism with traditional imagery found in the New Testament, particularly her favorite biblical passage, Revelations 21, known as the "gem chapter," for its pearls of wisdom. Her experiences of spiritual unity occur in meditation on high peaks of volcanoes, a place of *hieros gamos,* holy marriage, with the Gods.

Spiritual Democracy is a difficult concept to grasp because it can only truly be known through experience. Yet, America's finest visionary poets are able to convey its meaning by use of scintillating metaphors. Emily Dickinson does this beautifully in "Snake," where she says:

A narrow Fellow in the Grass . . .
I more than once, at Noon
Have passed, I thought, a Whip lash
Unbraiding in the Sun
When stooping to secure it
It wrinkled, and was gone—
Several of Nature's People
I know, and they know me—

I feel for them a transport
Of cordiality—
But never met this Fellow,
Attended or alone
Without a tighter breathing
And Zero at the Bone—[3]

Here's the idea of Spiritual Democracy captured beautifully in metaphorical imagery. At noon, sun consciousness, "Zero at the Bone—" and Zero with a capital Z. Dickinson gets at the meaning of Spiritual Democracy by descending through language to the lower brain centers, emotion, and the reptilian brain, or Snake. When she talks about being Zero at the Bone, she's saying that the origins of poetry appear to be cosmic, and therefore infinite. She starts with "Snake" and ends up with Zero, which is eternal. Dickinson's superb thought pattern in "Snake" is shamanistic; it originates in the right brain and the emotional brain and the reptilian brain accesses a different realm of existence that imparts shamanic wisdom directly through her experience of nature.

Dickinson's originality didn't fit well with the literary establishment of her time. She entered the field of her vocation—American poetry—and found herself in a standoff with editors and publishers who tried to change the structure of her line, her syntax, her punctuation, and the integrity of her poetic style with its marvelous use of dashes, particularly in "Snake." Refusing to submit to the publishers' demands, she stopped publishing her work altogether. Here Dickinson is a spiritual liberator for women. She takes her stand for Spiritual Democracy, and she too caught the spirit of the age, which was inspired by Alexander von Humboldt's *Cosmos*. In her poem numbered CXXVI (126), Dickinson wrote:

The brain—is wider than the Sky—
For—put them side by side—
The one the other will contain
With ease—and You—beside—[4]

It's ironic, moreover, that the quarrel Dickinson engaged in with editors was over "Snake." By the time "Snake" was published, she'd already decided publication was the "auction" of the mind of man. She refused to sacrifice her vocation for her career. Dickinson being a wild force—a "force of Nature," as was said of her—would have none of the judgments of patriarchal thinking about language, where women's natural voices, their natural intelligence, and their Spiritual Democracy was oppressed. She was, like Whitman and Melville, a fierce rebel for Spiritual Democracy, and she would not submit to external standards of authority. Only seven out of 1,775 of Dickinson's poems were published in her lifetime. This is staggering. She possessed such a supreme gift for elocution, for language-creation, and for metaphoric thinking. The silencing of such a natural gift for poetry in her lifetime is tragic.

Dickinson's rebellion was uniquely American. Her revolution through language against the forces of oppression in a patriarchal society harks back to the American revolution of 1776. Dickinson's mental penetrations into cosmic awareness in her breakthrough moments are stunning: "The brain—is wider than the Sky—"! By touching "tap-root," Dickinson transcends the space-time barrier to perceive the operation of religious equality in its eternal ground of being. Such transcendent moments shaped her life and prepared her soul for its transit to the "beyond." The Zero state that Dickinson talks about is the closest we can get to nothingness, no-thing-ness, like the Buddha's nirvana. A full treatment of Dickinson's work requires a book of its own, for she stands alone among her male contemporaries as a solitary in a class of her own.

The Snake, as Jung pointed out, is the most chthonic of all spirit-animals in the psyche—it is a literally grounded creature. As a medicine-woman, Dickinson found a way to heal herself of her own "sickness." She was, like Whitman and Melville, a revolutionary with a religious aim. She was, like the Biblical Jacob, a God-wrestler. Her poetry, and that of her male contemporaries, raises the question: Is same-sex marriage part and parcel of the American spirit, part of a living religious myth of who we are as a nation and a world?

In *Art and Artist: Creative Urge and Personality Development,* the author Otto Rank, who, along with Alfred Adler and Carl Jung, was one of depth psychology's intellectual giants, explored the relationship between the artist and society. One of the best insights in his book is his exploration of the "meaning" of the "changes in the idea of the soul."[5] If Rank is correct—that the transformations that took place in the "religion of genius" born in the Middle Ages, which gave birth to the sonnets of Michelangelo and Shakespeare, was the self-immortalization through verse via an "externalization" in art of the "presence of the beloved youth"[6]—then we might inquire how Whitman's, Melville's, and Dickinson's ideas of homoeros, homoaffection, and homospirit expressed toward same-sex lovers differed from the soul-love of their predecessors.

The shamans of the world, among whom we might number Jesus, receive the light of the cosmos, and it's this light Emily Dickinson taps into with her vision of a blaze at noon. The Buddha's similar achievement of cosmic awareness is not dissimilarly symbolized in the Japanese shogun tradition by altars of copper-colored metal that, when lit by candles, seem to radiate the many suns of consciousness. Rumi, Hafiz, Confucius, Laozi, and St. Francis of Assisi all had similar experiences, and the great Chinese sages and Jewish, Christian, and Islamic mystics did as well.

We've seen that the idea of religious equality has its source in shamanism. The first significant personages to incarnate what the Whitman-influenced Canadian psychiatrist Richard Maurice Bucke in 1901 called "cosmic consciousness" were Siberian and North American shamans who linked what they knew, and therefore consciousness itself, to the pulsating emanations of twinkling stars. All these shamans perceived their animal allies traversing the earth around them. This pan-cosmic energy-field of the shaman forms an ancient archetypal riverbed in the human psyche, and this is the archetype Whitman celebrated when he wrote in the lines of "Song of Myself" (1855): "Walt Whitman, an American, one of the roughs, a kosmos."[7] In the final 1891 "Deathbed" edition of *Leaves of Grass,* these lines read simply: "Walt Whitman, a kosmos, of Manhattan the son."[8] With these words, reminding us of Manhattan's Native American past, Whitman opened the floodgates to the shamanistic mind. He announces in his preface to *Leaves of Grass,* "There will soon be no more priests: their work is done. / They may wait a while, perhaps a generation or two, dropping off by degrees. / A superior breed shall take their place; / The gangs of kosmos and prophets en masse shall take their place." He argues that the old religious order will soon be replaced by a "new order" of American "poets" and "kosmos" who shall be the "priests of man, / And every man shall be his own priest"[9]; a view that we find in perceptions of America's visionary poets that world culture continues to benefit from today.

Whitman's religious vision sought to transport the reader's consciousness to the summits of knowledge in the living temple of the human body—your body, my body—by way of transport to the vastness of inner and outer space. The body is divine, Whitman was saying. And in his view Spiritual Democracy is here, right now, in all of us, if we can experience the grandeur of it in the "All," within and around us. The New World opened this vista to him. The experience of Spiritual Democracy is everywhere, Whitman was saying, and it is wherever we are; Spiritual Democracy is a potential living experience in everyone. The question is: How do we tap into it? To answer, Whitman relocated himself in the shaman's religious practice of participation in the universe.

The American democratic vista that informed Alexander von Humboldt, Ralph Waldo Emerson, and Whitman had a political aspect. This is what the famous nineteenth-century French political thinker and historian Alexis de Tocqueville focused on in his famous travels in the United States—the prospect of democracy. Whitman brought similar visions of his own to his notion of "vistas" of democracy. But for Whitman, there was a key religious aspect: a religious democratic vista that celebrates not only the soul, as the medium of the spirit, but the body as the vehicle of the inner marriage and, hence, of cosmic awareness itself.

The question of religious democracy comes to the forefront around the marriage question today. We find superior models of the syzygy, the connection of corresponding things, in American's prodigious poet-shamans. Whitman had the ingenious idea that all bibles must be made new, and that we each have a bible of our own that we need to write. In the experience of his own divinity he'd realized that he was one of an unending average procession of poets who would build his own church: "The churches built under their umbrage shall be the churches of men and women. / Through the divinity of themselves shall the kosmos, and the new breed of poets, / Be interpreters of men and women, and of all events and things."[10]

Emily Dickinson added her own view when she wrote: "The Bible is an antique Volume / Written by faded Men."[11] And she went so far as to say her parents worshiped an eclipse—which meant she had to find a way to write her own New Bible. Not unlike Jung, who wrote his own *Liber Novus,* Dickinson concluded the church she needed was within her. She didn't need to go to Sunday school. She had a place of worship within her own room, where she wrote her poems—a place of communion.

In our own more crowded vista of competing ideologies, these American poet-shamans speak to us in words that resonate in modern ears. Their time has come. Indeed, they seem to be our contemporary role models. The fact that Whitman was the first man who openly avowed same-sex love to serve in the U. S. military, as a volunteer nurse, is almost shockingly relevant today in our own nation. In this and other issues, American poet-shamans were far ahead of where we are now. When we think of same-sex marriage, we have Herman Melville to thank for his generosity in providing us with an image as well. He made a place for such a union in *Moby Dick,* in a scene that comes early in the novel, when Ishmael and Queequeg are wed. Melville even calls it a "marriage"![12]

What a contemporary gay sensibility might read into this is not merely sex, but a heightened sensitivity to the responsibilities of companionship, something Melville himself definitely took aboard his voyage. Melville, sailing back to the mainland from his South Sea idles on the iron U.S. Navy frigate *United States,* observed a brutal flogging. His subsequent book, *White Jacket,* written in 1849, did more to outlaw flogging in the U.S. Navy than any other book. Whitman would employ the same basic strategy in his preface to the 1855 edition of *Leaves of Grass,* where the poet's companion and fellow explorer of the regions of inner and outer space is none other than the reader—you or I—him- or herself, a bi-erotic unity of all animate and inanimate life in matter. Listen:

> Whom he [the greatest poet] takes
> He takes with firm sure grasp into live regions previously unattained—
>   thenceforward is no rest—
> They [the American poet and reader-companion] see the space and
>   ineffable sheen that turn the old spots and lights into dead vacuums.
> The companion of him beholds the birth and progress of stars and
>   learns one of the meanings.
> Now there shall be a man cohered out of tumult and chaos.
> The elder encourages the younger and shows him how.
> They two shall launch off freshly together till the new world fits an orbit
>   for itself,
> And looks unabashed on the lesser orbits of stars,
> And sweeps through the ceaseless rings, and shall never be quiet again.[13]

We are living in uncertain political times today. They are turbulent times, times of upheaval, uphill battles, and tumultuous political unrest. We have reached a major turning point in American politics where the nation can no longer look to the framers for answers, whether on issues of gun control or same-sex marriage. Politics lags behind religion, as stage one of Whitman's visions; the political stage, lags behind stage three, the spiritual dimension that Whitman inaugurates along with his compatriots, Melville and Dickinson. We might be wise to turn to our American poets and the new visions of democracy they created for us one hundred fifty years ago to find inspiration for the issues of marriage and gender and war that are currently besieging us. The time for a change in American politics is at hand, as there is a new wave of liberalism and egalitarianism sweeping the nation and the world. The visions of America's poets are still at the forefront of this; they speak to everyone today with a newness and freshness of spirit that only a poet-shaman can bring to the problem of the world's great religions. Thanks to the first principle of American democracy—the freedom of religion—Whitman, Melville, and Dickinson were all able to provide us with vistas of spiritual liberation made possible by the advent of science. We've seen that Whitman turned a concentrated light on a central issue regarding the institutions of religion: "What religion is the most universal?" Again, his answer resonates: All are equals. He speaks equally to all religions of the globe from an intuitive vision of the universality at the heart of all faiths.

Revelation, for the American transcendentalists, does not end with the Bible;

it continues to unfold in the depths and heights of individual conscience. High up in the vistas of the world soul, Whitman posited an equivalent value—an equivalence of civil, scientific, and religious faith—in Spiritual Democracy as the cornerstone of his new spiritual attitude. In his transcendent view, he agreed with the U.S. Constitution that all women and men are created equal; all are his brothers and sisters. But this cornerstone of Spiritual Democracy is not Whitman's alone. It is ours; it is Humboldt's; it is Emerson's; it is Henry David Thoreau's; it belongs to every American, as our spiritual legacy on this continent. As we've seen, its roots go back millennia, before Christ and Moses, to shamanism. Spiritual Democracy is the rock, the alchemical philosopher's stone, on which the American poets built. They may have gotten elements of it from Emerson and Thoreau, but it was Humboldt who gave them the vision of science to make it intelligible as a uniting principle anteceding all of the great world religions.

When Whitman began reading Humboldt is uncertain, although he did leave notes in the margin of a newspaper article in 1849 that makes reference to the famous Prussian botanist, scientific traveler, and author of the five-volume set *Cosmos: A Sketch of the Physical Description of the Universe*.[14] This naturalist, whose vision of the ultimate interconnection of all phenomena, from the furthest expanses of the Milky Way to the minutest particles of nature, strongly influenced not only Emerson, Thoreau, and Dickinson but Charles Darwin and John Muir as well. Already by 1847, Whitman in his notebooks is finding in literary creation a new poetic function of transcendence for the reader, which makes poetry itself a cosmic, world-uniting phenomenon.

Whitman first uses the term *kosmos* (he retained the German "k") in the 1855 edition of *Leaves of Grass*. Cosmos was the very idea that made Humboldt the most famous scientist of his generation upon returning from his five-year trek (1799 to 1804) through the New World from South to Central to North America. It is also the idea of vista that would so fascinate and rise to the level of a transcendent principle for Walt Whitman. The famous Humboldt, had reciprocally embraced the New World and American democracy. An explorer as well as naturalist, Humboldt and his three companions, one an Indian guide, scaled the highest peak ever ascended in South America. On their transformative climb, Humboldt passed through each climate zone to nearly the top of Ecuador's extinct volcano, Chimborazo, to a height, by his barometer, of 19,286 feet. This was a world record that would stand for thirty years.

From her home in Amherst, Massachusetts, Dickinson claimed her own stunning feat: a shamanic trek, alone, via ecstatic transport in her creative solitude, to the volcanic peak of Vesuvius and also to the Canary Islands.

Melville, too, asked his friends and readers in chapter 104 of *Moby Dick* to "Give me Vesuvius' crater for an ink stand!" Yet, the ever-fluid and visionary Walt Whitman would boast of having dipped his pen in deeper wells and traveled farther, when he wrote: "My ties and ballasts leave me, my elbows rest in sea-gaps, / I skirt sierras, my palms cover continents, / I am afoot with my vision."[15] This was a vast, Humboldtian vision. It was Humboldt whose example gave Whitman the cosmic ambition to behold the entire universe in person and thereby to transcend it, not only for science, but for the spiritual welfare of all humankind.

In Whitman's oeuvre, the spiritual ambition extends to demanding a new religion and a new metaphysical, political, and physical base for marriage. Well before some Christian ministers began preaching about the equality of religions, of men and women, and of heterosexuals and homosexuals, America's poet-shamans—Whitman, Melville, and Dickinson—were all beating their separate figurative serpent-skin drums to announce new churches of God. The drumbeat for a tolerant animism became their transports to the divine. What they chant as visionary poets are universal songs of equality for all people—songs, no doubt, that are as old as human culture itself. Their generosity in embracing all races, all nationalities, and all sexual orientations with equal affection is one of the best human virtues they bequeath to us. The idea of spiritual marriage is present in their writings as a "vista"—once again, a Humboldtian idea. Whitman wrote the "Calamus" cluster in such a democratic way that his poems speak as if on a cosmic high, to the people of all nations, who indeed are still hearing it today. This notion is captured in the Humboldt-influenced image of the cosmos as an equalizing principle. In Humboldt's introduction to volume one of *Cosmos,* we find these noble words:

> Nature is a free domain, and the profound conceptions and enjoy-ments she awakens within us can only be vividly delineated by thought clothed in exalted forms of speech, worthy of bearing witness to the majesty and greatness of creation. . . . Among the colossal mountains of the Cundinamarca, of Quinto, and of Peru, furrowed by deep ravines, man is enabled to contemplate alike the families of plants, and all the stars of the firmament.[16]

The passage beyond cosmos to new vistas of shamanic seeing could not have been made possible, however, without Humboldt's travels on the American continents. These journeys were not only geographic but linguistic. The explorer compiled large lists of native vocabularies, grammars, idioms, and tongues from countless native South American tribes, taking note of over two hundred separate languages in Venezuela alone.[17] He turned these lists over to his elder brother, William von Humboldt, for linguistic analysis. William's attempts to write a unified theory of language were known to Walt Whitman, and turned out to be of great use to the poet, whose own vehicle for vista was, of course, language. The American poet makes explicit use of William's ideas to advance his own linguistic theory for the first time in his essay collection *Rambles among Words* (1856 to 1859). However, where "William flatly rejected that any language was superior or inferior to any other,"[18] Whitman makes the case for American English as the universal language. Whitman wrote in his 1855 preface: "Marriage, health, free trade, / Nothing too close, nothing too far off—/ The stars not too far off. / . . . The known universe has one complete lover and that is the greatest poet. / . . . There shall be love between the poet and the man of demonstrable science. / . . . As the attributes of the poets of the kosmos / Concentrate in the real body and soul and in the pleasure of things / They possess the genuineness over all fiction and romance."[19]

As an American bard, then, Whitman was already a poet of the cosmos. He did not just write about the unity of all life in the universe, he claimed for himself as poet the title of a kosmos while raising his voice in a language that could address the universe, as if he was the nation's best and most cosmic singer of religion. His American identity is the deepest part of identity itself. Whitman's *Rambles among Words* consists of three prose essays written across a four-year period, from 1855 to 1859, marking the period of his most climactic midlife[20] transformations, and culminating at the age of forty, when he let the heroic phase of his life development dissolve into a new and more personal sense of identity that he called the "real Me." The deeper personhood he claimed after forty is what the ancient Hindus called "the atman" and what Carl Jung, translated as "self" (his followers would capitalize Self to distinguish it from ego)— the master-concept of the process and goal of mature individuation that includes all opposites.

For Whitman, the traditional idea of heaven found in many world religions is replaced by the Humboldtian notion of cosmos, a scientific notion. But there is a more ancient image that also launches the poet's vision. In his great poem "Out of the Cradle" (1859), the recovery of Whitman's "real Me" is coincident with the chant of the mockingbird that sang to him as a barefoot boy on the sands of Paumanok, Long Island. Birds have spoken to shamans throughout human history. Whitman is no exception to this. In 1859 Whitman wrote:

O baffled, balk'd, bent to the very earth,
Oppress'd with myself that I ever dared to open my mouth,
Aware now that amid all that blab whose echoes recoil upon
    me I have not once had the least idea who or what I am,
But before all my arrogant poems the real Me stands yet
Untouch'd, untold, altogether unreach'd,
Withdrawn far, mocking me with mock-congratulatory signs
    and bows,
With peals of distant ironical laughter at every word I have
    written,
Pointing in silence to these songs, and then to the sand
    beneath.[21]

This profound sense of having been balked and baffled by the very presence of the God of nature from his earliest years left Whitman feeling utterly devoid of a personal orientation to give his life and even his poetic work a basic significance and meaning. Whitman knew well that every nation of the world had forged its own language as the expression of its spiritual character, and what characterizes the American language most is its earthiness, the ground of its democracy. Why was this utterly profound sense of failure necessary?

Jungian analyst Joseph Henderson can help us understand this. "The theme of failure of initiation," he says, "seems to imply some tendency of the initiate to forget to honor (or even notice) significant vestiges of the old feminine religion of the earth."[22] This honoring of the feminine is something Humboldt never seems to have forgotten, for his five-year trip to the Americas (true virgin territory for a European) had taught him to honor the ultimate equality of all people, all races, and all religions. Whitman, caught up by America's post-Louisiana Purchase ideas about its Manifest Destiny in the New World, had been gripped by the same sense of exclusiveness that had given birth to many, if not most, of the world's great religions. But, thanks to the American spirit, his own idea of a new religion was that to be truly democratic it would have to embrace everyone's religion with the same equality, freedom, and liberty. Thus, Whitman was already in transit from an American assertion of national superiority to a myth of inclusiveness that would not permit American exceptionalism, and this demanded a certain death of religion as he knew it.

The total acceptance of death that we see at this time in Whitman's inner evolution coincides with the moment of his tremendous shift from heroic nationalism to nonheroic transnational equality. His egalitarian dissolution of his ego into an identity with the universal self was a death of narrow individualism in his writings. From then on everything in the cosmos, and not even Brahman, Jehovah, or Zeus—or some overvalued intellectual idea—became his subject, and his relationship to that totality became the key experiential fact of his individuation. His transcendence of all separative God-images was made possible through the transport beyond earthly categories provided by the lens of astronomical science.

In midlife, the youthful literary hero and sexual pioneer Whitman had to give way to his vocation into a more cosmos-embracing integrity. The years 1859 and 1860 were momentous for Whitman, for during this time he gave up his Quaker ancestry, his "white privilege," and his belief in the superiority of a post-Enlightenment Christianity. Also in this time he accepted Emersonian transcendentalism, let go of his American exceptionalism, and turned more modestly toward Spiritual Democracy and animistically embodied Native American spirituality. What is most central to his move from ego to what depth-psychology today would call "Self," however, is his 1860 disclosure of his own self-identity as bi-erotic, that is, a unity transcendent of gender categories, so that he can now view both male and female objects as well as his own heterosexual and homosexual feelings equally. One value, however, had to be sacrificed for that unity to come into being, and that was the idea of God the Father—including the American legacy of founding fathers. In short, the move to unity required Whitman to give up patriarchy as an ideal. Cosmos could only be realized under the sign of the divine feminine. (Whitman's idea has been repeated in our time, with regard to the ecological unity of the earth, as the Gaia hypothesis.) Using a term that the ancient Chinese philosopher Laozi would have applauded, Whitman refers to the integrity of the cosmos as "the Mother of All."

Vocalism: The Divine Power to Speak Words

Like Daoism, Whitman's Spiritual Democracy was at its core a shamanic vision of restoring the world and returning it to the sacredness of its origins. Whitman's spiritual and sexual innovations correspond to his embrace of a much older initiatory tradition, that of the archaic shaman. It was while reading the works of the two Prussian Humboldt brothers that Whitman found the basis of his poetic language. He believed what was to be said during peak moments of shamanistic seeing was the highest pinnacle of language possible. It enabled the poet to take the achievements of science forward into the uncharted domain of a new religion that was at the same time very old, and which could inspire its readers to form in its embrace of an "All." After opening ramble eleven with an epigraph from William Humboldt, Whitman goes on to express his understanding of the Humboldt brothers' language theory thus:

> Each language is a living organism; the totality of languages a grand series of organisms, all built after the same archetype, the same skeleton; but each presenting its special structural stamp, as fish, reptile, bird, mammal, are all modifications of one primitive Idea. Yes! Language is indeed alive! Primordial creation and manifestation of the mind, Language throbs with the pulses of one life.[23]

Whitman crafted his idea of Spiritual Democracy with what he'd learned from the Humboldt brothers, but, true to his vocation, he took their intuitions of a new level of synthesis into a manifesto for America's destiny. Whitman saw the findings of science as providing the democratic vistas that nineteenth-century America was dreaming of. This was an ecological vision, which Whitman voiced in his poem "Song of the Redwood Tree," as unveiling "vistas of coming humanity."[24] In *Rambles among Words,* Whitman gets at taproot when he invokes the word "archetype" as the basis for the "one primitive Idea." He was seeking the root metaphor of the aboriginal shaman as the master of initiation, his poetic guide for signing up for a nonheroic mode of human existence coequal with nature. Not surprisingly, it was the younger brother, Alexander von Humboldt, who provided the uplift. Whitman, like many nineteenth-century readers, followed his trek along the spine of the Andes and his study of the religious artifacts of countless Indian tribes and took in their significance.

After celebrating, in *Rambles among Words,* the "Teutonic genius" and the "glory of the English that is essentially modern—essentially unclassical,"[25] Whitman identified the heart of American English as "Anglo-Saxon," then wrote further: "This is the spine upon which the structure of our speech is hung."[26] Whitman's use of the word "spine" to describe the Anglo-Saxon language is reminiscent of Jungian analyst John Beebe's use of the term "spine" in his book *Integrity in Depth.* In brief, by "spine," Beebe means that aspect of character that moves a person to stand erect, upright, with a sense of right conscience, which for Whitman meant a spiritual or religious conscience.

Whitman, being a language-maker, knew that every nation depends for its growth on the integrity of its language to give native expression to its national identity. Such a language depends to a great extent upon the outgrowth of linguistic forms from an organic compact between the individual and the collective— self and society. In ramble twelve, for instance, Whitman writes, "The growth of words runs parallel with the unfolding of a nation's life,"[27] and this national life has its foundation in the words of our founding fathers.

In the poet's view, the "third" spiritual stage of democracy arises, as we have previously seen, out of the first (theoretical/constitutional) and second (practical/material) stages toward an overarching vista, which can crown the first two with completeness. "Transported to the new and vaster arena of America," Whitman asserts for the New World: "The English language has vista in it—vast vista in America."[28] Such vista was made possible by the First Amendment of the U.S. Constitution, and the fate or destiny of Spiritual Democracy hangs upon its foundational sixteen-word formulation of religious freedom: "Congress shall make no law respecting an establishment of religion, or prohibiting the free exercise thereof." It was the appearance of the religious clauses in the first continental Congress, on June 8, 1789, that truly marked the birth of America as the *locus classicus,* a prime example, of the God-image. Likewise these clauses marked the American nation as the ground of religious liberty, and as a country that was meant to circumnavigate the globe[29] in a resurrected vision of the divine for which the Enlightenment conscience would not have to apologize. On the other hand, according to one historian, Edward F. Humphrey, the papers of the Congress were "so filled with Biblical phrases as to resemble Old Testament ecclesiastical documents."[30]

It's fascinating to read about the emergence of the First Amendment in light of Whitman's achievement, for we can clearly see the lines of evolution out of which Whitman emerged as a poet-shaman of one a "primitive Idea"—one idea that announces many "eternal meanings"[31] and yet is quite specifically grounded in what had already practically emerged in the United States. Although they were not traditional Christians, the framers of the U.S. Constitution were not irreligious in the least. In fact, most subscribed to Deism and Freemasonry, which had become alternatives to Christianity. Benjamin Franklin, for instance, prized his membership in the Masonic movement. In 1779, he became Grand Master of the most prestigious Freemason lodge in France, the "Nine Sisters," to which Voltaire had also belonged.[32] These belief systems emphasized transpersonal unity in a way that anticipates the Jungian "Self" as one way to know God. Three of the original five who drafted the Declaration of Independence—Franklin, Adams, and Jefferson—were later brought together by Congress to design the permanent insignia signifying the beliefs and values of the new nation. The symbol they created—a pyramid with an eye enclosed in a triangle at the top—is well known today as "The Great Seal of the United States." In this seal, the God of Nature speaks in the Latin motto e pluribus unum: "out of many, one."

This motto emblematized in the seal was originally intended to express the union of the thirteen states, but its symbolism goes much deeper than that, into the very impulse that led the colonists to leave Europe in a quest for religious liberty.[33] The Declaration emphasizes the individual's right to determine his or her own religious beliefs and to act freely with an open conscience and without any coercion whatsoever by government upon those beliefs.[34] Religious liberty—the religion of the Goddess, and Liberty as the Goddess—was viewed by the framers as a natural human right.[35] America's religion is widely known today therefore as a "civil religion" independent of any institutionalized religion, because its conception of God is to be found solely in one's individual conscience and in the truths of nature.[36]

When Alexander von Humboldt stopped off at the end of his five-year voyage to visit Thomas Jefferson at the White House in 1804 he brought with him a store of scientific knowledge that was greatly beneficial to the American president. The meeting was of course mutual, as Humboldt later wrote to Jefferson: "I could not resist the moral obligation to see the United States and enjoy the consoling aspects of a people who understand the precious gift of liberty."[37] It is not surprising, furthermore, that Humboldt succeeded in removing not only all biblical references, but all references to the word "God"[38] in his five-volume set of *Cosmos*, his own scientific contribution to the idea of a transpersonal unity informing everything and everyone.

Whitman retained the word "God" throughout much of his writing, but followed the founding fathers in widening the meaning intended by that hallowed word. He eventually traced it to the one "primitive Idea"—referring either to "Nature," as Emerson would have it, or "Cosmos," as Humboldt had argued—either way, the transpersonal natural world source of Spiritual Democracy. And again, for the poet, language played the decisive role in this transit to a higher vista of seeing. In ramble twelve, Whitman speaks of the "marriage of several stocks and tongues."[39] Such marriage symbolism came later in Whitman's writings, in 1871, and extended to include all races, nations, and peoples.

In "Song of the Redwood Tree," Whitman hears the wood spirits come out from their haunts in the great redwood forest in coastal California to chant in chorus of the "vistas of coming humanity," the "new society at last, proportionate to Nature." In this poem Whitman's visions of Spiritual Democracy are located in the "common kind, the race,"[40] meaning it's in all of us, and the language necessary for such vistas is to be found, again, in the elevations made possible in our country by American English. From such vistas Whitman moves in *Rambles among Words* toward what he aptly terms a "spinal fact":

And here a spinal fact is the composite character of our language: to what new realizations is it [the English Language] lifted in America! . . . Where is the theory of literary expression that stands for the new politics and sociology? that puts itself abreast the vast divine tendencies of Science, that absorbs the superb suggestions of the Grand Opera? . . . Over the transformations of a Language the genius of a nation unconsciously presides—the issues of Words represent issues in the national thought.[41]

In *Rambles among Words,* Whitman is shaping his own views about American English as a vehicle capable of the highest vistas of speech, and these vistas he thought would be made accessible to the average person through his own achievement as a poet and by the poets to come—the American bards and writers who would fulfill his vision. The next stage of democracy would depend on our individual American voices, and the attitudes informing them might best be described, as the religious-liberty advocate James Madison would have preferred, as a religion of personal conscience.

Such "vistas" of coming human individuation are captured beautifully by Whitman in his 1860 poem "Vocalism," which celebrates the individual voice. This, he asserts, has "the divine power to speak words," or, expressed a bit differently, in an 1847 notebook: "Every soul has its own language."[42] This is to say that we each have our own unique language and one of our primary tasks in life is to discover what it is.[43] As a language-shaper, Whitman provides a technique through which such discovery can happen.

For Whitman the cosmos was the vehicle for the vocation of many in the one, who, by using an individual voice, answered the call to unity. Each person on the planet, in other words, is called to voice "the unspoken meanings of the earth."[44] As we've seen, the technique of this individuation is vocalism, a poetic practice for every person's attempt to comprehend the whole by speaking his or her own truth. Whitman writes:

The altitude of literature and poetry has always been religion—and always will be. The Indian Vedas, the Nackas of Zoroaster, the Talmud of the Jews, the Old Testament, the Gospel of Christ and his disciples, Plato's work, the Koran of Mohammed, the Edda of Snorro, and so on toward our own day, to Swedenborg, and to the invaluable contributions of Leibnitz, Kant, and Hegel— . . . the religious tone, the consciousness of mystery, the recognition of the future, of the unknown, of Deity over and under all—exhibit literature's real heights and elevations, towering up like the great mountains of the earth.[45]

In this passage, Whitman is proclaiming a new vista, the spinal language of literature as a way to access the whole of creation. Literature, as sublime language, taps a root strong enough to return each of us to the "primal Idea" of the God over and under all, the root-metaphor of shamanic intuition. "In preparing his trance," writes Eliade "the shaman drums, summons his spirit helpers, speaks a 'secret language,' imitating the cries of beasts, and especially the songs of birds. He ends by obtaining a 'second state' that provides the impetus for linguistic creation and the rhythms of lyric poetry. . . . It is from such linguistic creations, made possible through pre-ecstatic 'inspiration,' that the 'secret languages' of the mystics and the traditional allegorical languages later crystallize."[46]

Whitman shows us just how shamanistic he is in the following passage:

> Standing on this ground—the last, the highest, only permanent ground—and sternly criticizing, from it, all works, either of the literary, or any art, we have peremptorily to dismiss every pretensive production, however fine its esthetic or intellectual points, which violates or ignores, or even does not celebrate, the central divine idea of All, suffusing universe, of eternal trains of purpose, in the development, by however slow degrees, of the physical, moral, and spiritual kosmos. . . .
> It is not entirely new—but it is for Democracy to elaborate it, and look to build upon and expand from it, with uncompromising reliance.[47]

This passage is at least as practical as it is mystical. Whitman knows that poetic practice can enable anyone to lead his or her voice to expanding the physical, moral, and spiritual cosmos Whitman happens to have discovered as an American poet. And here again we can see him dividing an American vision of Spiritual Democracy up into three stages: political/constitutional, material/economic, and spiritual/religious. Despite the fact that the founding fathers refrained from giving any definite description of what they meant by "God," Whitman vocalizes his own belief that it means the "divine idea of All"—the divine cosmos in all and in each of us. And while vocalizing from such a vista of what humanity might be, he does not neglect to bring his mystical belief in the soul's immortality to the fore as a prerogative open to anyone possessed of the American idea of liberty.

"On the Beach at Night" is the poem in which he most clearly articulates this vision. In this remarkable work, a young girl stands with her father, facing east on the beach, where they see Jupiter and the Seven Sisters star cluster, the Pleiades. Black masses of clouds descend from the sky to cover the immortal orbs, and the little child holding the hand of her father begins to weep. "Weep not," Whitman as a spiritual father says to the little girl, "Weep not, my darling,

/ With these kisses let me remove your tears, / The ravening clouds shall not be victorious," and he reassures her that the "the Pleiades shall emerge." Immortality becomes Whitman's password to the little child and the Pleiades her initiators into the reality of the immortality of the soul. "Something there is," he reassures her, with his soothing words, "Something there is more immortal even than the stars, / Something" that shall endure longer even than lustrous Jupiter, and even the "radiant sisters the Pleiades."[48]

Here, Whitman takes a leap of faith beyond Humboldtian science. But he has made his confession of faith objective by appealing to the stars to confirm it. In the same year he was to write: "Greater than stars or suns, / O sun and moon and all you stars! Sirius and Jupiter! / Passage to you!"[49] The "you" referred to is God, the ultimate aim of any passage of the soul to the divine feminine as cosmic void (Buddhism), darkness (Daoism), or night (Dickinson).

In Whitman's view, the greatest sayers of words are those that give voice to the "all": "Ethereal, pervading all, (for without me what were all? what were God?) / Essence of forms, life of the real identities, permanent, positive, (namely the unseen,) / Life of the great round world, the sun and stars, and of man, I the general soul."[50] Now, in this passage from "Chanting the Square Deific", wherein Whitman posits a new, transnational, four-sided God-image in human history at the end of the Civil War, is a real Humboldtian idea and it was first articulated clearly in Whitman's 1860 poem "Kosmos," which appeared in the "New Bible." So if we want to understand Whitman's calling as a poet of Spiritual Democracy, we must turn to the 1860 edition of *Leaves of Grass* to recognize why "Vocalism" is so central to Whitman's verse technique.

On the very first page of his "New Bible" Whitman speaks of the art of "vocalizing all."[51] This is Whitman's calling as an American bard: to evoke (that is to say: to arouse, conjure, or induce) an awareness of "all" in his listeners in an effort to transform human consciousness and spur readers into action. As Whitman progresses through his "Chants Democratic," he comes to chant twelve and announces:

> To oratists, to male or female,
> Vocalism, breath, measure, concentration, determination,
>   and the divine power to speak words.
> Are you eligible?
> Are you full-lung'd and limber-lipp'd from long trial?
>   from vigorous practice? from physique?
> . . . .
> O now I see arise orators fit for inland America,

. . . .

And I see that power is folded in a great vocalism.[52]

A great vocalism is the movement he later names for us: Spiritual Democracy. It can only be realized through the human voice and the breath, which he calls Santa Spirita, using a feminine name to signify the divine feminine as the "breather, life, / Beyond the light, lighter than light," the "Ethereal, pervading all."[53] In volume 1 of *Cosmos*, Alexander von Humboldt had indicated that his vocation was to "bring together a unity in diversity of phenomena; a harmony blending together all created things, however dissimilar in form and attributes; one great whole animated by the breath of life."[54] Thus, in the first words of "Vocalism," Whitman includes breath in a true Humboldtian idiom, and in "Chanting the Square Deific" he ends: "Here the square finishing, the solid, I the most solid, / Breathe my breath also through these songs."[55] Thus, "Vocalism" provides a key for what follows after the Civil War, namely the notion of Spiritual Democracy. But just before the outbreak of the war, Whitman proceeds to chant to the "Poets to come!"

In "Poets to come!" Whitman is addressing poets, oratists (orators), singers, and musicians of the future to "justify" himself and "Democracy," and what we, as a global species, are really for. Whitman declares in 1860, with limited powers of speech he has developed by this time that a "new brood, native, athletic, continental, greater than before known" must arise to "justify" him. "Indeed, if it were not for you, what would I be?" Whitman asks each reader to consider; for "What is the little I have done, except to arouse you?"[56] Arousal is a seminal word here. If the reader has not been aroused by Whitman's songs, then she or he has not awakened to the truths of the "unspoken meanings of the earth!"[57]

Whitman understands that he depends on "being realized, long hence." The word *hence* or henceforward implies the future; henceforth: his call is to evoke singers from across the prairies, Oregon and "California inclusive" who will justify him. More, he expects all states will eventually come to "understand" and "love" and "enjoy" themselves with him. "Of to-day," he chants, "I know I am momentary, untouched, I am the bard of the future." Hence, Whitman advances "a moment, only to wheel and hurry back in the darkness."[58] He realizes that his body is mortal; but his spirit, and his soul's body and breath are immortal. Whitman is well aware in 1860 of the undeveloped nature of his thoughts on Spiritual Democracy, yet he has already received an intuition of its as-yet-unspoken-meanings, which he will bring forth a decade later. He has left it to readers, for now, to "prove and define" what he means: "Expecting the main things from you."[59]

"Poets to come!" was first published as number fourteen of the "Chants Democratic" and it was considerably shortened in all future editions of his collected poetry. The poem cannot be understood on its own and must be viewed from the broader vista that gave it birth, and that is the vista of the "all" he says is his vocation to vocalize in "Kosmos." He is going to do the job von Humboldt left unfinished, with regards to the unification of all religions, and that is to vocalize "the *universal all* in a manner worthy of the dignity of the word *Cosmos* in its signification of *universe, order of the world,* and *adornment* of this universal order,"[60] but in a new way that will unveil the unspoken meaning of the word *religio.*

In Whitman's view, spiritual "power is folded in a great vocalism,"[61] and it is the words of poets to come, the great sayers of words of the earth, orators, mediums, and singers of the future to bring this powerful force about and spread it across the globe, as a new religion of Spiritual Democracy. "All religion," Whitman says in his "Poem of the Road": "all solid things, arts, governments, all that was or is apparent upon this globe or any globe, falls into niches and corners before the procession of Souls along the grand roads of the universe."[62] Whitman begins his chanting of powerful earth words in "Poem of the Road" using a French word that he repeats in rhythmic measure with twelve strong exclamations: "Allons! Whoever you are, come travel with me! / . . . Allons! We must not stop here! / . . . Allons! The inducements shall be great to you! / . . . Allons! With power, liberty, the earth, the elements! / . . . Allons! Yet take warning! / . . . Allons! After the Great Companions! / . . . Allons! To that which is endless, as it was beginningless, / . . . Allons! Whoever you are! come forth! / . . . Allons! Out of the dark confinement! / . . . Allons! Through struggles and wars! / . . . My call is the call of battle, I nourish active rebellion, / . . . Allons! The road is before us! / . . . Allons! Be not detained! / . . . Mon enfant! I give you my hand."[63] *Allons!* means "Let's go!" He is urging us to go along with him on the open road, to celebrate freedom, liberty, equality, the earth, the infinite Kosmos, companionship, and democracy. The exclamations are all quite commanding and they are all meant to strike home to the foundation of the Soul inside each of us, to arouse, excite, and move us each into rebellious action, and call us forth out of dark confinement: into the "light, lighter than light" of Spiritual Democracy.

This chant was written on the cusp of civil war, so when he incites us to action he is enflaming us to use new words, our words, Nature's words, that are uttered, not from our heads, but from our hearts and bodies, as all words of the earth are *embodied* words and must be felt deeply to evoke their native significances. And the most embodied of all words in Whitman's lexicon is the word "all" because this is a metaphor for Kosmos, or the universal whole, which is at the center and heart of all religions.

Now, in the seven-page poem, "To the Sayers of Words," Whitman uses several words to make a distinction between words spoken from the head and words spoken from the heart, or words pronounced from intellect (book knowledge) and unuttered words: words that can never be said fully and can only be approximated through speech. "To the Sayers of Words" originally appeared in the 1856 edition of *Leaves of Grass* under the title "Poem of the Sayers of the Words of the Earth." In 1881 Whitman retitled it "A Song of the Rolling Earth."

The idea of vocalism, vocalizing all, or voicing wholly, pivots on earth words that Whitman says are of Nature. One of these nature words in "To the Sayers of Words" is *amelioration:* the idea of improvement, to make, or become better; or using effort and will to better oneself through vocal practice and refinement of the human voice: "Amelioration is one of the earth's words."[64] Another earth word appears in French, and as we've seen, Whitman has been using French in his "New Bible" profusely during his chants, such as in "Salut au Monde!" (Salute to the World!), "Enfans d'Adam," (Children of Adam), "Mon enfant!" (My children) and "Allons!" (Let's go!). Another powerful earth word that appears suddenly in his seven-page, tour de force poem, "To the Sayers of Words," is: "Accouche! Accouchez!" *Accoucher* in French means to bear, deliver; or childbirth; and *accouchez!* is a verbal imperative: "Give birth!" or more idiomatically, "Out with it!" As Whitman says, "why don't you let it out then?"[65] Giving birth and midwifery are pivots for "Vocalism" and "Kosmos." What he is saying in all of these poems, but in "To the Sayers" in particular, is that the divine power to speak words is within you, in your soul's body; and ample, or real, words are not to be found outside, in any specters of books; they are within your body and need to be birthed: "No, these are not the words, the substantial words are in the ground and sea, / They are in the air, they are in you."[66] Real words are more "delicious" than any words whether out of our friend's mouths, or our teacher's mouths. Real words are somatically located. In Whitman's view, "Human bodies are words, myriads of words" and: "In the best poems re-appears the body, man's or woman's, well-shaped, natural, gay."[67] Your body is a vehicle for the divine word that speaks itself and needs to be born in you through a calling.

Vocalism is the gateway to bring the divine word to birth through sacred actions of the body. But spoken words are not of the earth and merely specters; they are not really living words. To embody the words of the earth, the voice of the earth, the amplitude of the earth: that is the task of the masters. "The great masters, the sayers, are the earth's words,"[68] and such masters are the poets, orators, musicians, and vocalizers of the all he has been referring to.

As the poem unfolds we come to realize that the greatest master or earth's word is a person, whether male or female, who is a *birth giver*. What she, or he, gives birth to through words of the earth, is the self as a word. "Accouche!" is used with an exclamation point and it implies that the birthing of the self is a sacred obligation. In order for development to occur, for self-betterment to happen, effort is required, and this necessitates the exertion of *vocation*, the act of giving voice to a calling or summons from the divine to speak up. For this emergence as a word of the earth, midwives are needed. As a poet, who is about to realize his second vocation as a male nurse in the Civil War, Whitman does this magnificently, first by aligning himself (not identifying, but bringing himself into alignment) with "the words of the eloquent dumb great mother," whose "true words never fail" and "whose reflection does not fail."[69] She, the great mother and the "beautiful sister," who holds up in her hand what looks like the character of a mirror, and whose eyes glance back from it while reflecting on the beauty of her face,[70] represents the reflective function of the world soul that the poet-shaman is seeking to give voice to. Whitman says he is going to attempt to give voice to the eloquent mute great mother, who lacks power of speech and the beautiful sister, who tirelessly holds the mirror, day and night, and needs a vehicle to convey the earth's messages to the world's children through lyrics. For this to take place, practiced speech is needed.

Speech, Whitman says, is the twin of his vision. Speaking, talking out loud, vocalizing active words assumes a place of honor, coequal with the basic activity of visioning. In "To the Sayers of Words," however, vocalizing is supreme, and outstrips even the basic capacity for imagination. He has already had an intuition of this in 1855. As he said in section twenty-five of "Song of Myself": "My voice goes after what my eyes cannot reach, / With the twirl of my tongue I encompass worlds and volumes of worlds. / Speech is the twin of my vision, it is unequal to measure itself, / It provokes me forever, it says sarcastically, / *Walt you contain enough, why don't you let it out then?*"[71]

Walt contains "multitudes," and in "To the Sayers of Words," the mature Whitman whose mind is on fire lets it out, becomes a midwife to the nation and the world, and gives birth to the new idea: the transnational self, or the words Spiritual Democracy, as the way of the globe's future. "Accouche! Accouchez! / Will you rot your own fruit in yourself there? / Will you squat and stifle there?"[72] In these powerful lines, Whitman is confronting us each with what is essentially a psychological problem: for each of us has a divine child within, a seed, or fruit of futurity. The question is: will the fruit be stillborn, or, will we find a vehicle, a vocation to make it truly living? The idea of giving birth is central to the psychology of individuation and it is a generally recognized metaphor for the process of the second birth that is found in all rites of initiation throughout all cultures of the world. Stated psychologically, then, Whitman regresses (his psychic energy retreats, that is) to the domain of the "eloquent dumb great mother" and the "interminable sisters," the "ceaseless cotillions of sisters, . . . centripetal and centrifugal sisters, the elder and younger sisters" to "The beautiful sister we know dances on with the rest."[73] She, the most beautiful one, is the divine sister we all love because she is the anima mundi, the mirror-holding soul of the earth and universe. Because shamans arose during the aegis or age of the Great Mother religions, Whitman, by regressing, has entered the domain of the first artists, the poet-shamans and artist-shamans, and the beautiful sister of the world who dances in all of us is the word of the earth he is called to speak for. As a shaman-poet, who taps into the all, Whitman retreats to the matriarchal stage in the evolution of human consciousness dominated by the Great Mother religions and becomes a vocalizer of the unarticulated meanings of a nuclear, structural imprint in the human psyche that emerged during the time of the earth Goddesses. He becomes a poet-shaman of Gaia, who gives voice to the central aim of the religions of the Great Mother: giving birth.

Mother images in archeological residues, discovered by physical anthropologists over the last two hundred years, have unearthed a plethora of figurines of the Great Mother as a birth-giver. The cotillions of sisters are more modern versions of her ancestral lineage, for a cotillion in French is a complex dance that was popular in France in the eighteenth century. The beautiful sister is an image representation of the anima mundi, or world soul, an archetype of the earth Whitman says we all must seek to embody as words, during our practices of vocalism. "Whoever you are!" Whitman exclaims (and here he introduces the metaphor of a sailing ship that we find in Egyptian mythology and that he will use again and again until the end of his days): "The divine ship sails the divine sea for you. / Whoever you are!" He ends this magnificent stanza with the breathtaking line: "For none more than you is immortality."[74] We are all immortal. We all have a capacity to achieve immortality within ourselves, through our own efforts, and the primary vehicle to immortality is not through meditation alone, but through active speech, language, birthing earth words. Here, Whitman outstrips the linguists.

His vocalizing of the all is in advance of his vision, and he has transcended the linguistic field through speech, leaving us all as language-makers behind him in a trial of his dust and debris, like the tail of a comet hurling through space. The way to immortality, vocalism, or free verse, is to utter ample words from human bodies that, like the beautiful sister, are "the amplitude of the earth"; this, he tells us, is the way of the self as a word of God—the path to physical and spiritual completeness: "I swear the earth shall surely be complete to him or her who shall be complete!"[75] The main thing is to become a birth giver, or midwife to the self, as a word, and we will either let our fruit rot, squat, and stifle on the ground, or be born. Vocalism, not only active visioning, becomes a way to wholeness via word-images, or eidólons.

For the poet-shaman, speech is even more central than visioning, for it goes after what the eyes of the earth cannot reach. "No politics, art, religion, behavior, or what not, is of account, unless it compare with the amplitude of the earth."[76] Here, Whitman names it: *the amplitude of the earth is more primal than visions of the earth, hearing more pivotal than seeing, when it comes to bearing the fruit of Spiritual Democracy as a word of God. To arrive at such breadth of hearing, silence is needed.* "I swear I begin to see little or nothing in audible words! / I swear I think all merges toward the presentation of the unspoken meanings of the earth!"[77] All words aim toward one thing: "the presentation of the unspoken meanings of the earth!" This is the poet's job.

The unspoken significance of the mute Great Mother, the first religions of the earth, needs to be voiced, and she and her interminable sister-children need a *presenter:* someone who presents her unspoken word-meanings. This is the shaman's task; it is the analyst's task, and the writer's task, to make the reflective instinct conscious in us all.

The "unspoken meanings of the earth!", What is that? Whatever it is, Whitman assures us it is in the body, your body, my body, sounds of your body, your voice, sayings. That's it. Whitman makes it transparent that his poem is for "the sayers of words" and his words are merely "hints at meaning."[78] Sayers of the earth's words are individuals, whether male or female, who can tap into the shamanistic domain of the objective psyche and birth new words that are the only words worth speaking, out of the shamanic foundation of human consciousness. He provokes us to go beyond imitation to an approximation of his own spirit, to vocalize, which is the gift of language he bequeaths to us and he calls free verse. "Say on, sayers!" Whitman chants to the great masters of words, "Delve! mould! pile the words of the earth! / Work on, / . . . When the materials are all prepared the architects shall appear."[79] Here, Whitman is speaking to the poets to come: the coming poets are architects of Spiritual Democracy. This is a new notion he is giving birth to as a midwife on the verge of civil war: vocalizing all, for the nation and the world.

Whitman is certain at this point (he knows) they (the architects or build-ers) shall appear: "I swear to you the architects shall appear without fail!"[80] Of these creators "the greatest amongst them shall be he who best knows you, and encloses all, and is faithful to all."[81] The "he" of course is the future Whitman: the bard of Spiritual Democracy, the midwife of the great idea.

Thus, in "To the Sayers of Words" Whitman is not only conveying the unconscious meanings of Alexander von Humbotldt's "all" that is the whole Kosmos, he is also transmitting a transnational vision of earth words made pos-sible by his older linguist brother, William von Humboldt, the great German language specialist. "Language, more than any other attribute of mankind," writes William von Humboldt, "binds together the whole human race."[82]

So, Whitman is arriving in the above poem (in English, as well as through the use of French words), at the articulation of the unspoken earth-meanings through an international language he is midwifing. Just as there are four direc-tions, north, south, east, and west, and four elements, air, soil, water, fire, so too does Whitman say that his qualities, like ours, interpenetrate these, and that though the quaternary nature of such elements may be told in "three thousand languages," they know nothing of his name,[83] or your name, or my name. Here, then we see his synthesis of the works of the von Humboldt brothers, in a beauti-ful fusion of language that includes geography, in "Salut au Monde!", linguistics in "To the Sayers of Words," astronomy in "Kosmos," and the science and art throughout. Glancing through the mirror, with our beautiful sister, Whitman beholds and vocalizes the all of the Kosmos.

Finally, Whitman speaks, as a midwife to the masses, in an attempt to deliver us all from our fruit-rotting and squatting and stifling: "I swear to you, he [the greatest architect] and the rest [all other "singers of the songs of the body, and of the truths of the earth"] shall not forget you, they [the greatest poets] shall perceive that you are not an iota less than they [namely, we are all equals]," and finally, he ends this chant by asserting: "I swear to you, you shall be glorified in them."[84] Echoing the words of the prophet Isaiah, we shall all be glorified, he says, by the poet.

This unity of influence by the von Humboldts, Alexander and William, is coined in the mother lode phrase "the amplitude of the earth." Whitman is a birth giver, a male mother who is not eloquently dumb, but eloquently brilliant, because he has made the unconscious meanings of the earth conscious for us through the power of his speech. "To the Sayers of Words" is a forerunner of the design that will become his manifesto on Spiritual Democracy, "Democratic Vistas," in 1871. Whitman is one of the constructors, perhaps *the* centermost draftsman of this sacred notion, since he names it for us through active speech: Spiritual Democracy. As such, he can be credited with being the engineer of a transnational language he calls vocalism. Vocalism can be spoken in any language, it may be used cross-culturally, and it is transcendent of any one nation, because its reference of diversity is the Kosmos, which is itself a Word of God, "who makes the dictionaries of words that print cannot touch."[85]

During Whitman's later, halcyon days as a famous poet living in Camden, New Jersey, he wrote *Specimen Days*—in which the sense of cosmic silence and stillness as a self-fulfilling emptiness is palpable. In that book he ponders, "What communion with the waters, the air, the exquisite *chiaroscuro*—the sky and stars, that speak no word, nothing to the intellect, yet so eloquent, so communicative to the soul."[86] This echoes his earlier tribute to Alexander von Humboldt in his poem "Kosmos," published in 1860, where one finds no separation between man and God nor democracy and nature, because the cosmos unites them:

> WHO includes diversity, and is Nature,
> Who is the amplitude of the earth, and the coarseness and sexuality
>   of the earth, and the great charity of the earth, and the
>   equilibrium also,
>
>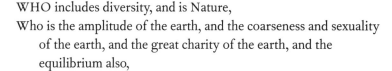
>
> Who believes not only in our globe, with its sun and moon,
>   but in other globes, with their suns and moons;
> Who, constructing the house of himself or herself, not for a day,
>   but for all time, sees races, eras, dates, generations;
> The past, the future, dwelling there, like space, inseparable
>   together.[87]

Such objective sympathy is founded on not knowing, or what the Buddhists might term *emptiness*. In Whitman's early poetry, particularly section forty-four of "Song of Myself," the word kosmos extends beyond the known universe to include the unknown: "It is time to explain myself—let us stand up," Whitman says, as if speaking to a lecture room full of scientists. He then exclaims further: "What is known I strip away, / I launch all men and women forward with me into the Unknown."[88]

Thus, the spinal-nature of language opens up vista to vocalism and enables a shamanic transport to an unknowable cosmic beyond, which can nonetheless be symbolized. "As in a waking vision, / E'en while I chant I see."[89]

IO

WHITMAN AS PRESERVER OF THE PSYCHIC INTEGRITY OF THE COMMUNITY

Traditionally, shamans fill key roles for their people. They are healers, they are conduits between the physical and the spiritual realms, and they can connect others with the past and the future. In his epilogue to *Shamanism: Archaic Techniques of Ecstasy*, Mircea Eliade discusses another essential function of shamans—as preservers of "the psychic integrity of the community."[1] A closer look at the way Walt Whitman fulfilled this role will shed light on a deeper understanding of what he means by Spiritual Democracy. We've previously looked at the deeper substratum of shamanic identity in American poetry. From there we'll uncover the meaning of Whitman's vocation in search of that elusive element—integrity.

Integrity, Jungian analyst John Beebe writes, is a time-honored word in the English language, which comes from the Latin root *integritas*. The word can be traced to the famous orator Cicero, who advocated Stoic notions of personal virtue during the Roman Republic. It also has roots in the writings of the Roman Catholic theologian St. Thomas Aquinas, for whom it meant the aesthetic "essence of wholeness."[2] As a value to be upheld in the new United States, the term was foregrounded by Benjamin Franklin in reference to something he found in his own personality: "my Character of Integrity."[3] The Stoic understanding of *integritas*, however, as Beebe notes, pointed "to the part of us that is general Intelligence, always seeking to live in accord with Nature's law. This part of our nature is actively interested in maintaining a continuity of Nature's intent." This definition of integrity accords with the meanings Whitman gives it. Integrity is a classic biblical idea, and, as Eliade has shown, its roots are shamanistic. In the psychology of personality, it has to do with the connection between the higher and lower forms of consciousness, the uniting of which Beebe calls the "spine" of the personality.[4] "Real integrity" Beebe writes, "ultimately depends upon the claiming of this spine in each of us; it is the inner basis of the 'uprightness' we look for in ourselves and in each other."[5]

In his "New Bible," Whitman's intent is to instill in the moral and spiritual conscience of America a new understanding of what is at the core of democracy itself: integrity for all. The words Whitman uses to describe integrity might best be defined as "nature," "spine-character," "conscience," "upright," "one's-self," "happiness," "justice," "call," "democratic," "personality." In 1860, when Ralph Waldo Emerson asked him to take references to sex out of *Leaves of Grass*, his "New Bible," Whitman declined. In that instance he exhibited the "uprightness" of character that suggests that he was indeed following the way of nature, or what Alexander von Humboldt, whom he read with interest, called the "cosmos." In the King James version of the Bible (which Whitman knew from front to back), Solomon says, in Proverbs 11:3, "The integrity of the upright shall guide them." And David says in Psalms 25:12, "Let integrity and uprightness preserve me: for I wait on thee." In the old Hebrew sense, "integrity" has to do with justice and walking with erect carriage before God (Proverbs 19:1; 20:7), and Whitman uses this metaphor throughout much of his early poetry. In the Hebrew language, integrity is written as *tumah*, or *tumah-tee*, meaning "mine integrity."

Integrity is what preserves a person in the presence of one's enemies, and Whitman seems to have felt, near the end of his life, that he had endured much abuse. "Public criticism on the book and myself as author of it shows mark'd anger and contempt more than anything else—('I find a solid line of enemies to you everywhere' wrote a correspondent from Boston in 1884)."[6] What is it that enabled Whitman to endure much criticism and to insist on his correctness and uprightness, even at the risk of his own career?[7] The poet-shaman's way of preserving the psychic integrity of the community is not unlike that of the psychotherapist, who must first attend to his or her own character and then to that of patients. The goal, which must partly be pondered out by examples, involves helping to align people with the general intelligence of the universe. Whitman's responsibility to all people can be seen in his insisting on the principle of human equality as the highest principle in a Spiritual Democracy. This is akin to Beebe's reflections on the therapist's obligation to protect the psychic integrity of patients, as well as of the institution of psychotherapy itself, which can be harmed by careless behavior.[8]

Whitman's moral courage to add new meanings to the world's understanding of marriage by answering America's call for a "new husband" in "Calamus" part 3 was an act of integrity that came not only from the domain of his personal passion and instinct, but from a moral foundation that is present in the teachings of all world religions.

> Here to put your lips upon mine I permit you,
> With the comrade's long-dwelling kiss, or the new husband's kiss,
> For I am the new husband, and I am the comrade.[9]

As we saw previously, Whitman, like Emerson, was never satisfied with the teachings of the churches of his day, as they did not embody the "relative attitude toward God, toward the objective universe." Among the transcendentalists, and even the Unitarians, there seems to have been a general feeling of dissatisfaction with the American churches in general for making Jesus himself, rather than the concepts he preached, their focus and goal. In his Divinity School Address, for instance, Emerson criticized Unitarians for subordinating our "nature to Christ's nature." And rather than settling for the messiah in Jesus, he suggested moreover, in complete agreement with his own scriptural interpretations, that Jesus had merely prepared the way for the "newborn bard of the Holy Ghost."[10] Whitman, like Dickinson and Melville, believed that he himself had answered this call, yet he eventually realized, more modestly, that he'd merely paved the way for the "poets to come." Nevertheless, in 1856 we can hear why he was so incensed with organized religion, and what may have been at the root of his momentary self-inflations.

As "to manly friendship, everywhere observed in the States," Whitman wrote in his lengthy and laudatory letter to Emerson, "there is not the first breath of it to be observed in print. I say the body of a man or woman, the main matter, is so far quite unexpressed in poems; but that the body is to be expressed, and sex is."[11] On a walk with Emerson in 1860, Whitman found Emerson's criticism of the "Children of Adam" poem cluster (where Emerson was the talker and Whitman the listener) simply "unanswerable" in its persuasive correctness, yet he ultimately did not heed Emerson's advice: "More precious than gold to me that dissertation—it afforded me, even after, this strange and paradoxical lesson; each charge of E's statement was unanswerable, no judge's charge more complete or convincing, I could never hear the points better put—and then I felt down in my soul the clear and unmistakable conviction to disobey all, and pursue my own way."[12]

What gave Whitman the confidence to hold to his language experiment and to boldly exemplify it without any further doubts? Here Whitman speaks for himself: "The actual living light is always curiously from elsewhere—follows unaccountable sources, and is lunar and relative at the best."[13] By "relative" he means a competing alternative to organized religion, a Religious Democracy, in which each individual is called to find her own personal relationship to God and that no God-image is better than another. In this view, all God-images of humanity are part and parcel of a Spiritual Democracy that is inclusive of the whole: "One main contrast of the ideas behind every page of my verses, compared with establish'd poems, is their different relative attitude toward God, toward the objective universe, and still more (by reflection, confession, assumption, &c.) the quite changed attitude of the ego, the one chanting or talking, toward himself and toward his fellow humanity."[14] This different relative attitude toward God is at the center of Whitman's experiment in Religious Democracy.

By staying true to his own integrity, Whitman was working on an expansion of the meaning of marriage for all continents, all nations:

I see O year in you the vast terraqueous globe given and giving all,
Europe to Asia, Africa join'd, and they to the New World,
The lands, geographies, dancing before you, holding a festival garland,
As brides and bridegrooms hand in hand.[15]

Despite the friendly caution of Emerson's criticisms about "The Children of Adam" cluster in 1860, Whitman felt he had to remain true to his own destiny, his vocation: "If I had cut sex out," Whitman reflected later, in a conversation with Horace Traubel, "I might just as well have cut everything out—the full scheme would no longer exist—it would have been *violated in its most sensitive spot!*"[16] The feeling of violation is a sure sign that his vocation was on the line, and by *"sensitive spot"* he means both the genitals and sex, not as a sign, but as a symbol. What Whitman foresaw is that the meanings behind his words were what mattered most, as he felt they would duly emerge and be lifted into a different light and atmosphere in the future. This is the lunar light he says is relative, because it reflects the actual living light, which is the sun. What Whitman experienced in relation to Emerson is what Beebe calls "a literal violation that demands a concrete response,"[17] and such a response was accomplished, it seems, through an assertion of what Beebe calls "lunar masculinity," which led directly to the publication entire of Whitman's "New Bible." "It is this sense of internal twinship, of a comfortable tension between solar masculinity that is aggressive and a lunar masculinity that is receptive,"[18] writes Beebe, that makes for a marriage of sames in men, or a wedding of solar and lunar conscience.[19]

Emerson insisted on a response to his stern demand that Whitman alter *Leaves of Grass* to make it less morally shocking for the times. "What have you to say then to such things?" he asked Whitman, while pausing after delivering what Walt later called his "review, attack, and pressing home, (like an army corps in order, artillery, cavalry, infantry)." Whitman appears to have listened calmly and with respectful reserve for the entire lambaste before answering: "Only that while I can't answer them at all, I feel more satisfied than ever to adhere to my own theory, and exemplify it."[20] We might all learn from the integrity of Whitman's example how to stand up and speak for our passionate convictions.

This is precisely the point that Beebe makes about integrity: it is that part of the personality that puts a person in accord with his or her innermost nature and permits one to speak with the moral certitude that is indicative of the highest quality of what it means to be human. In the third stage of the American experiment that he calls Spiritual Democracy, Whitman says that "All affection shall be fully responded to, the secret shall be told, / All these separations and gaps shall be taken up and hook'd and link'd together."[21] Thus, Whitman is a conjoiner of the whole, a cosmic linker, a person who sees into the developments of the future along evolutionary lines, and provides missing metaphors for our benefit. For Whitman this spinal function allowed him to perceive the lines of the "original intent" in the U.S. Constitution during the first stage of democracy: all are created equal.

In the wake of the legalization of gay marriage in a dozen states over the past few years, it's obvious that the United States is calling for a better understanding of the meaning of "marriage" than ever before, not for the country's own benefit, but for the benefit of a spiritually liberated global society. For it cannot be doubted that most objections to same-sex marriage are religious in nature and, ultimately, if Whitman is correct, all moral, legal, and constitutional objections will need to be wrestled with on religious grounds.

In the poem "Passage to India," Whitman provides us with his own subjective vision of faith, after a long period of suffering and grappling with ideas of the heart. Marriage is an archetype and as such it has an a priori meaning that is patterned upon a particular instinct, namely the nesting instinct, or the call to the mate. Its analogy is spread throughout all of nature, and it is not without significance that Whitman would meditate on same-sex love as a calling from "nature." Whitman's pivotal childhood recollection as a boy on the Long Island sea coast in "Out of the Cradle" was of a mockingbird that had lost its mate. He felt in his gut that the bird was singing uniquely to him. Flying around its nest, with four spotted eggs resting in it, the male he-bird called out frantically to its missing partner. Whitman, the curious boy, looked and listened long, ever so patiently by the lone seashore, and felt deep in his bones that he alone had heard its myriad meanings—the cries of unsatisfied love. It was at that point in his childhood latency, the poet says, that his vocation was "awakened" in him, and by reflection this memory in midlife—the call to sing to the United States and the world the song of the "new husband," the bi-erotic lover of all people—was made conscious in him at an archetypal level.

Whitman's acute awareness of the inherent relationship between sexuality and spirituality shows clearly how his understandings of the poet-shaman's function as a preserver of the psychic integrity of the community relates to the "All," and is aligned with the most progressive spiritual traditions. In Hinduism and Judaism, for instance, sex and spirit are not split off from the body. Rather, they are united on a plane of mystical realization, where the heavenly marriage and earthly marriage are intertwined as one. Jung has a salient passage about this kind of embodied marriage in *Mysterium Coniunctionis* that illuminates this meaning. He says, concisely: "Sexuality does not exclude spirituality nor spirituality sexuality, for in God all opposites are abolished."[22] That is Whitman's point exactly.

Might it be wise for the integrity of depth-psychology to make same-sex marriage pivotal in the discussion of all branches of psychotherapy today, when marriage is becoming such a pressing issue for our nation? It seems so, particularly as Whitman's important vision of Spiritual Democracy holds up a non-prejudicial possibility for the present cultural and political debates, and for the practices of psychotherapy across the helping professions as a whole. Let us listen to Whitman, in the early candlelight of old age, speak for himself a century and a half ago:

> From another point of view "Leaves of Grass" is avowedly the song of Sex and Amativeness, and even Animality—though meanings that do not usually go along with those words are behind all, and will duly emerge; and all are sought to be lifted into a different light and atmosphere. . . . Difficult as it will be, it has become, in my opinion, imperative to achieve a shifted attitude from superior men and women toward the thought and fact of sexuality, as an element in character, personality, the emotions, and theme in literature . . . the spirit in which they are spoken, permeate all "Leaves of Grass," and the work must stand or fall with them, as the human body and soul must remain as an entirety.[23]

What Whitman brought to the field of American poetry is a unitary awareness of the body and soul as equals, of men and women as equals, and of heterosexuals and homosexuals as equals, and of sex and spirit also as equals. Unlike all previous religious dispensations the world over, Whitman rendered the consummate marriage of the soul with God, not in heterosexual imagery, but in bisexual imagery, which certainly might have met with the approval of Freud. He did this for an important reason: his celebration of the democratization of the whole person began with himself as a "Personality,"[24] as one democratic "Individual": a "Human Being."[25]

Whitman sidestepped convention and allowed the light of the lunar masculinity he embraced as a route to the wholeness he was envisioning to reflect a "different relative attitude toward God." In so doing he paved the way toward a fairer and more democratic nonbiased future. This is where Whitman speaks like an Old Testament prophet, with the voice of liberty, conviction, and justice, as an American. He corrects for the violation done to same-sex couples by insisting that the foundation of the world—the body and sex—be preserved as sacred.

Whitman's religious idea of Spiritual Democracy appears to be based upon a trinitarian notion, and in this sense his anticipations are in accord with the predictions of Emerson that America would produce a "newborn bard of the Holy Spirit." Whitman added to this that many would follow him toward personal fulfillment. In this sense, Spiritual Democracy appears to be post-Christian and ecumenical. In "Passage to India," Whitman puts it this way:

> Trinitas divine shall be gloriously accomplish'd and compacted
>   by the true son of God, the poet,
> . . . .
> Nature and Man shall be disjoin'd and diffused no more,
> The true son of God shall absolutely fuse them.[26]

Here again is the idea of the poet-as-preserver, but for Whitman this function of integrity extends to the poet's duty to protect the environment, as well, with "ardor like mine." By putting his own personality on record as having a particular "nature," Whitman was advancing a new theory of the relativity of our individual means of accessing God in a way that had never been voiced before. He knew that the meanings behind his references would duly emerge in a different science, one that would accept individual differences in the way nature is embodied.

This led Whitman, in common with other American shamanistic poets, to voice the case for same-sex marriage as an archetype of the sacred in American poetry. We are speaking of a narrow period of nine years here, when Herman

Melville, Walt Whitman, and Emily Dickinson all put forth their independent hypotheses of a new archetype of marriage emerging on the American continent. This period of history is generally spoken about as the American Renaissance, but it's more accurately called the shamanistic movement in American poetry, which captures the meaning of the poetic genre with regards to marriage equality in the United States. It needs to be acknowledged that these poet-shamans were not weak, neurotic, or delicate personalities in the least, but rather they were strong and upright individuals. Their strength of character shows in their personal, professional, and family relationships, including Dickinson's, which might come as a surprise to some given her reputation for reclusivity. She was, in fact, aligned in her poetic imagination with Vesuvius, and her "little force" could erupt at any time.

All of these poets were in touch with a tremendous reservoir of psychophysical energy that flowed through them and their verses. "All waits or goes by default till a strong being appears," writes Whitman; "A strong being is the proof of the race and of the ability of the universe, / When he or she appears materials are overaw'd, / The dispute on the soul stops, / . . . What are your theology, tuition, society, traditions, statute-books, now?"[27] Awe is a good way to put it, as Dickinson referred to herself as a "Bride of Awe." Her own most "lesbian" poem, "The Soul selects her own Society—/ Then—shuts the Door—/ To her divine Majority—/ Present no more—"[28], places her squarely in advocacy for same-sex marriage, no matter what others might think.

The idea of marriage equality is vital today because of the particular focus in the world right now on all three stages of democracy. Judging by developments such as the recent mass movements in favor of reform in the Arab world, our spirits are yearning for Spiritual Democracy, and we see the birth pains starting. It seems clear that Spiritual Democracy is insisting on being born in the world soul today.

From a psychological point of view, the archetype of the "new husband" is an emotional-image, a thought-form, or mythologem (metaphor) that we do not find anywhere in the major religions of the world. Although some of its roots may be found in the New Testament, it appears to be original with Whitman, because he brings the body and sex back into the image, where the prophets, apostles, and mystics appear to have left it out. Whitman, writing in a multicultural, multispiritual, and internationally awakened (post-Enlightenment) democratic society, inserted into his Spiritual Democracy the seeds for the institutionalization of same-sex marriage in his "Calamus" cluster. We are seeing it reemerge now as an equivalent principle alongside the heterosexual marriage institution. Same-sex marriage is now legally recognized in Argentina, Belgium, Brazil, Canada, Denmark, France, Iceland, Netherlands, New Zealand, Norway, Portugal, Spain, South Africa, Sweden, United Kingdom, Uruguay, and several sub-national jurisdictions, including parts of Mexico and the United States.

The effort to legalize same-sex marriage in the United States has been a piecemeal battle fraught with conflict with traditional organized religions. In California, for example, same-sex marriage could be legally performed for part of 2008—until the state's Supreme Court ruling in support of the practice was reversed when voters passed the contentious Proposition 8. This prohibitive ballot measure was funded primarily by the Church of Jesus Christ of Latter Day Saints (the Mormons) and the Roman Catholic Church. However, since that major setback, public opinion has shifted perceptibly in favor of legalized same-sex marriage, and several states have passed legislation to allow it. Significantly, New York's lawmakers voted to legalize same-sex marriage in 2011, making that state the largest in the nation where gay and lesbian couples may wed. The momentum from the legalization promptly injected new energy and vigor into the national gay-rights movement. Such decisions would certainly have been applauded by Whitman, who was born on Long Island and for a time considered himself a proud New York City resident ("Walt Whitman, a kosmos, of Manhattan the son").[29]

The turnaround in momentum at a personal level is best illustrated by President Obama's "conversion" in favor of legal gay marriage. Obama, a Christian, opposed Proposition 8 in 2008 and stated afterward that his attitude toward the idea of legalizing same-sex marriage was "evolving"—a statement Whitman would have found respectable, since his own goal was to evolve consciousness, not dictate it. By the 2012 presidential debate, Obama was fully supportive of legalizing gay marriage, which was the first time same-sex equal rights were supported by a U.S. President. Undoubtedly Whitman would have celebrated the stirring words from president Obama's second inaugural address, on January 21, 2013, one hundred fifty years after Whitman's stunning breakthrough beyond traditional morality. In a historic moment, Obama said: "Our journey is not complete until our gay brothers and sisters are treated like anyone else under the law. For if we are truly created equal, then surely the love we commit to one another must be equal as well. . . . We, the people, declare today that the most evident of truths—that all of us are created equal—is the star that guides us still; just as it guided our forebears through Seneca Falls, and Selma, and Stonewall." It's not difficult to imagine that inspiring oration bringing Whitman to tears of joy.

The type of open-mindedness that President Obama came to embrace is at the foundation of a more progressive view of God than what we find in the Bible. It is this very open-mindedness that Whitman calls Spiritual Democracy. This is not a new dogma, for Whitman stood for no dogmas. Whitman never sought to take away from the Book of Prophecy, nor did he want to take anything out of the Holy City, where the "Spirit and the bride say, Come" (Revelations 22: 16–19). What Whitman brings forth are not the old laws, judgments, nor canons (of Genesis, Psalms, Matthew, Mark, or John), but rather a new metaphor of marriage equality. Whitman gives the Old Testament prophets and Christ full credit for discovering the idea of cosmic brotherhood, but he distinguishes between brotherhood and marriage, as they are not the same. The archetype of "cosmic brotherhood" is different from his more radical understanding of marriage as cosmic and bi-erotic, as he in his relativity experiences it.

Whitman, of course, never leaves sex and the physical body out of his democratic theory. Instead, he recognizes the body as sacred and creates a new institution of man's love for his fellow man on all levels of betrothal and engagement. Neither does Whitman presume to "contravene" the Bible, for this is impossible, he asserts, in his prose passage the "Bible as Poetry." In it, however, he goes beyond belief in any one religion to "marry" the cosmic lover in each of us.

In a Spiritual Democracy, where religious belief is free, there are no dualisms regarding marriage. Equality is what democracy teaches: "I will make cities and civilizations defer to me, / This is what I have learnt from America—it is the amount, and I teach it again."[30] Eventually, once psychology and religion catch up with Whitman's ecumenical vision, marriage equality may in time become free and the mantle of Spiritual Democracy might cover not only our nation but the entire world.[31]

In the third level of democracy, Whitman predicts, we may all be embraced in marriage one day, without religious, social, legal, and psychological misjudgment. This is of the utmost importance from a psychological angle, because when marriage rights are granted—such as they were in California in 2008—and then are taken away unconstitutionally by a ballot proposition funded primarily by the religious right, individual relativity is wounded, and sentient human beings suffer from the sanctioned prejudice, the onus, the emotional injury, and the discrimination. Whitman's visions of Spiritual Democracy enables us to see further than biblical statements about marriage to the shamanistic foundation underneath institutions.

Whitman claims a more complete embrace with the archetype of marriage than in any other religious metaphor, except Dickinson's, which is just as compelling. Like her, Whitman presents a complementary narrative to the prevailing religious narratives of the heterosexual majority that have dominated the West for three millennia, whether in Greece, Israel, Rome, or Mecca. We do not find this archetype of Spiritual Democracy formulated into a metaphysical or psychological theory anywhere in European, Eastern, Near Eastern, or Middle Eastern history, including the wisdom texts of the East and the King James Bible, which Whitman and Dickinson thoroughly studied and loved.

Whitman's vision has an equalizing message for all faiths across the globe and this can at least give us hope: We are all really the same, he says; we are all brothers and sisters internationally. He understood that all people are divine and need to be given freedom to pursue their own sexual preferences and religious faiths, whatever they might be. Spiritual Democracy levels all religions to their "religious root-ground" in a globalized world by making us all equals. And he is not alone in this vision.

Melville, too, shared a similar vision in his shamanizing from the pulpit in chapter 9 of *Moby Dick*, aptly termed "The Sermon." Father Mapple, in his sermon, delivered in the Whaleman's Chapel in New Bedford, Massachusetts, addresses the problem of vocation to the seafaring community. By analogy, however, he is speaking to all of us who must negotiate the fluid New World context as we struggle to shape our identities. He is speaking to every American and to everyone in the world, as well. Father Mapple teaches in the Sermon that a "far, far upward and inward delight" will be to him or her that has courage enough to stand up for his or her "inexorable self."

Without the body, and without the vision of the body as sacred, Whitman asserts, "reality would seem incomplete, and science, democracy, and life itself, finally in vain."[32] There is not only meaning in sex as a personal, relativizing, yet universal symbol but meaning in embodied sexual experience; and this is the meaning Whitman envisioned for the coming "Bards of the great Idea!"[33]— "Trinitas divine," or Spiritual Democracy.

(Democracy, while weapons were everywhere aim'd at your breast,
I saw you serenely give birth to immortal children, saw in dreams your
    dilating form,
Saw you with spreading mantle covering the world.)[34]

Democracy's mantle, for Whitman, is spread by marriage: "The dear love of man for his comrade, the attraction of friend to friend, / Of the well-married husband and wife, of children and parents, / Of city for city and land for land."[35] We see the archetype of marriage expressed in virtually every culture of the world, in every religion, every nation, and most often, the meanings of the marriage symbol are portrayed in grand heterosexual imagery: the royal couple, the king and queen, bride and bridegroom. Yet, under the light of Whitman's Spiritual Democracy, he is the bridegroom of women and the "new husband" of comrades. This is because he has traced the religions of the world to their archetypal source in shamanism, and, as a new American bard, he is called to speak a new revelation of God where the democratic God is to become relative to all others. In 1860, Whitman vocalizes from the religious foundation: "For I say at the core of democracy, finally, is the religious element. All the religions, old and new, are there."[36]

Another exception to the heterosexual convention about marriage may be found in shamanistic societies worldwide, where marriage also takes on a same-sex form. This suggests that the oldest spiritual traditions of the world may be more politically democratic in some indigenous societies than even the newest, because they have the most religious tolerance. A return to this ancient non-discriminatory practice on a societal level, therefore, is really a return to our religious origins. As Whitman correctly observed in this regard: "The primitive poets, their subjects, their style, all assimilate.—Very ancient poetry, of the Hebrew prophets, of Ossian, of the Hindu singers and ecstatics, of the Greeks, of the American aborigines, of the old Persians and Chinese, and the Scandinavian sagas, all resemble each other."[37]

Whitman's view of the relativity of our ways of God corresponds to a sea change in American society in the country's "evolving" (to echo President Obama's word) view toward marriage, as evidenced by growing public acceptance of homosexuality and same-sex marriage's legalization in numerous states. Whitman's putting of his personality on record as a democratic individual who embraced the bi-erotic may have helped to pave the way for the breakthrough to a new moral conviction, for he showed Americans a century and a half ago that speaking up for equal rights can lead to a more peaceful type of war—the War of the great Idea:

> Bards of the great Idea! Bards of the peaceful inventions!
>   (for the war, the war is over!)
> Yet bards of latent armies, a million soldiers waiting ever ready,
> Bards with songs as from burning coals or lightning's fork'd
>   stripes!
> Ample Ohio's, Kanada's bards—bards of California! inland bards—
>   bards of the war!
> You by my charm I invoke.[38]

Whitman's metaphor of bi-erotic marriage applies to the psychological and spiritual unity of all people. What is to emerge in our age of ever-increasing globalization has yet to be seen; nevertheless, Whitman was writing out of a heightened envisioning state of mind that has the longest history on this planet—the archetypal field of the shaman. Because he touched taproot, he arrived at the main thing—singleness of character and integrity: "These States, what are they except myself?"[39]

Whitman *is* America. Because he reached taproot in an archetype that strikes a common chord in the life-ways of all nations, he could take the teachings of the Hebrew and Christian Bibles further: "Low hangs the moon, it rose late, / It is lagging—O I think it is heavy with love, with love."[40] Developmentally we are speaking of the grief of a man in the throes of midlife, here at the age of forty, whose tears evoke the eternal child: "by these tears a little boy again."[41] Thus, the integrity of Whitman's vocation has its origins in his latency, early childhood, and infancy. His integrity is sourced in his loving relationship with his mother Louisa, who was a Quaker, and in his subconscious connection to the land (Paumanok), and in the voice of the he-bird's call in nature.

The problem of humanity, Whitman wrote in *Democratic Vistas*, is "social and religious." The answer to these problems will take the form of literature presented by a modern poet—the "divine literatus." In these states, the function of such a person is to speak to the spirit of the modern (and today we would add postmodern), and the way to do this is to arrive at democracy's living core, namely equal rights, legal rights, civil rights, spiritual rights, and environmental preservation, in the body politic through an archetypal language that accords with nature's intent. "At all times, perhaps the central point in any nation, and that whence it is itself really sway'd the most, and whence it sways others, is its national literature, especially its archetypal poems."[42] By "archetypal," Whitman means poetry that gets at the roots of the body's meanings, nature's meanings, and not only its surface meanings, but its spinal and cosmical meanings: "It must have for its spinal meaning the formation of a typical personality of character, eligible to the uses of high average men—and not restricted by conditions ineligible to the masses."[43] This is the same union of high and low Beebe postulates for the spine of individuals.

The central element that Whitman sees as fit for the states is the "simple, unsophisticated Conscience, the primary moral element."[44] Whitman, exalted, called for American literature and poetry to be incarnated and endowed with "grand and archetypal models—to fill with pride and love the utmost capacity, and to achieve spiritual meanings, and suggest the future—these, and these only, satisfy the soul."[45] What the soul needs and did not have, before Whitman wrote, was a bi-erotic understanding of the soul's body. This is what he intended to supply the new nation and the world in *Leaves of Grass:* "the radical pride of man in himself, (the radical foundation of the new religion.)"[46] But "pride" here doesn't mean the pride "that goeth before the fall," or arrogance, or what today we would call "inflation," but rather radical truth-telling in accordance with the laws of the cosmos, even if it is at times unrelenting, or even ruthless.

Why Whitman felt that "intense and loving comradeship, the personal and passionate attachment of man to man"[47] was so important to the soul, literature, and the United States likely has to do with the fact that here was a man, a son of Long Island, who knew who he was as a whole and upright person, a human being, who had the sense of "absolute Conscience, moral soundness, Justice"[48] to speak to the world in a bardic voice about the need for marital equality, when no other American writers except Herman Melville and Emily Dickinson, his shamanic compatriots, were sounding their own songs. And the aim of such relativity toward God and the changed position of consciousness toward a unitary conscience lead to the same basic aim: human wholeness. Listen again:

> Much is to be said—but I may say here, and in response, that side by side with unflagging stimulation of the elements of religion and conscience must henceforth move with equal sway, science, absolute reason, and the general proportionate development of the whole man.[49]

By ministering to 100,000 sick and wounded soldiers of the North and South, and by confronting a need for political reform in the army medical department and the army's operations as a whole, Whitman took moral responsibility and was accountable for the "evil" he himself was contributing to through the writing of his war poems. Looking back at his poetry after the Civil War, Whitman came to realize that "one deep purpose underlay the others, and has underlain it and its execution ever since—and that has been the religious purpose."[50] Indeed, for Whitman, the calamus grass so integral to *Leaves of Grass* was a religious symbol for God. Not God, as an abstract sense, but God as a living presence: a touch, a breath that filled his body with the spirit of life.

This was such a profound experience for him that he was led to see that the relative positions of God and man had changed. God was no longer superior to man. If God spoke to Whitman in the form of a new metaphor of marriage, that was all he needed. If it came to him from nature, he was satisfied. Nothing could sway him from this emotional truth, because it was his subjective experience, his call to the nations of the world from his place of vista, and his vantage point in the New World. In a notebook entry written during the 1860s called "A Spinal Thought," Whitman says: "The whole scene shifts.—The relative positions change.—Man comes forward, inherent, superb,—the soul, the judge, the common average man advances,—ascends to place.—God disappears."[51] By "Spinal Thought," Whitman means that he's vocalizing thoughts from the "spine" of his emotional personality, his democratic character, his own union of high and low, which is to say from the intent of the cosmos itself to realize spirit in individual bodies. "It almost seems as if poetry with cosmic and dynamic features of magnitude and limitlessness suitable to the human soul, were never possible before."[52] "Cosmic" here means integral, and as climate change is threatening us all, we realize that if we do not dispel our "godlikeness," we all as a species shall surely perish.

As we have seen, during his childhood latency Whitman turned to nature for solace in a United States that had patterned its views toward sexuality on the old conventional stereotypes of the Bible, where the majority were represented but the minority were not. He eventually answered the he-bird's call during the depressions of midlife by writing his own "New Bible." That Walt Whitman could dare to write "Children of Adam" and "Calamus" in 1860 and stick to the ancient path of nature's intent has much to do with the integrity, not only of his mind but of his conscience, which was for him a matter of right feeling. This idea, too, has biblical roots: "Yeah, I know that thou didst this out of the integrity of thy heart" (Genesis 20:6).

It's nothing short of a miracle that Whitman stuck to his moral conviction to stay true to his vocation, and "unstopp'd and unwarp'd by any influence outside the soul within me" asserted in the end: "I have had my say entirely my own way, and put it unerringly on record."[53] This unwavering devotion to his calling is a clear indication of his being untouched by convention, by collective opinion, and by outworn religious laws.

Yet, at the same time, Whitman was among the most religious of American poet-shamans on the verge of the Civil War, and he was being moved by forces in the American psyche that were part of a great groundswell of human history. Whitman was riding the crest of a giant wave that was not without shadow. In an ironical comment about "Calamus," Whitman exclaimed about his homoerotic cluster late in life: "Calamus! Yes, that is Calamus! Profuse, rich, noble, upright, emotional!"[54] Here, again, is the uprightness of character Beebe identified as the hallmark of integrity, and that very uprightness is portrayed in symbol of the Calamus leaf, a new religious symbol for the compact of marriage he shares between himself and all women and men.

To call on the collectivity to realize the inherent self-esteem of each individual is the primary job of the poet, shaman, and psychotherapist. Whitman has amazing integrity in this regard; his poetry extrudes from itself anything that does not belong to it. He listens to his call, which turns out to be the voice of the United States and the world calling for new metaphors of identity, sex, and marriage. These reflections raise an important question about the link between integrity and what he called "works" (vocation). Whitman's poetry reveals his integrity, his uprightness. He took responsibility for what the United States had left out of its Constitution regarding the institution of marriage, and he then created a new institution. As a protector of the self-esteem of American citizens, he was also promoting the moral and spiritual-spinal character of the world's people. He makes clear in his final prose statement that he imagined his poems would be immortalized by the world soul's acceptance of his ideas, which to a great degree has begun to happen.

It would greatly benefit the world's people if Whitman's bi-erotic Spiritual Democracy would inform the integrity of the new globalism. Its roots are already located in shamanism, which is the common root of most of the world's spiritual traditions. This foundation is one to which Whitman assigns the term "Mother of All," unknowingly echoing the ancient Chinese philosopher Laozi in the classic text *Daodejing*, but with a similar intent, to invoke the integrity of the entire cosmos—in the service of personal spiritual breadth.

Beebe compares Eastern and Western conceptions of integrity and arrives at the same conclusion about the recent shifting of the relative attitude toward God: "Both conceptions of integrity [East and West] presuppose a connection with ourselves that permits an ethical connection to everything else in the universe."[55] Integrity in a psychological sense means becoming a carrier of the feeling of wholeness, and this feeling state might be likened to being at a wedding. When we read of Whitman's celebration of the archetype of same-sex "marriage" in the 1855, 1856, 1860, and 1871 editions of his *Leaves,* it is hard not to feel a certain degree of delight, which is, in Beebe's view, the primary emotion that tells us we are living according to nature's intent.[56] Whitman puts it emphatically in section 4 of the poem "I Sing the Body Electric" when he declares: "I do not ask any more delight, I swim in it as a sea."

What Whitman teaches is that bi-erotic imagery belongs to the imagery of the soul; that same-sex love is integral to the individuation process, and that the union of sames forms a necessary stage of spiritual evolution in the integration of the self in all peoples. We'll take up this idea in light of Herman Melville's

Moby Dick, where the recent fall of the national regimes we saw dissolve during the overthrow of entrenched Middle Eastern dictators (Hussein, Mubarak, and Kaddafi, etc.) has parallels in the death of Captain Ahab. At the end of the tale the narrator Ishmael survives by clinging onto his male "wife's" coffin in the sea, and he is able to go on to tell his story.

Part Two

I I

MOBY DICK
The Evolution of a New Myth
for our Times

Myths are typical stories that express the unconscious life of different peoples, cultures, and nations. Sometimes they reach religious heights in their visionary scope. Certain myths are so powerful in their essential core truth that they get outside of individual and national concerns and reach the transnational dimension of the world soul and touch a corresponding chord in the souls of everyone.[1]

Such myths are typically known as the world's great religions, and their founders have left a rich literary legacy that's often expressed in the grand language of poetry.[2] We see this in such literary achievements as the Bhagavad Gita, the *Odyssey*, the *Daodejing*, the Koran, the Zend Avesta, the Old Testament, and the New Testament. Out of such texts, theologies have sometimes arisen that are somewhat different from local creeds. Like *Leaves of Grass* and Dickinson's *Complete Poetry*, Herman Melville's masterwork *Moby Dick* aims at the same universal significance. The story of Captain Ahab and the sailor Ishmael of the whaling ship the *Pequod* constructs a transnational myth that puts forth a vision that includes multireligious, multiethnic, and multicultural symbolisms. It needs to be interpreted psychologically to be understood.

Few read *Moby Dick* (known in Great Britain as *The Whale*) and escape without undergoing some kind of initiation—a figurative Jonah-like ritualistic death followed by rebirth. That indeed is the book's aim. The reader is to be *changed* by it in some way. Ultimately its aim is to lead the reader to an encounter with the self, a transformation, which opens us to the possibility that even God can be changed by a shift in consciousness.

Melville's novel truly offers a myth for our times. Key elements in the story address current global issues. These include themes of:

1. Separation from nature and the animal world, and the current efforts to revive the ecological base of our existence;

2. Shifting from top-down patriarchal myths of domination toward more horizontal, feminine, and earth-based assertions of the wisdom of interdependence;

3. Religious movement away from fundamentalism and creedal theology toward a more unifying Spiritual Democracy;

4. Illumination of the inevitable darkness in humanity to provide a basis for integrating good and evil into our very notions of divinity; and

5. The need for dictatorships to fall, in light of the twin dangers of hubris and the mass destruction of nature, as well as the resulting collapse of freedom that they invariably produce.

It's clear in the minds of many psychological, religious, and literary critics that Melville was writing, and aimed to write, much more than a personal myth that could contain his own complicated psyche. His myth is objective in the sense that it speaks to certain universal concerns that are present today in the conscience of the "Global Village." Melville knew his story would touch a chord in the American psyche, knew that it was multireligious in its spiritual vision, and knew that it sets forth a transnational myth of unity achieved through diversity. For this reason, we have to understand that Melville was not only working through his personal life story of his whale-hunt experiences in the South Pacific in a deeply archetypal way, but trying to tell a universal story of the problem that has plagued humanity for eons—the problem of man's disseverance from "Nature's God," which is the very story of Adam, told in the Old Testament of the Bible. It's this natural God that's symbolized by the great White Whale: Moby Dick himself.

Critics from various fields have noted that Melville was a "prophet"—that he foresaw certain things in the world's future. While he did have a rather prescient view, it's more helpful to examine how various aspects of the myth Melville found speak to our times and to explore how the myth illuminates the aims of Walt Whitman in a way that he, and his feminine counterpart, Emily Dickinson, could not quite articulate. It's helpful, also, to look at Melville's work in terms of the findings of the tradition of analytical psychology, where Melville's work has often been seen as seminal. The connection between analytical psychology and American poetry, Melville's poetry in this case, has provided a basis for an empirical investigation into myth.

Moby Dick is a famously long and dense book. A summary and overview of the book is a helpful place to start in a discussion of Melville's contribution to Spiritual Democracy.

A Synopsis of Moby Dick, Focusing on Ten Basic Elements in the Story

1. *Moby Dick* is a novel about the monomaniacal hunt of an enraged captain of an American whaling ship who obsessively searches for an albino sperm whale, one believed to have been hunted many times over for its bounteous stores of sperm oil. The whale turns out, at the end of the story, to be indestructible, unattainable, and immortal. The captain's name is Ahab, and he is so named after the biblical king of Israel that the "One God" of the Old Testament hated more than any other. The White Whale has its prototype in that ancient text's image of Leviathan-Rahab-Tiamat, the Babylonian sea dragon. Isaiah, the great Hebrew prophet, wrote: "In that day the Lord with his sore and great and strong sword shall punish leviathan the piercing serpent, even leviathan that crooked serpent; and he shall slay the dragon that is in the sea" (Isaiah 27:1); and again: "Was it not thou that didst cut Rahab in pieces, that didst pierce the dragon? Was it not thou that didst dry up the sea, the waters of the great deep; that didst make the depths of the sea a way for the redeemed to pass over?" (Isaiah 51: 9–10) It is important to point out, as we look for contemporary parallels, that whales were the most lucrative source of oil in the nineteenth century, and that the biblical Babylon was located in what is now the southern tip of Iraq.

2. The action of the drama takes place through the eyes of a fictional character who calls himself Ishmael, which is the name of one of the legendary sons of Abraham in the Hebrew Bible. Biblical Ishmael is the spiritual father of monotheism and the main ancestor of the nation of Islam. In chapter 1, Ishmael gives his reasons for going to sea. He writes:

    > *"Grand Contested Election for the Presidency of the United States."*
    > *"WHALING VOYAGE BY ONE ISHMAEL."*
    > *"BLOODY BATTLE IN AFFGHANISTAN."*[3]

    What might this statement about a bloody battle in Afghanistan have meant to Melville? We know that on January 3, 1841, Melville sailed on the whaleship Auschnet out of Fairhaven, Massachusetts, from New Bedford harbor, for the South Pacific. We have no idea if he was moved to do so by any external conflict, such as a battle in Afghanistan, but he was under great internal stress.

3. Ishmael meets a Polynesian whale hunter named Queequeg before the adventure takes place. The two men sleep together like "husband and wife" in the same bed and in a short while they become "bosom friends." Queequeg worships a black ebony idol from Africa, has Polynesian tattoos inscribed all over his body, smokes from a Native American "tomahawk pipe," and observes the highest Muslim religious rite of Ramadan. Thus, Queequeg is simultaneously a polytheist, a pantheist, and a monotheist, and he leads Ishmael to develop respect for "anybody's religious observations."

4. Before the ship sets sail, an old man and an old woman appear to warn Ishmael about the dangers ahead. Their names are Elijah, after the biblical servant of God, who was sent to warn Ishmael of God's wrathful side, and Tistig, a Native American seeress who predicts that the adventure will "prove prophetic"—which, of course, it does. The name of the ship is *Pequod*, so named after the Pequot Indians of the Eastern seaboard who were ruthlessly and violently exterminated by English Puritan settlers.

5. On board the *Pequod*, Ishmael and the ship's crew meet up with Captain Ahab. Ahab's leg, we soon learn, was ripped off by the devouring jaws of the White Whale in a previous battle. Ahab has an elongated scar running down his face to the full length of his body, where lightning hit him during that battle. He walks on an ivory stump, made of whale bone. His dismemberment by the whale occurred off the coast of Japan.

6. Ahab offers a golden doubloon, a Spanish coin, as a reward to anyone who sights the White Whale. Ishmael and the ship's crew make a pact with Ahab to hunt *Moby Dick* to his death. Ahab expresses his deep rage, violence, and hatred toward the White Whale. After the pact to hunt the White Whale has been made, we learn that it was only after Ahab's "torn body and gashed soul bled into one another; and so interfusing," made "him mad," on the homeward voyage, that the "final monomania" hit him.

7. On board the ship, five mysterious phantoms make themselves present prior to the hunt. The central figure is named Fedallah, an Arabic word which means "God's assassin," "ransom," or "sacrifice." The men on

board the *Pequod* begin to suspect that Fedallah is an agent of Satan. He is referred to as the *Parsee*, which means "Persian." Before the hunt for the White Whale begins in earnest, Ahab remembers his previous incarnation as a Zoroastrian fire worshiper. Fedallah becomes the primary instigator of Ahab's fate as a tragic hero.

8. Ishmael refers to Fedallah as "Ahab's shadow." The Parsee prophecies that Ahab will not be buried in the usual manner, and that only "hemp"—rope—can kill him. He prophesizes, furthermore, that Ahab's "hearse" will be immortal.

9. The hunt for the White Whale begins after the mystical sighting of a herd of whales is spotted heading east—toward the sun. The ship arrives at a pod of whale mothers, swimming in concentric circles, with their whale-children nursing delightedly at their breasts.

10. The White Whale is sighted. Ahab and his crew attempt to kill *Moby Dick*. Ahab is caught in a tangle of his own hemp ropes, attached by his harpoon to the back of the immortal White Whale. Ahab is dragged, against his will, to his death, with *Moby Dick* as his hearse. The enraged creature turns its head like a "battering ram" against the *Pequod*, and the ship is sunk. Only Ishmael escapes, on the "life-buoy" of Queequeg's coffin, left like a modern Job to tell his story. It is said in the epilogue that Ishmael was ordained by the Fates to take the place of the Parsee—as Ahab's bowsman—after the Parsee's death. In the final scene, Ishmael is picked up, like just another "orphan," by the cruising ship "Rachael."

In a key chapter, "The Sermon," Father Mapple preaches in New Bedford's whaling chapel before the ship sets sail. The preachers' words illuminate the way in which Melville insists we each must take moral responsibility for correcting for the darkness in humanity and God by speaking out of our own individual conscience. These words provide a sense of the majesty of Melville's postbiblical language in this powerful chapter:

> Jonah, bruised and beaten—his ears, like two sea-shells, still multitudinously murmuring of the ocean—Jonah did the Almighty's bidding. And what was that, shipmates? To preach the Truth to the face of Falsehood! That was it! . . . Woe to him who seeks to please rather than to appall! Woe to him whose good name is more to him than goodness! Woe to him who, in this world, courts not dishonor! Woe to him who would not be true, even though to be false were salvation! . . .

But oh! Shipmates! on the starboard hand of every woe, there is a sure delight; and higher the top of that delight, then the bottom of the woe is deep. Is not the main truck higher than the keelson is low?[4]

Later in "The Sermon," Father Mapple says that by speaking truth he means the art of speaking truth from "one's own inexorable self." This touches on the topic of his myth and its current relevance in the mythopoetic mode of imagination: Speaking truth from one's own individual standpoint, putting forth one's own myth and not a theology is, finally, what *Moby Dick* teaches. Melville's biblical-sounding words express the powerful nature of his *vocation* from the self to speak to the world a truth of his own subjective story for our times.

What feelings or thoughts might the mention of self in "The Sermon" evoke in us today? Readers would do well to take note of what the personal resonance might be in these words as he or she reads this chapter, for delight is surely Melville's way of expressing the same thing as Whitman about the joys of writing poetry, enjoying the ecstasies of love (including, of course, sex), and being in the presence of the beauty of the sea, the coast, and nature.

To set the context for what "The Sermon" is teaching, if we imagine the Pacific Ocean is space, then it is space that creates the breakthrough in moral rigidity to the foundation of individual conscience. The concept of individual conscience was vitally important to the early founding fathers, and it became a kind of touchstone for vocational certitude in American poetry. James Madison, for instance, argued vociferously that individual conscience be part of the Declaration of Independence. By this he meant a personal vocation to speak one's truth, one's essential calling—a sentiment at the heart of Spiritual Democracy.

This basic principle comes through loud and clear in "The Sermon." Father Mapple is a character based on a real person, Father Taylor of the famous Seaman's Bethel in Boston, who had awed Emerson, Whitman, and Melville with his oratory and elocution. Today, when watching director John Huston's 1956 black-and-white movie version of the epic novel, one hears the actor Gregory Peck recite Melville's prophetical lines as Ahab and truly gets an immediate feeling of the power of the voice Melville was channeling through this character. When Peck returns in a 1998 color version of the film, as Father Mapple, the postbiblical language of the Old Testament story of Jonah and the Whale soars when he delivers "The Sermon," and the pure majesty of American English, as the very voice of the self, is even more transcendent than what he had vocalized in the earlier character.[5]

Melville's tracing of the history of religion to its source is both to the God of the Bible, as here with Father Mapple, and also to the "God of Nature," which is referred to in our Declaration of Independence. Later in *Moby Dick*, furthermore, Ishmael assumes the guise of a geologist and speaks to us in a sermon that integrates the natural sciences and religion in a new way.

The whale, symbolized as "Nature's God" is traced to the finds of fossil whales throughout many parts of the world. The paleontological reference deepens our spiritual understanding through connecting us to our ancestral roots. Melville embellishes this image in a myth. By embodying the archetype of a geologist and giving us his scientific credentials, he asserts his aim to encompass all the sciences. This remarkable passage, echoing Humboldt's *Cosmos*, comes from chapter 104 of *Moby Dick*, entitled "The Fossil Whale":

> One often hears of writers that rise and swell with their subject, though it may seem but an ordinary one. How, then, with me, writing of this Leviathan? Unconsciously my chirography expands into placard capitals. Give me a condor's quill! Give me Vesuvius' crater for an inkstand! Friends, hold my arms! For in the mere act of penning my thoughts of this Leviathan, they weary me, and make me faint with their outreaching comprehensiveness of sweep, as if to include the whole circle of the sciences, and all the generations of whales, and men, and mastodons, past, present, and to come, with all the revolving panoramas of empire on earth, and throughout the whole universe, not excluding it suburbs. Such, and so magnifying, is the virtue of a large and liberal theme! We expand to its bulk. To produce a mighty book, you must choose a mighty theme. No great and enduring volume can ever be written on the flea, though many there be who have tried it.[6]

In order to expand to the "bulk" of his "large and liberal theme," Melville encompasses science and religion and magnifies his mighty text. The theme is *Moby Dick*, the whale, as a new symbol for the "Democratic God" that connects us with nature. *Moby Dick*, as a living symbol for Nature's God, requires us to develop an idea equal to him, one that recognized our relationship to the cosmos and at the same time sees the world thus united as holy.

"Ere entering upon the subject of Fossil Whales, I present my credentials as a geologist,"[7] Ishmael says. A geologist! This is a confession of the cosmic project on Melville's part. He's admitting his aim to develop a science of what today we would call "the biosphere," and that in his mind there is no split between science and religion.

Ishmael goes on to say that, during the time of the fossil whale, "the whole world was the whale's; and, king of creation, he left his wake along the present

line of the Andes and the Himmalehs."[8] This passage seems almost to anticipate Whitman's call for "science of God," though there is no evidence that
Whitman was thinking of Melville when he sounded it in 1871. Melville is certainly speaking as a paleontologist when his "geologist" tells us that "Leviathan
left his pre-adamite traces in the stereotype plates of nature."[9] "Pre-adamite"
suggests before Adam, and "king of creation" suggests a prebiblical God. Here
Melville invokes the primeval earth.

It is, therefore, not only the biblical God but the very same biological divinity that was later immortalized by Humboldt and his admiring follower, the
naturalist John Muir. Ishmael's Leviathan existed in an era prior to that of the
Old Testament's Book of Genesis. Its remains are "fossiliferous," and in these
pre-adamite traces, he says ironically, we find "the unmistakable print of his
fin"—a play on the concept of the traditional God of the Bible creating and
shaping the earth.[10] He's taking readers back to a vision that would be captured
in the late twentieth century by American theologian Matthew Fox's Creation
Spirituality—a democratic God-image transcendent of the three monotheisms.
For Melville, however, this spiritual center of unity within diversity could only
be reached through the power and majesty of poetic language.

Ishmael says that the pre-adamic antiquity of the whale, "having been
before all time, must needs exist after all humane ages are over."[11] The belief
expressed here is that the whale species is more durable than humans and will
outlast man. As a "geologist," Ishmael's quarrel with God traces the whale to
pre-adamite sources, back down to the dawn of all creation: the very cosmos—
the spiral galaxy of Cetus, the constellation of the whale!

The vocation of hunting whales is analyzed by Melville further as part of a
split in divinity itself; it's a brutal, butchering sort of business that's destructive
to spirituality. What's more, Ishmael leaves readers to silently worship not in a
synagogue, church, or mosque, but in an "Afric Temple of the Whale" off the
Barbary Coast. In our own time, this is the very region of the Arab Spring: the
coasts of Tunisia, Libya, and Egypt.

Moby Dick attempts to set straight the problem of religion. Nineteenth-
century Christianity, to which he was reacting, had forced Melville to recognize
the problem of the religious head being divorced from the human heart, a condition that was totally unacceptable to him. *Moby Dick* attempts to put us back
in accord with the God of biology: nature. The meaning of the myth is to be
found in its ability to extract from the reader's mind a virus, an infection, a collective epidemic we all share—our hubris, titanic ego inflation, and selfishness
as a species. Our separateness from the sea, from animal life, from the figurative

great Sperm Whale, is civilization's sickness. Ishmael uses it as a God-symbol to confront humanity with its complicity in collective evil and its duty to transform even God in this regard. "It is not surprising," Ishmael asks us to consider, "that some men have been mistaken by the apparently serene orderliness of God-in-Nature and, swept up into hubris, have attempted to blaspheme against it and to set themselves up as antagonists."[12] The only alternative to this was to engage God on the problem of natural evil.

"The Fossil Whale" enables readers to look from Melville's shoulders, or from a scientific-yet-spiritual vista in Humboldt's Andes, to a new notion of divinity, one that leaves out neither the necessity of incarnation nor the unsolved problem of embodied evil that is the task of human individuation to realize and transform. Where Humboldt took "God" out of his empirical investigations of the natural sciences, Melville, Whitman, and Dickinson all put God back in. Melville reminds his readers to silently worship in the "Afric Temple of the Whale": "In this Afric Temple of the Whale I leave you, reader, and if you be a Nantucketer, and a whaleman, you will silently worship there."[13]

A look at the psychological aspects of this view of divinity sheds light on Melville's intent. In an 1896 lecture on exceptional mental states given in Lowell, Massachusetts, William James examined the phenomenon of the witch-hunting epidemic that swept through Bavaria, France, and Cape Cod, Massachusetts. This penetrating investigation might help us better amplify the meaning of the whale hunt in Melville's masterpiece. James showed his audience that the epidemic began in 1250, catalyzed by a widespread belief that, in order to be a witch, one had to make a pact with Satan. The devil's period really began to heat up in 1484, eight years before Colombus's "discovery" of the Americas, with Pope Innocent VIII's issuing of a papal bull (proclamation), which was supportive of investigations against magicians and witches. This was followed by the 1486 publication of the *Malleus Maleficarum*, or Witches' Hammer, a treatise on the prosecution of witches by the German Catholic clergyman Heinrich Kramer. The *Malleus* helped spread the cruel witch-hunting epidemic to France, England, Italy, Ireland, Scotland, Mexico, and North America, especially Salem, Massachusetts, as well as to many other parts of the world. James told his audience: "a curious, gruesome, rathole feeling exuded from it."[14]

This epidemic, of course, was a subject that greatly interested Melville's friend and mentor, Nathaniel Hawthorne. In the witchcraft lecture James looked at the historical evidence of the German Inquisition and determined that most of the women accused of witchcraft were hysterics. Furthermore, he found that the torturers themselves were possessed of a certain morbidity of mind, resembling insanity. James pointed to the repressed sexuality of monks, who, struggling with their own vows of celibacy, projected their own hatred, unlived desires, and stifled impulses onto the female sex and tortured these poor women mercilessly.[15] James asserts, in words echoing Melville's: "There is no worse enemy of God and man than zeal armed with power and guided by a feeble intellect."[16]

Yet, Melville was far ahead of his times with regards to his own prepsychological investigations into this witch-hunting epidemic. Melville's astute analysis of this frenzied plague goes deeper than any historical look; it's a searing critique of all creeds, all fundamentalist religions, and all theologies, including Hinduism, Buddhism, Islam, Judaism, and Christianity. The split from Nature's God is depicted in an aberrant attitude of God himself toward his own creation, namely God's disdain for Leviathan, his *Chaoscampf* (chaos fight), in the Old Testament. This split from Nature's God is personified most demoniacally by Ahab, who lords over the whale from his "dictatorship" aboard the ill-fated *Pequod*.

The union of high and low that Melville himself espoused is critical. Ahab's supreme arrogance is an aspect of the American self, as well as of all world religions and nations of the globe. Melville capitalizes on this in the chapter called "Sunset," where Ahab is said to have the "high perception," but lacks the "low enjoying power":

> This lovely light, it lights not me; all lovliness is anguish to me, since I can ne'er enjoy. Gifted with the high perception, I lack the low, enjoying power; damned, most subtly and most malignantly! Damned in the midst of Paradise![17]

Ahab lacks a connection to emotion and sexuality, to eros and to human warmth. He is all head and no heart, like the German prosecutors who tortured women accused of witchcraft. It is this blackness that Melville sets out to illuminate for us in order to enlighten us on the problem of the projection of the human shadow. *Moby Dick* attempts to set straight the problem of religion that is at its roots the problem of our heads divorced from our hearts, our dissociation from the very core of our human survival drive: our basic instincts. Melville came full circle to include all the sciences in his vision of harmony and unity.

Melville was reading Fredrick Douglass's slave narrative shortly before he wrote his masterwork. This influence leaves its mark on *Moby Dick* in sections of the novel where African American music shines through beautifully particularly in words by thirteen-year-old Pip, who plays his spangling tambourine in full glory while dancing a jazzy jig for the whalers on board the ship. As Sterling Stuckey writes:

Melville's use of music—within the context of dance—in Moby Dick is one of his most remarkable literary achievements. Inspired by *Narrative of the Life of Fredrick Douglass*, he creates characterizations, dialogue, and story lines that are shaped in part by the music of the *Narrative*, and more generally by his understanding of the importance of music and dance to black culture.[18]

Pip, caught up in the beauty of his own joy, music making, and dancing, presents a vision of a person whose head and heart are united in harmony—a sharp contrast to the stern, violent, and emotionally vengeful Ahab.

We've seen that Melville's work touches on the theme of *personal* religion—which dovetails with Jung's idea of finding one's subjective myth as an antidote to fundamentalist religion. Melville makes his stand, in part, by choosing his characters' names carefully, in line with the very foundations of Western and Middle Eastern religions and modernity, such as the name of young Pip, which means a small seed of a fruit, or the action of breaking through the shell of a seed or egg in hatching. The boy's name is a prescient synonym for what was about to happen as a cultural breakthrough in the form of unequivocal ethnic, racial, and cultural equality between blacks and whites, as justification and vindication for the unalienable rights of the democratic self.

Other monikers were strategically picked based on actual personages from the Bible: Ishmael, Elijah, Rachael, and so on. "Ahab," in particular, is a very complex name and character. The captain is named after a reviled Old Testament character, the hated Hebrew king, and in *Moby Dick* he represents a slew of negative characteristics and historic atrocities: the Inquisition, the Crusades, Indian hating, Islamophobia, colonization, industrialization, the market economy, Manifest Destiny, and the institution of slavery in the American South.

Ahab's relationship with the Islamic figure Fedallah is highly significant, particularly in light of world events. Fedallah is also called the Parsee after the Parsee religion of followers of Zarathustra who were chased from Persia to India under Islamic persecution. Fedallah is a religious fundamentalist, and radically Islamic. The Melville scholar Dorothee Finkelstein traced his character back to the Fedayeen, or Muslim assassins, who Melville was reading about from 1849 to 1850.

The pairing of Ishmael and Queequeg, on the other hand, is not governed by fundamentalism, but rather by religious freedom and multispiritual rituals and practice. Thus, democratic freedom and fundamentalism form a complementary pair to each other. So do slavery, Indian-hating and the Judeo-Christian aversion to Islam. Ishmael's calling to vocation is captured in the following famous lines from the first chapter in *Moby Dick*, "Loomings": "Who aint a slave? Tell me that." His solution to the problem of the monotheisms is homoerotic and Sufi—brotherhood between the nations, love and peace, not hatred: "all hands should rub each other's shoulder-blades, and be content."[19]

In the chapter entitled "The Candles," we hear about the phenomenon of St. Elmo's fire, or *corpusants,* a weather phenomenon in which brilliantly lit plasma is created in a strong electric field in the atmosphere, and sometimes upon the masts of ships at sea. Sailors often regarded these light displays as the descent of the Pentecostal fire—or the Holy Spirit upon the ship. "Look aloft," cries the young chief mate Starbuck, "The corpusants! The corpusants!" and second mate Stubb, too, says in fright: "The corpusants have mercy on us all!"[20] In Christianity, Pentecost is a time the Holy Spirit comes down closest to humanity, and it's meaningful that this incident occurs during the penultimate passage where Melville has Ahab speaking in a transnational voice, in many religious tongues. "The Candles" anticipates Jung's dictum in chapter three that the aim of individuation is *making the darkness conscious.* In "The Candles," Melville shows that the confrontation with evil is the masterpiece of the process of integrating diverse elements of the personal and cultural psyche into a higher synthesis of world peace and conscious self-realization—individuation—as a transcultural phenomena.

In the final actions of the story, and with the aid of Fedallah as an incarnation of the dark side of the Islamic deity, Ahab accepts his tragic fate. Ahab's alignment with Fedallah, and Ahab's fall from power into the depths of the ocean, has parallel in the fall of dictatorships worldwide. The descent of the Holy Spirit coinciding with the toppling of malevolent regimes points to the death and rebirth of religion, especially all three monotheisms as they have been previously believed in by fundamentalists, as separate from the one God of religious freedom and enlightenment, offered through the vehicle of worldwide compassion.

As we have seen, Melville brings something into the American mythos that we cannot find anywhere else in world religions regarding the emergence of Spiritual Democracy as a global phenomenon. With few notable exceptions, Melville appears to be in his own original field when he speaks about evil and the shadow as aspects of divinity. In "The Candles," for instance, Ahab calls himself a "true child of the fire," and in using this term he is defying Allah and the traditional Christian trinity of Father, Son, and Holy Spirit. This self-reference reveals his contamination by the archetype of the *children of Satan* in the Koran: the "companions of the fire," or "people of the fire"—suggesting the evil, unworthy people who shall burn in hell. Ahab's too-close contact with Fedallah has so infected him with this anti-Islamic archetype that he has become a fire-breathing Ibliss: "O, thou clear spirit, of thy fire, thou madest me, and like a true child of the fire, I breathe it back to thee."[21]

Taken literally by anyone who lacks a grounding in comparative religions, pragmatism, analytical psychology, or Creation Spirituality, the Koran could be naively taken as a "Book which cannot be doubted" (Sûrah 2:2), and the people of the fire as infidels (or *kafirun*), disbelievers whose "sight is dimmed and a terrible punishment awaits them" (Sûrah 2:7). "Deaf, dumb, and blind; they shall never return" to the right path of Allah (Sûrah 2:18). "The lightning takes away their sight; when it flashes they walk on, but when it darkens they stand still" (Sûrah 2:18). Such references from the Koran were probably on Melville's mind when he wrote "The Candles," for they appear to form the guiding motif for Ahab's speech where he says defiantly:

> Thou canst blind; but I can then grope. Thou canst consume; but I can then be ashes. Take the homage of these poor eyes, and shutter-hands. I would not take it. The lightning flashes through my skull; mine eyeballs ache and ache; my whole beaten brain seems as beheaded, and rolling on some stunning ground. Oh, oh! Yet blindfolded, yet will I talk to thee. Light though thou be, thou leapest out of darkness; but I am darkness leaping out of light, leaping out of thee! . . . Through thee, thy flaming self, my scorched eyes do dimly see.[22]

Fire, lightning, and being struck by blindness are also metaphors for divine punishment that hark back to the Old Testament of the Bible, as in 2 Kings 6:18 where the loyal servant Elisha prays to God to smite the Syrians with blindness, shortly after the death of Ahab in 1 Kings 22:35. What the American Ahab is saying, however, is that through such divine cruelties he dimly sees God's shadow. This shadow, in all three of the major monotheistic religions—Judaism, Christianity, and Islam—is darkened by violence, hate, and war among nations, as well as violence against the sea and nature itself.

Ahab's mental state is highly dangerous. For just prior to Ahab's scene quoted above, the Parsee is said to be kneeling beneath a Spanish coin, a golden doubloon, in front of Ahab, and at this moment Ahab puts his foot on Fedallah, while his left hand is situated on the "lofty tri-pointed trinity of flames"—imagery invoking the Satanic.[23] Melville, as Ahab, says further, again in anticipation of Jung: "I know that of me, which thy knowest not of thyself, oh, thou omnipotent."[24] Ahab's attitude toward Muslim fundamentalism is one that is gripped unconsciously by evil rather than transforming it by reflecting on it as an aspect of his own personal and national character. Thus, by pursuing the White Whale to his death, he becomes, in his monomaniacal hubris, a jihadist against the great democratic "God," Moby Dick.

But Melville is not renouncing the God, who needs the gnosis, the knowledge of self, of human consciousness. Thus, as well as declaring that he is *darkness leaping out of light* (in essence the shadow side of God in all three monotheisms leaping into consciousness of itself), Ahab is saying that he possesses superior knowledge over the all-masculine divinity because he is fighting a fated battle on behalf of the American self for the inclusion of the feminine face of God, which is found in the roots of human spirituality. All religions, including polytheism, paganism, and Hinduism, can be traced, to the ancient Goddess religions, which embraced the inherent divinity of nature.

Fedallah and Ahab in this sense are mirror images of each other. Ahab is determined to become a world ruler, like Suleiman the Magnificent, Genghis Khan, or Tamerlane. Ahab with his foot on the Parsee, in front of a golden doubloon, suggests moreover, the conquests of South and Central American tribes by the Spanish conquistadores, as well as our present day America's potential for world domination. Ahab's pact with Fedallah is just as problematic when we consider the same potential for the West's exploitation of oil, or fossil fuels, feeding the current clash of frenzied civilizations anxiously vying for hegemony in the Middle East, with the reprojection of evil coming out of radical Muslim groups as an unconscious response to what president George W. Bush outrageously and deceptively called "a crusade against evil" prior to the U.S. invasion of Iraq. Ahab and Fedallah form a shadowy pair that illuminates the evil side of God, when seen as part of a new transnational mythos that is striving to be included into the divine totality of a transformed, more conscious, more inclusive, and finally more compassionate godhead.

Melville realized, after he returned from his four-year voyage on a whaling ship to the South Seas at the age of twenty-five, that he possessed a calling, a vocation. He wanted to bring attention to the massacre and depletion of the great ocean-dwelling mammals. Today, environmental groups such as the Sea Shepherd Conservation Society and Greenpeace fight to stop Japanese whaling vessels from killing these grand cetaceans. Yet, it took a collective movement spanning decades to arrive at a moment where killing whales is regarded as immoral by millions of people around the world. In the early 1850s, Melville must have realized there was nothing he could do to stop such an epidemic of slaughter—except write a mighty book. The power was in his pen: his condor's quill. It's been said that the greatest weapon against evil in human history is the pen—and the word. This is what Father Mapple teaches: the necessity of following the way of vocation, of speaking out.

This form of vocalism is also what Melville accomplished in his novels *Mardi and a Voyage Thither* and *Moby Dick*. He spoke to a collective need for a new myth that he knew includes what nineteenth-century Christianity excluded from human consideration as essentially ungodly—namely the feminine, the often homoerotic as well as heteroerotic body, Islam, and evil. He took on the creeds, theologies, and religions of the world and showed us that the main problem with humanity is our power-driven inflation—our arrogance—as nations.

In "The Fossil Whale" chapter, Ishmael encompasses a vision not only of human history but of the whale, and of the stars, which are embodied in the constellation of Cetus. This is Spiritual Democracy, the attempt to unify all world religions in a new spiritual vision that is inclusive of Humboldt's cosmos. We are all, to some degree, interdependent on one another on this beautiful green-blue planet spinning in space. To discover the *gold* of the feminine, the "Mother of All," for ourselves and others, we must remain modest in our religious attitudes.

What all three of our American poets—Melville, Whitman, Dickinson—teach is that the aim of the mythopoetic imagination is self-reflection, as the ultimate expression of what is divine in us, and of our capacity to become more conscious. To let the golden light of the cosmos shine through, the ego must work to make the darkness of the unconscious personality—the Ahab-Fedallah in us—conscious, and bring it into the light of day. And if shadow is not made self-aware, there can be no light and peace. By contrast, Ahab is *darkness and violence leaping out of light*. By bringing Ahab's image to mid–nineteenth century America, Melville opens our national consciousness to its potential for evil. Today, we can read his urgent myth as an impetus toward the Spiritual Democracy Whitman was calling for at the same time. Melville was Whitman's dark twin, and they are the Dioscuri of American poetry, still lighting our way to a greater wisdom than the arrogant inclinations of Manifest Destiny.

Moby Dick strides beyond all national mythologies to embrace the collective psyche—the world soul—of perennial philosophy, uniting the great chain of being and touching a potential chord of feeling in the whole human race. What the myth reveals for our times is what we are seeing in many parts of the Middle East today. People there are getting fed up with arcane, oppressive governments and are valiantly attempting to overthrow dictatorships. Their speaking up for equal rights is a way to make manifest the sacred activism that may bring the light of Spiritual Democracy to all people.

12

HERMAN MELVILLE
The Quest for Yillah

The central meaning of Herman Melville's third book, *Mardi and a Voyage Thither,* formed the background for *Moby Dick* and became the very symbol of Spiritual Democracy. This symbol is made luminous through the medium of poetry, a vehicle for carrying Melville and his readers into the realms of religious experience.

The perception of such a transporting experience is sensed by a "tingling" that Melville believed only true poetry can convey. He understood that not everyone who reads his work will experience such a feeling—but that was his aim. Translated into the language of analytical psychology, such tingling feelings are sensations in response to the presence of not-yet-embodied archetypes "accorded" to "the Romancer & Poet."[1] These are best described as indices of spiritual experiences, what comparative religion scholar Rudolph Otto in 1917 called "The Idea of the Holy." Such tingling in the face of the numinous and magical is an empirical event that many poets have described. Spiritual experiences also occur during psychological treatment in what William James and Carl Jung call "exceptional psychic states,"[2] such as during the writing of poetry.

In "The Conjunction," the final chapter of the *Mysterium Coniunctionis,* Jung argues that all theologians, no matter what denominations or religious creeds they represent, claim their standpoint represents the metaphysical truth about which there can be no argument. Not only do these zealous representatives of organized religions insist that their particular brand of faith is "the only true one, and, on top of this, that it's not merely a human truth, but the truth directly inspired and revealed by God. Every theologian speaks simply of 'God,' by which he intends it to be understood that his 'god' is the God."³ But, as Jung wisely points out, these are all only images of "God," formed by archetypal emanations. (Walt Whitman, drawing on the Greek concept of apparition or phantom, called them "eidólons.") These God-images, Jung said, can be empirically demonstrated in the human psyche in ways that are common to all people everywhere.

To counter this tendency, Jung asserts that the human psyche is structured by a multiplicity of God-images, and any one may presume to represent the central archetype of wholeness in the human personality, which is the "self." In a more modest view, they all form part and parcel of the "One" that dwells within all of them, the transcendental background, or the cosmos. The alchemical hypothesis of the unus mundus, the "one world," postulates a unitary world inside and outside the psyche, where what is common to every individual is the experience of the self. In alchemy this is known as the lapis, philosophical gold, or philosopher's stone—symbolizing wholeness. Thus, what makes all religions equivalent is their common shared experience in the archetype of wholeness.

This notion of religion, which is so clearly derived from William James's *Varieties of Religious Experience*, is in many ways an American one, despite Jung's own Swiss Protestant background, for it is exactly what Walt Whitman and Herman Melville and Emily Dickinson arrive at in their visions of Spiritual Democracy.

The equality of all religions suggests that what is valid in the human psyche, as the medium of religious experience, is the common factor of the self in all religions. As we've seen, in Spiritual Democracy all religions are valid in their own individual way, but none represents the absolute metaphysical truth. Melville captures the meaning of the numinous notion of God in a flourish of poetic versification in *Mardi*, and it is to this third novel in his canon that we turn to construct the literary background for *Moby Dick*.

The story of *Mardi* is essentially a romance, a symbolic quest undertaken by the main character of the novel, Taji, and his three traveling companions, Mohi, Babbalanja, and Yoomy, who are all in search of an elusive feminine figure called Yillah. While Yillah is never attained in the end, many dreams, visions, and mystical experiences happen to the four roaming companions, who are all transformed in consciousness during the quest for her. The name Yillah, in fact, just so happens to be the Arabic word for God, the divine absolute—Allah—or, in incantation "La ilaha illa-llah" ("There is no God but God").⁴

The fact that all four male characters are in search of an other-than-masculine aspect of the divine suggests that there's a need for integration of the feminine face of God in religious experience if Spiritual Democracy is to be complete. This is the object of Melville's quest in *Mardi*. Because its main aim is to unveil the feminine face of divinity, the meaning of the quest is to arrive at a more democratic whole. These visions of cosmic seeing, where inner and outer worlds coalesce, are experiences that widen the horizon of Melville's consciousness, as well as his readers' consciousness, toward a one-world-notion of Spiritual Democracy that has its roots in Judaism (with the deity of Shekinah), Christianity (Christ), and Sufism (Yillah). One cosmos or transcendental background of experience moves through *Mardi*, traveling toward greater vistas of spiritual relativity in a psyche transcending all creeds—a democratic truth telling that is equalizing at its empirical core. This is also the illuminative consciousness Melville brings to his greatest novel, *Moby Dick*. The method used by Melville to achieve such vistas in *Mardi* is mythopoetic.

Like Melville's first two novels, *Typee* and *Omoo*, *Mardi* brings forth the illuminative theme of the revitalization of Christianity by the incorporation of primitive, pagan, and primal elements from Polynesian culture into a superstructure of a postmonotheistic conscience that includes the body, the feminine, and good and evil. The book melds them into a God-concept capable of holding all religious tensions together on an equalizing plane. However, what Melville adds at this point in his religious visioning is a portrait of divinity that actually centers on the evolution of the God-image in Islam and its final synthesis with a post-Christian and post-Hebrew vision that is transcendent of any of the limitations of the three major patriarchal monotheisms—Judaism, Christianity, and Islam.

Melville's chief concern in the writing of *Mardi* is the discovery of a technique of free verse in preparation for a "flight" that will give birth, in *Moby Dick*, to a notion of Spiritual Democracy transcendent of nationality. Melville puts forth his realization of this necessity in a letter from January of 1848: "Well: proceeding in my narratives of facts I began to feel an invincible distaste for the same; & a longing to plume my pinions for a flight, and felt irked, cramped & fettered by plodding along with dull common places."[5] We have to grasp the enormous significance of this realization that occurred for Melville shortly before the California Gold Rush of 1849, for what he was creating in *Mardi* is the foundation for a new alchemy of the West, an imaginary method to "cruise" in free verse after a "gold moidores, the Cachalot"—or sperm whale—"whose brain enlightens the world."[6]

For Melville, the career of a travel writer was simply not enough to lead him to the life of the whole man, the man he knew himself capable of being, with all of his psychic functions in conscious operation. He longed for what Jung would later call the "constellation" of the self, a phenomenon that is the *sine qua non*, the essential element, of personal individuation—the process by which the unique self develops out of the undifferentiated unconscious. It's a voyage whose realization is never entirely completed, yet, there is a way, a path, that can accelerate its manifestation, and if one remains true to this track, the gathering up of one's energies may be increased so that the realization of self may be quickened.

The philosopher's stone, gold, or alexipharmic that Melville sought for his psychic healing in the writing of *Mardi* was mythopoetic, and as such it provided a pathway for anyone who employs a literary technique to achieve wholeness. He needed poetry to create a golden world for himself and for readers, and free verse provided him with a key. For the reader of this book, writing itself, in the way Whitman taught it in "vocalism," as the release of the divine power to speak words, may become, as Melville illustrated before him, a practical method to incarnate Spiritual Democracy.

During the writing of *Mardi*, as Melville began to slip the moorings of conventional narrative for the freedom provided through the method of free verse, he left his safe and "sane" haven as a travel writer and began to venture more courageously, like Whitman in his notebooks, into the deep-sea waters of the collective unconscious, the Pacific. Also like Whitman, he was in search of a panacea that could cure the world of its religious quarrel concerning the metaphysical nature of the divine. By allowing for the divine immanence in everyone, he transcended all the theological arguments of the earth.

Like Jung, who recognized the unity of all religions in a psychoid realm of possible religious experience transcending all creeds, Melville sought the universal remedy, or philosophical gold, or *medicina catholica* in "one cosmos" that, as Jung asserts, is in fact "a *unus mundus*."[7] The echoes of Alexander von Humboldt's grand vision in *Cosmos* here are clear, though it's likely they came back to Europe and Jung through the latter's reading of William James's work. For Melville, this unitary world of the alchemical opus forms an experience of what Jung calls the "transcendental psychophysical background" of all empirical knowing, by which he means an objective cognition of the world of matter and spirit via the careful observation of meaningful coincidences, or synchronicities, that cross our paths in our everyday encounters with the chance linkages between inner and outer reality.[8] This is made self-luminous in the title he chose for *"Mardi,"* a word he repeatedly refers to as the "world."

When Abrazza, one of Melville's fictional characters in *Mardi*, asks the philosopher-poet Babbalanja why the historian Lombardo would "choose a vehicle so crazy" as poetry, Babbalanja replies: "It was his nature, I suppose."[9] This is as pragmatic a justification for poetry as a vehicle for individuation as we can find. Natural individuation is a risk, a spiritual adventure, and a vocation well worth taking when the results are the attainment of a vision of a self-realized human being. Undertaking this precarious endeavor is likely Melville's aim in the writing of *Mardi*.

If indeed the "common background of microphysics and depth-psychology is as much physical as psychic and therefore neither, but rather a third thing, a neutral nature which can at most be grasped in hints since its essence is transcendental"[10] then it is highly possible, even probable, that Melville penetrated into this background of the empirical world of the unus mundus during the writing of *Mardi*. The pragmatic evidence for this is that there are literary references that exist between Melville's writing of *Mardi* and the writing of *Moby Dick* that show with increasing regularity that the "balsam or elixir of life, as a life-promoting, strengthening, and rejuvenating magical potion" was becoming abundantly present in his writing. As Jung has shown, alchemical symbols for the "desired realization of the whole man" could lead the adept—and in this case Melville—to the "healing of organic and psychic ills,"[11] and such therapy was beginning to manifest itself increasingly through the vehicle of his vocation as he moved toward a more all-encompassing vision of the world and broke through, in each consecutive chapter of his whaling novel, into the unus mundus. As Melville was writing *Mardi*, he was also reading the mystical literature of the Talmud, a Jewish mystical text where the Holy Spirit is represented as the Shekinah, the form of divine immanence, or indwelling Glory of God. He was also reading the mystical poetry of the great Sufi masters, as well as the *Narrative of the Life of Fredrick Douglass*, which gave him his idea for the African spirituality of the on-deck "Circle Dance" in chapter 40, "Midnight," of *Moby Dick*.[12] Clearly, he is seeing the unitary threads of the Divine in all of these religions.

Critics have noted that writing *Mardi* changed Melville's life from that of a travel writer to a literary genius, yet few critics have commented on the role of poetry, romance, and music in his transition from prose writer to the author of *Moby Dick*. In *Mardi* we can hear the music. In the novel, Melville makes evident the notion of Spiritual Democracy through the writing of poetry, not prose, and poetry becomes Melville's vehicle to lead him to the unitary world. The one truth of the unus mundus—Spiritual Democracy—is the main truth in *Mardi*. This is not a new metaphysical truth to be proselytized throughout the world but a subjective truth that is as much psychological as it is religious, because it's based upon an empirical ground of self-realization of an all-encompassing nature beyond the ego and its individual concerns, with its tragic fate and its consequences. The destiny of the self is an individual realization and can only be grasped in clues.

As we've seen, mardi simply means "the world." Not the outer world or the inner world within Melville, but the third thing, the unitary world. The aim of religious experience through the writing of *Mardi* is to arrive, not at the conventional truths of religious creeds, but at the one emergent truth of "round *Mardi*," with Vivenza (North America) as the "new *Mardi*."

That this is also a quest for universal truth in *Mardi* is made clear by the narrator, Taji, whose name in Arabic means "my crown." Taji could be compared to Jung's prince in a dream the psychotherapist wrote about.[13] During his travels to Tunis in 1920, Jung dreamed of a "handsome, dark Arab" who attacked him and tried to knock him down. The two men "wrestled," and, after falling into a moat, the Arab man tried to drown Jung. Jung then turned the Arab over and pushed his head under water, but eventually let the man go out of compassion. The men entered an octagonal room together in the center of a citadel, and on the floor was an open book with black letters written in magnificent calligraphy, on milky-white parchment. Jung had a religious feeling that it was his book; he had written it. The young man sat to Jung's right on the floor, and Jung forced him to read his book. Jung then says he knew in the dream that it was "absolutely essential" that the man read his book. The young man's attempts to kill Jung, was seen, moreover, as an "echo of the motif of Jacob's struggle with the angel."[14] Today it's important to reflect on these historical parallels to understand the meaning of Jung grappling with the shadow of the self in Islam. Whatever branch of Islam the prince may have arisen from in the Muslim world, this emissary of the self is religious in nature and is patterned upon a fundamentalist split in the Persian God-concept underneath. Jung's "making friends" with the shadow of the self in Islam calls us to fill in the missing cultural pieces, as it pertains to the present ongoing crisis in the Middle East.

In conjunction with his three traveling companions, all of whom bear Islamic names—Mohi, Baballanja, and Yoomy—the protagonist Taji leads the quest for Yillah, whose name, as we've seen, is the Muhammadan word for God inscribed as feminine. The central figure in the narrative, however, is the character Yoomy, who wears a turban with a bird-of-paradise feather as its plume.[15] Yoomy is a Persian poet, and in this sense he represents an archetype in the collective psyche that Melville was in touch with during his experiments with free verse. This archetype is the carrier of a "Romance of Polynesian Adventure,"[16] a marriage of two cultures.

Sufism is the inner, mystical dimension of Islam. It's an elaborate system of esoteric knowledge and symbolism, of wine, light, flowers, and of mystical love for the beloved, and it asserts that its central doctrine may be found in every religion of the world. So it was from Sufi poets like Hafiz that Melville drew deep and lasting inspiration. His aim was to use poetry to promote a unitary vision of God that could show that "Polynesia," like mystical Islam, provides "a great deal of rich poetical material" that had "never been employed hitherto in works of fancy." Such great richness was the subject of what Melville called a *"real romance"* that "is no *Typee* or *Omoo*, & is made of different stuff altogether."[17] In chapter 119 of *Mardi*, entitled "Dreams," Melville writes:

> Like a grand, ground swell, Homer's old organ rolls under the light frothy wave-crests of Anacreon and Hafiz; and high over my ocean, sweet Shakespeare soars, like all the larks of spring. . . . In me, many worthies recline, and converse. . . . Zoroaster whispered me before I was born. I walk a world that is mine; and enter many nations, as Mungo Park rested in African cots; . . . Yet not I, but another: God is my Lord; and though many satellites revolve around me, I and all mine revolve round the great central Truth, sun-like, fixed and luminous forever in the foundationless firmament. Fain would I hurl off this Dionysius that rides me.[18]

Taji, then, is a gentle warrior on behalf of this cosmic vision, and he is rather like one of King Arthur's knights on a legendary grail quest. This Persian prince or "emir" becomes the central vehicle for Melville's vocation as a questing poet who begins to subsume many religious archetypes (Homer, Hafiz, Zoroaster, Milton, Shakespeare, Dionysius, African Ashanti dance music, etc.) in his search for one corresponding image of the feminine face of the divine as the foundationless firmament of the cosmos. Yoomy, who is named after Jami, the last of the truly great classical poets of Persia, sings ecstatic verses throughout the novel, and this pronounced character is clearly Sufi.[19] Thus, as Melville pressed poetically ever deeper into the creative depths and heights of the psyche, to the central truth, the same truth of Spiritual Democracy that had spoken to Whitman and to Dickinson was revealed to him—the oneness of all religions. This is nothing other than a vision of what Jung would later call "the self," the generative center of all human individuation, including that of poets. As Babbalanja says about the poet-philosopher, Lombardo, who "got deeper and deeper into himself": "I have created the creative."[20]

The crown Melville sought after writing *Mardi* was not the ordinary cap of occupations but the spiritual coronet of his creative genius: his vocation to the music of the spheres, his muse to poetry. Melville arrives at truths in *Mardi* that are illuminating psychologically because they point to the central factor of religious experience without which the self could never be made known—namely, the otherwordly tingling sensation. The philosopher-poet seems to indicate that this feeling-sensation is a numinosity that can be felt from sole to crown. When Babbalanja asks the youthful poet, Yoomy: "Did you tingle, when that song was composing?" Yoomy replies, "All over, Babbalanja." "From sole to crown?" Babbalanja asks. "From finger to finger," Yoomy answers.

In this dialogue, two aspects of Melville's personality—the soaring poet and the deep-diving poet-philosopher—are working together in tandem to convey to the reader that religious experiences have little to do with creeds and more to do with mystical experiences that link together the common effects of the unconscious on all of us. The surest indicator of religious experience is not denominational religion but the instinctive apprehension of the self, or what Melville's character Babbalanja calls "self-tingling": "For this self-tingling," Babbalanja says, "is the test" of true poetry. "And infused into a song," Yoomy says, "it evermore causes it so to sparkle, vivify, and irradiate, that no son of man can repeat it without tingling himself." Babbalanja begins to get at the very heart of the principle of Spiritual Democracy here: the notion of the one unitary world, the self, can only be realized through the ego because the only vehicle for religious experience is to be found within individuals, never in creeds. Melville is clear on this point when he says: "As the sun, by influence divine, wheels through the Ecliptic; threading Cancer, Leo, Pisces, and Aquarius; so, by some mystic impulse I am moved."[21] In the Aquarian Age, our own era, the archetype of the self reigns supreme over all creeds.

Moved by the music of the spheres, Melville says, "Oh, reader, list! I've chartless voyaged," and then adds, "But this new world here sought" is "the world of mind; wherein the wanderer may gaze round, with more of wonder than Balboa's band roving through the golden Aztec glades."[22] The mystic impulse is an instinctive reality in the human psyche. It's an urge for self-realization in every individual, and for Melville, as for Whitman and Dickinson, poetry provides the key. The "new world" of golden verses he discovered, the Polynesian world of *real* romancing, is not to be found in some religion external to the self, for it all exists in the natural world of mind: *the mine of gold within*. This is the world of instinctive truth that he feels will prevail when the world's religions are made equal in a paradise of diversity.

In the following lines Melville gets at the heart of Spiritual Democracy, which is to become and then to show our own worlds: "Ego is the key," the philosopher-poet notes, "and all mankind are egotists. The world revolves upon an I; and we upon ourselves; for we are our own worlds; . . . let us show our worlds," he says. Yoomy then answers: "Of all mortals, we poets are most subject to contrary moods. Now, heaven over heaven in the skies; now layer under layer in the dust. This, the penalty we pay for being who we are . . . all our agonies operate unseen. Poets are only seen when they soar."[23]

One might be tempted to diagnose this spiritual moodiness as a bipolar illness in Melville, just as in Whitman we might speak of hypomania. Yet, the contrary cyclothymic moods he is describing in the Persian-Polynesian poet, Yoomy, are much more than a psychiatric condition, for such moodiness has many historical antecedents in the Sufi tradition. Such split moods need to be understood as stages in the apprehension of God, who discloses Himself by turns of emotion as wonderful as they are terrible, not as an indication of literal madness. Spiritual Democracy has a long history in the world, and the genius of Melville is that he traced the history of the "new Mardi" to the Middle East and Africa. Melville saw what Jung saw when he stared into the fathomless foundation of the spirit of the depths. As Babblanja says: "The essence of all good and all evil is in us, not out of us."[24] But what is in us, finally, is God.

Because the self is brighter and darker than the ego, Jung says, the task of self-realization "confronts it with problems it would like to avoid,"[25] by which he means moral conflicts. In Melville's case this created the problem of acknowledging that the essence of all good and all evil is in us, not out of us—nothing short of a millennial undertaking in an age of Spiritual Democracy. Melville became a victim of a decision to speak the truth of good and evil that was made over his head and in defiance of his heart. The numinous power of the self had him in its grip, and there was little that he could do to free himself from his duty except to speak the truth as it was dictated to him. "For this reason," Jung says "the experience of the self is always a defeat for the ego."[26]

The immense good that came from Melville's reading of the *Arabian Nights*, Zoroastrianism, and Sufi poetry, and Frederick Douglass's musically inspired *Narrative* came at a cost. The previously unconscious conflict that he'd begun to wrestle with during his attempts to create a narrative portrait of the "new Mardi" for the United States was brought to the surface in the realization about good and all evil: *It is in us, not out of us.* This awareness of the reality of good and evil existing in all people and in all religious personalities imposed upon his consciousness a heavy responsibility, as *it,* Melville's ego consciousness, was now expected to solve the conflict that the transcendentalists had avoided: the problem of the inclusion of the body, the feminine, the homoerotic, and nature into a God-concept more all-subsuming than any of the three monotheisms because it includes a healthy respect for the human shadow and for evil in all religions. Melville appears to have known that he would be defeated in speaking his truth because this perception did not hit on a consensus of opinion during his lifetime, as it was not yet "in the air," even though it was "spoken from the heart."[27] In the Bible, Mark 3:21, it's said by friends and family of Jesus of Nazareth that "He is beside himself." The same would be said about Melville. The experiences of the divine that Melville describes in *Mardi* during his dialogues with the poet Yoomy and Babbalanja and his other companions "happened" to him and he became, as it were, their "willing or unwilling victim."[28]

Certainly Melville became isolated after his failed attempt at a great and good friendship with Nathaniel Hawthorne. We find little evidence of any effort to connect with the other great American writers of his day—no attempt to correspond with Walt Whitman, Mark Twain, or Henry James, and no meetings with them. The danger of such isolation can be excessive subjectivity. Whatever the nature of the psychophysical background of reality is, namely the unknown dimension of God, one thing is certain: We can't know what it is no matter how enlightened we might be, and it's more modest to refrain from claiming one's own subjective truth as the truth. On the other hand, such isolation can favor the emergence of an archetypal vision that is astonishingly objective. "We know," writes Jung, "that an archetype can break with shattering force into an individual life and into the life of a nation."[29] The temptation when this occurs is to call it "God" and claim it for oneself or one's nation. Such an inclination is an ego inflation, for the "possessing" factor, as Jung says, is an archetype. The more modest attitude in a Spiritual Democracy is to not claim the self (cosmos or godhead) and presume to pronounce metaphysical judgments about it that are incommensurable with human reason.[30]

For Melville, this domain of the mind is the mystical world of creative inspiration, the essence of which is infused. "My lord," Babbalanja says to Abrazza, "all men are inspired; your highness is inspired; for the essence of all ideas is infused; and in ourselves, we originate nothing. When Lombardo set about his work, he knew not what it would become. He did not build himself with plans; he wrote right on; and so doing, got deeper and deeper into himself."[31] Melville is gaining on the truth that will make itself self-evident in *Moby Dick* as the central truth of the Aquarian Age: the truth of Spiritual Democracy. This notion that asserts that not only rare people of genius but all people are inspired and infused with a certain kind of brilliance or vocation is a conception that is remarkably astute psychologically, because it was revealed to Melville through a form of visioning Jung later calls "fantasy" thinking. "Call it as you will, Yoomy," asserts Babbalanja, "it was a sort of sleep-walking of the mind."[32]

In *Mardi*, the main goal in Taji's quest for Yillah is the transformation of carbon into diamonds, and lava into pure gold. To "create the creative" suggests that Melville's ego is being moved by forces that may unite matter and mind, continents with continents, and African spirituality with Polynesian and Native American shamanism. In the novel this unitary world is infused into the writer Lombardo by poetic "reveries" produced by "imaginary beings" during the writing of his sacred Kotanza, a book of poetry written in the secret script of worldwide spiritual equality where his breakthrough to the unus mundus is unmistakable. Steering his ship away from all borrowed forms, Lombardo plunged "deeper and deeper" into the domain of poetic reverie until he touched taproot in the primordial urge of all language at its archetypal depths. He actually creates a self-portrait of an instinct of ancient activity, an urge of the world that is primary to the formation of languages, and it is this basic perception of an intuition made self-conscious of itself that Babbalanja speaks for when says: "Though Lombardo abandoned all monitors from without; he retained one autocrat within—his crowned and sceptered instinct." This crowned instinctual world of Taji is the unitary world, where "matter and mind, though matching not, are mates."[33]

Anticipating this final union with the self to be the goal of the later stage of his individuation, Babbalanja, the philosopher-poet, describes what can only be a series of mystical experiences that happened to Melville during the writing of the book. The writer experienced dreams, visions, and ecstatic episodes, where the everlasting feeling was that "there are no interregnums; and Time is Eternity; and we live in Eternity now."[34] As the book nears its close, the realization dawns on the four travelers in quest of Yillah that in Alma there are no priests but one, and this is "Alama's self."[35] "We are apostles, everyone" and the truths of *Mardi* are "for this time present" whereby "we are all immortal."[36] Not Christ alone, but "Right-reason, and Alma, are the same" in all nations; and "The Master's great command is Love; . . . Love is all in all. The more we love, the more we know; and so reversed."[37]

The objective truth Melville was after in his developing isolation from his contemporaries becomes increasingly clearer in *Mardi*, until, near the end, he writes: "As poised, we hung in this rapt ether, a sudden trembling seized the four wings now enfolding me. And far oft, in zones still upward reaching, suns' orbits off, I, tranced, beheld an awful glory. Sphere in sphere, it burned:—the one Shekinah! The air was flaked with fire."[38] This is the consciousness Melville carries forward into the writing of *Moby Dick*. The fact that Melville's quest for a new vision of Spiritual Democracy ends with a vision of the Shekinah suggests that his notion will integrate Islamic and Christian themes with Jewish mysticism, and through this synthesis of the three major monotheisms of the Near and Middle East, he will create a vision of religious equality that will truly embrace the world. Such an embrace will subsume an empirical God-image that is light and dark, good and evil, and, in this effort, he will contrast the love and truth of right-reason with the hate and falsehood of religious fundamentalism. *Mardi* provides the imaginal seeds for such a confrontation. In his penetration to the third factor in human experience, the empirical background of all religious statements, Melville will put forth a new, enlightening vision of the American self.

13

TOWARD A HYPOTHESIS
OF THE BI-EROTIC

The archetype of mystical marriage between two men is not new in the history of religious ideas. We find it in Judaism and Christianity, Hinduism and Buddhism, Sufism and Islam, Greek philosophy and Daoism. Yet, when we turn to American art-speech as a spiritual discipline and practice in its own right, what we find extraordinary is the particular accent it places not only on unification with the soul and spirit of the beloved, but on mergings with the *body* of the man onto whom the archetype is transferred energetically.

This is accomplished via emotional projections—the transference of physical-affective desire for bonding that brings the archetype down to a more concrete level than the old religious traditions portray, to a place of ultimate meaning and supreme delight. The elevation that the same-sex marriage concept then attains becomes a wedding between two hearts, two minds, and two bodies. Such portraits have previously not been provided by most celebrations of divine love, at least to the same degree of psychophysical intensity and intimacy, due to the stigma of sin attached most commonly to homosexuality.

To engage with the archetype of spiritual marriage as a fuller religious trope in the United States, we need to turn first to the evocation of the marriage symbol in the domain of the personal relationship between an older and a younger man, such as in the bond of affection between Emerson and Whitman that helped the latter produce the "Calamus" poem cluster in *Leaves of Grass*.

With the bonding between Herman Melville and Nathaniel Hawthorne, on the other hand, we're dealing with a more personal desire for union that emerged in transference of eros by a younger man (Melville) onto a man who was not the younger's equal (Hawthorne). While the close union transported Melville in his writings into a region of pure mastery of his poetic craft, it nevertheless failed to bring lasting peace of heart, soul, and mind that is accorded only to those deeper types of human friendships, where homophobia has been fully dissolved.

In Sufism, a transcendent symbol for lasting love between men is found in the love of the Green Man for the beloved poet Hafiz. While most Sufi poets leave the body out of their metaphors of same-sex unification with men, Melville, like Whitman, brings it in in ways that are sometimes shocking even to modern ears. We'll take a look at how Melville's love for Hawthorne failed to be materialized in the personal domain of a lasting friendship, then at how Melville brought his homoerotic love down into a work of art that immortalized him.

During the initial stages of writing of *Moby Dick*, Melville reviewed a work by Hawthorne that leaves a distinct impression that he was in the grip of an Islamic archetype, the archetype of Khidr, the Verdant One from chapter 18 of the Koran. Virtually everywhere in this review he mentions the "mystical, ever-eluding Spirit of all Beauty, which ubiquitously possesses men of genius," as a feeling made self-evident in Hawthorne's book that refreshes him with its "perennial green."[1]

Melville seems to be enchanted by the repressed Puritan anima that haunts Hawthorne's writings like a phantom complex. He says of Hawthorne: "His wild, witch voice rings through me"[2] as "the very religion of mirth."[3] It's here that he begins to discuss his notion of the dark side of Hawthorne's soul as a "blackness, ten times black," or as a "mystical blackness" that has a touch of "Puritanical gloom," or some yet-to-be-realized "blackness of darkness beyond."[4] "Now it is that blackness in Hawthorne, of which I have spoken," he continues, "that so fascinates me."[5]

Melville then begins to discuss William Shakespeare, and it's here that his thoughts begin to soar. Clearly the archetype of the poet had him in its grip when he says about Shakespeare:

> But it is those far-away things in him; those occasional flashings-forth of the intuitive Truth in him; those short, quick probings at the very axis of reality;—these are the things that make Shakespeare, Shakespeare. Through the mouths of the dark characters of Hamlet, Timon, Lear, and Iago, he craftily says, or sometimes insinuates the things, which we feel to be so terrifically true, that it were all but madness for any good man, in his own proper character, to utter, or even hint of them. Tormented into desperation, Lear the frantic King tears off the mask, and speaks the sane madness of vital truth. . . . And if I magnify

Shakespeare, it is not so much for what he did do, as for what he did not do, or refrained from doing. For in this world of lies, Truth is forced to fly like a sacred white doe in the woodlands, and only by cunning glimpses will she reveal herself, as in Shakespeare and others of the great Art of Telling the Truth,—even though it be covertly, and by snatches.[6]

It's apparent that these words anticipate those of *Moby Dick*'s Father Mapple in chapter 9, "The Sermon." In a sense, Melville's review is a commentary on his own "Art of Telling the Truth,"—the truth of Spiritual Democracy, and it's a truth that is revealed in the novel through "far-away" things in him. The occasional flashings-forth of the intuitive truth in Melville—the short, quick probings at the very axis of reality—are what we feel to be so terrifically true in him.

Notably, Melville says, "And if I magnify Shakespeare." Can it be that Melville had the audacity to attempt to magnify Shakespeare? Or is it that, as with Hawthorne, Melville projectively identifies with the anima, the soul, in Shakespeare's writings? If some of this is Melville's projection, we have to consider what in the manner of channeling a poetic muse that Shakespeare left out, or could not do, that only a poet-shaman like Melville could accomplish. Melville says explicitly: "In this world of lies, Truth is forced to fly like a sacred white doe in the woodlands." The sacred white doe, an anima figure, is an early example of what would become a self-figure as well, the Great White Animal: Moby Dick. "Only by cunning glimpses will she reveal herself," he says. Thus, the White Whale, as a symbol for Spiritual Democracy, was revealed to Melville "covertly, and by snatches."

Melville here is in the process of creating the great American novel through his own literary individuation, which would both isolate and differentiate him from all his peers. And, early in this process, he announces, in a review of Hawthorne, that he wants to be believed when he says Shakespeare's inapproachability is about to be superseded. "Believe me, my friends," he says, "that Shakespeares are this day being born on banks of the Ohio." And then he reveals the clincher: "You must have plenty of sea-room to tell the Truth in; especially, when it seems to have an aspect of newness, as America did in 1492. . . . This, too, I mean, that if Shakespeare has not been equaled, he is sure to be surpassed, and surpassed by an American born now or yet to be born. . . . Let America then prize and cherish her writers; yea, let her glorify them . . . Not that American genius needs patronage in order to expand."[7] These are clearly autobiographical statements, as he is writing his great whaling novel.

Melville will go on to embrace—not avoid—difficult topics in *Moby Dick*.

To write about Spiritual Democracy was no easy task. Possibly he rejected Walt Whitman's work on the subject because Whitman made it seem so easy. Although Melville knew that his own era in America was not ripe for Spiritual Democracy's acceptance, he was certain that its time would eventually arrive. The experience of the self would indeed become a defeat for Melville's ego, and with this awareness of being overpowered, he said: "It is better to fail in originality, than to succeed in imitation. He who has never failed somewhere, that man cannot be great. Failure is the true test of greatness." Melville desired originality from his own country's writers. "We want no American Miltons. Let us away with this Bostonian leaven of literary flunkeyism toward England."[8]

Melville's truth of Spiritual Democracy would be preached to the face of falsehood in a time when religious equality had not yet come. But, like Walt Whitman and Emily Dickinson, he readied the way for its emergence. "While we are rapidly preparing for that political supremacy among the nations, which prophetically awaits us at the close of the present century; in a literary point of view, we are deplorably unprepared for it," Melville wrote.[9] In hailing the work of one literary countryman, Hawthorne, he was willing to recognize a peer. In this American novelist Melville was also recognizing all "meritorious writers that are our own;—those writers, who breathe the unshackled, democratic spirit of Christianity in all things, which now takes the practical lead in this world, though at the same time led by ourselves—us Americans."[10] By praising Hawthorne before he set out on his own lonely course, he was embracing in our national literature the "whole brotherhood. For genius, all over the world, stands hand in hand, and one shock of recognition runs the whole circle round."[11] He then goes on to discuss the subject of the "coming of the literary Shiloh of America"[12] and here again he is speaking of himself. As we will see, the truth in *Moby Dick* cannot be found in any creed, but only in what lies hidden in one's own inexorable self.

In his novel *Mardi and a Voyage Tither*, Melville tells us that when a shell of a sea creature was held up—"one of those ever moaning of the ocean"—Yillah the "maiden oft held it to her ear, and closing her eyes, listened and listened to its soft inner breathings, till visions were born of the sound, and her soul lay for hours in a trance of delight." Yillah has a bird-soul: "a milk-white bird, with a bill jet-black, and eyes like stars" that would come to her "at night" and fold their "wings in her bosom."[13] In all of the sequences of visions there is a focus on infusion by the transcausal factor of "delight" as a primary emotion that transports the poet-shaman to vistas of Spiritual Democracy. Such infusion produces an experience of unitary consciousness accompanied, as Danae experienced

Zeus, by showers of pure gold: "Gold, gold it is, that sways the nations: / Gold! gold! the center of all rotations!"[14] But this is not the ordinary gold of miners, but the spiritual gold of his poetic vocation, a consciousness of the ego's rooted-ness in the self, a pantheistic Spiritual Democracy, whose roots are broader and deeper than the Pacific.

"Deep, Yoomy" says Babbalanja, "deep, true treasure lies; deeper than all Mardi's gold, rooted to Mardi's axis."[15] We discover the ego-self axis in living, world-uniting form, as anima mundi, in the golden caverns of the universal mind, the consciousness of Spiritual Democracy, a fervor capacious enough to carry him deep into delightful states of being.

Like Whitman's search for "happiness" in his *Notebooks*, Melville's quest for Yillah is a search for delight, an embodied, affecting experience of the self that can yield the alchemical gold of knowing one is participating in a living mystery of spiritual brotherhood. It's a poetic quest, as well as a philosophical one, and its goal—like chant fifty of "Song of Myself"—is mystical, cosmic, unitary. It's a quest for the ultimate aim of the poet-shaman's art: the feminine Godhead, the "Mother of All," who can feel, mirror, and celebrate Spiritual Democracy. As we've seen, this is the world of the "one autocrat within," the self in which "matter and mind, though matching not, are mates."[16] What is at play in *Mardi* is a quest for the "spiritualization of the soul" (that is, illumina-tion). But what kind of spiritualization is it in Melville's work?

The pouring of a cornucopia of gold from this soul, celebrating spiritedness itself, to Melville's literary dream-ego in *The Confidence Man* reveals how much a mental transformation, a *metanoia*, had occurred in him through the writing of *Mardi* and *Moby Dick*. The successful search for Yillah led Melville to a higher integration of his consciousness, because Yillah had mediated his discovery of an American self.

Melville's isolation and solitude received some relief and comfort during the final years of his life, when he found, in his reading life, a soul-companion, a philosopher-friend, with whom he intellectually and philosophically aligned. This chosen companion, in what had become a thought experiment, was Ger-man philosopher Arthur Schopenhauer, a great mind of the age. Schopenhauer, one of the very first Western thinkers to look to both Hinduism and Buddhism, believed that for the *"better consciousness* to be active within," a person's "pain, suffering, and failure are as necessary" as "weighty ballast is to a ship, which attracts no draught without it."[17]

Melville did not begin reading Schopenhauer's depth-psychological phi-losophy until his later years, when he acquired the complete seven volumes of the philosopher's works. It was then that he found the metaphysical gold he had been seeking. In 1813, Schopenhauer wrote in his philosophical diary: "Personality and causality do exist in this temporal, sensory, comprehensible world; indeed they are necessary. But the better consciousness within me lifts me up into a world where neither personality nor causality, nor subject nor object, exist any more."[18] Such words must have resonated deeply in Melville, who had experienced this kind of sublimity of transport during the writing of *Mardi* and *Moby Dick*.

One hundred years after the advent of psychoanalysis and the advancement of depth-psychology in a number of different fields, it is becoming increasingly clear today that what the early German philosophers—Schopenhauer, Kant, and Nietzsche—and the depth-psychological psychiatrists who followed them—Jean-Martin Charcot, Pierre Janet, Sigmund Freud, Alfred Adler, William James, and Carl Jung—were, each in their own ways, converging upon the outlines of a new world mythos: a pattern of development extending from the Judeo-Christian-Islamic dispensations toward a more global religion in the future. The "gold" Melville discovered from 1847 through 1849, when he was writing *Mardi*, was Spiritual Democracy, and Schopenhauer confirmed and validated that discovery for him by making it philosophically respectable.

Of course, Melville was already a champion at the art of striking through the mask of nineteenth-century Puritan America, to a new image of the American self, in which the shadow of homophobia, slavery, and Indian-hating are all revealed. In Melville's novel *Redburn, His First Voyage*, the personages of Orpheus, Krishna, Hafiz, and Dionysus are four cross-cultural examples Melville gives of this archetype of the democratic self, as an "immaculate friend" or eternal companion (Khidr) that accompanies Redburn on his return sea journey to America, as a male muse. Interestingly, it's Redburn's friend Harry Bolton who outfits Redburn in his new poetic mantle at the Golden Anchor Inn after offering to give him a handful of gold and before sauntering, hand in hand with him, into London.[19]

Early critics who saw Harry Bolton as an "implausible" figure or as a "major flaw" in the narrative[20] failed to fathom the symbolic significance of this androgenic figure. Bolton seemed to serve as a point of reference for Melville's spiritualization of the soul after the writing of *Mardi*, where the four male companions in quest of Yillah were all transformed in consciousness through a number of visions, dreams, and mystical experiences. Harry Bolton can be seen as part of the movement in Melville's psyche to attain a bi-erotic unity. But this unity is nothing other than the American self. Ishmael-Queequeg represents a further stage of this development. Their transnational and multira-cial relationship is a living symbol of worldwide Spiritual Democracy, but it is still based on the American model of Bolton.

Contrary to Schopenhauer, who experienced the "comedy of success" at the end of his lifetime, Melville suffered the ignominy of virtual anonymity, and he appears to have died feeling himself to be an unappreciated man. At his funeral, it was said that he was simply the author of *Typee* and *Omoo*, his first two sea nar-ratives, for which he had achieved a considerable degree of recognition. It would take the passage of another thirty years after his death, however, before literary scholars would agree with what Melville himself must have realized, that in *Moby Dick* the reclusive author had written the greatest American epic of his age.

In order to understand Melville's project as a process of transforming the God-image into a more complete soul-image than ever before, one that is tran-scendent of gender, it's important for the reader that it begins with his quest for an image of the divine feminine as the sacred gold hidden in the cosmos. The Jewish mystics know her as the Shekinah. Christians know her as Mary. The Sufis know her as the Rose. Like Whitman's Spiritual Democracy, Melville's new religious vision contains a glimpse of a larger human totality, as well as a divine one. As Melville said in *Mardi*, "We have had vast developments of parts of men; but none of many wholes."[21]

Writing decades before the emergence of the gay liberation movement in the United States, American literary critic Leslie Fiedler noted that the spiri-tual renewal that takes place within *Moby Dick*'s narrator, Ishmael, is a "natural renewal of the soul, the holy marriage of males, immune to the spiritual death implicit in fleshly marriage with women." This marriage, Fiedler writes, is an equalizing "alternative symbol."[22] While this spiritual renewal was clearly an anticipation of the emergence of current discussions about same-sex mar-riage, the sacred marriage of males wasn't anywhere as complete as Melville's or Whitman's incarnation of it because the body was included, and women were not excluded from Spiritual Democracy.

Like Whitman, Melville felt compelled to speak out against the general unconsciousness of his day, which means that he had to "magnify" the conscious-ness of the self. Unlike Whitman, however, Melville illuminates homophobia—without using the term—more brilliantly than any of his contemporaries. He lays a cornerstone of acceptance of bi-erotic marriage by casting a considerable beam of light on the problem of projection of the human shadow, specifically addressing Puritan antipathy toward same-sex coupling, along with depreciation of the feminine and crusading hatred of the Muslim diaspora. By illuminating these antipathies, he forces his readers to contemplate the shadow side of the American ideal of selfhood, and, like Jung, he insists on the value of the shadow. This is the gold he offers to his readers.

In chapter 99 of *Moby Dick*, aptly titled "The Doubloon," Melville writes, "Some certain significance lurks in all things, else all things are little worth, and the round world itself an empty cipher, except to sell by the cartload, as they do hills about Boston, to fill up some morass in the Milky Way."[23] This was likely an incisive criticism of the "gaping flaw" Melville saw in Ralph Waldo Emerson. For the vision of religious history in *Moby Dick* is so vast that it lead him to declare his equality with the antique dispensation, the last time in Western discourse when shadow and virtue could so easily converse. In a letter to Hawthorne, Melville wrote, "I would sit down and dine with you and all the gods in old Rome's Pantheon."[24]

Melville was in this regard a bit like the adventurous traveler Alexander von Humboldt. His four-year voyages at sea were mostly with men. According to American literature professor Laura Dassow Walls, "Humboldt could surround himself with what Walt Whitman would call the love of comrades. He never married, and while he and his family kept sexuality veiled, it was and remains an open secret that his deepest and most passionate attachments were with men."[25]

It seems that a homoerotic imagination[26] informs more than just the Ishmael-Queequeg "marriage" in *Moby Dick*. The novel presents an image of transformation in the male psyche that involved different unions of masculine opposites that are in search of a more stable godhead. This search for inner strength and wisdom is not just the familiar homospirituality of the traditional Christian Trinity, for it has as much to do with bodily affect and instinct as with spirit and religious emotion. In fact, the body, not the spirit, is the key to this knowledge. Neither the feminine, nor women themselves, are excluded from such embodiment. The type of image of human sexual individuation is, finally, bi-erotic.

Sigmund Freud, too, was captivated by the bi-erotic. He was looking not only for a new system of psychological analysis but a new style of free speech—a mythopoetic language through which the technique of psychoanalysis could be made available for all people, namely the "talking cure." His vehicle was not to be found in identification with such forerunners of modern dynamic psychiatry as French neurologists Jean-Martin Charcot and Hippolyte Bernheim, but rather in his identification with the writers, such as Johann Wolfgang von Goethe and Shakespeare and Sophocles, who had first assisted in the discovery of the unconscious.[27] As Freud pointed out, it was really "the great poets and writers" who had "preceded psychologists in the exploration of the human mind."

Canadian psychiatrist Henri Ellenberger explains this point further: "He [Freud] often quoted the Greek tragedians, Shakespeare, Goethe, Schiller, Heine, and many other writers. No doubt," Ellenberger says, quite convincingly, "Freud could have been one of the world's foremost writers, but instead of using his deep, intuitive knowledge of the human soul for the creation of literary works, he attempted to formulate it and systematize it." When a French playwright, Henri-René Lenormand, went to visit Freud at his office in Vienna, moreover, Freud is reported to have pointed to the works of Shakespeare and the Greek tragedians as his main source, saying: "Here are my masters." Freud maintained, Ellenberger concludes, "that the essential themes of his theories were based on the intuitions of the poets."[28] Thus, we can see a process of identification with literary giants during Freud's greatest period of psychological transformation.

A similar discovery by Melville, several years before Freud's birth, might best be explained as an example of what Ellenberger calls the "creative illness." This condition, coupled with the initiatory search for "truth" that leads a person with such an illness to an experience of "recovery," is preceded by an intense period of emotional, mental, and physical ailments, through which the creative person eventually passes to a "termination stage." The final stage culminates when a great artistic, religious, scientific, or philosophic truth is discovered and revealed for the benefit of humanity.[29] In Melville, such a revelation would lead him to feel "indissolubly united with the conviction of having discovered a grandiose truth that must be proclaimed to mankind."[30] Ellenberger clarifies this experience of vocational insight further. Throughout the period of creative illness, "the subject never loses the thread of his dominating preoccupation. . . . he is almost entirely absorbed with himself. He suffers from feelings of utter isolation, even when he has a mentor who guides him through the ordeal (like the shaman apprentice with his master)."[31]

Melville experienced and emerged from such a state. "I am mad to think how minute a cause has prevented me from reading Shakespeare," Melville wrote to his editor in February 1849. "By chancing to fall in with this glorious edition, I now *exult* over it, page after page."[32] Such exalted feelings are characteristic of what Ellenberger defines as the "termination" phase of the creative illness, which is said to be "rapid and marked by a phase of exhilaration."[33] Freud, for all his revolutionary recognition of the presence of a pansexual lust in all our lives, seems to have wrongly theorized the aim of libido to be bisexual, rather than bi-erotic, as Whitman and Melville and Dickinson all do.[34] Whereas Freud used the word "bisexual" in a narrow way to define bisexuality directed toward male or female objects with only one concrete meaning denoting sex, I use the term in a broader connotation to define soulful and spiritual love that is inclusive of the possibility of same-sex marriage. For Melville, Shakespeare connected him to a bi-erotic exaltation of language hitherto unrealized by his reading of anyone except the biblical prophets, Sufi poets, and Jesus.

Walt Whitman formed a transformative "close friendship" in adolescence, and Dickinson had several close female friends whom she called her Amherst girls. A similarly significant relationship began for Melville in October of 1830, in his eleventh year, when he joined his nine-year-old cousin, Stanwix, at Albany Academy in Albany, New York. It is not entirely clear from historical records what the nature of their friendship was, but from Melville's own pen it's clear that a "love" relationship did in fact ensue between the two boys. Melville found in Stanwix a soul-companion, a brother, friend, and confidant who looked up to him and admired him, and this admiration and mirroring of Melville by the younger and more passive boy had a direct impact on the future novelist's verbal and intellectual capacities. In Melville's chapter "The Cousins" in his novel *Pierre or The Ambiguities,* he tells us that shortly after he was reacquainted with Stanwix in 1830, he was awarded as a scholarship prize a volume of the *London Carcanet,* a book containing passages from distinguished writers. Melville seems to suggest that it was not only the system of Lancastrian education, with its emphasis on debate, disciplined study, and critical thinking that evoked the archetype of the thinker in him, as some scholars have speculated, but also, and perhaps more significantly, the more than cousinly friendship that was awakened in the two boys. In chapter 15, "The Cousins," Melville tells us clearly:

> In their boyhood and earlier adolescence, Pierre [Herman] and Glen [Stanwix] had cherished a much more than cousinly attachment. At the age of ten, they had furnished an example of the truth, that the friendship of fine-hearted, generous boys, nurtured amongst the romance-engendering comforts and elegancies of life, sometimes transcends the bonds of mere boyishness, and revels for a while in the empyrean of a love which only comes short, by one degree, of the sweetest sentiment entertained by the sexes.[35]

The "one degree" is obviously sex. While love letters were exchanged between the two cousins from late adolescence to early adulthood, little is known about the actual nature of their preliminary "love-friendship of boys." Nevertheless, it seems plausible that the homoerotic feelings evoked, like those between Freud and Silberstein, allowed for the archetype of the same-sex twin to emerge and for the archetype of the poet to be evoked in Melville's "love" for Stanwix.

The problem for Melville, as we have seen, was how to take Shakespeare forward into a new American idiom, through an embodied speech that was not afraid of revealing man's yearning for union with his fellow man on all three levels: body, soul, and spirit, which is the only means of bonding through which spiritualization of the soul can be fully achieved. Shakespeare achieves some of this in his sonnets, perhaps inspired by "Mr. W. H." But the American poets would turn the gold of Shakespeare's language into something far more meaningful for the future of the race—what amounts to a new dispensation of religious ideas that would place sexuality on the same level as the spirit and turn the monastic and ascetic practices of all religious, with their focus on excess sexual repressions, into pure delight.

In June of 1851, prior to Hawthorne's sudden departure from his home in the Berkshires of Massachusetts, Melville wrote his penultimate letter of appreciation in which the full extent of his dark meanings were revealed for us: "This is the book's motto (the secret one),—Ego non baptiso te in nomini—but make out the rest yourself."[36] The motto of *Moby Dick* that Ahab deliriously howls—"Ego non baptiso te in nomini patris, sed in nomini diaboli"—("I do not baptize thee in the name of the father, but in the name of the devil") is the secret that wounds us. The book was written wickedly for a very important reason: to broaden, paradoxically, Christ's teachings of love. Because of the book's unprecedented accent on male homosexuality, pantheism, violence, and evil, it would take one hundred fifty years before scholars of world literature, psychology, and religion would begin to comprehend how such a change in eros and consciousness had occurred in Melville, and what its meaning might be for postmodern times. In *Moby Dick*, America is the patient while Melville is the exorcist: the poet-shaman of America, whose function was to extract the most damaging virus in the world's religions that was ailing the collective psyche. Today this cultural sickness is called *homophobia*, and its roots can be traced to the Judeo-Christian-Islamic God-complex, which is the very power structure Ahab embodied in 1850.

Melville excluded the traditional Trinity of Christ, the Father, and the Holy Ghost from his dark benediction to Hawthorne not to destroy the Judeo-Christian-Islamic message of love in God, Jesus, or Allah, but to fulfill it. Melville fairly cooked and "broiled" the book in blood and hellfire in an effort to make the dark side of the self conscious in us, and in this way he was attempting to further the Christian message of caritas, selfless love, not to spread a gospel of Ahabian hate. American literature scholar Charles Olson quotes a significant passage that Melville left on the last flyleaf of the final volume of his Shakespeare set, one that contains the major plays Lear, Othello, and Hamlet: "—madness is undefinable—/ It & right reason extremes of one, /—not the (black art) Goetic but Theurgic magic—/ seeks converse with the Intelligence, Power, the / Angel."[37]

By being America's first champion of homosexuality, Melville knew he was standing completely alone with his Whale. In Melville's view, to write about homosexuality and evil and the feminine Islamic face of God (Yillah) in America was not goetic magic (black art), but rather theurgic magic (white art), which leads to the higher kind of intelligence, the love and wisdom he was after. "The more we Love the more we Know," he wrote in *Mardi*.

In *Moby Dick*, Melville is the poet-shaman of America whose function it is to extract a virus that was ailing the anima mundi most. This cultural illness is man's fear and hatred of his fellow man, leading ultimately to atrocities like Indian-hating, Islamophobia, racism, and Jew-bashing. Melville rounds this idea out by including Islam and the Far East in this equation.

Both Freud and Jung overlooked the significance of the homophobic complex in their explorations into the destructive instincts (Freud) and the archetypal shadow (Jung); yet Melville can be credited with being the first "thought-diver" in the West who explored this terrain. This is what makes Melville's contribution to the psychology of the unconscious so vitally important for all psychotherapists, theologians, and literary critics: he gets at the heart of the marriage problem that faces us all today at a political and religious level. Melville felt "spotless as a lamb" and liberated at the end of his "wicked" truth-telling book, because he knew, in his Ishmaelian heart and mind, that he had practiced "right reason" (Alma's religion of love) throughout the whole ordeal of "cooking" (that is, integrating) the symbolical gold (spermaceti) of the phallic white whale, with all of its homoerotic implications. Because he had performed an important function of exorcism on the "witch-hunting" spirit (Ahab) in the American psyche as a whole, he was liberated from the spell of its darkness.

By writing his homoerotic benediction on the whale, Melville was making the shadow of homophobia, and the destructive instinct, conscious for all people. In so doing he charted a path no less pioneering than Whitman's toward the latter's Spiritual Democracy. In our time Whitman's big idea is becoming increasing evident in the world as a way of visioning self-realization. It's similarly linked to scientific notions of a single cosmos in which all of us can realize ourselves—men and women, heterosexual and homosexual—just as in the heady nineteenth-century days when Whitman was reading Humboldt: "Whence come you, Hawthorne? By what right do you drink from my flagon of life? And when I put it to my lips—lo, they are yours and not mine."[38] These surprising words—"they are yours and not mine"—had their literary antecedents in the words of Redburn to Harry Bolton in the novel *Redburn:* "But they are yours, and not mine, Harry." "Yours and mine, my sweet fellow," Harry remarked in reference to the "gold" he would share with him in London.[39] Melville's words to Hawthorne at the completion of his great shaman novel confirm the fact that the "gold" Melville was seeking in the writing of *Mardi*, like the new outfit Harry gives Redburn to wear in London, is the spiritual gold of his vocation, the mantle of a poet.

As is well known, the relationship between Melville and Hawthorne eventually fell apart. The axis of love, the center Melville felt so deeply—an "infinite fraternity of feeling" that both men might have shared and delighted in together as friends—didn't hold. Melville would spend the rest of his days exploring the problem of incestuous love that entered into the domain of his personal relationship with Hawthorne.

In his ponderous religious poem about his trip to the Middle East, *Clarel*, when Melville writes about the protagonist Clarel's longings for a man named Vine (who most critics now see as a symbolic stand-in for Hawthorne) he says, bluntly enough, "Prior advances" were "unreturned." But this did not keep Clarel from attempting a communion: "O, now but for communion true / And close; let go each alien theme; Give me thyself!"[40]

What might this statement "Give me thyself!" mean, psychologically? The demand is a reference to his love for the "inescapable twin brother," the treasure hard to attain, the rose, in Vine-Hawthorne. We can find evidence for this in the following account: "But Vine" did not suspect "Clarel's thrill / Of personal longing . . . / The heart's desire did interfere . . . / After confidings that should wed / Our souls in one:—Ah. Call me brother!—/ So feminine his passionate mood / Which, long as hungering unfed, / All else rejected or withstood. / But some inklings he let fall. But no: / Here over Vine there slid a change—/ A shadow . . ."[41]

In this November 1851 letter to Hawthorne, we can see Melville arriving at a Whitmanesque solution to the perennial Romantic problem of what to do with ecstasy. This solution, as we saw in Whitman's first notebook, is to give it generously to the people in a spirit of democracy. But Melville's mistake, if indeed he was partly to blame for the misunderstandings that ensued, is that he attempted to express this love directly with Hawthorne, who was not in the least prepared for such an emotional (or as the hunger metaphor implies, physical) demand. But this was Melville's response to Hawthorne's previous "exultation-breeding" letter in *Clarel*.[42] Melville provides a searing critique of his own charitable excesses in the personal relationship and an accurate awareness of how his efforts to incarnate the male-male coniunctio (the "heart's desire") greatly exacerbated his conflict with Hawthorne.

In *Clarel*, Melville explores the problem of homoerotic intimacy within the domain of the mentor-protégée relationship, where an approach at "communion" seems to have been attempted in the personal domain of the relationship constellated between the two men, described in chilling terms in the poem above. This dynamic of same-sex love, where a thrill of personal longing and heart's desire interfered with confidings that might have wed their souls into one, was experienced, rather, as a hunger unfed. Melville makes it explicit: "over Vine there slid a change—/ A shadow." Today we would call this the shadow of homophobia. "Shadow," a term developed through the nineteenth century, and later applied to the unconscious by Jung, is used here explicitly to refer not to homosexuality, but to homophobia. Homophobia was the shadow that clouded Vine's response to Clarel. As Clarel, Melville is able to get closer to the real source of the feelings of rejection that men typically feel when their love for another man is not returned. As Shakespeare before him had sketched out in his sonnets, spiritually what men are seeking from such a passion goes much deeper than gratification of instinctual desire. It is, at heart, a wish for mutual love of the beloved, the kind of relationship to the divine achieved between Krishna and Arjuna, David and Jonathan, Christ and John, Hafiz and Attar, Rumi and Shams, and Whitman and Peter Doyle.

Similarly, in Melville's elegiac poem "Monody," Hawthorne's "clostrel vine" is said to have "hid the shyest grape." This is a metaphor, which, as John Seele tells us, "looks forward to Melville's symbolic portrait of Hawthorne in *Clarel*. "Ambushed in leaves," a character in *Clarel* declares, "we spy your grape . . . Black but juicy one." "There is something vaguely sexual in this metaphor," American literature specialist John Seelye writes with droll understatement, "as there is in many of the figures Melville used when speaking of Hawthorne."[43]

The God Dionysus makes an appearance in the symbolic "marriage," or communion of two hearts: the field of transference between Melville and Hawthorne. In psychological terms Melville's attempts to keep his homoerotic transference (onto Hawthorne) conscious during the writing of *Moby Dick* were unsuccessful after the book's completion, but as he said in the chapter entitled

"Dreams" in *Mardi:* "Fain would I hurl off this Dionysius that rides me."[44] Thus, during the writing of his masterwork, the God of the vine was riding him hard.

In his book *Dionysos,* the Greek mythology scholar Carl Kerényi tells us that after Dionysus was sewn in tightly to his father Zeus's thigh, he experienced a "second birth" from the father, an image that places the emphasis of this symbol of a male divinity in the location just below the testicles. Yet more than this, Dionysus emerged from the father's body as a second womb. As a God of "juicy black grapes" and fermented red wine, Dionysus is the generative and natural principle of verdant vineyards, an archetypal image of indestructible life.[45] In the grip of this God, a "thrill of personal longing" entered the mentor-protégée relationship of Melville and Hawthorne, leading to a rift in their soul-communion and a concomitant loss of Melville's adhesion to the self, as the source of his ultimate poetic power. There appears to have been an attempt on Melville's part to concretize the relationship through some kind of an intimate, homoerotic union—an "advance" that was unreciprocated. He provided a psychological explanation for this in *Clarel,* when he wrote that after confiding that should have wed their "souls in one," the "Shadow" (homophobia) slid over Hawthorne.

To wed two souls together, in the form of a male coniunctio, means psychologically that Melville attempted to unite a Dionysian part of his soul with Hawthorne in the form of a male-male communion. The experience of Spiritual Democracy is preserved in Melville's words to Hawthorne as a felt sense of universal union with divinity, an infinite fraternity of feeling that extends to the cosmos: "I feel the Godhead is broken like the bread at the Supper, and that we are the pieces."[46] This is the essence of Spiritual Democracy, whose source, as Whitman also says, is both fraternal and maternal. Like the Dionysian God—he "with two mothers"[47]—the second birth of a man from the body of a mentor-male is an archetypal image that is religious at its roots: a moral and ethical problem, which the early poet-shamans (Melville, Whitman, and Dickinson) all attempted to resolve aesthetically for nineteenth-century America. Their efforts to depict their sexual androgyny in religious-spiritual terms intended to engage the reader's feelings and thoughts into acts of critical self-reflection. They also encourage emotional as well as intellectual understanding of a new paradigm shift toward wholeness. Their depictions of an American self shines a light on homophobia, racism, Indian hating, Islamophobia, love and hate, and good and evil within us.

Thus, when Melville began to read Shakespeare seriously for the first time, in 1849, we can see, concomitantly with the discovery of gold in California, the forging of a new alchemy for the West. It was at this time that he arrived at the mindset of what Whitman called Spiritual Democracy. Since the "second birth" of a man from the father's body makes up an important part of the imaginative products of American poetry, it's important that we analyze the meaning of Whitman's and Melville's images of male coniunctio at a significant time in American history when our culture seems to be calling out for a more-than-personal understanding of its symbolic import. Thus, we can extend Jung's notions of psychic energy into the area of masculine-feminine individuation in light of the discovery, in American poetry, of the bi-erotic as a central aspect of wholeness. "Wholeness is a combination of I and You," wrote Jung, in *The Psychology of the Transference*, "and these show themselves to be parts of a transcendent unity."[48] Jung makes room here for the possibility that Melville's projection of the divine feminine, Yillah, onto Sufi men may indeed bespeak something of the missing element of love in American culture that is typically discouraged or denied between heterosexual men as open expressions of homoaffection, usually in a homospiritual rather than homosexual way, but no less erotic for that. As we've seen, Whitman placed special emphasis on this in his notion of adhesiveness.

As long as Melville was projecting the Dionysian aspect of himself onto Hawthorne, he seemed to be participating in a state of delight. But this emotional state, which was numinous, ecstatic, and charged by a new emerging God-image of Spiritual Democracy, could not last when the shadow of homophobia crept over Hawthorne, leaving Melville bereft. Such breakages in male affection are common to adolescent and young adult friendships. Yet, it's equally possible that such bonds may remain intact in their integrity, leading to friendships lasting for a lifetime. Whitman surrounded himself with a large group of male friends who became his disciples, whereas Melville sought the inner union with his soul (Yillah, Hagar, Rachael, the Shikinah) to heal his hurt. He also read Hafiz as a cure.

Psychological and literary criticism concerning the Hawthorne-Melville friendship has become increasingly precise over the last century and has been converging on a contemporary theme that forms a cornerstone of the imagination that structures Spiritual Democracy as an ideal in the poets' America: the transformative power of homoeros on the genesis of psychological and literary creativity. Melville was in the grip of a religious archetype, a numinous face of God (Yillah) that seized him with an emotional force. This force was building toward a climax that might best be compared with the volcanic explosion of

Krakatoa, which erupted in 1883 with an energy Jung reported sensing across the globe in Switzerland when he was eight years old. Through his travel writing and in his poetic experiments with a new kind of free verse in *Mardi*, Melville had been attempting to give birth to a new form of spiritual alchemy for the West, coinciding with the California Gold Rush: a method of vocalism that, as an American, he hoped would surpass even Shakespeare's union of high and low forms of discourse within a trancelike, dramatic, and incantatory new art-speech.

By 1951, the centennial of the publication of *Moby Dick*, Freudian and psychosexual interpretations of the Melville-Hawthorne relationship began to center on the question of a possible homosexual aim on Melville's part as the pursuing, more ardent of the two men.[49] This assumption, however, is too narrow, and has led to an inaccurate interpretation of their relationship.

To paint a portrait of Melville as suffering from either overt or "latent homosexuality" in the form of an intrusive, unconscious complex would be to mistake the archetype of same-sex marriage as a mere instinctual image, as opposed to seeing it more correctly, from a Jungian angle, as a religious need, a symbol for transformation and spiritualization of the libido into a truly bi-erotic love. By definition this symbol transcends such literal concretizations as what Melville would have regarded as far-too-ordinary shipboard sodomy. The kind of reductive criticism that would have made Melville "gay" before his time reached its heyday after the riots at Stonewall in 1969, where the old latent homosexuality hypothesis was merged with the new gay liberation movement. In this era Melville was written off as a man with a repressed homosexual urge that he couldn't quite handle—someone who, when already disillusioned in his marriage, had hoped to find a father figure and a loving soulmate in Hawthorne, who could at best have mirrored, understood, and loved him as a poet-brother.[50]

To his credit, writing in the 1980s, Melville scholar James Wilson called for "new hypotheses" to explain the actual nature of the influence involved in the Hawthorne-Melville friendship: "The question of mutual influence remains as important as ever, but one would hope the future critics would concentrate less on the 'details' and more on synthesizing them into a coherent theory that would attempt to explain the exact nature of that influence."[51] Today, one hundred years after the birth of psychoanalysis, and during an era partly characterized by a movement to legalize same-sex marriage across the United States and throughout many nations of the world, it's easier to see the archetype of same-sex marriage that Melville discovered, along with his American compatriot, Walt Whitman. This model embodies "homosexuality" in a manner that does not deny its sacramental potential. It's unwise, though, to make inferences or draw conclusions about Melville's literal, personal sexuality, about which we really know nothing.

In his essay on Hawthorne, Melville made it clear that he was in the grip not of a sexual but a religious archetype. He noted about this "Mossy Man" that Hawthorne was, like Christ, or the "Green One" of Sufism, a Khidr, for he mentions him in light of a reflection on the "Assyrian dawn" and "our Savior," who "Jewish eyewitnesses" had "failed to see heaven in his glance."[52] A modern reader may immediately think of Rumi's encounter with Shams, or Hafiz's love for Attar.

Imported through Goethe, Humboldt, Emerson, and the Islamic Sufi masters, the archetype of same-sex marriage had arrived, as a transforming symbol for the West. Writing before Whitman, Melville confessed he'd heard in Hawthorne a "wild, witch voice." In Hawthorne's chapter on "Fire-Worship," Melville read about the alchemical gold latent in the "blackness, ten times black, a light leaping out of darkness" that would illuminate the world. Melville wrote: "You but touch it [Hawthorne's blackness] and you find it is gold."[53]

Hawthorne, however, had failed to grasp the enormous power of the archetype in his writings that had held Melville so in thrall. He likely would have been horrified to think that anything he wrote could have unleashed the power of the homoerotic imagination that informs *Moby Dick*. The magnet of Melville's metaphysical longings for the absolute was so intense it must have come as a shock to Hawthorne to be drawn into its demand for reciprocal attraction. The mystery of the relationship that did unfold lies in the factor of transpersonal delight, or ecstasy, evoked by the fortuitous meeting of the two men, an emotion Hawthorne was never able to accept, or fathom. He was too possessed by the Puritan spirit of Roger Chillingworth, the estranged husband of Hester Prynne in Hawthorne's masterwork *The Scarlet Letter*, to embrace such transporting passion. The failure of the men's relationship to reach that place of the spiritual maturity of Hafiz and Attar in the city of Shiraz, or Rumi and Shams in the city of Tabriz, or even the brief "bromance" of Freud and Jung, left Melville a "spiritual orphan." The resolution of the father-son and brother-brother, friend-friendship with Hawthorne would have to be found in Melville's lonely discovery, rather late in life, of the works of Schopenhauer, where he would find indeed another man possessed of the better consciousness he had attained during the writing of his final shamanistic novel, *Billy Budd*.

Before that, Melville simply failed to sustain a connection to the artistically procreative power of Hawthorne, the male muse. The ideal collapsed when the friendship failed to become what he dreamed it could be, when the man he had so venerated as an "equal" brother, to whom he had felt truly wed in spirit, was ultimately not his peer at all, in either a spiritual or sensual sense. Simply put, Melville's vision, and also his artistry, was beyond Hawthorne's. As Seelye rightly says, Melville "seems to have mistaken his man."[54] Most critics of the twentieth century failed to grasp this because they, too, were still under the spell cast by Hawthorne's own assumption that he was the first great American master of literature and thus, in a sense, unsurpassable. Specifically, these critics failed to answer several key questions:

1. What did the homoerotic undertones in the friendship between the two men mean psychologically as an imaginal construct in the American literary psyche?
2. What was the exact nature of the emotional image in the archetype at play in the relationship?
3. How, for Melville, was the archetype of male partnership conceived as a transport to the divine?
4. What role did the archetype of same-sex marriage play in the emergence of the notion of Spiritual Democracy that Hawthorne could not embrace?

These four questions are all key in understanding the literary relationship that has remained, as yet, unanswered by Melville scholars. Spiritual Democracy, as articulated by Whitman and made a darker reality by Melville, is never simply a feeling of being in love, although it may be felt as such at times, when the factor of the numinous sweeps over one, as it did when Melville authored his famous letter to Hawthorne.

> My dear Hawthorne . . . I can't write what I felt. But I felt pantheistic then—your heart beat in my ribs and mine in yours, and both in God's. . . . I speak now of my profoundest sense of being, not of an incidental feeling.

> Whence come you, Hawthorne? By what right do you drink from my flagon of life? And when I put it to my lips—lo, they are yours and not mine. I feel the Godhead is broken like the bread at the Supper, and that we are the pieces. Hence this infinite fraternity of feeling. . . .

> My dear Hawthorne, the atmospheric skepticisms steal into me now, and make me doubtful of my sanity in writing you thus. But, believe me, I am not mad, most noble Festus! . . . I am content and can be

happy. I shall leave the world, I feel, with more satisfaction for having come to know you. Knowing you persuades me more than the Bible of our immortality. . . . The divine magnet is in you, and my magnet responds.[55]

Hawthorne was shocked, and retreated, just as he had done when he wrote chillingly to his wife Sophia: "The real Me was never an associate of the human community; there has been a spectral appearance there, . . . doing me the honor to assume my name. . . . This Specter was not thy husband."[56] At Hawthorne's death in 1864, after Emerson lamented that he was never successful in his attempts to "conquer a friendship with Hawthorne" and took careful note of the "tragic element" in him,[57] Melville penned the quatrain "Monody" in tribute to his lost friend, a man he tried to love and spiritually wed, but who could never return this level of affection with anyone, man or woman:

> To have known him, to have loved him
> After loneness long;
> And then to be estranged in life,
> And neither in the wrong;
> And now for death to set his seal—
> Ease me, a little ease, my song! . . .
> Glazed now with ice the cloistral vine
> That hid the shyest grape.[58]

The grape Melville had sought in his wedding of two hearts, was of course, as Melville knew, a toast and a testament to feeling the celebratory grape-ardor of Didymus, also known as Hafiz: "To Hafiz in grape-ardor comes / Didymus, with book he thumbs: / My lord Hafiz, priest of bowers, " who "lauds the grape of Shiraz."[59] It was Hawthorne's loss that he could not admit Melville to its mystery—and in that sense Melville knew it.

14

MOBY DICK AND THE
TRICKSTER

No analysis of the roots of Spiritual Democracy in America can overlook the works of Herman Melville, who was, after Walt Whitman, nineteenth-century America's most outrageously homoerotic poet. Melville, of course, is known primarily as a novelist, and in the view of many literary critics, his poems were not as good as his best prose fiction. He came to poetry late, only after producing what is now considered to be America's greatest novel, *Moby Dick*. But even in *Moby Dick*, Melville had begun to experiment with a poetic style that would enable him to push the bounds of fictional prose into a free-verse technique that approaches pure poetry.

Melville's object in writing *Moby Dick* was to heal a problem in the religious attitude of the United States and the world, one that, for all his efforts, stubbornly remains with us. It's the problem of projecting the human shadow, in righteous alliance with a monotheistic, jealous God. As Carl Jung showed throughout his *Collected Works*, this is a problem that only a religious attitude can resolve—an attitude of self-examination that includes a willingness to take back projections. Facing the projection of the human shadow begins not with a change in the collective humanity in the direction of greater compassion, but with a change in heart in the individual, in our moral and mental frame, toward the ultimate reality of God. Melville already knew this, and in *Moby Dick* he illuminated the moral problem of the projection of evil in the psychology of Ahab's "dictatorship" aboard the whale ship *Pequod*. Melville brings to light the tremendous violence, rage, and hate in America's relationship with the animal world—our crimes against nature—and in so doing he attempts to transform our former conceptions of "God" through a shift in the center of gravity from the human world to the gods spread throughout in the animal world. This is not done by remaining aloof to the realities of life. Jung characterized such detachment as perpetuating the "One big myth" that has dominated the globe—that "time-hallowed archetypal dream of a Golden Age or a paradise on earth" with its hopeful illusion of "universal peace" and "equality" for all women and men, of "eternal human rights," of "justice and truth" for all or the "Kingdom of God on earth."[1] Rather, Melville models a full participation in life through the living out of his spiritual vocation as a writer. By signing up for a whale hunt, Melville immunized himself, so to speak, with a dose of collective evil, and made himself into an instrument of psychic resistance against the general human infection that was moving like a plague across the globe during his day. This epidemic was the rapid spread of the market economy, greed, human arrogance, and titanic inflation, which was and continues to be the central problem in the world today, as we witness the demise of material democracy in so many nations of the world. *Moby Dick* is an excoriation of the economic strata of democracy that threatens us all with universal mayhem. The solution Melville offers to the accompanying religious problem of greed for spiritual and economic hegemony (the scramble for the moral high ground) was very like Whitman's Spiritual Democracy. Melville's symbol, moreover, was similar—a same-sex marriage, between a Christian with a Muslim pseudonym, Ishmael, and a Polynesian, Queequeg, who stood for a more polytheistic, animistic worldview than any monotheism could offer, and was a person of color to boot.

In *Moby Dick*, Melville's calling was directed forward with the goal of exposing the shadow that America's deism had ignored: whaling as industry, with the whale ship as a gigantic factory for big business, and whale oil and spermaceti as its main object, and all of it going down, like the crash of the market on Wall Street, with the ruthless Captain Ahab at the ship's helm. Melville feels the repressed anger, rage, and hatred of the "Nature God" toward the psychic infection of man (Ahab-Fedallah) that was rising in the nineteenth century like a plague. He offers a counternarrative to help create balance and harmony in what had gone wrong with the human psyche in the course of human evolution and was resulting in environmental degradation, the decimation of countless natural species, Indian-hating, plantation slavery in the South, and increasing industrial pollution. Through his exercise in active imagination, Melville eventually arrived at a personal and objective myth that offered him and us the possibility of healing.

One of the central ways he opened up the problem of the shadow to a literary

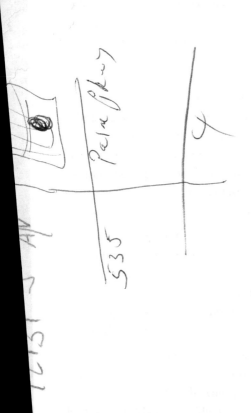

archetype of "the Trickster." In mythology
goddess, a person, or an animal who flouts
he trickster archetype is found throughout
:haic religions to the most modern. It was
in religious practices, yet, it did not seem to
i that the transcendentalists had taken up by
Goethe, the Sufi poets, and the Upanishads.
pe was explored by the American cultural
dy of the Lake Michigan Winnebago Indi-
type in North America became recognized
tury. In his preparatory note to the 1956
merican Indian Mythology, Radin writes:

:ntly, identified with specific animals,
r, but these animals are only second-
animals. Laughter, humor, and irony
)es. The reaction of the audience in
nd his exploits is prevailingly one of

"is admittedly the oldest of all figures in
in all mythologies";[3] and "Among the
, the North-west Coast of Canada and
ates but generally he is given an animal
name.[4] "Among the physical traits the trickster possesses amid a large number of tribes, moreover, the most important in Radin's view "are his enormous
penis and large intestines."[5] We've seen this frank exposure of parts of the body,
which nineteenth-century middle-class Americans were teaching their children
to hide, in Whitman's "Children of Adam" and "Calamus" poem clusters in
Leaves of Grass.

For Melville, on the other hand, the attempt to trace the origins of the
myth of spirituality to its source in the oldest of all religions moved beyond the
humanistic and anthropomorphic aspects of God to the indigenous foundation,
where his God, the trickster, is given an animal name: Moby Dick. The name
itself speaks volumes: the Great White Sperm Whale is the archetypal progenitor of the species of Leviathan that "was there swimming as of yore; was there
swimming in that plainisphere, centuries before Solomon was cradled,"[6] and
"comes floundering down from the head-waters of the Eternities."[7] This is, of
course, an image of sperm itself, squeezed out, as we shall see, when we look at

Melville's prose, by a spermatic imagination. Spermaceti wax found in the cav-
ity of the sperm whale's head and in the bones is symbolically equivalent to the
logos spermatikos, the seminal intellect of divinity.

It's likely Melville saw clearly that, through American poetry, he might illuminate (with the symbolic oil of whale fat) a theological truth across all nations
from an aesthetic point of view. This truth is one that may ultimately usher forth
a new spiritual realization in the world at large: the myth of same-sex marriage
and human equality and light as central messages of Spiritual Democracy. As
we've seen, for Whitman's Spiritual Democracy to exist in the world, same-
sex marriage will need to be institutionalized as coequal with heterosexual marriage. What the myth tells us, in light of recent controversies swirling around the
world, is that the archetype of same-sex marriage adheres to the American soul.

In Melville's view, same-sex marriage is not simply a civil matter; it's a religious matter, and it must finally be met on spiritual grounds. As a poet-shaman
Melville etched an unforgettable portrait of the quintessentially American character in his portrait of Moby Dick, a trickster that is essentially religious. "The
symbol which Trickster embodies," writes Radin "is not a static one. It contains
within itself the promise of differentiation. For this reason every generation
occupies itself with interpreting trickster anew. No generation understands him
fully but no generation can do without him. Each had to include him in all its
theologies, in all its cosmogonies."[8]

The point of Melville's myth is the transcendent mystery: the mystical wedding underlying conjunctive symbolisms. Psychology is too limited
to take this issue to its spiritual ground unaccompanied. Melville's books, like
Whitman's and Dickinson's, are meant to stimulate action in the world, to call
us to sacred work, to spiritual embodiment, and to move us all into the joy,
ecstasy, and delight of holy work. It took American poet-shamans to make the
reconnection to the trickster archetype first. In his famous letter to Nathaniel
Hawthorne, Melville draws Hawthorne's attention to the prepsychological fact
that male-male marriage is a bridge to union with the divine, and to the archetype of twinship that is indigenous to North American religious experience. It's
an experience that transcends all longings, all wants, and all desires, because it
has to do with one of the pivotal subjects of analysis: the healing of the cultural
wound of homophobia in the hearts and bodies of women and men. In Melville's
view this is a pantheistic experience as well as a monotheistic one.

What Melville's portrait of same-sex marriage suggests is that it must be
reckoned with on its own terms and on its own democratic ground. Gay and
lesbian people need "rites of incorporation" in betrothal and "rites of transition"

in marriage[9] every bit as much as heterosexual people do to celebrate their personal and cultural transformation. When same-sex marriage is banned, or when rights that have been granted are taken away, we all suffer from an attack on our Spiritual Democracy, which nourishes our individuation, regardless of our sexual orientation. Marriage is a democratic right and it's shamanistic in its native ground. The gender of the bride or bridegroom needn't matter. The important thing is the linkage to the marriage *typos* (archetype) during the process of individuation, an imprint that extends to the animal world and the cosmos (the constellation of Cetus, the whale). Melville's portrait of same-sex marriage in *Moby Dick* provides empirical evidence for a transcultural myth that has universal significance for his times and ours.

It's in this chapter, well into his narrative of facts, that the trickster, the whale, really begins to take center stage. In "A Squeeze of the Hand," Ishmael experiences the same-sex marriage portrayed in chapter 10 in a communal sense while he and Queequeg, his Polynesian husband or wife, are engaged in the avocation of squeezing lumps of cooled and crystallized spermaceti into an unctuous and musky-smelling fluid, an avocation in relation to the brotherhood of men. This might be interpreted as a metaphorical or literal act of mutual-masturbation, a symbol of transcultural transformation between men. There is a direct association to masturbation in Melville's repeated use of the word "sperm," which he sounds over and over again throughout this hilarious chapter. The act of "squeezing" becomes a reciprocal process between the men and the symbolic link between the writer and his audience is intended to be a political and a religious one as well—not merely economic (with Ahab representing production, capital, and technology). Readers can partake in the ritual action metaphorically and emotionally as an image for Spiritual Democracy. Masturbation becomes a metaphor for the activity of sperm squeezing that is economically, politically, and religiously self-liberating and self-healing for everyone when the walls of homophobia are melted down on a transcultural level and the spirit of equality is experienced through liberation of feeling.

Melville presaged the development of a political program for America that, concomitant with Whitman's revelations in the "Calamus" poems, make the incarnation of the archetype of same-sex marriage self-conscious as a living symbol for all Americans to celebrate. Prior to the writing of *Moby Dick*, Melville provided a mandala-image of a circle of shipmates at the end of *White Jacket* that depicts the experience of a communion of male brothers conjoined together homoerotically around a ritual masthead: "We main-top-men are all aloft in the top; and round our mast we circle, a brother-band, hand in hand, all spliced together."[10] In "A Squeeze of the Hand," this "brother-band, hand in hand, all spliced together" has become a circle of men engaged in an act of sperm squeezing.

Here Ishmael is speaking in a blasphemous voice as an American trickster under the mask of a whale-shaman; the use of irony and metaphor has turned this playful chapter into a sermon, which transforms the shadow of relative evil, envy, and enmity into an outrageous treatise on divine love. The core idea in Melville appears to be illuminated, like Whitman and Jung, by the notion of unitary conscience, where the trickster and shamanism are included. This means that compassion and evil (in its relative form, not absolute) are not necessarily seen as opposites; evil may also be good in some instances. Although very difficult for conservative theologians to swallow, but taken in small doses, such a healthy dose of homosexual humor can be liberating and ultimately conducive to religious liberty and spiritual freedom. But the important thing to keep in mind theologically and psychologically is not to make absolute evil and absolute good equals, otherwise genocide is praised too. That is why Jung saw early on that relativity of the God-concept is so vitally necessary for a transformation of the gods. Here is the American trickster speaking:

> Squeeze! Squeeze! Squeeze! All the morning long; I squeezed that sperm till I myself almost melted into it; I squeezed that sperm till a strange sort of insanity came over me; and I found myself unwittingly squeezing my co-laborers' hands in it, mistaking their hands for the gentle globules. Such an abounding, affectionate, friendly, loving feeling did this avocation beget; that at last I was continuously squeezing their hands, and looking up into their eyes sentimentally; as much as to say,—Oh! My dear fellow beings, why should we longer cherish any social acerbities, or know the slightest ill-humor or envy! Come; let us squeeze hands all round; nay, let us all squeeze ourselves into each other; let us squeeze ourselves into the very milk and sperm of kindness.[11]

These passages are all packed with economic, political, and spiritual meaning. But we cannot ignore the engagement with the body and depths and heights of feeling in them. Psychologically, when Ishmael says "let us all squeeze ourselves into each other; let us squeeze ourselves into the very milk and sperm of kindness," he is describing a resurrection process. This process transformed Ishmael through the function of his homoerotic imagination in relation to Queequeg and the ship's crew into a political and spiritual agent of transformation for the nation. The accent on "touch" brings the meaning of the same-sex marriage symbol down to a physical plane of shared religious experience. The religious dimension he reaches is what makes "A Squeeze of the Hand" transformative for world culture. It is the affectionate, friendly, loving feeling that this symbolic avocation begets that makes it so ingeniously illuminating, because it's in accord with the ostensible basic aim of all religions: universal oneness, compassion, and the brotherhood of man.

The transcendent position Melville arrived at, in which the avocation of sperm squeezing can be seen as synonymous with both mutual masturbation and a higher "spiritual sympathy" existing simultaneously with his fellow men, is accomplished through a metamorphosis of the poet-shamans fingers into eels, or snakes. The hands of the writer, in other words, are turning the sexual instinct into pure eros and spirit, not unlike the dervish who spins himself into an ecstasy and then writes a ghazal, a form of poem. Such a change in body-soul consciousness amid the violent activities of the whale-hunt leads Ishmael to formulate, after he has set down to write his own "Sermon" for America, where "melting" become synonymous with the economic, political, and religious process of breaking down the walls of homophobia in individuals in the nation and the world. From the United States as a nation of many nations and as the greatest producer of sperm-whale candles in the world (its hub being Martha's Vineyard, off the coast of Massachusetts), Melville hoped to illuminate all the sacred shrines and sanctuaries of the globe.

In Melville's depiction of Ishmael's participation in the sperm squeezing, the statement: "I squeezed that sperm till I myself almost melted into it" is particularly relevant. The root of latent meaning of this passage is found much earlier, in chapter 10, "A Bosom Friend." In that chapter Melville-as-Ishmael writes: "I began to be sensible of strange feelings. I felt a *melting* in me. . . . This soothing savage [Queequeg] had redeemed it."[12] As we will see, Ishmael's ritual action of taking up Queequeg's Native American *calumet* or "tomahawk pipe" and drawing in smoke with Queequeg before the two men "undress" and lie in bed together, like man and wife, "a cozy, loving pair,"[13] takes place directly after Father Mapple's (Melville's) "sermon" on the necessity of following one's vocation in obedience to the dictates of the divine will. Queequeg initiates Ishmael into the sacred mysteries of America's God, which includes the trickster. Religious freedom and evolution of moral laws cannot be complete without the trickster, as Spiritual Democracy must make plenty of room to advocate for equal rights, even if it means turning sacrosanct religious values on their head and using the most paradoxical parodies of monotheistic absolutism about sin and evil.

In "A Squeeze of the Hand," it's Ishmael who steps up to the pulpit in the shape-shifting role of the trickster to deliver own his "sermon" to America prior to the discovery of petroleum to replace the manufacture of whale oil and before the outbreak of fratricide during the U.S. Civil War. As a poet-shaman, Ishmael is preaching a new way of homoeros for the modern and postmodern world. Here same-sex marriage takes on a cultural significance for all women and men, and the "sermon" Melville delivers is meant to strike through the barriers of homophobia to the hearts of all women and men, to a transformation of our ethical and religious values. The impulse for the movement toward change in American politics and the market economy must start with individuals (as it did with Ishmael and Queequeg). The change begins with an inner transformation and spreads outward from the merchant mentality to the rest of the community— the men aboard the ship—and from there to each reader, at the level of the heart.

As we will see, Ahab is the economic man who can never stop long enough to do the inner work of uniting gender opposites within. He cannot achieve the same-sex marriage, so he can never experience a union with the divine feminine. He piles upon "the whale's white hump the sum of all the general rage and hate felt by his whole race from Adam down." He descends into madness, and once the final monomania seizes him, he becomes a "raving lunatic lashed in his hammock; and, though unlimbed of a leg, yet such vital strength lurked in his Egyptian chest"[14] that his chest becomes a mortar ready to explode its hatred and fury onto the whale that took his leg in a symbolic castration. Ahab then seeks, through homophobic revenge, to enact a marriage-death sacrifice that will culminate in his final destruction.

Following Melville's meditation on the avocation of sperm squeezing, he attempts to engage his Puritan and post-Puritan audiences in a loosening up process, at a "little lower level," whereby his "sermon" on the virtues of masturbation is transposed into the politically charged arena of the Catholic Church. This is the trickster at work.

Through the narrative voice of Ishmael in chapter 95, "The Cassock," Melville describes the peculiar office of the "mincer," who "stands in the full canonicals of his calling" in "that unaccountable cone,—longer than a Kentuckian is tall, nigh a foot in diameter at the base, and jet-black as Yojo, the ebony idol of Queequeg. And an idol, indeed, it is; or, rather, in old times, its likeness was. Such an idol as that found in that of the secret groves of Queen Maachah in Judea; and for worshiping which, king Asa, her son, did dispose her, and destroyed the idol, and burnt it for an abomination at the brook Kedron, as darkly set forth in the book of Kings." Arrayed in the flayed skin of this gigantic

Sperm Whale's penis; or the "grandissimus, as the mariners call it," Melville, in the sacred habit of the mincer, occupies "a conspicuous pulpit; intent on bible leaves." Here Melville pokes fun at the Catholic Church by presenting the mincer, quite outlandishly, humorously, and paradoxically as "a candidate for an archbishopprick, what a lad for a Pope were this mincer!"[15]

Melville's playful jabs at Christianity are not meant to offend or provoke his democratic audiences so much as they are to induce us to laugh with him, and to break down the walls of homophobia dividing us all as women and men. We have to understand that when the archetype of the trickster is at work in a religious work of art in prebellum America, whether in our examination of Whitman or Melville, the function of the poet-shaman is to lead the culture to an experience of sexuality as an aspect of the sacred, without shame. God gave men and women sexuality, Melville is saying throughout his text, so how can sex with a man or a woman be shameful? This is the narrative strategy that informs *Moby Dick*. This is more than the Greek sense of men's love; it is uniquely American.

In "The Cassock," the black skin of the enormous whale's penis, the "grandissimus," is worn as a sexual mask, and this is consistent with the actions of Siberian shamans. As Mircea Eliade tells us, among the shamans of the Far North, there were "drawings of the human sexual organs," which helped "to sanctify the [shaman's] costume."[16] The poet-shaman, when he is in his right vocation, as Melville was when he penned his great novel, gets readers to melt: to experience joy, fun, or humor, by entertaining us and entering us with his outlandish sexual jokes, pricks, and pranks. Melville is a trickster-shaman par excellence, who, like Whitman, wears the sexual mask in order to transform and liberate society. Melville was attempting to heal us from the Judeo-Christian-Islamic stereotypes and belief-systems that made same-sex love morally wrong and illegal.

In the former quote Melville uses the skin of the whale's gigantic "jet-black" member to dismember the Church's overly spiritualized representations of Christ as a glorified "white" redeemer. He then reclaims the divine phallus, which was lost through Church doctrine concerning original sin. Like the segmented pillar of Osiris, the ancient Egyptian god of the afterlife, the Church divided the trickster up into opposites of human vs. animal and spiritual vs. bodily units. By reminding us of "Yojo, the ebony idol of Queequeg" in the passage above, he is making a connection between North American and African spirituality.

In the vast corpus of his prose, Melville consistently embodied in his deeply paradoxical, narrative voice—the image of the *shaman-as-trickster*—an archetype formed in many cultural traditions that fulfills the essential purpose of transforming outworn cultural forms. The aim of such ruthless disregard of conventions in a Spiritual Democracy is to break down personal rigidity and arrive at the oneness of all religions, including the most archaic ways the human race has found to realize its spiritual capacities. In the history of religious ideas the trickster had been increasingly split off from any definite assertions of what the God-image is and who its appreciators are. Thus, all heresies, even the psychological, were demonized from the prevailing cultural pattern in Puritan America. Melville's insistence on the dusky nature of the whale's bulk elevates the trickster to the theological level by insisting that the body and matter adhere to the highest values of divinity via the marriage archetype as the sacred institution of love's most enduring and endearing values.

In 1851 when *Moby Dick* was first published, the United States was projecting its shadow and evil onto any group that was aligned in any way with tricksterish opposition to Puritanical pietism. Targets included Native Americans, women (witches), homosexuals, and blacks, but mostly, to Melville's mind, the animal world (whales, buffalo) of which the trickster, Moby Dick, is an essential part. Melville's love for his fellow men goes farther, beyond humanity, extending to the animal world. His love of man exceeds even the Roman sense of love given to us by Shakespeare in *Coriolanus,* where the two captains Coriolanus and Aufidius meet and embrace.

Melville scholar Charles Olson tells us that this is the only place in the play that Melville heavily marked with his pencil: "I see thee here / Thou noble thing, more dances my rapt heart / Than when I first my wedded mistress saw / Bestride my threshold."[17] There is a homoerotic core to Melville's love theme. Man's love of man is his final lore: the love that ultimately leads to union with Yillah, the Rachael, the Rose, or the Shekinah. The union of "sames" is a way for men to integrate the trickster. In Melville's treatise on masculine individuation throughout the course of his life it's the central path to the mystical marriage that he found in many places, including the Island of Delights in Polynesia, among the prosody of the ancient Hebrews, the sayings of Jesus, the teachings of Mohammed, and the words of the Sufi mystics (Saadi, Rumi, and Hafiz[18]) and of Shakespeare.

The problem in the three Abrahamic monotheisms that have so far guided the Near East, Middle East, and West is what might best be called the problem of "pietistic fundamentalism" in all three. As a consequence of idealistic devotion to the patriarchal forms of worship discovered by the great founder-leaders, Jesus and Mohammed, the trickster—or what in common speech might be best described as a sense of humor toward all religious forms—is simply split off. When it attempts to resurface, it's demonized. The trickster has been historically severed from the God-image and repressed in the unconscious, or is fought against externally through projection onto an enemy, group, race, or nation. When this happens, cultural neurosis follows, or even a psychosis that becomes extremely dangerous. When the shadow side of God is hunted in other ethnic groups, other races, other sexual orientations, or other religions, or when a former friend is made into an enemy, it leads to the greatest danger to man: what Jung called "psychic infections." Atrocities as extreme as religious or civil wars and genocide can happen under these conditions.

No one illuminates this problem more ominously than Melville. While keeping his eyes on the sometimes not-so-apparent unity within diversity, he sees psychic epidemics as the recurrent fate of religion, and contrasting this fate, he inserts the hilarious destiny pattern of the trickster. Fundamentalism is a psychological state of being gripped by an archaic God-image, where the archetypal power of the favored myth is grasped to be the only true revelation of God and all other revelations are believed to be false. This, of course, is the reverse of Spiritual Democracy, which acknowledges the "One True God" in all religions.

By aligning himself, therefore, with the trickster in the American character, Melville attempted to accomplish the purpose of making the evil of fundamentalism conscious and evident in Puritan American and in the world. He turned his literary talents to promoting the trickster archetype with the point of making its *imago* transparent through a religious work of art that is both tragic and comic at the same time. Yet, we have to look deeper into the meaning of Melville's symbols to comprehend their significance for the psychology of the nation and the world today. Clearly Melville was not writing for himself alone, but for his American audience and, by extension, he was, like Whitman, attempting to speak to the religious conscience of the world. For this, he needed a vehicle, a *mysterium* of a—seriously religious—trickster work of art.

Such an attitude was made self-evident by Whitman in his paradoxical statement: "Do I contradict myself? / Very well then I contradict myself, / (I am large, I contain multitudes.)"[19] This, of course, is the trickster speaking through Whitman to America and to the world. The capacity for holding ambiguity, as we have seen, is widened by the largeness of the indigenous foundation in North America and the coextension of the trickster archetype across all world cultures, extending all the way back to our origins as a species in Africa, toward containment of the multitudes in a monotheism that makes room for all.

Joel Ryce-Menuhin writes in *Jung and the Monotheisms: Judaism, Christianity, and Islam,* "At a time when religious faith has played its part in violent political difficulties in many parts of the globe, it is valuable, as an aspect of peaceful intent, to consider *the unity-in-variety* of the three monotheisms. In his total self-theory of oneness and wholeness within psyche, Jung affirms an analogy to the comprehension of oneness in God or monotheistic revelation. Jung always believes in the unus mundus—the unified one world—an eventual understanding of the unitary mirroring of the microcosm in the macrocosm and vice versa, which enables man's psyche to carry a monotheistic religious belief. Jungian psychology is behind monotheism. This empirical fact has yet to be comprehended by all of Judaism, Christianity, and Islam."[20] In other words, Jung's theory of the self provides a model for the oneness of all monotheisms. The same is true about the unity in variety in *Moby Dick*.

Nevertheless, Jung was critical of creeds and was constantly worried about the spread of psychic infections. Indeed there is a trickster at work in many of his statements on organized religion, which, like Melville's, are sometimes ambiguous, and need to be considered gingerly, and perhaps taken with a grain of salt. For instance, Jung was never easy on evil, and he was not unaware of the shadow side of Islamic history, nor, as we shall see, was Melville. But they both, to their credit, consider the unity in variety of all three monotheisms.

In 1935, while he was conducting a five-year series of seminars on Nietzsche's *Thus Spake Zarathustra*, Jung said, with a tone of religious irony, "Islam has recognized all 'the people of the Book'; it was a law to spare the people of the Book, otherwise Mohammedanism spared no one."[21] To be sure, this was an exaggeration. The warlike aspects of the Prophet's teachings are anathema to the mercy and compassion of Allah. Yet Jung saw a shadow in all major religions, including Judaism and Christianity. And while he learned and wrote a great deal about the Middle Eastern figures of Gilgamesh, Marduk, Zoroaster, Mani, and the Gnostics, he left the history of the Persian Assassins out of his research. Jung appears to have reflected little on the historical splitting of Islam, after the Prophet's death, into the two major sects—Sunni and Shiite. Jung was well aware of the warlike side of Islam, and did not hesitate to criticize the political side of the Prophet's message in the Koran—another example of the trickster at work in Jung's thinking. Certainly Jung saw that there is a trickster element in the Koran, yet he also held to the unity of Islam. Had Jung taken the time to include the Koran in his analysis of the God-image in his book *Answer to Job*, he would have undoubtedly enlightened us on some of the shadow elements in Islam. Jung found the same trickster side of the divinity in the Old Testament, the New Testament, and the Koran, as is evidenced in the irony of his statement about Muhammadanism sparing no nonbelievers. But Jung is talking about fundamentalism here, not Islamic spirituality and Sufi mysticism.[22]

A trickster element runs through Islamic thought, where the Koran calls upon Muslims to be compassionate on one hand, and, on the other, to fight infidels (kafirun) to their death unless these heretics embrace Islam. This is the imagery Jung seems to have had a problem with in the passages above.

As is true in Judaism and Christianity, where the word of God is spoken to the prophets and their followers through fixed moral commandments that can never be broken, *Kalam Allah* means the *infallible* Word of God. This means also that the Koran, like the Bible, cannot be doubted, because it is absolute. This infallibility leaves little room for the trickster. The Bible and the Koran are sacred spiritual texts, and for adherents to take any of them literally, in a fundamentalist way, is a major problem in all monotheistic systems of interpretation that are based on religious absolutism and not the *unity in variety* of all three monotheisms. Yet this unity is what Muhammad taught.

Literally taken, religious truths are the furthest thing from what Whitman, Melville, and Jung mean by Spiritual Democracy. All three agree that the ultimate truths of the world's religions are essentially the same (although dissimilar in detail), and have to do with the arrival at a primordial religious phenomenon, an experience that begins with the trickster.

Spiritual Democracy in American Deism fully recognized its debt to the monotheisms. In fact, the famous inscription on the Liberty Bell in Independence Hall in Philadelphia was borrowed from the Bible, Leviticus 25:10, which reads: "Proclaim liberty throughout all the land unto all the inhabitants thereof." The debt owed to the monotheistic notion in the development of the U.S. Constitution is incalculable, and this is the same spirit of unity that Whitman and Melville each carry forward. We see this in the novel *White Jacket*, where Melville writes:

Escaped from the house of bondage, Israel of old did not follow after the ways of the Egyptians. To her was given an express dispensation; to her were given new things under the sun. And we Americans are the peculiar, chosen people—the Israel of our time; we bear the arc of the liberties of the world. Seventy years ago we escaped from thrall; and besides our first birth-right—embracing one continent of earth— God has given us, for a future inheritance, the broad domains of the political pagans, that shall yet come and lie down under the shade of our arc, without bloody hands being lifted. God has predestinated, mankind expects, great things from our race; and great things we feel in our souls. The rest of nations must soon be in our rear. We are the pioneers of the world; the advance-guard, sent on through the wilderness of untried things, to break a new path in the New World that is ours. In our youth is our strength, in our inexperience, our wisdom. At a period when other nations have but lisped, our deep voice is heard afar. Long enough have we been skeptics with regards to ourselves, and doubted whether, indeed, the political Messiah had come. But he has come in us, if we would but give utterance to his promptings. And let us always remember that with ourselves, almost for the first time in history of earth, national selfishness is unbounded philanthropy; for we can not do a good to America but we give alms to the world.[23]

Melville, along with Whitman, was sent through the wilderness to give "alms" to the world through the establishment of a New World literature that would place Spiritual Democracy as its cornerstone. As we shall see, the remarkable fusion and mirroring symmetry in the pairing of Ishmael-Queequeg, who see the unity in variety of all three monotheisms, with the fundamentalist duo Ahab-Fedallah, is instructive as a symbol of cultural, political, and spiritual transformation.

Melville's vision of Spiritual Democracy, no less than his teacher Milton's, instructs the world "under a masque" by making "the Devil himself a Teacher & Messiah."[24] As a visionary artist,[25] Melville is outlining a present and future possibility, not predicting any political or historical outcome to an age-old problem of fundamentalism in all three monotheisms that begins with God's slaying of Leviathan. By making Ahab God's champion and lord over Leviathan and Fedallah his devil, Melville's particular concern is not exclusively with the Hebrew or Christian God, but with the absolutism and fundamentalism of Islam as well. In amplifying Melville's images in the light of recent historical events, we see the psychological dangers for the world's soul in the United States' hunting down of dictatorships and oppressive regimes with a power-driven patriarchal attitude mirrored by the very regimes it hopes to change. We have to reflect that the Muslim fundamentalists have already succumbed to the danger of absolutism.

Melville was well aware that Muhammad came to establish new laws as a mediator between Jews and Christians. The Prophet came to restore people to the "true" monotheism of Abraham and Christ, that is, to a God-notion. The Koran was believed to be a continuation of the Book, in which the God of three men—Abraham, Isma'il, and Isaac—are all One God, the same God of Jacob, to whom Muslims and Christians and all devout Jews submit.

Muslims make no distinction between the God of Mohammed, Moses, Jesus, and the Prophets. They all receive truth from the same one God (Sûrah 2:140). In this *hanif* religion, truth is from God, falsehood from Ibliss. "Your God is

One God. There is no God, but He, the Compassionate, the Merciful" (2: 163). (As we shall see, truth vs. Falsehood is the same metaphysic Melville gets into chapter 9 of *Moby Dick*, "The Sermon.") Muslims are instructed to believe in the God of Abraham and Jesus and Muhammad and to refrain from saying "three," referring to Judaism, Christianity, and Islam, for "Allah is truly One" (Sûrah 4:171). The Prophet insisted on the one religion of compassion that they all have to offer, and this is what the Sufi poets transformed in their celebrations of wine (whether symbolic or real) and the rose: the oneness of divine repose.

In the United States, and in Jung's psychology, we find religious attitudes based on the assumption of a single deity, ascribed to one national identity or religious creed. But Spiritual Democracy is the very reverse of monoism: a pluralistic notion of "Many in the One," with the "One" being a transnational religious democracy that includes the goddess and the feminine. The three monotheisms, from an historical standpoint, are all based on the principles of equality, liberty, and religious freedom, and this is the basic human feeling that we experience in reading in *Moby Dick*. Yet, in his search for Yillah, Melville, like Whitman and Jung, added the feminine element to his Islamic God-notion. Such Spiritual Democracy puts the self forward as an *answer* to the problem of fundamentalist religions. The problem in the monotheisms is not their nationalism, it is their absolutism and fundamentalism. When any religion becomes monistic, it falls short of a Spiritual Democracy, for Spiritual Democracy is not morally absolute, but pluralistic in its receptive, unprejudiced, ethical attitude. Sometimes it is outrageously funny, as when the trickster appears. Spiritual Democracy is the reverse of absolutism, and it doesn't need a new book of commandments. Relatedness and interconnectedness are at its center, not a new moral code. Its aim, rather, is unitary conscience.

If the world is to advance toward a new spiritual standpoint made possible through the relativity of what Whitman called "the science of God," or what Melville called "The great God absolute! The center and circumference of all democracy!"[26], the trickster will need to be included. Then Satan, the Devil, or Ibliss himself will no longer be demonized, but become, in the poems of a great master, a teacher and messiah who instructs "under a masque."

We see the trickster in the poems of the great Sufi master, Shams-un-din Muhammad Hafiz (c. 1320–1389) from Shiraz. A majority of his verses were destroyed by fundamentalist clerics and fanatical Muslim rulers. He is the "only man" Ralph Waldo Emerson is said to have wished to be in his lifetime.[27] Hafiz has a humorous way of reminding us that the presence of the living God is not to be found in synagogues, churches, or mosques alone, but also, and perhaps most immediately, in the temples of our own hearts and minds. In Hafiz's poems, the trickster is preserved in such an ironical way that the aim of the verses is not to enforce fear and guilt and terror of hell, but to invoke ecstasy—love and humility, by means of divine laughter induced by wine, in every cell of our bodies. He gives us the "Golden tools" and the Dionysian "feeling that God / Just came Near."[28] Nearness for him moreover means delight—and fun. "If you think I am having more fun / Than anyone on this planet / You are absolutely correct."[29]

In this humorous sense, he is very much like the comical Whitman who tells us that if we want him again, to look for him under our boot soles, as our friend and lover. Hafiz, like Whitman, becomes the universal friend of women and men; he invokes the archetype of the great green Islamic mystic-spirit Khidr and becomes one with him. In this sense, Hafiz is also like Jung, who tells us how to befriend Khidr through active imagination. He invites us to unlock the doors of our eyes that keep us from knowing the "Intelligence / That begets love / And a more lively and satisfying conversation / With the Friend"[30]; "Come to my verse again tomorrow. / We will go speak to the Friend together"[31]; and "Hafiz / Is willing to share all his secrets / About how to befriend God."[32] Hafiz does not keep his secrets to himself. By revealing the mystery of self, at the center of each person, he evokes, like Whitman and Melville, the archetype of Spiritual Democracy to the entire world's friends. In fact, there can be no divine selfhood without you, and he says it again: "God belongs to only you! / Did you hear that? / Did you hear what Hafiz just said? / God belongs only to you!"[33]

We can understand why fundamentalist clerics felt threatened by his books and destroyed them, for Hafiz seeks religion in the transreligious domain of the human heart, which beats democratically in each of us. Today only Hafiz competes with the Koran for book sales in Iran. This would be equivalent to *Leaves of Grass*, or *Moby Dick*, vying with the sales of the King James Bible in the United States. Religious fundamentalism is losing a dying battle, with Ahab and Fedallah at the ship's helm. The fundamentalist ship of the world's religions might in time go down. Absolutism appears fated to Melville, in the sense that we can see rigid adherence to the old laws of monotheistic piety crumbling before our eyes as more and more people look for a way to embrace same-sex marriage without fear of fanatical religious judgments. In his delight of Sufism, Melville embraced the wine of Hafiz, as "meditation and water are wedded forever."[34]

In *Answer to Job*, Jung traces the problem of absolutism, the petrification of God's laws into terrifying commandments that can never be broken without judgment of eternal condemnation, to Satan: "We can hardly suppose that Yahweh would have played such a trick on himself; it is far more likely that his son Satan had a hand in it. He is a trickster and a spoilsport who loves nothing better than to cause annoying accidents."[35] In a parallel way Melville used the trickster, as well as Ahab and Fedallah, as a mask, to confront America with its own inherent darkness.

When Ahab boards a British ship, the "Samuel Enderby" out of London, for instance, the two captains, the one-legged American Ahab and the one-armed British Captain Boomer, cross arm and leg in a ritual way that is as much ironic as it is tragic. Boomer tells the one-legged American captain (Ahab) that he spotted three harpoons sticking fast to the starboard fin of the White Whale. Ahab exclaims "exultingly" that they were his irons. Boomer then proceeds to confirm Ahab's suspicion that the whale that bit off his arm was indeed Moby Dick: "Aye," Ahab says, "I see! an old trick—I know him."[36]

The delight makers in Melville's myth—the aspects of the trickster that are made self-conscious and induce us to laugh at ourselves and to see the evil in America, Europe, and Islamic fundamentalism—occur through the voices of several figures in his novel, including Pip, Ishmael, Queequeg, and Fedallah. As a religious figure the Polynesian Queequeg worships an African, ebony idol, smokes a Native American tomahawk pipe, and observes Ramadan. Thus, whereas Jung used psychological consciousness (the open expression of feelings and emotions as they occurred to him during his readings of the book of Job) to turn the tables on Satan, showing the proper relationship of a man who has integrated the trickster, Melville brings an Islamic figure aboard the *Pequod* to include the devil as Ibliss. He confronts God (Yahweh and Allah) in full moral consciousness about the split in His own nature—and sacrifices not a bit of his integrity along the way.

Melville had seen into the theological problem of the moral split in God, and he portrayed it through symbols in an American myth-narrative that rises to the level of a new American Bible—one that includes radical religious sects of Islam. In his version of an American "Gospels," Melville gives the trickster the main part in the play in the figures of Moby Dick, Fedallah, and Ishmael, whose narration gives voice to the teaching of his message. As Jung pointed out: "The so-called civilized man has forgotten the trickster."[37] He adds: "There is something of the trickster in the character of the shaman and medicine-man, for he, too, often plays malicious jokes on people, only to fall in his turn to the vengeance of those who he has injured."[38]

In *Answer to Job,* Jung notes that the Old Testament God-image always seemed to find fault for the taint in his creation in man's disobedience, "but never in his son [Satan], the father of all tricksters."[39] In *Moby Dick,* Melville's

Satan, the Christian Devil, and Muslim Ibliss are all completely at fault for the calamity that ensues, yet, like in the works of John Milton and Johann Wolfgang von Goethe, evil is not projected, but rather beloved. Melville does not let Satan off the hook in any of the three monotheisms; neither the Christian Devil, nor Muslim Ibliss is released from his line. Like Jung, he reels Leviathan in on his fishing rod.

Melville's main effort in *Moby Dick* was to remind us that the trickster had been split off through the advance of civilization in its movement toward modernity and to caution the world that comedy and tragedy go hand in hand. Like Ishmael, we must learn to laugh at ourselves and also to weep. Lament is the bigger part of Melville's work. The lamentations of the prophet Jeremiah and songs of Solomon and the grief of the Native Americans and blues of African American slave music were all important to him.

In *Moby Dick*'s chapter 100, "Leg and Arm," the British captain, Boomer, refers to Moby Dick specifically as a trickster: "Oh! Cried the one-armed captain," who lost his arm to the jaws of the White Whale, "I didn't then know what whale it was that had served me such a trick, till sometimes afterwards, when coming back to the Line, we heard about Moby Dick—as some call him—and then I knew it was he."[40] The irony of the British captain lies in the connection of his words to Ishmael's stated reasons for setting out on the whale hunt from the beginning of the story in "Loomings": "BLOODY BATTLE IN AFFGHANISTAN."[41]

The synchronicity of this statement with America's recent history is amazing. The "bloody battle" to which he probably referred to was the British-Afghan battle at Parwandarah, on November 2, 1840, led by the most powerful of the Barakzai Sardars, Dost Mohammed, who maintained the upper hand during the battle but surrendered to the British in Kabul the following day. Not long after, on January 3, 1841, "One Ishmael," Melville, sailed on the whaleship *Auschnet* from the New Bedford, Massachusetts harbor, bound for the South Pacific. Today, of course, it's not only the Afghans and British who are weeping. Americans, too, feel the pain and grief of such wars. Like Jung in *Answer to Job*—Jung's whale—Melville leads us to *feel* in *Moby Dick,* and the laughter that the trickster induces in us through the sexual irony prepares us for the anguish that follows comedy.

Among the most remarkable thing about the political-economic-religious significance of *Moby Dick* is Melville's awareness of homophobia as a source of Ahab's paranoid projections. Homophobia, a term that was not coined until 1969, is similarly linked up in the novel with the fear of the God of the

Indians (the Great White Animal) and with what has more recently been termed Islamophobia, the fear of Islamization or the Muslim's God (Allah), which was particularly pronounced in Britain and the United States during the Bush administration. As we'll see, Melville's myth brings these two notions—homophobia and Islamophobia—together in an ingenious way in the chapter entitled "A Bosom Friend."

15

THE MARRIAGE OF SAMES
"A Bosom Friend"

Early on in *Moby Dick*, in chapter 2, "The Carpet-Bag," Ishmael is making his way to the whaling yard in New Bedford, Massachusetts, and a question suddenly arises in his mind as to where he will eat, drink, and sleep for the evening. As he makes his way through the dank and slimy streets on a bitingly cold Saturday night in mid-December, he stumbles upon an ash-box and considers whether the box's "flying particles" that "almost choke" him are perhaps the charnel remains from that "destroyed city, Gomorrah?"[1]

In this passage, Herman Melville takes readers through the collective history of the Judeo-Christian-Islamic past to one of the principal cities of Biblical "sin"—Gomorrah. From a psychological standpoint, he is opening readers' minds to origins in the thoughts, beliefs, and imagery of "the big three" monotheisms in order to make a transformation of consciousness possible for all people. Melville's path to healing was through the homoerotic imagination and the feeling function. This healing path has biblical roots. In 1851, the same year Melville published his great American novel, he underscored the following Bible passage from Samuel II, 1:17, where David declares his affection for his friend Jonathan, who was killed in the civil war that pitted David's forces against those of Saul: "Thy love to me was wonderful, passing the love of women." A psychic truth corresponds with biblical truth: the homoerotic imagination etched an unforgettable portrait of the quintessentially American character. Melville uttered an unmistakable truth, that the homoerotic imagination is another face of God, a hidden side of the monotheistic God-image.

This is made possible by a movement beyond Jonathan's love for David, Rumi's love for Shams, Hafiz's love for Attar, or the love of Shakespeare for his fellow man in his first one hundred sonnets, because, like Whitman, Melville brings the body and sex into the equation. Only Saadi, who Emerson and Melville both read, introduces homosexuality into his moral code, in tale IV of the *Gulistan*, a book that was altered and bowdlerized by American editors by "changing the male for the female character" and thereby "castrating the English of it, to purify Gentius's text."[2]

If anything can be said about *Moby Dick*, it's that its spiritual aim is to transform our former conceptions of what God is, in an effort to unite all religions. "One Ishmael" is the primary vehicle for this.

In Genesis 19:24, it is said that Sodom and Gomorrah were destroyed by Yahweh with "fire and brimstone," for the "cries of iniquity" that went up out of that city. In Genesis 19:28, moreover, we read—following the outpouring of Yahweh's wrath upon those two cities—that the "smoke of the country" went up "as the smoke of a furnace." Surah 29:28 of the Koran goes further: "And (remember) Lot, when he said to his people: 'You are committing the foul act [Sodomy] which no one in the whole world ever committed before you.'"

This latter reference is almost surely to homosexuality. By presenting us with what has traditionally been viewed as "shadow" within the very language of the Hebrew-Christian-Islamic religious "complex," namely the "sins" and "wickedness" of that ancient city Gomorrah, in which homosexuality is said to have been practiced, Melville exposes the patriarchal values of the monotheistic God as isolating. Ishmael ponders these passages before he goes happily to bed with Queequeg. The paradoxical effect is to lead readers toward another consciousness, to reconsider the meanings of same-sex eros for modern and postmodern times. Spiritual Democracy presents another way of reading religious texts and of being "religious" that allows for a nonjudgmental approach to sexuality, women, and the body that is free of shadow projections of sin, damnation, and evil onto others.

By presenting us with the homosexual "shadow" in the Hebrew-Christian-Islamic God-complex, Melville was paradoxically turning the patriarchal ethical values of one aspect of the monotheisms on their heads and taking readers, potentially, to new vistas of consciousness about the meanings of same-sex marriage as a channel to the divine. By inhaling some of the charnel ashes from Gomorrah into his lungs and choking on them a little before smoking the tobacco-filled "tomahawk pipe" with Queequeg in bed, Melville-as-Ishmael was inviting Victorian and Puritan readers to breathe in some of the collective memories from that ancient city with him and to assimilate some of the split-off collective "shadow" of our Judeo-Christian-Islamic past into conscious-ness. Here Melville wants us to transform our awareness of the moral opposites through a depth of feeling for new emotional and ethical values. By lifting the ban on "sin" he is making same-sex marriage possible as an imaginal proclivity within all woman and men. In this sense his efforts were similar to Whitman's, and his calling was no less in earnest to create a foundation stone for Spiritual Democracy.

Ishmael's relationship to Queequeg, however, is not initially a harmonious one. It takes some coaxing on Melville's part to loosen Ishmael up and to dis-solve the homophobic anxiety and Islamophobia that their same-sex "marriage" portends. Ishmael takes us to the source of this moral anxiety early in the book, in chapter 3, the "Spouter Inn," where he encounters the deathly innkeeper, Peter Coffin. As Ishmael enters the inn he sees on the opposite wall of the entry a "heathenish array of monstrous clubs and spears. . . . Some were thickly set with glittering teeth resembling ivory saws; others were tufted with knots of human hair; and one was sickle-shaped, with a vast handle, sweeping round like a seg-ment made in the new-mown grass by a long-armed mower. You shuddered as you gazed, and wondered what monstrous cannibal and savage could ever have gone a death-harvesting with such a hacking, horrifying implement."[3]

This is the first impression we get of Queequeg, who can be viewed as Ishmael's "twin brother," husband, or same-sex wife. His harvesting tools, or primitive implements of violence and death, are all symbolic of his cannibal-ism and vocation as a Polynesian harpooner, but they are also metaphoric of his shamanic function: as a harbinger of death and transformation for collective humanity. All of these artifacts of the whaling profession represent Queequeg's phallic, killing, and penetrating qualities as a hunter, cannibal, and warrior, as opposed to his more receptive, lunar and friendly side as Ishmael's love-partner, weaver, and mat-maker.

This death-wielding side of Queequeg's nature at first frightens Ishmael. Unable to pay for his own sleeping quarters, Ishmael is asked by Peter Coffin if he would like to share a bed with this "queer" harpooner. Ishmael responds that he "never liked to sleep two in a bed," but, "depending upon who" the savage "harpooner might be" he would be willing to "put up with the half of any decent man's blanket."[4] When the deathly innkeeper tells him in the follow-ing passage that Queequeg prefers "steaks" done "rare," Ishmael begins to feel uneasy, anxious, and "suspicious" about "this 'dark complexioned' harpooner." Here the accent on "dark complexioned" is deliberately emphasized by Melville;

an indication that the collective "shadow" of white Elizabethan England and Puritan America are about to be opened up for public scrutiny.

It's clear from the outset that Queequeg is not just Melville's homosexual shadow. He is an aspect of the self associated with divinity, the body, primitive religions, India, and Islam (he even celebrates Ramadan). As Ishmael's suspicions and anxieties mount he begins to prate:

> No man prefers to sleep two in a bed. In fact, you would a great deal rather not sleep with your own brother. I don't know how it is, but people like to be private when they are sleeping. And when it comes to sleeping with an unknown stranger, in a strange inn, in a strange town, and that stranger a harpooner, then your objections indefinitely multiply. . . . The more I pondered over this harpooner, the more I abominated the thought of sleeping with him. . . . I began to twitch all over.[5]

From a psychological angle, Ishmael is beginning to experience symptoms of acute moral, physical, and emotional extremity here. His nervous twitching is a psychological symptom of panic over his being eaten (cannibalism), over the possibility of physical violence (masculine physical strength and aggression), over Queequeg's "other" religious orientation (transreligious), and over his fear of homosexual penetration (sodomy). All of these loose associations—embedded in Melville's metaphors of same-sex "marriage"—are expressions of what Jung called a "shadow invasion" from the collective archetypal psyche.

Ishmael now presents us with yet another aspect of the collective shadow: insanity, or madness. He says: "This harpooner is stark mad, and I've no idea of sleeping with a madman."[6] Contrary to suspicions, Queequeg proves to be quite friendly, loving, and sane. What we are seeing at this early point in the narrative is the factor of Ishmael's homophobic anxiety about taking in another man's point of view—his "strange" way of life, opposite sexual orientation, different customs, dark skin color, religious pluralism, and violent tendencies. We're also seeing Melville's penchant for entering states of psychological extremity that accompany the breakdown of traditional emotional, moral, and religious values. Puritan America feared what was unknown and "queer," and projected "madness" and "evil" onto whatever was foreign, dark, uncivilized, or nonego. But as a poet-shaman, Melville saw through such illusions. He'd been to the South Seas. He was quite well read in the nonhomophobic literature of Hafiz and other Sufi poets, such as Saadi, who had made such a profound impression on Ralph Waldo Emerson.

In 1842, Emerson published a poem called "Saadi" in the transcendentalist publication *The Dial* while Melville was on his whaling voyage. Saadi had become familiar to the American West through the works of Voltaire and Johann Wolfgang von Goethe, yet, where Emerson had laid stress on the moral purity of Saadi in his view of him, Melville, in his copy of Saadi's *Gulistan*, or *Rose Garden*, "marked a chapter on homosexuality," writes Melville scholar Dorothee Finkelstein, "which even after the attempted 'purification' of the translator has still to be faced by the reader as an integral part of Saadi's moral code."[7] Emerson missed Saadi's moral teaching completely, but Melville had the benefit of a point of view outside the United States to open his eyes to the need for unitary conscience, and this democratic spirit of equality is evident in his markings of Saadi's text. There are clear indications in Melville's annotations of his copy of the *Gulistan*, kept at the Yale University Library, that shows the extreme divergence in his spiritual outlook from Emerson's. With regards to Sufi homosexuality and its impact on the Spiritual Democracy inherent in his works, Melville's meanings are much more of-the-body and physical than Emerson's, and more in line with Walt Whitman's. Melville went to the "heart" of what was ailing white heterosexual America, and through Ishmael's authorial voice, he struck through the mask.

When Queequeg first makes his appearance and reveals his face by the flame of dim candlelight, Ishmael declares: "Good heavens! what a sight! Such a face! It was of a dark, purplish, yellow color, here and there stuck all over with large, blackish looking squares. Yes, it's just as I thought, he's a terrible bedfellow." A bedfellow! This is irony here—not actual homophobia—on Melville's part. Melville, who had slept in the same bed with a Polynesian *tayo* or "friend," in the same year that Emerson wrote his tribute to Saadi, had already dissolved his homophobia by 1842 and was well on his way toward the creation of a new moral code for America that would be more transparent than Saadi's in the *Gulistan* or Shakespeare's in *Coriolanus*. Thus, in the passage above, he is inducing us to laugh in an attempt to loosen us up for the image of same-sex "marriage" that is to follow, or perhaps even to experience the emotion of religious awe.

Now, we move deeper into the cultural aspect of the narrative. Ishmael recalls the story of a "white man—a whaleman too—who, falling among the cannibals, had been tattooed by them." Then, fumbling into his bag, Queequeg pulls out a "tomahawk, and a seal-skin wallet with hair on" it.[8] Queequeg now emerges into focus as an amalgam of many cultures, religions, and races: Black, Polynesian, Asian, Muslim, Hindu, African (Yojo), and Native American (tomahawk pipe). He is moving toward a democratic image of a Queequeg-Ishmael "marriage" that is uniquely American and transnational and transreligious.

As Ishmael takes this same-sex image of Queequeg in, he thinks of "slipping out of the window." But he quickly realizes that he's on "the second floor" and cannot possibly escape an embrace with his dark-skinned "brother," which will turn out to be a squeeze, beyond Shakespeare's Elizabethan embrace, with the democratic self. Before this clinch takes place, however, he has to dissolve his homophobic anxiety and the factor of shadow projection that typically stands in the way of the marriage of sames. Ishmael declares: "I must confess, I was now as much afraid of him as if it was the devil himself who had thus broken into my room at the dead of night." Here, Ishmael clearly projects the "shadow" of Puritan American onto Queequeg in the form of the Christian "devil," or absolute evil. But his awareness of the devil goes further than that: to the devil worshipers of Persia and to the murderous shadow of Islam toward homosexuality in the Koran. Here again, the "devil" is teaching, through Melville, under a mask—an American political-religious messiah-as-trickster.

Ishmael projects an internalized image of the "devil" onto Queequeg out of apparent unconsciousness, but we must remember that the trickster is speaking through him, and this projection is meant as pure irony. As Ishmael represents part of the American self that is aligned with Christ and the devil, Melville is not at all unconscious of what such a dark-complexioned "brother" of the homoerotic imagination who happens to observe Ramadan represents. This becomes clear as the story progresses. From the standpoint of the monotheisms, when read literally in a fundamentalist way, this is clearly sacrilegious, yet, from another standpoint Melville is getting at the very heart of Saadi's moral code in an unexpurgated subtext of Islamic mysticism.

As Queequeg undresses, Ishmael imagines further. He sees "a parcel of dark green frogs" that "were running up" Queequeg's legs, like "the trunks of green palms . . . A peddler of heads too—perhaps the heads of his own brothers. He might take a fancy to mine—heavens! look at that tomahawk!" As he reaches into his pocket, Queequeg reveals what appears to Ishmael to be a "curious little deformed image with a hunch on its back, and exactly the color of a three days' old Congo baby." Ishmael continues: "Remembering the embalmed head, at first I almost thought that this black manikin was a real baby preserved in some similar manner. But seeing that it was not at all limber, and that it glistened a good deal like polished ebony, I concluded that it must be nothing but a wooden idol, which indeed it proved to be."[9] So Queequeg worships a phallic "pagan" god, Yojo, at a self-constructed "shrine or chapel." This little ebony "Congo idol" appears to be from Africa. With its hunched back, this strange little idol proves to be a religious emblem or icon for phallus.

In chapter 95 of *Moby Dick*, "The Cassock," as we've seen, Melville undresses this phallic idol for readers by humorously drawing our attention to the peculiar office of the "mincer," who "stands in the full canonicals of his calling" in "that unaccountable cone,—longer than a Kentuckian is tall, nigh a foot in diameter at the base, and jet-black as Yojo, the ebony idol of Queequeg."[10] The outrageousness of this scene lies in the heretical fact that it flies in the face of Islamic fundamentalism, as well as the Jewish God's commandments that there shall be no worship of any pagan idols, and not so much as a mention sodomy. The pure monotheism of Abraham that Muhammad came to restore as the "Messenger of God" was originally divided into 114 surahs, or chapters, of the Koran and was sent down through the angel Gabriel in pure Arabic, directly from Allah. Under the leadership of Muhammad, Muslims were led as a political and religious body to capture Mecca in 630 AD, and the "Prophet's first move was to enter the Ka'ba, or Sacred Shrine, and destroy the pagan idols—said to number 350—housed in it, and to institute the rite of pilgrimage to the Sacred Shrine, which Abraham was said to have founded centuries earlier."[11]

Yet, unlike Ishmael and Queequeg, Melville is no idolater. He is a true believer in what Whitman calls Spiritual Democracy, and his pantheistic sweep is just as wide. In his pre-Adamite vision he sees that "the whole world was the whale's; and king of creation, he left his wake along the present line of the Andes and the Himmalehs" and the "unsourced existence of the unspeakable terrors of the whale," he adds, "having been before all time, must needs exist after all humane ages are over."[12]

As a poet-shaman, Ishmael is going into depths of the transnational unconscious here. He is asking Americans, and readers all over the globe, regardless of one's skin color, or sexual orientation, to withdraw projections of the "devil" onto all idolatrous forms of worship, which Yojo seems to represent. For what is Yojo but an image? And the whale is but a trace upon "Egyptian tablets, whose antiquity seems to claim for them [Leviathan or whales] an almost fossiliferous character."[13] He is confronting all men and women with their (or our) own homophobia and Islamophobia and fear of atheism or "Saturn's grey chaos,"[14] as such fears turn out to be religious at their root.

After Queequeg undresses, he takes his tomahawk up from the table, examines its "head for an instant, and then holding it to the light, with his mouth on the handle" puffs "out great clouds of tobacco smoke. The next moment," Ishmael says humorously, "the light was extinguished, and this wild cannibal, tomahawk between his teeth, sprang into bed with me. I sang out, I could not help it now; and giving a sudden grunt of astonishment he began feeling me."[15]

Now this passage is psychologically astute. For as Nathaniel Philbrick showed in his retelling of the *Essex* shipwreck disaster, upon which the story of *Moby Dick* was based, the central psychological factors that kept the men of that American whaleship from sailing comfortably to the Islands of Polynesia were fears of cannibalism—and homophobia.[16] Not only does Ishmael quickly accept Queequeg's sexual orientation as a tayo, but he assimilates his native savagery and cannibalism too: "I myself am a savage, owing no allegiance but to the King of Cannibals; and ready at any moment to rebel against him."

That Melville had the audacity to turn such a story as the tragedy of the *Essex* around in such a comic and paradoxical way suggests that Ishmael was not only making "friends with the shadow" in a classical Jungian sense, he was also "marrying" him. This is an irony that seems as startling as it's drolly democratic to a less disquieted audience. It makes the assimilation of the shadow of homophobia (and Islamophobia) transparent as a psychological and political problem for the transformation of the religious consciousness in all people, as seen from the new scientifically informed observatory of Spiritual Democracy.

Despite Ishmael's startled singing, he moves quickly beyond homophobic angst to a position of radical acceptance. The object of Ishmael's nervous twitching, the cannibalistic homosexual "shadow" that made him tremble all over with physical symptoms, has now become integrated into a transformed consciousness, and he assumes a comfortable and relaxed position beside Queequeg in bed. Smoking the Indian calumet together, the two men lie together for the first time in the embrace of a male-male sacred marriage of two hearts. This is a new image of marriage that is purely imaginal; it's not an outer marriage with a same-sex partner, but an inner psychological "marriage" with a same-sex lover: the homoerotic/homospiritual self.

To the degree that the pairing of Ishmael-Queequeg can be interpreted psychologically, religiously, and politically as a "uniting symbol" in the American psyche, Ishmael represents a democratic attitude of equality, love, and religious liberty toward his fellow man, regardless of race, faith, sexual orientation, or skin color. This is a new image of an American self that stands outside the tensions of homophobic anxiety that normally keeps men from examining their sexual antipathy toward other men. As Ishmael looks at Queequeg he says that the Polynesian's head reminds him a little of "George Washington's head, as seen in the popular busts of him" while being "cannibalistically developed."[17] Again, the aim is to illuminate the origins of Spiritual Democracy to America's founding father and first president.

George Washington, who both Whitman and Melville revered since child-hood, had made every effort to frame his own proclamations in a language that would be acceptable to all faiths. It was regressive that his successor, John Adams, called for Christian worship as the basic way to realize this dream. It remained to the efforts of Thomas Jefferson and James Madison to work out the details that would ensure that the U.S. Constitution would preclude any such private religious proclamations and guarantee that there would be no preten-sions toward the nourishment of a national religion,[18] especially a Christian one. Adopted on July 4, 1776, the Declaration of Independence—which is, according to Davis, "arguably the most widely known and influential political document in the history of the world"[19]—provided the backbone for Whitman's visions of Spiritual Democracy.

A look at the attitudes of the framers toward religion and the foundation of "original intent" in the Constitution illuminates how Whitman and Melville used the first, Constitutional stage of democracy to shape their political and spir-itual agenda toward the "third" stage, which seems to be attempting to be born in our own age. The dialectic in the tension between the founding fathers was situated within the opposites of atheism versus Deism from the Enlightenment, with Unitarianism (Jefferson and Adams) and Christianity as political fallbacks. Yet, the question of whether there will be an alliance or coalition between the government and religion became the rallying point of the Constitution's princi-pal architect, James Madison, who argued persuasively that a Bill of Rights was necessary to ensure that "the civil rights of none shall be abridged on account of religious belief, nor shall any national religion be established, nor shall the full and equal rights of conscience in any manner be infringed."[20] Madison, too, might best be described as a Deist, for he could defend the Constitutional gov-ernment by appealing to its progenitor as "God," whom he described as "the supreme lawgiver of the universe."[21]

The chief author of the Declaration, Thomas Jefferson, believed that the only way to know God's will was by discovering the "laws" of nature, or "Nature's God" (which was the term used in the Declaration of Indepen-dence).[22] Although a number of conservative Christian scholars complained that the admixture of biblical and Enlightenment influences on the shaping of the Declaration and especially the term "Nature's God" does not reflect the supreme "God of Scripture,"[23] the founding fathers—as well as Whitman and Melville—might have argued that any reference to the biblical God in Judeo-Christian terms would have violated the first article of the Constitution and its religious clauses. The term "Nature's God," a Deist notion (Thomas Paine,

The Age of Reason), made room for the practice of all religions, in a potentially multiethnic, multicultural, multispiritual United States. It's not the biblical God that's the author of nature, in Whitman's and Melville's views, but nature itself is the author of the political ideas governing the Declaration and the principle Whitman calls Spiritual Democracy.

Queequeg's harpoons, spears, and tomahawk are all symbols for the penetrating and aggressive qualities of the "solar" masculine principle, as opposed to the more receptive, loving, and feminine "lunar" aspects, which the "Congo baby," the tattoos of green tree frogs, and the Indian calumet represent. From a psychological angle, Ishmael's fear of being "felt" by another male is the horror of being penetrated by Phallus, the agent of death to the puerile ego. One symptom of this fear is homophobia; another is the fear of death to one's lopsided religious beliefs, and what has only recently been termed Islamophobia. In "The Counterpane," Melville takes us to the historical roots of this moral anxiety, which proves at bottom to be religious or spiritual. When Ishmael awakens in the morning with "Queequeg's arm thrown over" him "in the most loving and affectionate manner" possible, he says: "You had almost thought I had been his wife."[24] Here, the moral tension of taking in another man's position seems to have dissipated, and Ishmael leaves readers free to imagine whatever we might think transpired the previous evening. This is the beauty of the symbol of same-sex marriage: it can be interpreted in a number of different ways, and no one interpretation can claim to have the only right answer.

While many readers might see this symbolic union between the two men as the product of nineteenth-century attitudes toward sex, where two men sleeping together could have tolerated body-to-body contact without the complications of sex getting in the way, by today's standards such an interpretation of this scene following the gay liberation movement would be naive without a discussion of homosexual politics entering into the dialogue. But some kind of a metanoia of consciousness took place in Ishmael's body, spirit, and soul, for Queequeg's compassionate embrace dissolved any homophobia Ishmael formerly held toward him, when Ishmael says: "I felt a melting in me." What melted the homophobia and transformed it into a marriage of sames was a memory engram, or imprint of a numinous childhood dream.[25]

In *Moby Dick*, Melville worked through his homophobic anxiety, and he is asking us, as readers, to dissolve our own homophobia as well, for when we do, the force of love can flow toward our fellow men without obstruction. "Now, take away the awful fear," Ishmael says, "and my sensations at feeling the supernatural hand in mine [in the childhood dream the hand of God was upon him] were very similar, in their strangeness, to those which I experienced on waking up and seeing Queequeg's pagan arm thrown around me." Though Ishmael tried to move Queequeg's "arm—unlock his bridegroom clasp—yet, sleeping as he was, he still hugged me tightly, as though naught but death should part us twain." At last, despite the religious anxiety of being hugged by "a fellow male in that matrimonial sort of way,"[26] Ishmael managed to awaken Queequeg from his bridegroom-sleep. And just as he was coming to consciousness, Ishmael pronounced something quite meaningful for his generation, for our present generation, and for generations to come. He says:

Queequeg, do you see, was a creature in a transitional state—neither caterpillar nor butterfly. He was just enough civilized to show his outlandishness in the strangest possible manner. His education was not yet completed. He was an undergraduate.[27]

This passage may help us understand why Ishmael said in his narrative of "facts," that "if at my death my executors, or more properly my creditors, find any precious MSS. in my desk, then here I prospectively ascribe all the honor and the glory to whaling; for a whale-ship was my Yale College and my Harvard."[28] Melville himself dropped out of school at Albany Academy to help support his family after his father's untimely death, and he never got more than an eighth grade education. Yet, for this lack of formal education, he was remarkably well read. Like Whitman, Melville knew what it will take to arrive at world peace, and that is an acceptance of one's fate and all that happens to a person in our collective transit toward Spiritual Democracy. He asks:

What of it, if some old hunks of a sea-captain orders me to get a broom and sweep down the decks? What does that indignity amount to, weighted, I mean, in the scales of the New Testament? Do you think the archangel Gabriel thinks any the less of me, because I promptly and respectfully obey that old hunks in that particular instance? Who ain't a slave? Tell me that. Well then, however the old sea-captains may order me about, I have the satisfaction of knowing that it is all right; that everybody else is in one way or other served in much the same way— either in a physical or metaphysical point of view, that is; and so the universal thump is passed round, and all hands should rub each other's shoulder-blades, and be content.[29]

What Ishmael is modeling for us here is *amor fati*, love of one's fate. He's saying that we all have a destiny of some kind to live out our vocation, and this calling is part of the "grand programme of Providence that was drawn up a long time ago."[30] Like Whitman, his calling is to strike through the clothing of thick-coated shams to the way to Spiritual Democracy, the universal domain of light and love: "All hands should rub each other's shoulder-blades, and be content." In other words, we are all in this mess together!

Our religions are in an appalling state. Melville's saying we should all get into bed together and smoke the tomahawk peace pipe with Queequeg, a symbol that unites together all opposites, love and violence, good and evil, war and peace. The marriage ceremony is consummated by smoking the tomahawk pipe together in sacred union. As a symbol for global transformation, the tomahawk pipe is the best and most enduring weapon against religious fundamentalism, for it solves the problem of religious wars through a paradoxical solution. Smoking the tomahawk pipe on American shores, Ishmael seeks to restore the United States to its truest vision of democracy. What might Melville have been thinking when he created the transforming symbol of the tomahawk pipe? Clearly, the trickster is made translucent through this image of religious change in America. As the ritual smoke is consummated during the sacrament of same-sex marriage, it is meant to unite the opposites of war and peace.

Thus, the solution to the problem of religious fundamentalism and war in *Moby Dick* is presaged by the offering of the tomahawk pipe to Ishmael—and by extension to us—from Queequeg, as a peacemaker. In Whitman's visions of Spiritual Democracy we saw that in 1847 he said: "I remember I stood one Sunday forenoon, / (the Peacemaker)."[31] Melville too created a symbol for peace in a ritual of reconciliation with what the United States had become divorced from: indigenous American values.

Melville was initiated into the meaning of same-sex marriage on the Island of Nukeheva in the Polynesian Islands, when he apparently slept for several days next to a tayo, a homosexual of the tribe.[32] Whatever it was that Melville experienced on the whale ship in relation to his fellow men, or on land in relation to his Polynesian "friend," or in relation to his countrymen, his experiences with men became a turning point for a marriage symbol that was indeed in a "transitional state" in the United States.

We don't expect a whale to turn against man or a ship as it does in *Moby Dick,* but when the animal side of God (trickster) is hunted down with malicious intent as it is in the story, the self will turn against man with a vengeance and the trick will be on man, not God. Nature will rebel against man, as she is doing today, tragically in the sad phenomenon of climate change. Radical Islamic terrorists continue to wage jihad against the West in an effort to thwart its attempts to achieve economic, political, and religious hegemony. As a modern myth for our times, *Moby Dick* can help us understand some of these issues and provide some clues as to how readers can translate the alchemical gold in the book into principles for sacred action. These hints are not always made self-evident as truths, but that Melville knows the truth that Father Mapple preaches is indisputable for anyone who has meditated long enough on the text to make its teaching manifest.

Since the "universality" of the trickster is "co-extensive" with "shamanism,"[33] we would be wise to look to shamanism for a clue to the enigma of *Moby Dick*. At the center of Melville's invective is the factor of homoeroticism that forms a healing narrative in the novel. For Melville, for his nineteenth-century audience, and for us today, chapter 10, "A Bosom Friend," is intended to be hilarious, as are other sections of the book where the trickster emerges, not only to provoke comic relief in the midst of the more tragic and serious parts of the book, but to confront a moral evil that strikes at the very heart of Jewish, Christian, and Islamic mysticism: man's love for his friend (Khidr). As we have seen the association to Khidr, the Verdant One, is evident in the "parcel of dark green frogs" that "were running up" Queequeg's legs, like "the trunks of green palms." As Ishmael says, "What could I think of a harpooner who stayed out of a Saturday night clean into the holy Sabbath, engaged in such a cannibal business as selling the [New Zealand] heads of dead idolaters?"[34]

By integrating the trickster and confronting Satan in the American character, which is religious hatred in all its aspects, including hatred of "Nature's God," symbolized by the Whale, the Goddess, and sexuality, Ishmael turns the tables on religious orthodoxy or fundamentalism in the most ironic way possible: by using humor (comedy) as a way to instruct us that what we need today is not the old-time religion and its rigid set of moral codes, but new emotional and ethical values that may shift with the tides of history. He makes us all equals, including Indians, Maori, Polynesians, Muslims, Africans, blacks, homosexuals, men, and women—even bison and elephants and wolves and whales. He brings the animals into his narrative, so that we will not forget our instinctive inheritance and animal intelligence.

Melville's protest against the Old Testament and New Testament and Koranic images of God was directed against what was dead in the Judeo-Christian-Islamic myths and in need of resurrection: namely the repressed energies of the human Spirit-Soul-Body in all women and men, including not only sex but violence. Thus, for a further transformation of self-consciousness to occur in America, a radical democratic way of reimagining of the archetype of same-sex "marriage" was needed.

Biblical scholar Stan Goldman, in his 1993 book *Melville's Protest Theism,* saw correctly that the quest for homoerotic "touch" in Melville's epic poem *Clarel* is traced to a religious quest for "spiritual sympathy" between men. This approach, in contradiction to Feidler's, is limited by its accent on the religious and the spiritual, but he misses the homosexual reading that is Melville's main point at the political level of democracy. As we've seen, Melville referred to the "coming of the literary Shiloh of America"—and here again he is speaking of himself—as a "political Messiah." Melville added: "He has come in us, if we would but give utterance to his promptings."[35]

We therefore need to arrive at a symbolic middle ground in order not to get caught between the clashing rocks of the opposites, between a homosexual vs. a homospiritual line of interpretation, for clearly his book was prophetic of what we're seeing in politics today. For this practical way of reading his text, an archetypal-developmental method is needed, a symbolic and personal way of approach that pays as much attention to the affective and emotional aspects in Melville's character as to the spiritual-archetypal facets. Many a critic's ship has been sunk between the Scylla and Charybdis of the living symbol Ishmael-Queequeg.

A better way to go, then, as a possible solution to these problems, is to take up the meaning of the symbolism in general, where we ought be able to employ the tools of analytical psychology, if it were not for the fact that "even here," in John Beebe's words: "a certain homophobia has persisted, making it difficult to give equal consideration to images of male-male coniunctio that analysts and psychotherapists have so freely granted to male-female coniunctio, as evidence of individuation. Fortunately, a new breeze has been blowing in the less anima-biased direction of the interpretation of the *union of sames*—as a motif in literature, film, myth, and legend—within the past decade; and so, the Jungian critic has at last some conceptual light to shed on a theme that is quite central to the body of Melville's oeuvre, as it is within the genre of shamanic visionary literature generally."[36]

What such an exploration can yield is a new understanding of the role that the union of sames played in Melville's life and individuation, as well as in the poetical and political life of the new nation. By keeping an eye on the life-pulse of Melville's relations with his fellow women and men and on the factor of synchronicity at work in his destiny pattern, we will be in a better position to illuminate how the symbol of male-male marriage was incarnated through his relationships and art into a uniting symbol that is alive with psychological, religious, and political meaning for the benefit of all nations. The self does not always incarnate itself as bisexual or androgenic. It can also be incarnated as a same-sex image: an inverted integer. In Melville's work, the self is not typically bisexual, or androgenic; it is atypically homoerotic. The androgyny is "inverted" in Melville's oeuvre, in a same-sex sort of way.

Melville, in a laudatory review of Hawthorne's *Mosses From An Old Manse*, points out the somewhat intangible nature of Melville's relationship to homosexuality: "I feel that this Hawthorne has dropped germinous seeds into my soul. He expands and deepens down, the more I contemplate him; and further, and further, shoots his strong New England roots into the hot soil of my Southern soul."[37] The imagery in this passage is unmistakably homosexual, but we don't get the same feeling, as we do in reading Whitman, that Melville is talking about literal homosexuality here. The "marriage" of Ishmael-Queequeg may be homologous with homosexual coupling, but we can't quite believe it as a literal fact. There is a trickster element at play that continuously seems to elude us in our efforts to pin Melville down. That is because he is not writing out of the old myths of romantic love from Europe, Greece, or Asia.

Paradoxically, everything that is elusive, ambiguous, and problematic about Melville's controversial images of same-sex love is emblematic of what we find in shamanistic American poetry generally. The poet-shaman straddles the opposites in a peculiar sort of way, and we often don't know what he or she is talking about: Is Melville kidding us? A portrait of same-sex marriage in 1851 before the word "homosexuality" was coined? There is a paradox at play in Melville's myth that reveals the underlying archetype of the trickster-as-shaman at work in his imagery. As Hafiz says: "I know you have a hundred complex cases / Against God in court, / But never mind, wayfarer, / Let's just get out of this mess."[38]

What's truly astounding about Melville's uses of language, in contradistinction to Whitman's, is his prepsychological elucidation of the archetype of same-sex marriage as central to the American experiment. In their "heart's honeymoon," Ishmael and Queequeg lie in bed together, a "cozy, loving pair." There is nothing particularly instinctual ("lower") about this passage, yet it is remarkably astute psychologically because it gets at the meaning of love ("higher") through the heart, the area of religious emotion. Melville, like Whitman is trying to draw our attention to the prepsychological fact that male-male coniunctio, like the symbol of heterosexual "marriage" portrayed as the only form of matrimony sanctioned by God in the Bible and Koran, is a possible bridge to union with the divine. It represents a potential embrace between ego and self, friend and brother, man and man, man and nature, man and God, Muslim and Christian, American and Polynesian, Indian and African.

In Whitman's work, on the other hand, the sexual instinct is developed in great detail, but the image is not fleshed out. Whereas in Melville the image of same-sex marriage and its psychological and religious meaning holds ultimate sway over sex. The difference between these two poets is the difference between the image and impulse, instinct and symbol. We don't know as much about Melville's homosexuality as we do about Whitman's, but we do know that Melville valued the male coniunctio highly, so much so that he placed it as a cornerstone of the American mythos of Spiritual Democracy.

In Melville's portrait of the symbol of same-sex marriage we must remain "open" to the most liberal, democratic, and even literal aspects of his book so that we do not leave actual homosexuality or any religious belief out as a viable reading. This way of re-visioning and reinterpreting the same-sex symbol in *Moby Dick* is the only way to keep the image alive, without deadening it or getting caught in the clash of opposites that is rampant in the field of Melville criticism.

Such an ambiguous attitude toward the meaning of the symbol, where psychic and literal forms of homosexuality are held in consciousness at the same time, is the way Melville approached the enigmatic symbol of the White Whale, which proved to be white and black, masculine and feminine, good and evil. Most importantly, moreover, we need to arrive at a nonhomophobic style of interpretation that remains "open" to the democratic way of life of all people in a liberal society. This approach should be always ready to do battle with archaic laws and moral values that are out of touch with the spirit of the times. This is the meaning of the tomahawk pipe that Ishmael and Queequeg smoke together before the whaling voyage takes place. Queequeg is a peacemaker.

Thus, the spiritually democratic elements in *Moby Dick* symbolized by the tomahawk pipe and the "marriage" between Ishmael, the novel's narrator, and his New Zealand-Polynesian male "wife," Queequeg, are contrasted in the book with Ahab and the figure Fedallah, an Islamic name which means "God's assassin." On the one hand we have the tomahawk pipe Ishmael and Queequeg smoke together as a symbol of peace and Spiritual Democracy, while on the other we have the pair of Ahab and Fedallah, a symbol of fundamentalism and war.

Melville was the first to put forth same-sex marriage as a living symbol and a cornerstone of the new American myth of Spiritual Democracy. He contrasted this with a counter narrative of Ahab's fundamentalist pairing with Fedallah, in a religious work of genius. By cornerstone, we mean a sacred stone set at the corner of a new mythic construction of the American self, inscribed with a starting point (Melville, 1851) and completion date (Whitman, 1860; Dickinson,

1861), along with the names of the architects. To these three American poets, this sacred stone—same-sex marriage—is a rock that the builders of the monotheisms rejected, the head of the corner (Matthew 21:42). Same-sex marriage is therefore a rock, a spiritual foundation of the book *Moby Dick*. It is the ground on which Melville formed his marriage of two hearts with his friend and mentor, Nathaniel Hawthorne, the spiritual godfather of the book.

Thus, the archetype of same-sex marriage and the movement surrounding it during the opening of the twenty-second century are part and parcel of the new myth of Spiritual Democracy that Melville and Whitman and Dickinson all foresaw as divine and golden in us. This announcement of a New World myth takes place through the narrative voice of Ishmael.

16

MOBY DICK
The Characters behind the Names

Before progressing further into the heart of Herman Melville's new myth for our times, it's important to establish the identities of some of the major characters in *Moby Dick* so that we may enter into their "hidden" meanings in the context of our current world situation. This will shed light on why this particular novel, published more than a century and a half ago, in the fall of 1851, provides us with a complementary vision to Walt Whitman's notion of Spiritual Democracy, and why it's so relevant today as a myth for our times. We must first acknowledge that as Melville was the first American-born poet to put forth his visions of Spiritual Democracy for the benefit of the world, and because his way of approach to the meaning of God is through allegorical symbolism, reading him will require a bit of psychological elucidation.

ISHMAEL

Any reader of *Moby Dick* will immediately see the impact of the Old Testament of the Bible, as well as the Koran, and these sacred texts' remarkable influence in shaping Melville's myth. This becomes clear in the opening line of his first chapter, "Loomings," where the book's narrator famously says: "Call me Ishmael." Let's listen to Ishmael speak in this passage that conveys his peculiarly American state of mind:

> Call me Ishmael. Some years ago—never mind how long precisely—
> having little or no money in my purse, and nothing particular to interest
> me on shore, I thought I would sail about a little and see the watery part

of the world. It is a way I have of driving off the spleen, and regulating the circulation. Whenever I find myself growing grim about the mouth; whenever it is a damp, drizzly November in my soul; whenever I find myself pausing at coffin warehouses, and bringing up the rear of every funeral I meet; and especially whenever my hypos get such an upper hand of me, that it requires a strong moral principle to prevent me from deliberately stepping into the street, and methodically knocking people's hats off—then, I account it is high time to go to sea as soon as I can. This is my substitute for pistol and ball. With a philosophical flourish Cato throws himself upon his sword; I quietly take to the ship.[1]

Who was the "original" Ishmael? According to biblical legend, Ishmael was the illegitimate son of Abraham, the archetypal progenitor of the Jews and Arabs. In the Bible, the angel of the Lord said to Ishmael's mother, Hagar, that Ishmael "will be a wild man; his hand will be against every man, and every man's hand against him" (Genesis: 16:12). Born to an Egyptian maidservant, Ishmael was rejected by his stepmother, Sarah, for mocking the birth of his younger half-brother, Isaac. So we can see that the biblical Ishmael was himself a bit of a trickster. Going to sea is Melville's solution to the bipolarity of a religious experience of being momentarily gripped by the trickster. It's interesting to note that the archetype Melville encountered on his trip to Polynesia was the very model that is self-evident in Whitman's work: bi-erotic marriage. In Melville's case it was revealed to him in the polyandrous marriage practices of Polynesia, where it was not the man who took two or more wives (as Abraham did), but the woman. Earlier than Melville, Honoré de Balzac had asked the rhetorical question: "Should there be a little Hagar in each marriage establishment?"—meaning that to accept a little healthy shadow of monogamy in one's fantasy life at least can be a boon to one's individuation. Melville brought back with him an answer from the South Seas.

In anger, the biblical Sarah had asked Abraham to cast Hagar the Egyptian and Ishmael her son out from their home. Although grieved over this, Abraham listened to Sarah, because Yahweh, the Hebrew god, had told him he would preserve Ishmael's seed and make of him a great nation, even while leaving him a fatherless orphan. As a living symbol, Melville's Ishmael offers some way beyond the Judeo-Christian (and also Islamic) myth of the one monotheistic and just God toward a more all-inclusive standpoint of the democratic self that has integrated the possibility of a shadow side to God that has integrated the trickster. Despite the charges of heresy that Melville knew would be hurled against him, it was a task that he nevertheless knew was Christian—in the democratic spirit of things. He knew from his Protestant standpoint that to write a version of a new Gospels for his century—to admit a further revelation of the divine drama—would indeed be viewed as heretical, and that he would be harshly criticized for writing it.

As a whale hunter, Melville's "vocation" had amounted "to a butchering sort of business," yet, Ishmael also points out religiously that "almost all the tapers, lamps, and candles that burn round the globe, burn, as before so many shrines, to our glory!"[2] Melville was justifying the "vocation" of whaling because his calling as a writer was to bring illumination to the world, and without his experiences on the whale ship, the book would never have been written. He uses whaling ironically as a metaphor to cast light on the collective "evil" of the industrial civilization: what nineteenth-century America was doing to deplete the populations of whales and bison, as Asia had done to the population of elephants, and as Africa is still sadly doing today. But more important, beyond the obvious environmentalism inherent in the novel, is the religious irony—the confrontation of fundamentalism. In this sense, *Moby Dick* was the first novel to form an incisive criticism of the major monotheisms by opening them up to a greater inclusiveness that makes all of the shrines of the world holy, including the shrine of the pagan.

Melville's message in *Moby Dick* is to "civilize civilization and Christianize Christendom"[3] by making homophobia, Islamophobia, the neglected feminine (Hagar), and the trickster conscious in us. He is quick to remind us that oil from sperm whales was also used to "light up the world." The largest producer of sperm whale–oil candles on the East Coast was on Martha's Vineyard off the coast of Massachusetts, and it was from that small island that spermaceti candles were imported to many parts of the world. Thus, he originally saw the technology of the whaling industry as a divinely ordained vocation, a calling that made possible the continuing evolution of human consciousness on a collective scale.

Melville starts the book with an Old Testament story, the story of Ishmael. Significantly, he starts with a Hebrew myth, not a Christian or Islamic one. This shows us that he's attempting to take Puritan readers back to their origins in the books of the Old Testament, primarily through the stories of Jonah, Kings, Ecclesiastes, and especially Job. And he did this, like Whitman, without the benefit of a traditional education at a prestigious university like Harvard or Yale, but rather by drawing on his experience as an ordinary whaler. Recall that Ishmael calls attention to the legitimacy of his education at sea by saying: *"No dignity in whaling? The dignity of our calling the very heavens attest. Cetus is a constellation in the South! . . . ; if, at my death, my executors, or more properly my creditors, find any* precious MSS. in my desk, then here I prospectively ascribe all the honor and glory to whaling; for a whale-ship was my Yale College and my Harvard."[4]

The deep truth of this statement would not become apparent until the middle of the twentieth century, when it became widely agreed that Melville was the greatest literary genius that the United States had yet produced. However, this does not explain why the whale-ship became his Harvard and Yale. On his journey homeward on the U.S. Navy man-of-war vessel, Melville spoke of books that "we pick up by chance here and there; those which seem put in our hands by Providence; those which pretend to little, but abound in much."[5] Among such books picked up by chance, or with what Jung calls "synchronicity," was a book or books that dealt with a branch of a series of imams, or revealed prophets within Islam, who followed Mohammad. This is the sect of radical fundamentalist Islam known as the Ismailiya, and their particular belief is that the prophecies would stop with the seventh imam, Ismā'īl, the Arabic for Ishmael, to whom the religious texts refer to as the "hidden prophet."[6]

From one or more sources, Melville made it a special study to research this sect of fundamentalist Islam closely, and Melville scholar Dorothee Finkelstein tells us about this in her book *Melville's Orienda*. Finkelstein gives a comprehensive and compelling treatment of the "hidden" significance of Melville's naming of his narrator: Ishmael and his mother Hagar would be given transnational significance. For in chapter 2:158 of the Koran it's said that Safa and Mara, the names of two mountains in Mecca where Hagar is said to have run to and fro with Ishmael in quest of water in the wilderness, are surely "beacons of Allah." Thus, as we shall see, the opening line "Call me Ishmael"—perhaps the most famous line in American literature—is given a double significance. Ishmael is both the son of Abraham and Hagar *and* the hidden seventh imam.

In discussing the story of the man-child who is "caught up" to God in the Apocalypse of St. John, Jung writes in *Answer to Job:* "The story of Hagar may be a prefiguration of this."[7] Thus, Melville's Ishmael is seen in this light, not as a fundamentalist Ismaili, but as a "common seaman" called by Yahweh, Christ, and Allah in historical succession of monotheistic revelations to teach the true message of God to humankind. It's significant moreover that he would hear this call in a chapter called "The Sermon."

QUEEQUEG

Ishmael's individuation as an American does not truly begin to unfold until he merges his religious identity with the identity of the Polynesian wild man,

Queequeg. Queequeg might even be associated with the first principle of American democracy, namely the "freedom of religion." And Queequeg manages to represent at least five types of spirituality: Polynesian, Native American, African, Hindu, and Muslim. He is "fearful of Christianity, or rather Christians,"[8] however. And, no matter how "comical" his religious attitude might appear to religious orthodoxy, Queequeg is all-inclusively democratic in his spiritual outlook. He opens the same possibility to Ishmael. Through his relationship to Queequeg, Ishmael embraces the universality of all religious dispensations. Although his name identifies him as an ancestor of Islam, Ishmael was raised Presbyterian, and his general outlook is that of a primitive Christian. As a son of Abraham, he embodies the monotheistic spirit of Judaism, Christianity, and Islam. By turning paradoxically to "idolatry," as Queequeg's soul-companion, "twin" and "wife," he is moved to accept "everybody's religious observations,"[9] meaning that Deism, monotheism, paganism, pantheism, polytheism, animism, atheism, and shamanism are all included.

Queequeg is the embodied carrier of four polytheistic religions and a monotheistic one, Islam. Ishmael carries three monotheistic religions and adds to them the multivalent spiritual practice of his "bosom friend." Spiritually, Ishmael and Queequeg are mirror images of each other, coming from opposed cultural standpoints. Ishmael starts from so-called "civilized" monotheism, and works historically backward, to subsume the polytheistic religions of the earth's primal peoples. Queequeg, on the other hand, starts from the animistic polytheism of the Polynesian islands to work historically forward, subsuming the Muslim religion through his observances of Ramadan.

FATHER MAPPLE

Before Whitman and Melville emerged onto the literary scene, the notion of Spiritual Democracy in America was most clearly articulated by Ralph Waldo Emerson, the great backer of self-reliance and "nonconformity" even to "your people's law, or to what they call their gospel." Like the American poet-shamans of the mid-nineteenth century—Melville, Whitman, and Emily Dickinson—Emerson did not spend time expounding the gospels, but was content to settle for the "rural poverty" of writing his own sermons, essays, letters, journal entries, and poetry, where each individual's life and everyone's religious experience may, after his and others' examples, be valued and where "every man and woman makes his own religion, his own God."[10] Tracing the development of Spiritual Democracy to its source in Emerson's writings, we find its earliest conceptualization in 1830, not long after his attendance of a sermon by Father Edward Taylor (1793–1871)—the inspired Methodist preacher of the famous Seamen's Bethel in Boston. Immortalized by Melville in chapter 9 of *Moby Dick*, Father Taylor was ingeniously transformed into Father Mapple in "The Sermon."

Whitman, who went to hear Father Taylor speak when he visited Boston in 1859 and 1860, wrote about him in a pithy essay called "Father Taylor (And Oratory)." Whitman reported that Taylor's preaching and praying was so electrifying that it moved him to tears: "The *living feeling* advanced upon you and seized you with a power before unknown."[11] Taylor's gift of selfhood left lasting traces of the profundity of his preaching, but it was perhaps Melville who best captured the spirit of his overpowering religious emotion. William James, addressing such sublime states of emotion as this maverick preacher was in touch with, famously wrote: "The best thing is to describe this condition integrally as a characteristic affection to which our nature is liable, a region in which we find ourselves at home, a sea in which we swim." Such an emotional state, says James, is a "natural psychic complex, and carries charity with it by organic consequence."[12] In this view, religious experience is said to be patterned on a natural psychic complex in the human soma and soul, an organic factor, or religious instinct. Jung would later refer to this as the "religious function of the psyche." Taylor was apparently moved by this religious function in a sublimely eloquent way, so much so that three of the most prominent men of American letters were led to eulogize him.

Emerson exalted Taylor (who'd gone to sea as an orphaned cabin boy at the age of seven and who later became a Methodist minister in his youth) as one of the two truly great poets in America.[13] Perhaps it was the living feeling for religion—the fire and the abandon—that so gripped Emerson upon encountering the magnetism of Taylor's speech in 1829, which was prior to his own rise to the summits of American oratory.

Emerson's visions of Spiritual Democracy are an extension of his efforts as a Unitarian to formulate an idea of God that makes sea room for all peoples of the world, in all cultures, in all lands, to find their own authentic relationship to the divine. In December 1830, Emerson had been reading the remarkable records of Alexander von Humboldt's travels in his *Personal Narrative of a Voyage to the Equinoctial Regions*. At this time Emerson appears also to have reached a turning point in his ideas regarding the nature of divinity. By the spring of 1832, Emerson delivered a sermon on astronomy where his ideas on religion were ignited by the new sparks of knowledge provided by modern science and by Sufism. "Astronomy," he said, "irresistibly modifies all religion." In a journal entry during the same year, he adds: "Let us express our astonishment before we are swallowed up in the yeast of the abyss. I will lift up my hands and say *Kosmos.* "[14] Astronomy and the image of cosmos opens the human mind up to the notion of the immensity of God and thus to the Spiritual Democracy inherent in all of nature.

Coincidentally, in September of 1845, Emerson picked up the first book of Humboldt's five-volume *Kosmos* and began to delve deeper and deeper into the mystical wisdom literature of Islam and some major Indic texts as well. He was especially drawn to Sufi poetry, which had an illuminating impact on him.[15] According to Emerson scholar Robert Richardson, the greatest event of Emerson's discoveries in the area of religious unity came in 1846, when he bought a copy of Joseph von Hammer's two-volume set on the poet Shams-un-din-Muhammad Hafiz (c. 1320–1389). The following year, Melville was commenting on Hafiz in his third novel, *Mardi.*

The basic belief of Sufism, which Hafiz championed and Emerson and Melville took forward, is that the "secret" teaching of the divine is found in every religion and "its bases" are available and ready for use inside everyone: "in every human mind." Sufism, says Richardson, "has no mythology, no scripture, no church. . . . They [Sufis] are thus the heirs of Zarathustra, as Emerson recognized. . . . Emerson eventually filled a 250-page notebook with translations from Persian poets, mostly Hafiz."[16]

American poetry was looking for a way to carve out a national literature of its own and Emerson was at the forefront of this effort. Searching for a synthetic way to augment the meaning of the world's religions toward a point of transcendence that could be brought together in a succinct statement, Emerson captured the spirit of the moment in an 1851 lecture series called "The Conduct of Life" that galvanized the literary world in the same year *Moby Dick* was launched. In an essay in this series called "Culture," Emerson wrote that the goal of education is fulfilled in every individual: "Individuality is not only inconsistent with culture," he wrote, "but the basis of it. And the end of culture is not to destroy this [individual determination], God forbid! but to train away all impediment and mixture and leave nothing but pure power." In his essay called "Worship," Emerson wrote further, "God builds his temple in the heart on the ruins of churches and religions."[17]

The wisdom of the Sufi mystics—Persian poets such as Saadi, Hafiz, and Jami in particular—had been available in nineteenth-century America, via Goethe and Emerson primarily. Melville acquired a copy of Goethe's *Truth and*

Poetry in London in 1849 and also read Goethe's *Conversations with Eckermann*. It's also evident he was well aware of Goethe's views on Muhammad by the time he wrote *Moby Dick*.[18]

This is the intellectual climate out of which Whitman and Melville emerged onto the literary scene. True, Hafiz was a great poet, perhaps the greatest poet Islam ever produced, and Humboldt was without doubt the leading scientific mind of his age. Emerson synthesized such proponents of spirituality and science into a vision of a new gospel of religious experience that James called "pragmatism," but Whitman would take the insights of Emerson much further. "Whitman was the first to break the mental allegiance," wrote D. H. Lawrence. "He was the first to smash the old moral conception that the soul of man is something 'superior' and 'above' the flesh."[19]

But it took an American novel to create a revolution in ideas that would illuminate the shadow of religion in such a brilliant way that the basic tenets of Spiritual Democracy would be carried to a new level in the "Sermon," where Melville captures the quintessence of religious equality in his portrait of Father Mapple. The truths of Father Mapple are not God's truths in their absoluteness (there is no fundamentalism here), but he tells the truth in a more down-to-earth, subjective sense. It is Melville's truths given to him by the self that provide an answer to his experience of alienation from God in a conventionally creedal culture as a Calvinist.

Ishmael says: "Father Mapple . . . had been a sailor and a harpooner in his youth, but for many years past had dedicated his life to the ministry."[20] Thus, Father Mapple is a man who found his vocation as a preacher. In "The Sermon," Father Mapple asks his congregation: *"What* is this lesson that the book of Jonah teaches?"[21] In this evocation of a salty nineteenth-century sermon it's clear that Melville, Ishmael, Jonah, and Father Mapple are all somehow aligned. In the biblical story of Jonah, God commanded Jonah to go to the great city of Nineveh and cry out against it, for its wickedness had come up against him. But Jonah fled his call to the Lord (or self) and went down to Joppa, the modern-day city of Jaffa. From there he boarded a ship that was headed for Tarshish (Jonah: 1:1–1:3). It's important to note that the primary factor that led Jonah to refuse his calling to speak to the people of Nineveh (now the Iraqi city of Mosul) was the affect of *fear*. As we read in the book of Job: "Upon the earth there is not his like, who is made without fear" (Job: 41:33). Melville, too, must have felt such fright when he was called to write *Moby Dick,* for he knew what the consequences would be if he failed to answer the summons.

One way to develop the Judeo-Christian-Islamic myth, as Melville knew, was through the function of the creative imagination. By extending and ampli-fying the story of Jonah and the Whale and what he had learned from his read-ing of the Koran and Sufism, Melville tapped into the underlying archetype of the quest-myth and its meaning for our times. To grasp the gestalt or form of the main messages in the novel, one needs to understand the idea of "linked analogies." Melville's theory of correspondences provides his evidence for the existence of God. When one is enabled to see the pattern that connects by means of mythopoetic images, one can truly *know* God; otherwise one ends up short-handed. After mentioning St. Paul, Melville writes, in chapter 70 ("The Sphynx"): "O Nature, and O soul of man! how far above all utterance are your linked analogies! Not the smallest atom stirs or lives in matter, but has its cun-ning duplicate in mind."[22] The reference to St. Paul is an important one, for it was Paul who condemned homosexuality in Romans 1:26–28. Thus, the linked analogies that are threaded all throughout the novel refer to the cunning dupli-cates between the higher and lower aspects of homoeros, as we see in the title of chapter 10, "A Bosom Friend."

Ever since Melville had read about the famous Essex shipwreck disaster in the South Pacific, something miraculous had been playing through his mind; his mighty theme had been dallying and delighting there. Father Mapple's ser-mon, in its veneration for Jonah's path of discovery, can be read as the disguised spokesperson, even the apologist, for the path Melville had most deliberately chosen sometime between 1847 and 1850: the path of vocation or calling over and above the path of career. We have heard this in Father Mapple's statement: "Jonah did the Almighty's bidding. And what was that, shipmates? To preach the Truth to the face of Falsehood!"[23]

As we'll see, woe and delight are pairs of opposites sourced in Melville's reading of the Old Testament, from which he drew plentifully during the writ-ing of *Moby Dick*. In the words of Father Mapple, we can hear the echoes of the Old Testament prophets speaking to us in new American verses that are as wise as they are new. He loved Solomon and quoted from Ecclesiastes. The woe is self-evident in the following lines:

> So, therefore, that mortal man who hath more of joy than sorrow in him, that mortal man cannot be true—not true, or undeveloped. With books the same. The truest of all men was the Man of Sorrows, and the truest of all books is Solomon's, and Ecclesiastes is the fine hammered steel of woe. 'All is vanity.' ALL. This willful world hath not got hold of unchristian Solomon's wisdom yet.[24]

Melville would later write to Nathaniel Hawthorne in May of 1851: "I read Solomon more and more, and every time see deeper and deeper unspeakable meanings in him. I did not think of fame, a year ago, as I do now."[25] In his "Sermon," delivered in New Bedford Whaleman's Chapel, Father Mapple addresses the problem of vocation to the seafaring community, and by analogy to all of us who must negotiate a fluid New World context as we struggle to shape our identities, family lives, careers, and vocations. He is speaking to each and every one of us:

> Delight is to him—a far, far upward, and inward delight—who against the proud gods and commodores of this earth ever stands for his own inexorable self. Delight is to him whose strong arms yet support him, when the ship of this base treacherous world has gone down beneath him. . . . Delight is to him, whom all the waves of the billows of the seas of the boisterous mob can never shake from this sure Keel of the Ages.[26]

Delight is the most common emotion for the way of truth in the Hebrew Bible, the way of God: "Will he delight himself in the Almighty?" (Job: 27: 10); and "I delight to do thy will, O my God: yea thy law is in my heart" (Psalms: 40: 8). By preaching a sermon on "Delight," Father Mapple is offering a way to vocation for everyone in a Spiritual Democracy—each person who stands for his or her own inexorable self. This might be seen as Melville's sermon on wisdom. He does this from a point above the average man, which means that he is already somehow exalted. *Moby Dick*, however, goes beyond the Jonah and Father Mapple stories and the preacher Solomon King of Israel. He is also speaking as an American Ishmael, a "hidden" imam. The central quest in *Moby Dick*, the search for the great phallic white Sperm Whale, speaks from the depths of the collective American soul to a spiritual need of the new country to make an authentic religious connection with the numinous possible in everyone. This chance encounter takes place in the Pacific, which is a place that represents symbolically the deepest and therefore the most meaningful part of the collective psyche. This is the place where, like Jonah, we are in a state of refusal, where our souls have "fainted" (in Hebrew *heetatef*) and gone into a state of unconsciousness. "When my soul fainted," says Jonah, "I remembered the Lord: and my prayer came in unto thee, into thine holy temple" (Jonah 2:7).

Before the men of the ship heading for Tarishish threw Jonah overboard, Father Mapple recounts, an important question was asked: "'What is thine occupation? Whence comest thou?'" "'I am an Hebrew,' he [Jonah] cries—and then—'I fear the Lord the God of Heaven who hath made the sea and the dry land!'"[27] The question about Jonah's vocation is central to American Democracy. It is a question that holds a great deal of meaning for each and every one of us: Are we going to answer our vocational call or refuse it? If so, are we prepared to suffer the slings and arrows of fate and destiny, of woe and delight? To find the path between these opposites requires suffering, not neurotic suffering, but the suffering of work, of one's calling, of a religious devotion to one's inner voice. These are the stakes. For Melville, as for generations of readers of the English Bible, the people of Nineveh were the symbolic "I" and "you" in everyone.

Melville used Jonah and the whale story as a metaphor to confront us with the tragedy of the Industrial Age—the violence inflicted on Native Americans, gays, blacks, and others. He was speaking, like Whitman, to the "poets to come"—to a future generation of American writers, and, by extension, to the nations of the world, to listen for the word of God and to find a way to speak it in verse. It was as if Melville, by addressing his American public, was addressing the conscience of the world, which he hoped would one day listen. He realized his quest for fame in his lifetime would be in vain. Knowing his path as a path of sorrow, Melville adopted the persona of the trickster to confront us with the need to make conscious the evil effects of the "inner voice"—prejudice, homophobia, and hatred of "other" religions—within us. But Melville needed to confront and integrate that very shadow in order to discriminate his identity as an American personality. By "Call me Ishmael" Melville means a cast-off from the self that exists in every person and makes each of us part of a democratic whole, an ensemble, an individual within the collectivity, through which the world can be changed. If change is going to happen in the world, it will have to start with each individual person, and that means you and me. This is the teaching of Father Mapple. And as we've seen, it's also the teaching of Whitman and Jung and James.

Melville had what he would have called "heaven's sense" or "right reason" to integrate the unconscious trickster, the irony in the American project that was breaking through the foundation of the American psyche prior to the Civil War. By summoning the powers of his blackest art, Melville shared with the people of his Nineveh a truth he had clearly taken aboard from his rereading of the story of Jonah. As we can boldly translate it now his message is that a country cannot perpetuate crimes against oppressed groups of people and expect to be free from the law of *enantiodromia,* the curve into its opposite. As Melville predicted, nature will rebel; the spirit animals will rebel.

As we have seen, the meaning of the Jonah and the Whale story has much to do with the question of vocation, or what Melville calls (more pluralistically) "occupations." Sometime, during the process of lowering his head, and saying yes to his vocation, Melville must have gotten an idea that he hoped would speak to every American. As a poet-prophet, Melville disguised his secret intentions in allegory and symbol and assumed the persona of a preacher. *Moby Dick* is in that sense a "Sermon," in which Melville was able to vent his spleen by preaching to a wicked "Nineveh," the increasingly materialistic nineteenth-century America and a world rapidly spinning out of control in its dependence on fossil fuels (see "The Fossil Whale" chapter of *Moby Dick*).

Through his reading of the Bible, Milton, Dante, Goethe, Hawthorne, Shakespeare, the Koran, and other classics, Melville was secure in his own majestic verse to bring about a change in the dominant ideology of Judeo-Christianity, encouraging the traditional religion to make an experience of the shadow available to everyone. Obviously, in his own time, such integration wouldn't be accomplished without great pain and emotional suffering. Melville's lifting of the repression on homosexuality, in chapter 10 of *Moby Dick,* where Ishmael and Queequeg are "married," has generally been misunderstood. Early Jungian scholars tended to miss the profound significance of the male-male "marriage" as a living symbol for Spiritual Democracy, which now, in light of the recent progress in the gay marriage movement, is quite obvious to us.

By creating the first portrait of same-sex marriage in American literature even before Whitman, Melville was teaching the way of vocation, speaking up for right conscience, right thought, and right morality, long before there was a gay liberation movement and same-sex marriage was celebrated in California and other states. Melville confronts Americans and the world with what Jung calls a "Jonah-and-the-Whale complex," by which Jung means that the sexual libido regresses past the personal unconscious and "desexualizes itself by retreating step by step to the presexual stage of earliest infancy." In this process, the libido leaves the sphere of personal psychology altogether and "irrupts," as Jung writes, "into the collective psyche where Jonah saw the 'mysteries' *(représenta-tions collectives)* in the whale's belly."[28] One of these mysteries was the mystery of a marriage symbol that could not be found in the Bible nor the Koran.

Ahab in the Bible, and How Ahab Was Named

To better understand the parallels between Melville's visions of Spiritual Democracy and Whitman's, we must turn to the story of Ahab in biblical legend, which ends in the Bible at the second book of Kings. It's after this infamous king of Israel that Ahab is named. In Judaic mythology, Ahab ruled over Israel in the land of Samaria (an ancient city of central Palestine in present-day Jordan) for twenty-two years. There he married a wife called Jezebel who was a priestess of the Canaanite religion. Jezebel promoted the worship of Baal—known in the Bible as a "false god" or "idol"—whose mother-consort was the Goddess Astarte. Through Ahab's worship of Baal and the "wicked" acts he perpetrated in Samaria, Ahab "did more to provoke the Lord God of Israel to anger than all the kings of Israel that were before him" (I. Kings 16:33). This tells us something important about Ahab's character right from the start—he is *hated* by the Jewish God. Yet, at the same time, Ahab is a Hebrew king. He's therefore an ambivalent character, and not to be trusted.

Nevertheless, there is something redemptive about Ahab—and that is his anger and his hate. He allows readers to access feelings that are forbidden, or were particularly forbidden in Melville's day. God can hate Ahab more than any other king, but the biblical Ahab could not hate. Melville's Ahab is the reverse of this. He dies rebelling with massive hatred and rage. The American Ahab becomes an amalgam of the biblical Ahab, who assimilates Satan's anger, Adam's anger, Job's anger, Jonah's anger, the crucified Christ's anger, and all of their anguish and woe. Melville takes this anger and woe into himself until his chest becomes a psychological filled and spiritualized mortar. He challenges Yahweh's assertion that "None" would be "so fierce that dare stir him [Leviathan] up" (Job 41:10).

Melville knew the story of the Bible quite well. For in chapter 19 of *Moby Dick*, "The Prophet," we are faced with the enigmatical figure Elijah, the loyal servant of the Hebrew deity. Elijah was the chosen vessel of Israel who slew the worshipers of Baal in the brook Kishon. Melville places Elijah at the beginning of the novel to sound a clear warning to Ishmael, and, by extension, to all Americans, *not* to follow Ahab in worshiping Baal, but to integrate him as an aspect of the trickster into our collective consciousness. This is what gives Ahab his redemptive significance as an agent of spiritual transformation.

Elijah is also the prophet who Yahweh sent to confront Ahab with a threat of destruction if he persisted in his vile ways. We hear this most clearly in the story of Naboth the Jesrelite in the book of Kings. Naboth had a vineyard near Ahab's house that Ahab wanted so that he could grow herbs in it. Ahab offered Naboth a better vineyard or "the worth of it in money" (I Kings 21: 2). Naboth told Ahab, however, that he was instructed by God *not* to give away the inheritance of his father's house. But Jezebel, seeing Ahab was displeased, *tricked* Naboth. She "wrote letters in Ahab's name, and sealed *them* with his seal, and sent the letters to the elders and the nobles" in Naboth's city, saying: "Naboth did blaspheme God and the king. Then they carried him forth out of the city, and stoned him with stones, that he died" (I. Kings 21: 7–13). In order to get the land Ahab wanted, Naboth had to be killed, and this was done through Jezebel's trickery. Thus, Ahab's wife was a trickster. In his fury, God sent Elijah to deliver a stern warning to Ahab: "Thus saith the Lord, Hast thou killed, and also taken possession? . . . In the place where dogs licked the blood of Naboth shall dogs lick thy blood, even thine" (I. Kings 21: 19). When it came to pass that Ahab heard these words, he rent his clothing, fasted, and put on sackcloth (I Kings 21:27).

In *Moby Dick*, after Ishmael asks Captain Peleg to see Ahab before the ship sets sail, Peleg names him: "He's Ahab, boy; and Ahab of old, thou knowest, was a crowned king!" "And a very vile one," Ishmael answers wittingly. "When that wicked king was slain, the dogs, did they not lick his blood?" Melville-as-Ishmael answered the question so that his readers would know that the narrator was a biblical man. He leads us to think about the meaning of Ahab as an allegory with cultural significance, for his times and ours. "Come hither to me—hither, hither," Peleg says, with significance in his eye that almost startles Ishmael. Then Peleg continues: "Look ye, lad; never say that on board the *Pequod*. Never say it anywhere. Captain Ahab did not name himself. 'Twas a foolish, ignorant whim of his crazy, widowed mother, who died when he was only a twelvemonth old. And yet the old squaw Tistig, at Gay-head, said the name would somehow prove prophetic."29

Ahab has a distinct function in the story in relation to Spiritual Democracy. Looked at historically, the story is a disguised parable on what the U.S. government was doing to the Indians (Tistig is a Gay-head Indian from Martha's Vineyard). This is supported furthermore by the fact that all the best Indian whalers in the novel come from Martha's Vineyard. Tashtigo, for example, is also a Gay-head Indian, one who symbolizes the best strength from that island. Tashtigo's senior, an old Gay-Head Indian among the crew, is also the one who tells Ishmael that Ahab received his facial scar where the lightning hit him and left its mark on him, "not in the fury of any mortal fray, but in an elemental strife at sea." The Indian also notes that Ahab lost his leg to the jaw of the whale Moby Dick, "dismasted off Japan."30

Thus, in *Moby Dick*, when Ishmael asks Elijah: "The dogs, did they not lick his blood?" he appears to be referring ironically to the retribution that God (the self) would perpetrate in America if she (America) allowed Ahab to trick her into committing further immoral atrocities against indigenous peoples and against the God of Nature. Essentially, Ishmael was saying: if America follows

Ahab, the same fate will befall America as potentially would have befallen the biblical Ahab had he not repented.

America, however, did not repent, at least in Melville's opinion. In an 1850 review of Parkman's *Oregon Trail,* Melville wrote: "Let us not disdain, then, but pity. And wherever we recognize the image of God, let us reverence it, though it hung from the gallows."[31] This reference is to the certainty of God's existence in all cultures and religions of the world—Native American, African, Islamic, Polynesian, or otherwise. It shows us just how close Melville's thoughts were to Whitman's regarding the need for Spiritual Democracy, only Melville went far deeper into the historical unconsciousness of America to confront the heinous crimes the cavalry was committing against Indians. On this subject, Whitman was silent.

Melville used the same metaphor of the image of God hanging "from the gallows" in his antebellum poem "The Portent" (1859), where the unhealed wound of John Brown's head was used to signify the outbreak of destructiveness during the Civil War. This ruthless honesty toward the shadow side of American civilization and culture is the clearest indication of Melville's shamanic function as a preserver of the psychic integrity of his community.

Thus, Melville used the story of Ahab as an allegory for America. He asked readers to see through the biblical referent imaginably, not literally. Melville was pushing readers to move past literal interpretations. He does not see Baal as a sign, but as a symbol. What does Baal represent psychologically to Melville? Like the city of Nineveh, Ahab and Baal are likely disguised symbolic representations for America, with its greed for land, gold, oil, and its mid-nineteenth-century unconscious hatred of Indians, animals, homosexuals, Muslims, and blacks. If Baal is anything in *Moby Dick,* it's the power over dark races, the worship of land and the market economy, or the *solar* (Baal was a sun god) rather than the *lunar* aspects of the masculine God-image (Queequeg's "idol," and the phallic white whale).

Elijah appears at the beginning of the novel to sound a clear warning to Ishmael-America and the whaling industry not to follow Ahab in the worship of Baal. We can look to Melville's use of irony in his last major novel, *The Confidence Man,* which was built up around a host of figures who are all tricked and made fools and knaves by money. In *Moby Dick,* before the ship set sail, Elijah the prophet says to Ishmael: "Good bye to ye. Shan't see ye again very soon, I guess; unless it's before the Grand Jury."[32] It's important to know that Melville's father-in-law was Judge Lemuel Shaw of the Superior Court of Massachusetts. The irony in Elijah's statement about the grand jury extends to all

Americans. We know this because of the association Melville makes between the prophet Elijah and the old squaw Tistig at Gay-head. They both serve a similar function as prophetical voices of the unconscious to sound a clear warning to America not to follow in Ahab's footsteps—and Ahab is homophobia incarnate. We must all accept our portion of the collective responsibility for what was done to Native Americans, blacks, gay and lesbian people, and nature itself, and then work to repair our highest ideals of Religious Democracy, striving toward the essential unity of the human species with the trees, rivers, plains, mountains, deserts, and oceans, and the animals and birds that inhabit them. When Elijah asks Ishmael if he has "heard anything about his [Ahab's] having lost his leg last voyage, according to the prophecy?" Elijah adds wryly, "Who knows that? Not all Nantucket, I guess."[33] This suggests that Ishmael's ability to see into the future as a "hidden" imam is provided for by both Tistig (a Native American woman) and Elijah (a Hebrew prophet). As Ishmael looks upon the harpooner Fedallah, "Ahab's Dark Shadow," and his crew, he recounts how he had seen these "tiger yellow creatures" creeping onto the *Pequod* during the "dim Nantucket dawn," and he recalls also the "enigmatical hintings of the unaccountable Elijah."[34]

Melville does not conflate the two distinct phenomena of the fear of Islam and the fear of radical Islam in his novel. Instead, he places them together in the story, side by side, where the comic aspects of the Ishmael-Queequeg "marriage" appear before the more tragic Ahab-Fedallah pairing. Islamophobia, as Melville views it in *Moby Dick*, is much more than social anxiety; it's a psychological phenomenon that's based on the projection of evil onto "other" religious groups or sexual orientations. In North America, it begins with the problem of Indian-hating.

In *The Confidence Man*, Melville traces the roots of religious hatred to the problem of projection of the human shadow in a brilliant chapter called "The Metaphysics of Indian-Hating." Melville's fictional character, Colonel John Moredock, is said to have "hated Indians like snakes."[35] "For you must know," his narrator says, "that Indian-hating was no monopoly of Colonel Moredock's; but a passion, in one form or other, and to a degree, greater or less, largely shared among the class to which he belonged. And Indian-hating still exists; and, no doubt, will continue to exist, so long as Indians do."[36] Melville attributes the problem of "Indian-hating" ironically to the "Indian blood-thirstiness" and "Indian diabolism" that was so reprehensible to the "backwoodsmen" of his day: the "deep abhorrence with which the backwoodsman regards the savage." Such a metaphysic was viewed ironically as a "vocation whose consistent following" involves the "renunciation of ambition" and "the efficacy of a devout sentiment."[37] Note the accent he places on devout. This chapter gives us a clue to the origins of Ahab's hatred against the great white animal as a symbol for the divinity or Great Spirit in indigenous North American societies. Hatred against Indians or Jews or Blacks or Muslims, too, can be a religious devotion, as is hatred by Islamic fundamentalists against Americans and Western allies.

How many vineyards did Ahab-America steal from the Indians? How many Indian children were killed by the projections of American Jezebels (tricky-paranoid animas)? God commanded the Indians, like the early Hebrews, not to give away the land that their forefathers and the Great Spirit had bequeathed to them. For their defense of their land, countless Indian tribes were decimated. In fact, Melville was working out a cultural problem here. One of Melville's grandfathers had helped to torch Mohawk villages, and for this he was dubbed "commissioner of the Iroquois." So Melville, acting in rebellion against hero worship in America and against the canons of his own family and culture, created a new language disguised in parables. It was an American poetic, which he hoped would speak to his Puritan audience before it was too late.

Moreover, it's also said in the first book of Kings in the Bible that the house Ahab built in which to worship Baal was an "ivory house" (I Kings 22:39). Thus, we can see why the myth of Ahab spoke so personally to Melville: The *Pequod* is white, with white chaste whale bones, like Captain Peleg's white teepee and the ivory matter of Ahab's whalebone leg. Melville uses a Gothic story to send all of this whiteness down once again into the sacred dimension, from which it arose, to the bottom of the Pacific.

Thus, there is also a self-sacrificial side to Ahab that we must learn to love and laugh at as our very own blood. As Captain Peleg, one of the chief proprietors of the *Pequod* tells us: "stricken, blasted if he be, Ahab has his humanities!"[38] "Ahab of old thou knowest was a crowned king!"[39] As a light bearer of our culture, the American Ahab is a culture hero for modern and postmodern times because he helps us make the darkness conscious. In Melville's view, America needs to see that we have an inner wounded and castrated king in us who is mad, like William Shakespeare's Lear, Hamlet, and Macbeth; Milton's Satan; Goethe's Mephistopheles; and the Hebrew Ahab. This madness in America and the world needs to be consciously integrated if humans are to continue to evolve.

We learned a little bit more about Ahab's madness in "The Ship" (chapter 16), where we heard that Ahab did not name himself. He was given his name by his "crazy" mother, who died when he was a year old. Thus, the American Ahab is the son of a crazy widow and he has been infused with his mother's madness.

Psychologically, Ahab's illness is a hereditary one, coupled with an abandon-
ment depression, stemming from the early loss of his mother in infancy. This
makes him an orphan, like Ishmael, although Ahab has a peculiar psychic dispo-
sition that makes him a vessel for divine conflict. He's a bearer of two sides of
a split within the God-image that extends much further than Israel and Christendom, all the way to Islam. He's also Persian and Mongolian, an amalgam of
many cultures.

Job's Whale

In chapter 32, "Cetology" (a disquisition on the nature of the whale), Ishmael
asks readers:

> What am I that I should essay to hook the nose of this Leviathan! The
> awful tauntings in Job might well appall me. 'Will he (the Leviathan)
> make a covenant with thee? Behold the hope of him is in vain!' But I
> have swam through libraries and sailed through oceans; I have had to
> do with whales with these visible hands; I am in earnest; and I will try.[40]

A little further in the narrative, Ishmael tells us that Ahab was a "grey-
headed, ungodly old man, chasing with curses a Job's whale round the world."[41]
And in the epilogue, Ishmael quotes these final lines from the book of Job: "And
I only am escaped alone to tell thee."[42] No less than Carl Jung in his *Answer to
Job*, Melville located the paradigm for the crisis of modern consciousness in the
sufferings of Job: *"The whale no famous author, and whaling no famous chronicler?*
Who wrote the first account of our Leviathan? Who but mighty Job!"[43]

As a writer attempting to hook the nose of Leviathan, Ishmael is a figure
who recounts the tragedy of our modern era, the tragedy of our disseverance
from the earth and from the sea, and our disseverance from the cosmos (Cetus),
and therefore from Spiritual Democracy. Melville uses the Old Testament metaphor of God's fight with Leviathan to deliver a stern message that it's a danger
when man attempts to have dominion over nature. The arrogant Ahab does not
accept his humility in the face of nature.

Elijah warns Ishmael that a person must have respect for the power of nature
and not follow Ahab to doom. Gabriel repeats this warning. All throughout the
novel, God's messengers send clear warnings that the God of Nature needs to
be revered and respected. This is all very American. As author and chronicler of
the whale, Melville's calling was to heal this hurt.

In the above passage, we can see the twin activities (vocations) that inform

Moby Dick: "essaying" and "hunting." Melville was called equally to both. Ishmael is the "essayist" who attempts to "hook the nose" of Moby Dick by writing about him with his condor's quill just as Melville, as a literary artist, was called to spread the news of Spiritual Democracy—that man is part of nature and equal with it. Ahab, on the other hand, is the defiant and rebellious economic whale hunter who chases Leviathan out of revenge and hate in an attempt to confront, destroy, and subdue the vengeful side of God through the ritual of hunting.

From an analytical standpoint, to hook the nose of Moby Dick is equivalent to making the symbol of Leviathan apparent to Americans—making the unconscious fire (the positive and negative poles of the Christian "devil," or shadow) conscious in us. Melville-as-Ishmael, as much as any contemporary essayist, is asking Americans to consider: How can Americans perpetuate violent crimes against indigenous Americans, women, gays, and blacks, without feeling shame? How can we let such terrible tragedies occur as happened during the Salem witch trials, without experiencing fear, grief, or despair? What has happened to our humanity?

In the light of the Job story, Ishmael's answer to such questions is that we have to disentangle the human shadow from the invisible spheres of the God-image. By what "evil magic" over America's collective soul were our Puritan forebears so possessed that Ahab's hate could have seemed "almost" theirs? What Jung writes in *Answer to Job* is that we all have a Satanic Christ that seeks an individual answer to the problem of human suffering. In his prepsychological reflections, we can see that Melville located the problems of antihomosexuality, slavery, witch hunting, Indian-hating, and the destruction of nature in the collective occupations of the white race in general. This was epitomized by the California Gold Rush of 1849 to 1851, when strip mining killed the salmon—sacred to Native Americans—along the Klamath, McCloud, and Sacramento Rivers, as well as by the buffalo hunts of the 1860s, the bloody Indian wars, the brutal plantation system of slavery, and the excess and tragedies of the whaling industry itself.

For Melville, *Moby Dick*, no less than the story of Job for Jung, provided a symbolic solution to the problem of the human shadow. Jung as a psychologist would later convert his own intuitive insights about Job into psychological consciousness. Certainly Jung knew *Moby Dick*, calling it the "greatest American novel" by 1930,[44] and someone must have opened the door to it for him. Jung had become aware of his own darkness, as well as humanity's darkness, through the tragedies of the First and Second World Wars, as well as through his own political mistakes in the early thirties, when he stumbled in his relationships with his Jewish friends. But by the time he wrote *Answer to Job*, he could hold such a contentious mood and make it pay off. The trickster in his own character seems to have been integrated to such an extent that we have more than a proud diatribe.

Melville had seen this problem in his symbolic imagination too, but he lacked psychological language to explain it. But both men were actually hunting the shadow side of God. Jung would take the Judeo-Christian trickster (Satan) by his jaw. He would use psychological consciousness to turn the tables on the Old Testament God-image and the half-conscious awareness of his son (the Devil) in the New Testament. And they saw their projects in similar ways. In a short letter to his secretary Aniela Jaffe in May of 1951, Jung wrote: "I have landed the great whale; I mean *'Answer to Job.'* I can't say I have fully digested this tour de force of the unconscious. It still goes on rumbling a bit, rather like an earthquake."[45] In June of 1851, Melville wrote similarly to Hawthorne: "Shall I send you a fin of the Whale by way of a specimen mouthful?"[46] Almost exactly one hundred years apart, these two books, *Moby Dick* and *Answer to Job*, found their completion. The first book was written by an American poet-shaman who was still struggling to integrate the trickster and free himself from the strangle grip it laid upon his traumatized soul; the second was written by the great analyst of the twentieth century in whom the paradoxical wound of God had been made conscious at an unprecedented level of psychological and moral development. We have to view these two books, therefore, as deliberately epochal in the evolution of the Judeo-Christian God-image. And it would not be amiss to regard both as products of the continuing evolution of the divine drama, in which God's nature is revealed to men and transformed by man's consciousness of it.

FEDALLAH AS A TRICKSTER

In order to understand the complexity of the figure of Fedallah as a trickster in *Moby Dick*, we must first come to terms with the Iranian prophet Zarathustra (also known as Zoroaster), for Ahab's link to Fedallah rests in their common religious origination as Zoroastrian fire worshipers. The splitting tendency that we find in the Zoroastrian holy text the Zend Avesta, and also in the Hebrew-Christian Bible, was continued historically in the teachings of Mani, who lived in Iran in the second century AD. The same dualism is present in the Koran, and, perhaps especially, in historical Islam. Melville was well aware of dualistic notions in the monotheisms, Zoroastrianism, and Manichaeism through his reading of the folio volumes of the seventeenth-century French Dutch

Reformed Calvinist, Peter Bayle.[47] Similarly, Mircea Eliade traced the dualistic conceptions of the deity to "Iranian influences."[48] So the fact that the character of Fedallah has an unquestionably Arabic name is highly significant in the overall meaning of Melville's myth and its relevance to our times.

As a trickster, Ahab is an ambivalent figure, as we've seen. He's a reincarnation of a Persian fire worshiper, a crusader, and an anti-Islamic "child of the fire." His Christ-like characteristics are even more evident in the following description: "He sleeps with clenched hands; and wakes with his own bloody nails in his palms."[49] But Ahab is no Christ. He does not follow Jung's edict that "everyone will be crucified on his destiny, i.e., upon his self" as Christ was. He is a trickster. The irony of the trickster is made self-evident also through the young crewman Pip, who says in chapter 99, "The Doubloon": "Ha, ha! old Ahab! the White Whale; he'll nail ye!"[50] Here Jung's proclamation regarding the need for symbolic death at midlife (Ahab is forty) is reversed, and he is nailed and crucified by Pip's irony.

In *Moby Dick*, Melville is teaching under a disguise, and beneath this mask is the trickster. The trickster's moral ambivalence makes Ahab an incarnation of God and Satan, Christ and the Devil, Allah and Ibliss. He carries not a dual principle of absolute good (Christ) and absolute evil (Ibliss) as a "split" in the Crown of Lombardy that he wears, but rather an ambivalence in the figure of Ishmael, who narrates the story and summons us to integrate the opposites, rather than identify exclusively with the good and project evil outwards. Ahab's powers as a trickster are in preponderance in Melville's portrait of him. Ahab stands on a "barbaric white" ivory "leg," which was fashioned at sea from the "polished bone of the sperm whale's jaw."[51] Moreover in "The Ship," we learn that he has "fixed his fiery lance in mightier, stranger foes than whales."[52] By this, Ishmael means, ironically, the animal side of the deity (Leviathan). Ahab's half-animal, half-human presence leaves us with an impression that he is part sperm whale, part man, and part "crowned king," part Leviathan. He's a bearer of an instrument of divine power, a spear (harpoon) that holds the potential to inflict pain and consciousness on the inhuman side of God, to make the unconscious God, Christ, or Allah (Satan, Devil, Ibliss) conscious as a principle of psychological relativity and relatedness in man.

As a bearer of the mechanism of psychological projection in the collective psyche, Captain Ahab carries a mythological key, therefore, to self-reflection in God-consciousness. He carries aboard his ship the diabolical figure of Fedallah, an Islamic assassin, to whose cultural and religious fate as a radical Muslim fundamentalist Ahab is inextricably tied. Ahab's pact with Fedallah similarly reveals a pact to make the dark side of God conscious. It's hard to trace Ahab's historical character to any one specific cultural region. His name, however, clearly reveals his Hebrew origins, and his having been tricked by God's avenging angel, who happens to be a suicide assassin, gives him the vengeful power of tragic rage to become an agent in God's self-healing. Through Ahab's pairing with his Islamic "shadow," Fedallah, he is linked to the fire-worshiping Parsee, and his fate is bound to the "white-turbaned old man"[53] with a cord. Ahab has sold his soul to the fire-worshiping Parsee and given up his moral freedom just as Fedallah and his assassin group of five have subordinated their fates to Ahab as dictator aboard the *Pequod*. The trickster figure is further illuminated in Ishmael's description of the ship: a "cannibal of a craft, tricking herself forth in the chased bones of her enemies."[54]

In Ishmael's alignment with Ahab aboard the ship and Ahab's pairing with the figure of Fedallah, two inextricable split aspects of the God-complex (God-Satan/Christ-Devil/Allah-Ibliss) are engaged in a battlefield of mutual projections against a common foe, Moby Dick, who represents the so-called "unreasoning" side of God. In them, the trickster's aim is to make the unconscious God in human history conscious. For instance, Ahab smuggles the Parsee on board the *Pequod* before the ship sets sail, which suggests that the whole crew has been "tricked" from the start.

As we've seen, Melville had read about God's ambivalence in the Bible, particularly the book of Kings. He also knew about the history of the Fedais or Fedayeen, from which he coined the name Fedallah, literally in Arabic *fedai* (*fidāʾi* and *dāʾi*): a "devoted one" who "offers up his life" in service to Allah in the form of a divine calling.[55] Thus, Fedallah and his five assassins are avenging ministers or "destroying angels" that assist Ahab in his attack on the White Whale, suggesting that they are all fundamentalists. Melville also mentions Fedallah's "rumpled Chinese jacket" and his "tiger-yellow complexion" that is "peculiar to some of the aboriginal natives of the Manillas."[56] In the post-9/11 era, warnings of the rise of Islamic fundamentalism began in earnest on Mindanao, the Philippines' second-largest island and home to most of the nation's Muslims. The spread of the fundamentalist and restrictive vision of Islam has been fueled by foreign states through funds, preachers, and mosques, and terrorism has recently been on the increase there.

The wisdom of the trickster at play in the novel is reflected, furthermore, in the interactions between the British Captain Boomer and the ship's surgeon, Dr. Bunger. Boomer says to Bunger in Ahab's presence, "'No more White Whale's for me; I've lowered for him once, and that has satisfied me. There would be great glory in killing him, I know that; and there is a ship-load of precious sperm in him, but, hark ye, he's best left alone; don't you think so, Captain?'—glancing at the ivory leg." The British captain attempts to reason with Ahab about the madness of continuing the chase to hunt Moby Dick. Dr. Bunger steps forth and "like a dog, strangely snuffing," takes a lancet from his pocket and draws near Ahab's arm. Ahab throws him against the bulwarks and Fedallah, knowing the White Whale is heading east, toward the sun, asks in whispering voice: "Is your Captain crazy?"[57]

Thus, the Parsee Fedallah carries knowledge of the trickster in his consciousness too, and he uses this trickery to turn the tables on Boomer and Bunger in his diabolical pact with Ahab. Using the trickster's cunning consciously by questioning the English captain's sanity, Fedallah uproots the logical process of "right reason" in favor of "heaven's sense." He holds God to task for being the author of his own evil. Thus, the Parsee uses the trickery inherent in God to trick the American crew into believing that, by turning back along with Boomer, Bunger, and the Samuel Enderby's crew, one would have to be "crazy"; for the terrorizing agent or principle of evil in its projected form is believed to be out there in the feared and hated "other" (the White Whale). Continuing with the hunt for Moby Dick in this state of insanity, therefore, seems the only logical course. And there is wisdom in this. For the trickster to strike through with its ironic conclusion, irony is needed. This course of action is sheer blasphemy in the eyes of God—and Bunger, Ahab, and Fedallah all know this.

Ahab surrenders his will to Fedallah. In fact, he enlists him and his crew of five assistants in an experiment in the evolution of human consciousness. Ahab, who acts under orders, implies during the final chase scenes that events are predestined by calling himself "the Fates' lieutenant" and by saying that the whole act was "immutably decreed" and was "rehearsed by thee and me a billion years before the oceans rolled."[58] Ishmael goes along as a scribe, not because he has free will of his own, but because, like Ahab, he believes that the voyage is preordained. Echoing Ahab, Ishmael asserts similarly: "And, doubtless, my going on this whaling voyage, formed part of the grand programme of Providence that was drawn up a long time ago." Ishmael continues, "I cannot tell why it was those stage managers, the Fates, put me down for this shabby part of a whaling voyage, when others were set down for magnificent parts in high tragedies."[59] Here he submits to the archetype of his destiny. Thus, absolute knowledge was present in Ahab's pact with Fedallah before the American ship ever sets sail, and while Ishmael does not presume to know why, Ahab and Fedallah are fully aware of why.

In reading Melville's myth for our times, Fedallah takes center stage, both as Ahab's "shadow" and as a trickster who assists Ahab in his quest to make the dark side of the monotheistic God-complex conscious in America and the world. This is perhaps his chief function as an agent of transformation in Melville's visions of Spiritual Democracy: to make the shadow of fundamentalism in all its forms—Christian, Islamic, Judaic, Hindu, Buddhist, and Confucian too—conscious in us, so that we can practice religious tolerance pragmatically wherever we are on the planet. Americans also need to be aware that fundamentalism includes belief in literal interpretations of our Constitution's principles, such as "the right to bear arms," a statute used by the National Rifle Association to justify the purchase of automatic weapons. Practicing religious tolerance for such beliefs might include taking an attitude of compassion toward the NRA's position on the right to bear arms, while speaking up against lax policies that are harming us as a society. It means confronting ignorance with uncompromising integrity and justice.

By making Fedallah a Parsee and Ahab a reincarnation of a Zoroastrian fire worshiper—and both impious heretics, moreover—Melville shows us that these two hostile "brothers" are colluding together to bring the greatest amount of light to the world through their mutual unveiling of the ambivalence in God. In *Moby Dick*, this function of bearing responsibility for the split in God is carried by Ishmael—the spiritual progenitor of a new myth of the trickster on American shores.

AHAB AND FEDALLAH: THE FAILED CONIUNCTIO

Before unmasking the sinister character of Fedallah further to see his relevance to current affairs, it's important to note that Ahab, who he serves to the end, is referred to by Melville as a "dictator," a "Grand Turk," a "sultan," "Genghis Kahn," and "Khan of the Plank." Such references are ominous in light of our present-world situation.[60] As an archetypal son of the Great Mother, Ahab has preserved his line of continuity from patriarchy to matriarchy and the earth's primal peoples. He is a king of Israel who claims mastership (after God) over Leviathan, portrayed in the biblical books of Isaiah, Job, and Psalms, and he also incarnates some of the treachery as John Milton's Satan in *Paradise Lost,* the cunning of Johann von Goethe's devil character Mephistopheles in his tragic play *Faust,* and the light-bearing qualities of Zoroaster, Moses, Christ, and Mohammad. On the other hand, he's an inflated world ruler, like Tamerlane and Suleiman the Magnificent; an incarnation of the sun god Murduk of Babylonian religion who slayed Tiamat, the oceanic chaos monster; a worshiper of Baal; and a representation of Manifest Destiny, witch-burning, slavery, Indian-hating, and empire-building.[61] As a character then, Ahab is an embodiment of the dark side of the American national complex. In our own times, we see this play out in events like the presumptive "preemptive" strike against Iraq in 2003, which was justified by falsified reports about the existence of Iraqi-held weapons of mass destruction. Ahab is also a materialization of the ego inflation and subsequent demise of power-driven "dictatorships" in the Middle East. He crosses national lines.

The figure that embodies the fundamentalist Islamic side of the God-complex in its most sinister aspect is the "white-turbaned old man."[62] This old man, Fedallah, is an avatar of the Old Man of the Mountain, the historical and legendary chief of the Persian Assassins[63] who was a threat to Marco Polo and a terror to Christian Crusaders during the Middle Ages. A historical line of succession can be drawn from this Old Man of the Mountain to Fedallah and to Osama Bin Laden, holed up in Torra Bora, who waged jihad against the American ship of state from the mountains of Afghanistan on September 11, 2001. His group of five assassins traveled in the four planes that were sent as envoys on a mission to terrorize the United States. These attacks still haunt us as a nation and a world today.

Fedallah is the central figure in Moby Dick who encourages Ahab to pursue the White Whale to his death. His positive significance lies in his function as an Islamic trickster: again, in his ability to make the dark aspect of God conscious to the world. Why Melville chose to coin this Islamic name for his Mephistopheles is a mystery, as there are no written records referring to Fedallah anywhere in notation in Melville's pen. Nevertheless, it's clear that before the publication of *Moby Dick*, Melville had read portions of the Zend Avesta, the Arabian Knights,[64] Islamic Sufi poetry, and substantial portions of the Koran. He was also influenced by accounts that he probably read in newspapers of the British battle with Afghan soldiers at Parwandara, shortly before he left for his four-year whaling adventure to the South Seas in 1841. These had convinced him that the Moslem threat had constellated and melded with Christian evil.

While there are rough notes Melville left on a flyleaf on the last volume of his set of the plays of Shakespeare that provide us with a mythological key to deciphering Melville's intentions in the creation of the characters of Ahab, Pip, Bulkington, and Ishmael,[65] the figure of Fedallah is as elusive as Bin Laden was himself until he was finally found near a military complex in Pakistan and shot to death by Navy Seals. As events following the 9/11 attacks have made clear,

Fedallah's place in the formation of Ahab's pact with Satan, Devil, Ibliss, or absolute Evil has proven to conform to the tragic outworking of the transnational narrative that Melville correctly intuited for us 160 years ago in details that are shocking to anyone who has studied them in depth.

Thus, *Moby Dick*, as a prototype for a myth that accurately portrays our present clash between Islam and the West, couldn't be more precise in pinpointing the diabolical transcultural pairing between warlike elements contained in the Judeo-Christian-Islamic complexes of many nations. These manias are highly contagious and toxic to civilizations and tend toward projection and reprojection of evil, due to splits that exist in all four major patriarchal religions of the Middle East since the time of Zoroaster. The search for a more all-inclusive God-image that adequately represents the nature, structure, and dynamics of the self in the world soul must inevitably go on until our religions, politics, economics, and psychology have caught up with civilization's need for new guiding myths that supersede the patriarchal gods (Yahweh, God, Christ, and Allah) with a myth that includes "the All."

What America was doing to its Native peoples was enough to make Melville weep. Thus, *Moby Dick* might be read as a lamentation, a grief song, for the lost vision of Spiritual Democracy that the uniting figures such as Hiawatha and Pocahontas had brought to the white man newly venturing onto an unspoiled continent.

17

THE FALL OF THE DICTATORSHIPS AS PORTRAYED IN *MOBY DICK*

In his 1957 correspondence with the scholar H. L. Phillip, Carl Jung warned, "We are threatened with universal genocide if we cannot work out the way of salvation by a symbolic death."[1] We all must be crucified on the cross of our own destiny, Jung said, in order to survive.

Such an inference clearly has its origins in Christianity but is ultimately a post-Christian view. Jung's words do not restrict their application to Christians, any more than the anxieties that informed *Moby Dick* apply to the tensions of a pre–Civil War United States bedeviled by industrial pollution, the mass slaughter many species of wildlife on land and in the air and seas, Indian Wars, and slavery. Jung's words are ominous, no less ominous than Melville's in *Moby Dick*. To be crucified upon one's destiny, as Melville was, means he pushed his egotistical will as far as possible so that it could be sacrificed to the greater will of the self, which beckoned him beyond the possibility of anticipating the outcome with its inexorable call to wholeness.

As Melville says in *Moby Dick*, Ahab stands before his shipmates with a "crucifixion in his face."[2] Ahab also wears the Iron Crown of Lombardy, which was forged from the nails of Christ's cross and worn during the coronation of the holy Roman emperors. About this crown, Ahab says:

I, the wearer, see not its far flashings; but darkly feel that I wear that, that dazzlingly confounds. 'Tis iron—that I know—not gold. 'Tis split, too—that I feel; the jagged edge galls me so, my brain seems to beat against the solid metal; aye, steel skull, mine; the sort that needs no helmet in the most brain-battering fight![3]

As a post-Christian symbol, therefore, Ahab carries the fundamentalist principle of absolute evil as a "split" in the very Crown of Lombardy he wears. The fact that it's iron, not gold, also suggests that Melville deliberately placed this crown in contrast with the Taji's "crown" in his novel *Mardi*, as well as with the gold of Spiritual Democracy. This intuition is further reinforced by the following statement from Ahab during "The First Lowering": "Hurrah for the gold cup of sperm oil, my heroes! Three cheers, men—all hearts alive!"[4]

In *Moby Dick*'s chapter 99, entitled "The Doubloon," Ahab promises the namesake coin as a prize to anyone on deck who first spots the White Whale. "On its round border it bore the letters, REPUBLICA DEL ECUADOR: QUITO. So this bright coin came from a country planted in the middle of the world, and beneath the great equator, and named after it; and it had been cast midway up the Andes."[5] As we've seen, in Alexander von Humboldt's introduction to volume one of his masterwork *Kosmos*, we read that: "Among the colossal mountains of the Cundinamarca, of Quinto, and of Peru, furrowed by deep ravines, man is enabled to contemplate alike the families of plants, and all the stars of the firmament."[6] Anyone who has read "The Doubloon" chapter of *Moby Dick* knows that there are many references to the stars and the zodiacal constellations. So for the doubloon to have been found halfway up the Andes suggests that Melville must have had Humboldt in mind. Unlike Ahab, who nailed the doubloon to the mast pole of the *Pequod*, and was nailed by the White Whale in the Pacific, Melville sacrificed his life on the cross of his destiny.

This important chapter starts with the religious question, "What is truth?" This, of course, is the teaching of Father Mapple—truth is some "certain significance that lurks in all things." Melville puts Father Mapple's insistence on the truth all religions teach in the mouth of Ahab, speaking of the spiritual equality between gold and the self: "This round gold is but the image of the rounder globe, which, like a magician's glass, to each and every man turns but mirrors back his own mysterious self."[7] Thus, it's clear that the alchemical gold is to be found in "gold cup of sperm oil" that Ahab and his crew are after.

What then did Jung and Melville intend by valorizing symbolic death? For Jung, "universal genocide," though a literal threat, probably meant the symbolic egotism that he felt was ruining humans' possibility of taking their proper place in the cosmos. For Melville, the symbolic meaning of Ahab being killed on the back of the White Whale is less certain. Melville had certainly seen the decimation of many species of whales, as well as giant tortoises of the Galapagos, and his is a narrative filled with the hard facts of whaling. He does not spare us the violence, greed, stupidity, and evil of this antiecological activity. Yet his story also shows a human affection between men that can triumph over this grim exercise in mastery. The alternative is couched (literally) as same-sex love—Ishmael's love for his Polynesian friend Queequeg, who is multireligious and with whom he essentially enters into a same-sex "marriage," while connecting with the Divine Feminine in the process. Thus, the cross that crucified Melville on his own destiny was not so much a Christian one as a Jungian play of opposites, in which love for nature, God, the feminine, and his fellow man intersect with the insistence on power-driven mastery that was his birthright and original problem as an American in the age of Manifest Destiny.

Melville, like Walt Whitman and Emily Dickinson, knew the religious clauses of the U.S. Constitution. He knew the framer's central purpose—"to protect *religious liberty*" at all costs[8]—and it's perhaps for this reason that he made Queequeg multireligious. From the beginning of his narrative of facts, he followed the dictates of his own conscience, free from civil coercion and any established church in the new nation. He chimes in with Walt Whitman with an emergent, quintessentially American solution to the realization of this spiritual ambition by emphasizing, through the surprising image of the sacred marriage of shipmates locked in erotic embrace, that if anything is sacred, the human body is sacred, as body is coequal to the soul. Sexual expression, therefore, is its sacrament.

As we've seen in chapter 10, "A Bosom Friend," Ishmael gets into bed with the Polynesian harpooner, Queequeg, whom he "marries." This prototypical same-sex marriage in a mid-nineteenth-century novel and their marriage vow, traditionally restricted to heterosexual couples, was certainly groundbreaking. For Whitman, Melville, and Dickinson, however, no such categorical distinction among heterosexual and homosexual applies: sex, soul, and spirit are necessary to incarnation as partners in the dance of love, and their union is unimaginable without a homoerotic variable that brings one as close as possible to one's own experience of being sexually gendered, mirrored unavoidably in another person of the same gender—a "cozy, loving pair."[9]

Jung showed that the opposites of "higher" and "lower," as well as sexuality and spirituality, are abolished in God. Jung undoubtedly exhibited a cultural homophobia, which was very common in his day, as was Sigmund Freud's ambivalent attitude toward the possibilities of homosexuality as love. Jung joined Freud, however, in appreciating the value of homoerotic fantasy. Fantasy, for Jung, is the "bridge" to the transcendent function, a psychic capacity that arises from the tension between consciousness and the unconscious and supports their union. As if to confirm him in advance, all three of these American poets—Melville, Whitman, and Dickinson—engaged in homoerotic imagination for purposes of both personal and cultural transformation well beyond what they could have lived in "real life."

In the writing of *Moby Dick*, Melville allowed homoerotic fantasy to flow freely into his culture's dying riverbeds of body and soul to construct what Jung calls a *"symbol of God's renewal."*[10] The bedrock on which this new flow could proceed was the symbol of same-sex marriage, which Whitman went so far as to make the cornerstone of his Spiritual Democracy. In *Moby Dick*, Melville uses the same image as a symbol of cultural renewal. Such renewal was necessary because Melville had seen firsthand the results of a one-sided patriarchal ambition: the decimation not only of countless animal species but of numerous indigenous tribes and religions in the name of white Anglo-Saxon "family values."

In *Moby Dick*, the death of traditional religion and the motif of God's replacement by something new—Spiritual Democracy—becomes the primary theme. Melville's novel shows that transformation of the old through sacrifice and death will be followed by the rebirth of new values. This rebirth is symbolized by the union of same-sex peers of different races and religious backgrounds, and by God symbolized in the form of an animal divinity that defeats all human presumptions to dominance over nature. In order for Spiritual Democracy to come about, former religious forms and their values, such as Victorian heterosexual marriage, must undergo an experience of cultural death followed by rebirth. As we've seen, in the words of Whitman: "Development, Continuity, Immortality, Transformation, are the chiefest life-meanings of Nature and Humanity, and are the *sine qua non* of all facts, and each fact."[11] By "facts" Whitman seems to mean the empirical experience of the truths of the heart. If there is no change in the heart, in *feeling*, there is no rebirth, and no transformation. In his centennial 1876 poem, "Prayer of Columbus," Whitman says: "Haply the lifeless cross I know, Europe's dead cross, may bud and blossom there."[12] European Christianity may indeed bud and blossom through the principle of transformation, latent in its seed in every religion, including Christianity.

Carl Jung, too, saw the necessity of transformation through facing darkness. Certainly one of the most interesting letters he exchanged with Freud, after their trip to Massachusetts' Clark University in 1909, occurred a month before Jung's second trip to the United States, in March of 1910. He said, rhetorically, that we must "love evil if we are to break away from the obsession of virtue that makes us sick and forbids us the joys of life."[13] "Religion can be replaced only by religion," he wrote. "2000 years of Christianity can only be replaced by something equivalent."[14] This is the germ of Jung's revolutionary attitude toward the shadow. It shows that from the start he saw it as the basis of a new religious attitude.

At this time, Jung was in the grip of an intuition when he identified how "dead" religions can be revived, as were Melville and Whitman and Dickinson when they wrote their masterpieces. Jung's early, naive, and eventually renounced desire to replace Christianity with "sexual freedom" was rather quickly transformed by the inspiration and support he received from William James, the father of American pragmatism. As a consequence Jung's psychology became spiritualized, emerging in his maturity as a passion for a variety of world religions. Still, Jung's central aim was to replace Christianity with something better:

> I think we must give it [psychoanalysis] time to infiltrate into people for many centers, to revivify amongst intellectuals a feeling for symbol and myth, ever so gently to transform Christ back into the soothsaying god of the vine, which he was, and in this way absorb those ecstatic forces of Christianity for the one purpose of making the cult and the sacred myth what they once were—a drunken feast of joy where man regained the ethos and the holiness of an animal. . . . only this ethical element can serve the vital forces of religion.[15]

Jung must have known about the "love fest" of the early Christians to have written in this way. This letter, written to Freud in February 1910 during a moment of inspiration, states Jung's intention to give voice to a new millennial vision that he was in search of but had not yet found. It's important to note that this letter was written one month before his second trip to America, in March of the same year, when Jung planned to visit with William James again. It's likely that Jung had realized by this time that he was called to revivify Christianity through his writings by transforming Christ back into "the soothsaying god of the vine" (that is, Dionysus), a God of Nature, and shamanistic ecstasy, not unlike what Melville did to the whale in *Moby Dick*.

Melville's intention was not to destroy the Christian message of love but rather to fulfill it—to "breathe" the "unshackled, democratic spirit of Christianity in all things."[16] To this endeavor he would add the rose, the light, the grape, and the wine of Judaism, Christianity, and Sufism. The fact that Ishmael is described in chapter 10 ("A Bosom Friend") as a "good Christian; born and bred in the infallible Presbyterian Church"[17] implies that Melville's hero, by entering into a love union with Queequeg, was not simply "going native" in reversion to paganism, but beyond that carrying forward the Christian consciousness of his generation and ours. It's in this way that Melville intended to transform creedal religion through the writing of his "Gospels"—no matter the personal cost. In a letter to Hawthorne, Melville wrote: "Though I wrote the Gospels in this century, I should die in the gutter."[18]

This transformation of Christian consciousness was intended to take place through the poetic quality of Ishmael's voice, which is to say, through the lulling cadences of Melville's lyrical mood itself, and from the return to the animal powers, symbolized by the whale, that Christianity had forcibly removed from the Church long ago. Self-named for the symbolic father of the nation of Islam, and inspired by lines from Hafiz and cabalism, Ishmael is consciously accepting, in a positive way, of the darkest shadow of our Christian civilization—its longstanding Muslim enemy. This acceptance is particularly clear when Ishmael and his male companion, friend, and spouse, Queequeg, celebrate Ramadan, the holiest of all Muslim holidays. Once again, it's worth noting that "Ishmael" does this as a Christian with a consciousness that's been transformed by influences including cabalism, Ashanti dance music, and Sufi mysticism, hence the Spiritual Democracy out of which his vision is born.

Melville seemed to be attempting to heal a split in the monotheistic psyche by providing his American audience with a compensatory image of an American self that could lead his age and ours closer to the goal of "completeness," as it's commonly understood in analytical psychology today. He provided us with an image of God that's carried forward the Puritan vision of John Milton in *Paradise Lost*—itself a challenge to Puritanism to integrate its own shadow—in an attempt to heal the split in the deity for Christendom.

Death and Rebirth of God

Maurice Friedman, the biographer of the Israeli philosopher Martin Buber, was partly correct in his assessment of *Moby Dick*. The novel, Friedman said, presents us with "the basic situation with which the problematic of modern man develops" and that is the "death of God."[19] While the German philosopher Friedrich Nietzsche is famously credited with the stunning late-nineteenth century utterance "God is dead," the need for radical spiritual renewal was sounded even earlier in the United States by Whitman, Dickinson, and of course Melville. The most powerful example of this is depicted in the destructive action of the White Whale that turns the economic hunt for sperm-whale oil into a horrifying nightmare for the American ship of state through Ahab's diabolical pact with the Islamic fundamentalist assassin Fedallah. At the end of Ahab's "dictatorship" aboard the *Pequod*, the American ship is sunk while Ahab is caught in a tangle of his own harpoon lines, attached to the back of the White Whale, Ahab's "hearse." The way of death fulfills Fedallah's prophecy of doom and his prediction that the captain would die by rope: "Hemp only can kill thee."[20] Ishmael alone survives on the flotilla of Queequeg's coffin to tell his story. With these two symbols juxtaposed together—the death of Ahab and survival of Ishmael—it's possible to reinterpret their meaning as representing *the death (Ahab) and rebirth (Ishmael) of the notion of God*. For each represents a portion of the God-image in the American psyche and the world that is striving, each in its own way, to establish a movement toward Spiritual Democracy.

The tyrannical Ahab's madness can be seen as a kind of psychic epidemic based on an archaic religion's archetype. The dictator-like captain was "infected" by a fellow shipmate, fate's "assassin" Fedallah—the Islamic fundamentalist who grips him with a religious fervor to pursue Moby Dick. In this madness, we see the parallels with the problems of dictatorship in more recent times, from the World War II regimes of Adolph Hitler, Joseph Stalin, Benito Mussolini, and Emperor Hirohito to U.S. policies in modern times. Since 2003, for example, hundreds of thousands of Iraqi people died due to the Bush administration's "Shock and Awe" campaign. We've also experienced the death of Saddam Hussein, Osama Bin Laden, and Muammar al-Gaddafi, and the sudden fall of the dictatorships of Zine el Abidine Ben Ali in Tunisia and Hosni Mubarak in Egypt.

In the Middle East, we also witnessed the hopeful phenomenon of the Arab Spring, starting late in 2010, when masses of people in many nations took to the streets to protest repressive regimes. But progress is not a smooth path. Egypt's democratic elections, for example, were followed by a rising tide of Islamic fundamentalism under the leadership of President Mohamed Morsi, whose policies aimed to create a new Muslim state that would undermine the rights of women and minorities and empower clerics to dictate laws clearly contrary to the principle of religious freedom. Such attempts to construct a divisive constitution run dramatically counter to Spiritual Democracy.

Fundamentalism and all limited views of religion, when they are believed in as the only creed, the only truth, will have to die so that a new age of Spiritual Democracy may rise. In this vision, democratic freedom is more focused on the environment and sustainability, and on political, economic, and religious equality, as well as tolerance toward all religions. Such a dispensation might in time come about as a global phenomenon, but only, of course, if we don't destroy ourselves and much of the planet first.

Jungian analyst Joseph L. Henderson's words about the meaning of the symbol of the whale Moby Dick may have relevance for readers who feel that we need our own limited images of God to be replaced with new myths to help us understand what's happening around us. Henderson said:

> The symbol of the White Whale is a symbol for death. Whiteness does not represent rebirth in itself; it represents death. There can be no rebirth without death. Symbols of death have a tendency to be weak unless they embody this white element. After destruction and death there can be rebirth, but not until that point. A ritual death creeps in where it otherwise might be left out.[21]

Henderson was speaking about what many religious people would prefer not to consider, namely that when we leave death out of our religious experiences, as during the death of the hero at midlife, a ritual death creeps in by way of outer events that happen to us as fate. As we've seen, Ahab's intention is to keep the hero myth *alive:* "Hurrah for the gold cup of sperm oil, my heroes! Three cheers, men—all hearts alive!"[22] But the heart that's still beating is not Ahab's; it's Moby Dick's. It is also the heart of Hafiz, and of Muhammad calling every Muslim to prayer. As a living symbol, the White Whale may in fact represent a world-shattering event in the collective psyche: the death and rebirth of the God-image in all three major monotheisms.

In this sense, Melville offers a myth through which to frame the need for a new religious attitude in America, an attitude of reverence for "Nature's God," with equality for all, as expressed by the founders. An age of psychological wholeness can only come about through death to the God-images we've held most dear. By clinging to them, what the Buddhist's call *tanha,* we only accelerate their dissolution in time.

Taking a closer look at the interactions between Ahab and Fedallah gives a deeper understanding of how these two figures provide a picture that reflects aspects of the current situation in the Middle East. In his Terry Lectures at Yale University in 1937, after paying a warm tribute to William James, Jung defined religion to a large academic audience as an "attitude peculiar to a consciousness which has been changed by experience of the *numinosum.*"[23] By numinosum, a term coined by Rudolph Otto in his book *The Idea of the Holy,* Jung meant a "dynamic agency or effect not caused by an arbitrary act of will. On the contrary, it seizes and controls the human subject, who is always rather its victim than its creator."[24] Jung based this view on the Greek word "πίστις," which means "trust or loyalty, faith and confidence in a certain experience of a numinous nature and the change of consciousness that ensues."[25] He added modestly that the "psychologist, if he takes up a scientific attitude, has to disregard the claims of every creed to be the unique and eternal truth."[26] Jung defined *"homo religiosus"* as "a man who takes into account and carefully observes certain factors which influence him and his general condition."[27] Moreover, Jung ominously predicted a "peculiar kind of new development" was building in Germany's youth and even warned that a "Wotanistic revolution" was soon to be "expected in Germany."[28] Jung's intuition could not have been more precise. Indeed, he saw what was about to happen in Europe through his visions in 1913, prior to World War I, and he began speaking up about his worries about a coming subsequent catastrophe as early as 1916, while the "Great War" was still waging.

Prior to his Terry Lectures, in his March 1936 essay "Wotan," Jung cautioned against the spread of psychic infections and their tendencies to swallow up individuals in mass collective movements. As we've seen, the idea of being gripped by religious archetypes, or archaic God-images that are affectively charged and contaminated with evil, is a general psychological phenomenon that was elucidated through Jung's extension of the German term "Ergriffenheit—a state of being seized or possessed. The term postulates not only an Ergriffener (one who is seized) but also an Ergriefer (one who seizes)."[29] Recall Jung's alarm about the madness, the furor teutonicus, that possessed and had so infected a whole nation to bring about such a state of insanity that "everything is set in motion and has started rolling on its course toward perdition."[30] On the other hand, Jung spoke more optimistically about Meister Eckhart, the thirteenth-century German mystic who was also Ergriffen. "The Ergreifer who seizes us is always "God," Jung says.[31] Repeating these cautionary words makes it possible to imagine a more positive potential in revolutions, such as the possibility for lasting reform that was launched in the Middle East with the Arab Spring.

In 1931, Jung wrote: "Religious thought keeps alive the archaic state of mind even today, in a time bereft of gods,"[32] which suggests that the gods were dying in the collective psyche in preparation for something new. This is an idea Jung had been attempting to articulate in his *Red Book* in the opening chapter: "The Way of What Is to Come." Despite these views, Jung tended to judge collective movements negatively. This is of course understandable, given that he lived through two horrific World Wars with a loss of over seventy million lives the world over. From an analytical psychological standpoint, the God-image that Whitman was summoned by between 1855 and 1871—the God *of Spiritual Democracy*—is the same deity that still captures the imagination of people around the world who are hoping for and working toward better forms of government.

Religious thought offers a model for how we might live our lives during a time of war and hope for world peace. But we cannot fail to confront evil in our own country while hunting evil down in the world. The pair Ahab and Fedallah, as the shadow side of Spiritual Democracy, forms a portrait of a transnational God-image that is riveting not only our nation, but many nations. A truly American psychology must start, as Jung did, with its national poets, as they are the gateways to deeper understandings of the meanings of the God-image that gripped them and is now clearly gripping us.

In *Moby Dick*, Captain Ahab is referred to as a Zoroastrian fire worshiper, "dictator," "Grand Turk," "sultan," "Genghis Kahn," "Khan of the Plank"[33] as well as a "dictator." He undergoes a horrifying death at the end of the novel, along with his fundamentalist Islamic crew of five Persian assassins. This strikingly contemporary myth forms a commentary on the shadow side of American Democracy and globalization, as well as on the fall of the recent dictatorships in the Middle East and on the death of Osama Bin Laden. In chapter 26 of *Moby Dick*, entitled "Knights and Squires," Melville writes about the American God-image—an image that still has us in its clutches:

> But this august dignity I treat of is not the dignity of kings and robes, but that abounding dignity which has no robed investiture. Thou shalt see it shining in the arm that wields a pick or drives a spike; that democratic dignity which, on all hands, radiates without end from God; Himself! The great God absolute! The centre and circumference of all democracy! His omnipresence, our divine equality! . . . thou just Spirit of Equality, which has spread one royal mantle of humanity over all my kind! Bear me out in it, thou great democratic God! . . . Thou who didst pick up Andrew Jackson from the pebbles; who didst hurl him upon a war-horse; who didst thunder him higher than a throne![34]

Jung postulated that, through fantasy thinking, "typical myths" may appear in the dreams of an individual through which a country's "national complexes" might be worked out via what Swiss cultural historian Jacob Burckhardt called "great primordial images" of culture. Through such national myths, Jung says, "every man has to discover *his* own being and destiny in his own way."[35] National myths are created by poets who embody the general sentiment or feeling of a collectivity they are meant to serve by way of a fate/destiny pattern, and they come from the national level of the unconscious that is often associated with the religious level of the psyche. In *Symbols of Transformation*, Jung writes: "Burckhardt seems to have glimpsed this truth, when he said that every Greek of the classical period carries in himself a little bit of Oedipus, and every German a little bit of Faust."[36] National myths are created by poets who embody the general sentiment or feeling of the collectivity that they are meant to serve from a national standpoint. In the United States, such a standpoint is transnational in scope. Thus, to carry Jung's insights further, every American carries in himself or herself a little bit of Ishmael and a little bit of Ahab, a little bit of Queequeg and a little bit of Fedallah.

Recall that Ishmael famously cited his reasons for going to sea in the following lines, which convey the realities he felt he had to escape, as well as the destiny he needed to embrace and the madness he was called to confront through the sacred action of novel writing:

"Grand Contested Election for the Presidency of the United States."
"WHALING VOYAGE BY ONE ISHMAEL."
"BLOODY BATTLE IN AFFGHANISTAN."[37]

This is precisely where the United States has been over the last decade: engaged in a bloody battle in Afghanistan. And Osama Bin Laden is dead, hearsed, and buried at sea by the U.S. Navy. Preaching truth from his "inexorable self," Melville attempted, like Whitman and Dickinson, to provide America and the world with a religious solution to the problems of violence, homophobia, reprojection of evil, religious fundamentalism, and war between nations. He strikes through the mask of the three Abrahamic religions and reveals a split in the major monotheisms of the world and traces them to Zoroaster, the first prophet of Iran that split the God-image into a pair of warring brothers, who represent the eternal feud between absolute good and absolute evil.

As Ishmael is visualizing the death of Queequeg, he takes us back in time to the awe-inspiring atmospherics in ancient Persia: "An awe that cannot be named would steal over you as you sat by the side of this waning savage, and saw as strange things in his face, as any beheld who were bystanders when Zoroaster died. . . . no dying Chaldee or Greek had higher and holier thoughts than those, whose mysterious shades you saw creeping over the face of poor Queequeg."[38]

Ishmael, Queequeg, and the entire ship's crew, moreover, were said to "live together" "in some primitive instances" like "an old Mesopotamian family."[39] Thus, by taking us back to the cradle of civilization in ancient Iraq, Iran, Syria, and Turkey, Melville's myth-narrative returns us to the realization that it's out of the voice of the self in all four patriarchal religions of the Middle and Near East—Zoroastrianism, Judaism, Christianity, and Islam—that the most urgent warning to the world needs to be sounded. He insists that we need to heed the lessons of man's "queenly personality" and her "royal rights" on our planet, and feel a reverence for "Her." This "queenly personality" is the spiritual ancestress of patriarchy exemplified within the Goddess religions in the form of a fate/destiny pattern encompassing the aspects of the feminine embodied in the Roman goddess Fortuna and the tripartite Greek Goddesses of Fate, which are united in the symbol of the ship the *Rachel* that saves Ishmael in the end.

In this sense, Ahab is both our destiny and our fate, as a nation of many nations, as is Ishmael. They are parts of our national complex, and, by extension, of an emergent transnational mythos of world culture that Whitman calls Spiritual Democracy. Only here in Melville's "gospels" do we get a clearer picture of democracy, which is inclusive of the dark side of the self.

Let's examine one pertinent scene in *Moby Dick* to illuminate this further. In chapter 117, "The Whale Watch," Melville recalls the story of four slain whales that are brought aboard the *Pequod* and of the interesting conversation that takes place between Ahab and Fedallah beside the body of one of the dead whales while the other four members of the Parsee's five man assassin-crew are fast asleep. Here the symbolism of four is highly significant, for four, according to Jung, is a symbol of wholeness. Melville writes:

> Ahab and all his boat's crew seemed asleep but the Parsee; who crouching in the bow, sat watching the sharks, that spectrally played round the whale and tapped the light cedar planks with their tails. A sound like the moaning of squadrons of unforgiven ghosts of Gomorrah, ran shuddering through the air.
>
> Started from his slumbers, Ahab, face to face, saw the Parsee; and hooped round by the gloom of night they seemed the last men in a flooded world. 'I have dreamed it again,' said he.
>
> 'Of the hearses? Have I not said, old man, that neither hearse nor coffin can be thine?'
>
> 'And who are hearsed that die on the sea?'
>
> 'But I said, old man, that ere thou couldst die on this voyage, two hearses must verily be seen by thee on the sea; the first not made by mortal hands; and the visible wood of the last one must be grown in America.'[40]

Of course we know that what the Parsee (Fed-Allah) is referring to by "two hearses" are 1) the immortal hearse of the White Whale to which Ahab is wedded in a love-death, tied and tethered to the feeling-toned object of his hate at the end of the novel, and 2) the mortal hearse of the *Pequod*, an American ship so named after the Pequot Indians, the wood of which was grown on our national soil, and is sunk at the end of the novel by the "battering ram" of Moby Dick. This "prophecy" comes out of the core element of the complex of religious fundamentalism represented by Ahab's hate, an emotion that the Parsee induces in him via a sort of infectious spell by which both Ahab and the ship's entire crew are bound in a diabolical pact with Ibliss or Satan. Fedallah, through archetypal possession by an archaic God-complex, leads Ahab to project evil by the very fact that he is absolute evil incarnate.

Here we must infer that Melville's vision of evil offers a diagnostic picture of a prospective tendency in the American psyche to project and reproject evil unconsciously, without reflecting on the archetypal source of evil in the God-complexes of the world that have a tendency to split evil off from the reality of God. We've seen that a quadratic constellation of four religious ideologies is emerging in the American psyche and the world in an effort to advance civilization toward a New World myth in which these God-complexes may be integrated into a quaternary spiritually democratic God-image that makes room for all religions. This new symbol of the Democratic God is threatened with destruction by the Ahab-Fedallah pairing. This is evident in Ahab's dream of the two "hearses."

> 'Aye, aye! a strange sight that, Parsee:—a hearse and its plumes floating over the ocean with the waves for the pall-bearers. Ha! Such a sight we shall not soon see.'
> 'Believe it or not, thou canst not die till it be seen, old man.'
> 'And what was that saying about thyself?'
> 'Though it come to the last, I shall still go before thee thy pilot.'
> 'And when thou art so gone before—if that ever befall—then ere I can follow, thou must still appear to me, to pilot me still?—Was it not so? Well, then, did I believe all ye say, oh my pilot! I have here two pledges that I shall yet slay Moby Dick and survive it,'
> 'Take another pledge, old man,' said the Parsee, as his eyes lightened up like fire-flies in the gloom—'Hemp only can kill thee.'
> 'The gallows, ye mean.—I am immortal then, on land and on sea,' cried Ahab, with a laugh of derision;—'Immortal on land and on sea!'[41]

This sounds a bit like the hubris of Saddam Hussein before his tribunal where he was found guilty of countless war crimes by his own people and then hung in a public square. The danger of possessing such an arrogant attitude in our relations with the countries of the Middle East is that through its immense military might, Ahab-America might think itself "immortal" and be incited by fundamentalist Islamic groups to engage in what in time might become a third world war. This potential is clearly outlined in Melville's vision of evil, which appears to come from an epidemic released by an Islamic figure goading the national complex of America to continue on its mad hunt and precipitating a potential clash of civilizations.

It's during Ahab's oppression of the Parsee that the captain goes through his past reincarnations and remembers his previous incarnation as a Persian fire worshiper:

> At the base of the mainmast, full beneath the doubloon and the flame, the Parsee was kneeling in Ahab's front, but with his head bowed away from him. . . .
>
> 'Aye, aye, men!' cried Ahab. 'Look up at it; mark it well; the white flame but lights the way to the White Whale!' . . . [Ahab] put his foot on the Parsee; and with fixed upward eye, and high flung right arm, he stood erect before the lofty tri-pointed trinity of flames. . . .
>
> 'But thou art but my fiery father; my sweet mother, I know not. Oh, cruel! what hast thou done with her? There lies my puzzle; but thine is greater.'[42]

Here the relationship between Fedallah and Ahab is clearly identified. Ahab's reference to his "sweet mother" is an allusion to the Goddess that was excluded from the patriarchal God-images in the Abrahamic religions and Zoroastrianism. Hence the danger is implicit in the Zoroastrian-Judeo-Christian-Islamic complexes of world nations that are currently vying for hegemony in a worldwide push toward increasing democratization and globalization during a time of simultaneous rising fundamentalism or religious radicalism. This portent of impending danger, amid new waves of hope, is most clearly represented in chapter 130 of *Moby Dick*, "The Hat."

In this chapter, Melville outlines the relationship between the Ahab-Fedallah pair and the *Pequod*'s evil-infected crew. At this point, the prospective dream of Ahab and Fedallah's prophecies of doom have so contaminated the men on board the American ship that we begin to feel that Ahab and the Parsee are merely mirror images of one another. In other words, the contaminating effects radiating between the men—from Fedallah to Ahab, and from Ahab to Fedallah—are seen in their mutually antagonistic forms as penetrating and enflaming one another to form an energetic center wherein their split-off nuclear dynamics could become explosive and cover the world with a cloud of poisonous hate. This nuclear center is a serious threat to the world's civilizations. About this massively destructive potential located in the world, Ishmael recounts:

> But did you deeply scan him [Ahab] in his more secret confidential hours; when he thought no glance but one was on him; then you would have seen that even as Ahab's eyes so awed the crew's, the inscrutable Parsee's glance awed his; or somehow, at least, in some wild way, at times affected it. Such an added, gliding strangeness began to invest the thin Fedallah now; such ceaseless shudderings shook him; that the men looked dubious at him; half uncertain, as it seemed, whether indeed he were a mortal substance, or else a tremulous shadow cast upon the deck by some unseen being's body. And that shadow was always hovering over there. For not by night, even, had Fedallah ever certainly been known to slumber, or go below. He would stand still for hours; but never sat or leaned; his wan but wondrous eyes did plainly say—We two watchmen never rest. . . . But though his [Ahab's] whole life was now become one watch on deck; and though the Parsee's mystic watch was without intermission as his own; yet those two never seemed to speak—one man to the other—unless at long intervals some passing unmomentuous matter made it necessary. Though such a secret spell seemed secretly to join the twain . . . Without a single hail, they stood far parted in the starlight; Ahab and his scuttle, the Parsee by the mainmast; but still fixedly gazing upon each other; as if in the Parsee Ahab saw his forethrown shadow, in Ahab the Parsee his abandoned substance.[43]

Such images point to the prospective of the unaccounted evil emerging in the American national complex to outline a potential conflict in the future—or what we may now be seeing in its incipient stages and looming large on the horizon. Such visionary images, according to Jung, "are no more prophetic than a medical diagnosis or a weather forecast. They are merely an anticipatory combination of probabilities which may coincide with the actual behavior of things but need not necessarily agree in every detail."[44] The Bush Administration may have thought that by attempting to destroy an affectively charged dictatorship in Iraq, the United States could have destroyed the beginnings of what President Bush called an "axis of evil" (of Iran, North Korea, and Iraq), or that if we had captured Osama Bin Laden "dead or alive" on his watch, America would have won his "Crusade against Evil." But, as Jung warned in *Aion* and *Answer to Job*, it's a shattering experience for a person to stare straight into the face of "absolute evil."

This is exactly what each of us must do today, to avert the possibility of a third world war on all four sides of the Zoroastrian-Judeo-Christian-Muslim religious complex: confront our own fundamentalism, in whatever way it might manifest itself as the shadow of sacred activism. But the real "axis of evil" is the projection and reprojection of absolute evil among each national power that engages in such dangerous conflicts of civilization. Melville was the first poet to give us an accurate picture of the ultimate aim of this dangerous God-complex as it relates to contemporary religion, myth, and politics, and we would be wise to take heed of his warnings. All of the Parsee's dreams and predictions come true. One by one, they are revealed to dark Ahab until, at last, the process of transformation that's destined to come about is made visible in the final death gaze of the glassy-eyed Fedallah, to whose radical Islamic vision of evil Ahab becomes transfixed in the end. As we've seen, Melville provides us with an opportunity to make our national evil conscious through the voluntary sacrifice of the Ahab-Fedallah pair.

> And yet, somehow, did Ahab—in his own proper self, as daily, hourly, and every instant, commandingly revealed to his subordinates,—Ahab seemed an independent lord; the Parsee but his slave. Still again both seemed yoked together.[45]

Ahab and Fedallah are "yoked together." The important thing is that the way to *symbolic death* is supplied to individuals, groups, and nations by the narrative-motifs of myth. By being "yoked" together in mutual warfare against a common foe, the whale Moby Dick, these two warlike brothers facilitate a metanoia, a self-correction of consciousness, in which all sides of the God-complex may indeed be transformed through Ishmael's survival aboard the *Rachel* and the narration of their tragic fate.

We've seen the inability to mourn expressed by our American political leaders following the traumatic events of September 11, 2001, where the external mobilization of archetypal aggressive energies in the war against terror in Iraq raged through the American polis during the Bush administration in order to keep citizens and politicians from feeling the lamentation and grief in their own collective pain. Most psychotherapists and political leaders were so caught up in the need to provide empathic mirroring and healing acceptance that many had trouble seeing the shadow of homeland security, national defense, Iraqi Freedom, or some other deceptive slogan for waging war against evil.

Immediately following 9/11, America took about three days to mourn the tragedy of the Word Trade Center and Pentagon attacks and the Pennsylvania plane crash before George W. Bush found his Christian creed's religious "calling" to seek vengeance against the United States' persecutors in Afghanistan, and then, against Iraq, which was not even involved in the attacks.

We might well wonder how a metanoia of consciousness can be facilitated by the work of a great visionary artist. How can a national myth such as *Moby Dick* mirror the process of psychic transformation in the collective psyche? How can his story inspire us as readers to translate its meanings into holy work? Melville's underscoring of forty passages from the book of Job makes it the most heavily studied section of his Bible.[46] This might lead us all to lament. For in the Pacific, where the *Pequod* went down in the whirling vortex created by Moby Dick's angry seething, there is now a whirling ring of plastic the size of Texas. Our burning of fossil fuels and pollution in the sea has contributed to the creation of storms so violent that God's wrath—nature's wrath—is no longer only a myth, but a horrifying and frightful reality. We'd all better use our vocations to do something about it—and quickly.

In chapter 126 of *Moby Dick*, "The Life Buoy," when the first man who mounted the masthead to look out for the White Whale was "swallowed up" Jonah-like, "in the deep," few men were "grieved at this event, at least as a portent; for they regarded it not as a foreshadowing of evil in the future, but as the fulfillment of an evil already presaged."[47] Dragged down, the men aboard the ship were tied to Ahab's evil fate as we too were tied to the fate of the American-led coalition during the Bush administration. A further portent is provided for by the Parsee's final death-glance:

> Lashed round and round to the fish's back; pinioned in the turns upon turns in which, during the past night, the whale had reeled the involutions of the lines around him, the half torn body of the Parsee was seen; his sable raiment frayed to shreds; his distended eyes turned full upon old Ahab.[48]

In a significant parallel, the Obama administration decided, according to Islamic law, not to bury the body of Bin Laden on land, but rather to give him a proper burial in a hearse at sea at some unknown destination in the Persian Gulf. In this scene Ahab and the Parsee's destinies become interfused, interwoven, intertwined, and interlinked, and two parts of a single God-complex are miraculously fused again. Ahab is determined to follow his unconscious fate to its end. "Befooled, befooled!" cries Ahab in the story, drawing in his last long lean breaths, as if in mirroring of a future event in the collective psyche where the beam in the Western gaze will become ever more visible to the entire world:

> Aye, Parsee! I see thee again.—Aye, and thou goest before; and this, this then is the hearse that thou didst promise. But I hold thee to the last letter of thy word. Where is the second hearse? Away, away mates . . . obey me.—Where's the whale? gone down again?[49]

The more the American ship of state strives for teleosis, through the denial of the feminine, the homoerotic, and through the reprojection of the evil onto Islamic terrorists throughout the Middle East, the more the weight of the collective psyche may accumulate until our excesses will expand to a bursting point and our national pride may lead us even deeper into perdition and economic gloom. Only then, according to Melville's prophecy of doom, may a new consciousness be born from the sea of the collective unconscious. We might then begin to carry God's moral imperfection and our own immorality, and our allotted portion of evil will hopefully teach us to grieve for the children of the world that have been senselessly lost, through which alone we may begin to enlighten the world with the good tidings of Spiritual Democracy.

As we've seen, Melville's religious symbols are multivalent, multiethnic, and multireligious in his narrative. Many images provide a contemporary solution to the problem of the projection of evil in contemporary politics, economics, and religious sectors of the world's population. Ishmael's survival points more optimistically to what might become, in time, a Political-Economic-Religious-Democracy.

As a great visionary artist, Melville saw into the latent meaning of the God-complexes of all religious cultures—to the feeling-toned intensity of religious emotions, affects, and ideas—to answer a need for closer human sympathy among all nations. By illuminating the affects of hatred, rage, and economic greed in the figure Ahab, and complementing this with the symbol of the whale ship the *Rachel*, he was illuminating a problem of possession not only in the Middle East but especially in the United States, and leaving us with a solution in our lamentations. Melville's archetypal images of the American self represent a complex of mythological and religious potentials, which point to a collective world-soul-spirit, symbolized in the White Whale and the "Grand Armada," that is in danger of being lost in the violent clash of opposing religious-political ideologies.

18

METAMORPHOSIS
OF THE GODS

Carl Jung defined *God-image* as an inner image or function that is in the process of transformation in the collective psyche. It's not the death of "God" that *Moby Dick* signifies, therefore, but rather the death of our images of God that Melville's myth connotes for our times.

God can never be fully known, according to Jung, except as an image in the human psyche, which has now been relativized by science. He writes:

> We thus arrive at the objectionable conclusion that, from the psychological point of view, the God-image is a real but subjective phenomenon. . . .
> To carry a God around in yourself means a great deal; it is a guarantee of happiness, of power, and even of omnipotence, insofar as these are attributes of divinity. To carry a god within oneself is practically the same as being God oneself. . . . As a power which transcends consciousness the libido is by nature daemonic: it is both God and devil.[1]

Anyone who witnessed the immediate aftermath of the attacks on the World Trade Center and the Pentagon on September 11, 2001, glimpsed the shadow side of God at work in the terrorists' beliefs that they were carrying out the will of Allah. Islamic fundamentalism was revealed in its most sinister form when Osama Bin Laden spoke on a video clip broadcast on international television and recalled with sadistic pleasure the planes hitting the buildings. People jumped to their deaths from the fiery buildings and the gargantuan buildings of the World Trade Center crumbled to dust—and Allah willed this? As Melville and Whitman and Jung all knew, God is both good and evil—a union of opposites.

"The 'relativity of God,' as I understand it," writes Jung, "denotes a point of view that does not conceive of God as 'absolute,' i.e., wholly cut off from man and existing outside and beyond all human conditions, but as in a certain sense dependent on him; it also implies a reciprocal and essential relation between man and God, whereby God can be understood as a function of God, and God as a psychological function of man."[2] Psychologically, God is a complex of religious ideas grouped around a powerful feeling tone, and these affects are personified in *Moby Dick* most powerfully by Captain Ahab. The solution to Ahab's problem of "dictatorship" can be found aboard the rescuing ship the *Rachel.*

We saw the dramatic splitting of opposites in American politics as the tension heated up during the 2004 presidential campaign, where, at the same moment that George W. Bush announced himself America's "war president," San Francisco's mayor Gavin Newsome galvanized the nation by challenging the values of the old Hebrew-Christian-Muslim ethic by legitimizing same-sex marriages and filing suit against the state of California for discriminating against gay people. In the Golden State, the political argument was seen as a clash of opposing religious ideologies in the polis of the United States, as the ballot initiative to roll back these rights, Proposition 8, was mostly funded by the Mormon and the Roman Catholic Churches. The split in the God-complex around the legitimization and delegitimization of same-sex marriage has been forcing American citizens and politicians to take an emotional and ethical stand on an issue that Herman Melville and Walt Whitman and Emily Dickinson imaged as central to American democracy over a century and a half ago.

In *Moby Dick*, the Ishmael-Queequeg relationship, which is described as a "marriage" between two men, and the union of whale sisters and mothers in chapter 86, "The Grand Armada," represents one side of the God-complex in the American psyche, which points toward God's renewal in the world soul. The other, shadow side is represented by Ahab and Fedallah and the emergence of a new God-image of Spiritual Democracy (symbolized by the White Whale).

Ahab's death on the back of the whale represents an end to religious fanaticism and the approach of a new era of a masculine-feminine deity that includes both God and the Goddess, inclusive of the wisdom traditions of all religions of the earth. The Ahab-Parsee pairing and the mad hunt for *Moby Dick*, on the other hand, represent the fundamentalist side of religious orthodoxy that is filled with destruction and evil, but will ultimately die out if the global attempt to unify the world's religious faiths into a Spiritual Democracy are successful. Perhaps the most hopeful indication of a movement in this direction was the coordinated efforts by Coptic Christians and Muslims to topple the dictatorship of Hosni Mubarak in Egypt during the Arab Spring of 2011. As Jung wrote in *The Undiscovered Self:*

> We are living in what the Greeks called the kairos—the right moment— for a "metamorphosis of the gods," of the fundamental principles and symbols. This peculiarity of our time, which is certainly not of our conscious choosing, is the expression of the unconscious man within us who is changing. Coming generations will have to take account of this momentous transformation if humanity is not to destroy itself through the might of its own technology and science.[3]

Through the voluntary sacrifice of the American heroic ego (with its masculine hubris and immense pride), Ahab achieves his greatness. In his moment of death, Ahab experiences his topmost grief. Only in death does Ahab arrive at the goal of his vision quest. His defiance against God and sacrilege against the sacred feminine becomes the signature of his failed initiation as a tragic hero, and the agent of transformation as a national instigator of war against Moby Dick is portrayed in a momentary signal of defeat.

Understood in this light, Ahab's final surrender to death at the end of the novel, as a conscious sacrifice as opposed to an unconscious one, is redeeming and presages the renewal of God. When the Ahab archetype is lived out in the unreflecting masses, however, its potential lethality is immense. As a symbol of transformation, Ahab is an extraordinary personality, who, like Father Mapple and Ishmael, hears the word of God and speaks it. Ahab hears not only the word of the Judeo-Christian God, but also the voice of Allah, as revealed through the whispering voice of his assassin, Fedallah, as a religious duty at the expense of the feminine. Ahab says in "The Candles": "whencesoe'er I came; whereso'er I go; yet while I earthly live, the queenly personality lives in me, and feels her royal rights. But war is pain, and hate is woe."[4] Through Melville's voice, this injured femininity in this former Goddess worshiper speaks aggressively and with war vengeance and hate. It's through Ahab's transformation, however, that Melville finds his prophetic calling to confront us all on the dangers of refusing to embrace a relativistic attitude toward God. A religious attitude that is at its root spiritually democratic might lead us to modesty.

But Ahab is interested in a confrontation with God, and his pact with the devil is with an Ismaili assassin, whose literary character is forged after the "Old Man of the Mountain," the grand master of the fanatical Islamic mystical sect known as the Fedais, whose aim was to wage jihad as a religious duty. Ahab is not, like Starbuck, concerned with how many barrels of whale oil he'll bring

in to the Nantucket marketplace. In *Moby Dick*, Ahab's goal, as a son of the
Mother Goddess and a world ruler of Fedallah, is to arrive at the "little lower
level," beneath the historical masks of God to include the wrath of the Babylonian Goddess, Tiamat, and become her agent—to provoke "Nature's God"
as a son of chaos to crucify him, as he cannot accomplish the aim of initiation
on his own. This transnational crucifixion of his quest for world dominion is
his conscious aim as a trickster aligned with Fedallah and as someone who carries the Goddess personality within him who "feels her royal rights" upon the
earth. The Ahab-Fedallah pair works in a joint effort to illuminate the darkness
of God.

Ahab is not fighting to preserve the living orthodoxy of the Father God.
Rather, his aim is to reclaim the heterodoxy of the Goddess, to fight for the
integrity of the beliefs he once embraced: the feminine, emotional, and ethical
values of the Earth. "Oh, thou magnanimous! now I do glory in my genealogy.
But thou art my fiery father; my sweet mother, I know not. Oh, cruel! what
hast thou done with her?"[5] What matters most in Ahab's efforts to kill Moby
Dick is his pact with Fedallah to reveal the hidden face of God in her feminine
form: their mutual quest is to make the darkness of God conscious. It's important to remember that, according to the Ismailiya that Melville had read about
before he created his characters, the prophets of Islam who followed Muhammad through a series of imams would stop with the seventh imam, Ismael, the
"hidden prophet."[6] *Moby Dick*'s famous opening line, "Call me Ishmael," takes
on a whole new significance in light of the events in our world since the first ter-
rorist attack on the World Trade Center, in 1993, which was also the work of the
hidden assassin, Osama bin Laden.

This, therefore, is Melville's aim as a spiritual seer: to strike through the
masks of God to what Jung calls the "relativity of the God-symbol"[7] and to
lead us to see the many in the "One," even the shadow side of God. Jung mentions in his "Definitions" in *Psychological Types* that symbol formation occurs
in the founders of religions during their "initiation period," such as during the
struggle between Jesus and Satan, Buddha and Mara, and Martin Luther and the
Devil.[8] In *Moby Dick* this opposition is represented by the struggle of Ahab and
Fedallah against a common foe, the great White Whale. The inception for this
period of initiation is 1849, when Melville wrote upon the flyleaf of his seventh
and last volume of Shakespeare:

> Ego non baptizo te in nomine Patris et
> Filii et Spiritus Sancti—sed in nominie
> Diaboli.—madness undefinable—

It & right reason extremes of one,
—not the (black art) Goetic but Theurgic magic—
seeks converse with the Intelligence, Power, the
Angel.[9]

This Latin benediction on *The Whale* forms the secret motto of *Moby Dick* and reveals precisely what the author's intentions were in the formation of his characters. Ahab invokes evil *(Diaboli)* to illuminate the darkness of the Father *(Patris)*, the Son *(Filii)*, and Holy Spirit *(Spiritus Sancti)*. Ahab's action thereby fulfills Whitman's call in the poem "Chanting the Square Deific" for the inclusion of Satan and the feminine (Santa Spirita) into his Deus Quadriune, and as well as Jung's later proclamation of the self in *Aion* and *Answer to Job* as the new symbol for divinity. What the new myth tells us is that cultural transformation toward Spiritual Democracy can take place only after human communities have made the inward darkness in the world soul conscious; only then may a new world order come about. As an international image for the pairing of cross-cultural opposites engaged in mutual "war" in the name of a higher insight into the nature of God ("Intelligence, Power, the Angel"), Ahab and the Parsee (Fedallah) push individuals, nations, groups, and particularly religious collectivities through death and destruction toward the annihilative edge.

Melville's answer to the problem of religious fundamentalism is given to us through Ishmael's suffering as the "hidden prophet" whose religious duty comes to him through the goetic realization that good and evil are inextricably entwined into one interwoven thread. This is the thread of each human life, the thread of fate and the fate of the world's nations, with many threads twined together in one rope, which Melville brilliantly calls the "monkey-rope," reminding us of our humble originations from apelike ancestors. By goetic, Melville is playing not on the German reference to Goethe's Faust but rather on the Greek connotation *goetos,* which, as Melville scholar Charles Olson tells us, means "variously trickster, juggler, and, as here, magician. (Plato called literature *Goeteia*.)"[10] Ishmael alone hears Father Mapple's Sermon out and speaks it through his narrative function as conductor of the entire chorus. Melville-as-Ishmael hears all of the characters' voices in the story and expresses them in symphonic resonance through the angelic power given to him via indwelling cadences of music, in concourse with the Holy Spirit. Such inspirational influences enable him to accomplish his poetic task through his vocation, his calling, as a post-Christian writer bringing forth a new revelation of "Gospels" for America and the world—a new myth through which the shadow side of Christianity will not remain unaware.

It's important to note moreover that two religious archetypes—the Ahab-Fedallah pair—do not fight each other in the outworking of the novel, as they do whenever good and evil are constellated as a pair of moral opposites projected between and among fundamentalist religious groups into the field of international politics. Rather in an effort to make the unreasoning side of "God" conscious in collective humanity, they fight against a common foe, Moby Dick, who represents an unconscious, animal side of the deity.

The purpose of *Moby Dick* as a national and international myth is to make conscious in readers the archetype of absolute evil in Islam, the Near East, and the West, so that we might mitigate the possibility of collective mass destruction by consciously reflecting on our own evil. Such a potential for transformation is depicted during the final scenes of Ahab's adventure into death, followed by Ishmael's rebirth. Ahab's transformation begins in earnest during chapter 132, "The Symphony," when this homophobic character that assumes command over the symbolic American ship of state declares to his first mate: "Close! Stand close to me, Starbuck; let me look into a human eye; it is better than to gaze in sea or sky; better than to gaze upon God."[11] Ahab sees in this moment of clear reflection the "bright hearth-stone," saying, "This the magic glass, man; I see my wife and child in thine eye."[12] Significantly, the reflection of his "wife and child" in Starbuck's eye is him seeing, through this reflection in the eyes of another man, the feminine face of God, Hestia, the Goddess of the hearth, or the Green One, Khidr, from chapter 18 of the Koran. It's a moment of pure clarity, where Ahab questions: "Is Ahab, Ahab? Is it I, God, or who lifts this arm?"[13] It's not the "I," Ahab's ego, that lifts the handspike, but rather fate. In this reflection through Starbuck's eyes, Ahab's humility is given back to him momentarily, through a sudden upsurge of human feelings of love, homoeros, and comrade emotions. This reflection results in eros, sympathy, and grief—the emotion Ahab represses. Pip, too, the little black cabin boy who serves Ahab loyally to the end, leads him to shed a tear in the Pacific. Ishmael says: "From beneath his slouched hat Ahab dropped a tear into the sea; nor did all the Pacific contain such wealth as that one wee drop."[14] The wisdom of this statement on Ahab's connection to his fellow human beings (Starbuck and Pip), arises when, for a brief moment, what led to reflection as a possibility of accepting an upsurge of same-sex sympathy is suddenly forgotten or repressed, as is the mirror-image of Ahab's wife and child in Starbuck's eye, in his captain's vengeful obsession to dismember his dismemberer[15]:

> Behold, Starbuck! is it not hard, that with this weary load I bear, one
> poor leg should have been snatched from under me? Here, brush this

old hair aside; it blinds me, so that I seem to weep. . . . I feel deadly faint, bowed, and humped, as though I were Adam, staggering beneath the piled centuries of Paradise. God! God! God!—crack my heart!—stave my brain!—mockery, mockery, bitter, bitter mockery of grey hairs, have I lived enough joy to wear ye; and seem and feel thus intolerably old.[16]

This correspondence between love and violence becomes clear a few lines earlier in the novel. Ahab's decision to move into deadly battle with Moby Dick is something that is determined by fate. Ishmael has access to such a prophetic insight in chapter 54, "The Town Ho's Story," when he recalls words he said to two young dons in Lima, Peru: "Gentlemen, a strange fatality pervades the whole career of these events, as if verily mapped out before the world itself was created."[17]

In Melville's view, when we're able to see the great gestalt or symbolic pattern in the mind of nature, we may come to know God as a democratic unity. Such gnosis, or self-knowledge, may inevitably lead to the transformation of God. Melville's visions of Spiritual Democracy are conveyed most clearly in chapter 87, "The Grand Armada," in the great scene depicting the image of the great whale-pod formation, and in the final rescue of Ishmael by the *Rachel*. These stunning passages represent the feminine deity as the containing matrix, or transcendent aspect of the godhead.

Melville's depiction of the whales swimming in a geometrical pattern evokes a symbolic mandala. Mandalas are symbols of healing that often appear at the culmination point marking a major change or transformation during a long course of psychotherapy; as such, they bring order and peace during periods of chaos and psychic disorientation. These depictions are universal God-images found transnationally in all religions, often including a unifying center and a containing circumference that may link individuals with the surrounding cosmos. As curative matrices of the mythopoetic imagination, mandalas are potent sources for creativity used universally as meditation devices and medicine for harmonizing self and society, such as in the Chinese yin/yang or Dao symbol, Navajo sand paintings, or the peace symbol, used widely in nonviolent protests during the height of the Vietnam War. The functional significance of such transcultural mandalas in establishing peacemaking marks them out as leading images in our global struggle toward Spiritual Democracy.

We may never fully come to know God in Melville's visions of Spiritual Democracy, for God is immense like the stars. This is suggested by his numerous references to the Milky Way, and Cetus, the whale constellation: "The dignity of our calling the very heavens attest. Cetus is a constellation in the South!"[18] Yet, as God spoke to humanity as he is once said to have spoken to Moses, "face to face, as a man speaks to his friend" (Exodus 33:18–23), or as a purified soul may behold the glory of the Shekinah, "eye to eye," so, too, does Melville enable us to behold the glory of the White Whale in our human eyes, as an everlasting image of the God in Nature. More than this, however, is the humanizing factor of relatedness when Ahab gazes into a human eye: "better than to Gaze upon God."[19] The idea of friendship, or male-male partnership, exercised across various ethnicities, cultures, and groups became Melville's answer to man's existential search for meaning, his wrestling with the problem of meaninglessness, hatred, and evil among men in the cosmos. This antidote to the inevitable human suffering has its ultimate dwelling place in the human heart of man. Melville's answer to God's indifference to the suffering of humanity is supplied, finally, by Ishmael's dramatic rescue by the whale ship *Rachel*. As Maurice Friedman writes:

> Ishmael's rescue by the *Rachel* suggests overtones of the redemption of the Shekinah—the imminent Glory of God of the Talmud and the Kabala. But it reminds us still more strongly that prior to that redemption, the Shekinah is traditionally pictured as in exile.[20]

While the exile of the Shekinah is what Freidman (echoing Martin Buber), terms the "death" or "eclipse of God"—which appears to be occurring in the clash of religious ideologies today—Ishmael's survival on the *Rachel* points to the coming glory of God through the force of a new spiritual revelation, in which the feminine, the bi-erotic, and evil may all be included into a new conception of God. Talmudic and cabalist scholars anticipated the coming of the feminine into monotheism in the symbol of the Messianic Banquet, a symbolic portrayal of the blessings of the age to come, in which the elect will share in a rich and righteous feast with the Messiah as their supreme and triumphal host in the Kingdom of Heaven. But the "marriage" made explicit in the notion of the Shekinah is without its homosexual shadow. This is what Freidman, like so many other commentators on the novel, fails to take into account. It's not the death of God *per se* that is being symbolized in Melville's visions of Spiritual Democracy, but a rebirth of a new God-symbol, the renewal of the bi-erotic and multispiritual religions of the earth.

Fear of fate is what makes the externalized war against evil possible as a political and environmental event in the first two strata of democracy, and this inevitability to react out of the various national complexes without right reason is captured in Ahab's words to Starbuck in chapter 134, "The Chase—Second Day," where we read, "Ahab is forever Ahab, man . . . Fool! I am the Fate's lieutenant; I act under orders."[21] This inability to act as anything other than the agent of fate is the miracle of reflective life at the center of the novel. Again, it's the eyes that reveal the hidden meaning of the book as a transnational narrative in the last lines of "The Symphony" chapter where Ishmael says, after observing the loving connection between Ahab and Starbuck: "Ahab crossed the deck to gaze over the other side [of the ship]; but started at two reflected, fixed eyes on the water there. Fedallah was motionlessly leaning over the same rail."[22] Trust in Spiritual Democracy as a third solution to the first two stages (political and economic) offers a compassionate and just option for a saner possibility, for rather than acting automatically out of unconscious fate, one reflects upon it. This affords a conscious choice to take moral action for the destruction one might engage in, either individually, as groups, or nationally, and most often at the expense of nature, eros, and the sacred feminine.

Melville ends his story *Moby Dick* with a note of hope, nonetheless, by pointing to the fact that Ishmael's survival heralds the coming of the integration of the shadow, the feminine (Mother Goddess), and the bi-erotic into our conceptions of the deity. This indwelling, or immanence, of evil, the Shekinah, and the self through bi-erotic marriage can only arise through the failure of fundamentalist monotheisms, which are currently infecting the globe with a psychic sickness perhaps more dangerous than anyone in America, Europe, Africa, Asia, South and Central America, or the Middle East might have foreseen in Melville's time.

In the end, Ishmael and Queequeg have what the Ahab-Parsee pair does not have: a nonhomophobic male-male friendship and a new religious attitude toward "Nature's God" in a coming Spiritual Democracy, which teaches simply that we are all interconnected. Such interdependence is required if we are to arrive at a "common destiny" between women and men and nations, if we are to move together toward a closer democratic goal of universal brotherhood and sisterhood—an interdependence that is necessary in the human-divine relationship.[23] Having sailed through these dark and treacherous waters of the shadow of death with Melville at our ship's helm, let's now proceed to sail more peacefully into the main message of his teaching, which is our spiritual destiny to bequeath to the world, and that is to love.

19

THE RE-EMERGENCE
OF THE FEMININE

In the epilogue of *Moby Dick*, Ishmael, the sole survivor of the whale ship *Pequod*'s sinking, echoes the biblical Job: "And I only am escaped alone to tell thee." After Fedallah's and Ahab's disappearance, it's the "hidden prophet" Ishmael, and not some fundamentalist lieutenant, who's ordained by the fates to take the place of "Ahab's bowsman [Parsee], when that bowsman assumed the vacant post . . ."[1]

The mysterious hidden prophet, according to Antoine Isaac Silvestre de Sacy's famous account, is the one called by Allah to teach the true message of God to humankind.[2] Thus, Ishmael is a narrator who teaches the way of Spiritual Democracy, and this equality is also reflected in his character and that of his multireligious, Ramadan-celebrating friend Queequeg. Ishmael is saved when the coffin of Queequeg shoots up out of the whirling vortex of the sea to serve as his life buoy.

Ishmael represents the capacity to endure and develop a new insight into life's present limitations and future possibilities. He's therefore a "self-figure" who's able to relate lovingly to a transcendent "other"; this we know from the Ishmael-Queequeg "marriage." Carrying the burden of the religious complex of monotheism, he offers healing through the unexpected solution of the repressed shadow of homosexuality and the realization of a reciprocal eros between men. The male-male marriage and a feminine symbol of completeness, the rescuing ship *Rachel*, were seen by Melville as developments in the world that may usher forth a new age of consciousness. In this era, evil may be held in awareness without being reprojected as archetypal hatred, as symbolized by the last line of the epilogue: "It was the devious-cruising *Rachel*, that in her retracing search after her missing children, only found another orphan [Ishmael]."[3]

It's this feminine side of the Hebrew deity, the whale ship *Rachel*, who picks up Ishmael from the life buoy of Queequeg's coffin and transports him back to American shores. The *Rachel* is "the Shekinah, the glory of God in exile, and its personification, Rachel weeping for her children, in whom the personal aspect" of the Goddess is preserved.[4] The anima figure-ship *Rachel* is the containing vessel in Melville's vision of evil for the new image of God, as seen through the reflective and feeling eyes of Ishmael, who bears the message of the creative and destructive sides of God, Christ, or Allah to the world's people. Because she's described "devious-cruising," we can say that she has integrated the trickster and thus can guarantee Ishmael's survival, and his ability to hold (and share) his vision. Called "devious" because she deviates from a "straight" course in her voyage back to the United States mainland, the *Rachel* arrives intuitively at her destination point at sea. With her fortuitous rescue of Ishmael on the sea she brings a divine feminine consciousness to our current global fate of religious wars, dictatorships, and climate change, which left unconscious of the highest vistas of equality between the world's spiritualities would surely destroy us as a nation if the shadow side of our democracy (inequality) were to be deviating in the slightest from the highest principles of justice, liberty, and equal rights for all people. As one of the main ancestral mothers of compassion and justice in the three monotheisms, the *Rachel*'s main purpose, therefore, is to integrate everything and everyone that has been historically left out by the big patriarchies.

The *Rachel* may link and ultimately transcend this trinity of male divinities in the Near East, the West, and Islam through her global remedy of environmental justice. The missing "fourth" feminine element appears at the end of the narrative to bring salvation to Judaism and Christianity by welcoming a rejected son of the three monotheism—homosexuality—and redeeming an orphan (Ishmael) long embraced by Islam aboard her nonprejudicial transpatriarchal ship, without leaving him behind on his "wife's" flotilla because of his newly acquired sexual orientation. As a transformational and perhaps transgendered personage across all nations and nationalities, moreover, Ishmael may then begin to bridge a gap between male and female genders, as a "two-spirit." The "devious" sailing vessel might become in time a healing container for personal and transnational transformation, in which the institution of same-sex marriage can be included at the political and economic stages of democracy. Her ability to mourn all of her lost children enables everyone—lesbian women too—to share in her bountiful grace, joy, and blessings, with equal rights and without unfairness, as a panacea for what is lacking in the first two strata of democracy. On this hopeful note Melville ends one of the greatest stories ever told by an American.

In the Hebrew Bible, the image of Rachel weeping for her children is found in a passage in the book of Jeremiah, and it's quoted by Matthew in the New Testament (Matthew 2:17–18) as follows: "In Rama was there a voice heard, lamentation, and weeping, and great mourning, Rachel weeping for her children, and would not be comforted, because they are not." Maurice Friedman tells us that Melville read not only the Bible but the Talmud, the ancient book of Jewish law, and that he may have known that in mystical Judaism the exile of Israel "became a central symbol not only for the destiny of the people but for the complementary destiny of God. In the Talmud, the Holy Spirit is hypostatized as the Shekinah, the form of the divine immanence, the indwelling Glory of God."[5] Thus, the implication of Melville's spiritual realization of the importance of the feminine side of the Holy Spirit, the Shekinah, is quite profound. The *Rachel* is a symbol for the United States and the world to follow. By bringing the neglected feminine (Rachel) and the homoerotic (Ishmael-Queequeg) together into one vessel, Melville takes his visions of Spiritual Democracy back with him to the mainland and thereby provides his answer to the sufferings of man by making the shadow of religious fundamentalism conscious.

In the end, Ishmael is not destroyed but rather enlightened by his tragic awareness of evil aboard the *Rachel*. The immortal White Whale escapes, though with Ahab's irons lodged into the gaping wounds in his back. The Whale, as an agent of the living God, must carry a newly found sensitivity to his own pain.

Thus, Melville ends *Moby Dick* not on a note of pessimism, recognizing that the Judeo-Christian-Islamic psyche has no vision of evil, but on an optimistic hope in Ishmael's relationship to his fellow women and men. Melville knew that if we could accept Ahab, Ishmael-Queequeg, and the White Whale as parts of ourselves, we might get along better in the world. "Wing ye down there, ye prouder, sadder souls! Question that proud, sad king! A family likeness! Aye, he did beget ye, ye young exiled royalties; and from your grim sire only will the old State secret come."[6]

Melville excluded women in his masterpiece *Moby Dick* for obvious reasons: there were no women aboard whale ships, and his myth is an allegorical portrayal of the actual seafaring "facts." Nevertheless, with a specific purpose in mind, Melville was called to write a new American myth of homoeroticism and love for nature that would include the feminine in her anima (whale), geophysical (the world's seas) and transcultural (multireligious) aspects. This is a new revelation of God. As we shall see, the experience of the same-sex marriage that

Ishmael brings on board the Rachal is actually contained and underscored by a much deeper same-sex union in the world soul, the anima mundi—by the theriomorphic side of God-as-a-Sea-Goddess—beautifully portrayed by Melville in *Moby Dick*'s chapter 87, "The Grand Armada." This is a pantheistic vision of the feminine face of God that Melville hoped could heal the mind-body-soul "split" in the Judeo-Christian-Islamic mythos.

Interpreted psychologically, Melville's images of same-sex eros reveals that the male-male marriage comprises three components: the sexual, the erotic, and the spiritual. These aspects of the allegory are all subsumed by the fourth principle—the feminine.[7] The three instinctive, soulful, and religious components—sexual, erotic, spiritual—make up a tripartite image of an innate urge for love that exists in all of us. That Melville realized same-sex union to be a sacred masculine "marriage" is remarkable for a man in 1851.

In *Moby Dick*, Melville said—possibly for the first time in American letters—that every man has within him an "inescapable twin brother" that must be acknowledged. In this vision the twin is an indivisible image in the soul that exists in every man and extends outward from a connecting bond toward other people.[8] Such an eros-link can be found in the symbolic "tie" that extends between Ishmael and Queequeg in chapter 72, "The Monkey-Rope":

> So, then, an elongated Siamese ligature united us. Queequeg was my own inseparable twin brother; nor could I in any way get rid of the dangerous liabilities which the hempen bond entailed. So strongly and metaphysically did I conceive of my situation then, that while earnestly watching his motions, I seemed distinctly to perceive that my own individuality was not merged in a joint stock company of two: that my free will had received a mortal wound; and that another's mistake or misfortune might plunge innocent me into unmerited disaster and death.

Melville-as-Ishmael then goes on to add something even more startling for a nineteenth-century readership:

> Still further pondering, I say, I saw that this situation of mine was the precise situation of every mortal that breathes; only, in most cases, he, one way or other, has his Siamese connexion with a plurality of other mortals.[9]

In analytical psychological terms Ishmael envisioned a masculine "twin" in the soul of every man that typically gets projected outward onto "a plurality" of people, men and women alike. Here Melville is emphasizing the phenomenon of psychological projection—the very phenomenon that so interested Jung. To experience one's "Siamese connection with a plurality of other mortals" might mean when one's same-sex soul-image has been exteriorized into a condition of multiplicity, and this situation is the typical condition of every human being. But, to recognize the inner "twin brother," or, by extension, inner "twin sister" in a homoerotic bond of brotherhood or sisterhood symbolized by "marriage," and then to engage this part of the soul in an inner dialogue through active visioning, or free-verse, is to participate in what Jung calls the "colloquy with the inner friend in the soul."[10]

For Melville to admit that he *loved* his mentors—his shipmate Jack Chase, author Richard Henry Dana Jr., and especially Nathaniel Hawthorne—suggests moreover that he was "wedded" to these men by a connection to the "twin"— the self—within himself. Through this inner relationship he forged a marriage with the anima mundi, the "many-in-the-one," that he took aboard with him onto the *Rachel*.

The literal meaning of the word *homosexual* is "of, relating to, or being of the same sex (—twins)"[11]; this is a meaning Melville captures brilliantly in his description of an inner marriage-bond of Ishmael-Queequeg and their connection via an "elongated Siamese ligature," with the term "Siamese" referring to conjoined twins. In Latin, *ligatura* means a "bond" or a "tie." Thus, the inner ligatura ties Ishmael and Queequeg together in a way that makes them inseparable and indistinguishable from one another—therefore *married*. They represent an imaginal marriage of twins in Melville's psyche, and they correspond to an archetype in the collective psyche of mankind. The same archetype is found in *Moby Dick*, as it applies to the feminine aspect of a man and to the bond of twinship between women.

The irony in debates surrounding same-sex marriage is that the archetype that the "religious right" is fighting against institutionalizing is present inside each of us! Marriage is a psychological state that represents a conscious realization of the self through an inner dialogue with the "brother" or "sister" in everyone. This includes the images of same-sex marriage as an essential aim of Spiritual Democracy.

At about this time in his creative unfolding, Melville wrote a letter to Richard Henry Dana Jr., who authored the best-selling book *Two Years Before the Mast*, where he clarifies the meaning of this same-sex symbol as it applies to everyone. In a letter dated October 6, 1849, Melville wrote that Dana had become a "fraternal" "sea-brother" by encouraging him to write his "man-of-war" book *White Jacket*. In the following letter to Dana, dated May 1, 1850—perhaps concurrently penning "The Monkey-Rope" chapter—Melville decoded the elusive meaning of the "Siamese" ligature-symbol further, as a metaphor for an "affectionate sympathy" that existed between the two men, a warm empathy based on their literary friendship. He writes:

> My Dear Dana—I thank you heartily for your friendly letter. . . . I am specially delighted at the thought, that those strange, congenial feelings, with which after my first voyage, I for the first time read 'Two Years Before the Mast', and while so engaged was, as it were, tied & welded to you by a sort of Siamese link of affectionate sympathy—that these feelings should be reciprocated by you, in your turn, and be called out by any White Jackets or Redburns of mine—this is indeed delightful to me, . . .[12]

Notice the special importance Melville gives to the emotion of delight. This is the meaning of same-sex marriage that Ishmael takes aboard with him onto the *Rachel*: a Siamese link of affectionate sympathy that fills him with especial delight. Yet, deeper still is the delightful image of the feminine face of God, the hidden face of the Shekinah in "The Grand Armada" chapter, and this delight is equally congenial. In this chapter, Melville takes us into the very heart of the book—the feminine mystery of creation—when "a continuous chain of whale-jets" is seen "up-playing and sparkling in the noon-day air." The *Pequod* presses after these "jets," which are produced by a herd of sperm whales, and the male harpooners, handling weapons, all cheer jubilantly from suspended boats. The Native American, Tashtego, then calls attention to a group whales ahead of them, and the suspended boats are lowered down to the masculine sea. Embarked in pursuit of the whales, Ishmael and two harpooners, Tashtego and Dagoo (an African American) wait in suspense while the third harpooner, the Polynesian Queequeg, hurls a heavy-handed harpoon into a whale's side. This wounded and bleeding whale drags Queequeg's boat and its men into what Ishmael calls "the innermost heart of the shoal." Melville-as-Ishmael writes, "As if from some mountain torrent we had slid into a serene valley lake. . . . in the distance we beheld the tumults of the outer concentric circles, and saw successive pods of whales, eight or ten in each, swiftly going round and round, like multiplied spans of horses in a ring; and so closely shoulder to shoulder . . ."[13] At this point some smaller whales, like "household dogs," come "snuffing round" the men "right up to our gunwales, and touching them; till it almost seemed that some spell had suddenly domesticated them . . . Queequeg patted their foreheads" and "Starbuck scratched their backs with his lance." Ishmael continues:

> But far beneath this wondrous world upon the surface, another and stranger world met our eyes as we gazed over the side. For, suspended

in those watery vaults, floated the forms of the nursing mothers of the whales, and those by their enormous girth seemed shortly to become mothers. The lake, as I have hinted, was to a considerable depth, exceedingly transparent; and as human infants while sucking will calmly and fixedly gaze away from the breast, as if leading two different lives at the time; and while yet drawing mortal nourishment, be still spiritually feasting upon some unearthly reminiscence;—even so did the young of these whales seem looking up toward us, but not at us, as if it were but a bit of Gulf-weed in their new-born sight. Floating on their sides, the mothers also seemed quietly eyeing us.[14]

At the innermost heart of the concentric spheres were the cows and calves of the herd, the babes and "nursing mothers." Within the center of this shoal-mandala rests the feminine archetype: the feminine face of God, the Shekinah, or hidden divine presence, which, with her creativity, reflecting eyes, and loving kindness, brings calm to the anxious whalers in the midst of more frightening uncertainties of impending castration, death, and doom at the periphery. It's the bulls of the herd that bring terror to the men, and particularly the one ominous white male bull spermaceti that awaits them with rage, ultimate destruction, and doom. The motherly females, on the other hand, offer the men a nurturing and peaceful presence.

The whale children seem to be drawn to the boat as if by some unknown thread of fate were drawing them closer for a kind of a ritual of spiritual transformation: a reciprocal divine-human/human-divine "touch" before the action of the chase. It's a kind of entrance within the mandala of the self, a *circumambulatio* around the feminine matrix, or center in which Melville-as-Ishmael attempts to "touch" the living God through the vehicle of his art. The experience of the mandala, the center and circumference of the self, gives the poet empirical evidence of God over and against the existential angst of non-being.

Again it's the homoerotic twin, Queequeg, who leads the poet (Ishmael) to the center of this shoal to achieve a momentary healing. In this sense, Queequeg provides an axis of communication for Ishmael and the crew to the archetype of wholeness. He forms this connection with the feminine symbol of the self and the delight that emanates from it. Ishmael's God is not the impersonal God of Ahab; it's the God of relatedness, connection, and human love, a fierce eros symbolized by Queequeg, who leads him to the center of the whale-mandala: the image of the maternal Goddesses with their whale children.

The anima mundi is a function of connection with nature here, a connection a man may provide for another man to the life-giving reality of the anima within and without, as Hawthorne and Melville provided for one another in the Berkshires. As a writer, Melville-as-Ishmael is the author who enters the whale-mandala with Queequeg and the other harpooners at his side. Together these five men penetrate the center, to the source of healing. The center is the feminine area of creation from which delight and transformation spring. Transformation is achieved through a reciprocal "touch" of the harpooners with the maternal ground of creation in the heart of the sea.

Ishmael leads Puritan America to see the feminine face of God at a "little lower level," as a mandala of revolving pregnant whale mothers, reveling in "dalliance and delight." It's here that Ishmael realizes the aim of Father Mapple's "Sermon": *Delight!* In the Hebrew Bible, delight is perhaps the clearest indication of one's following in God's ways, and Melville knew this. Ishmael says:

And thus, though surrounded by circle upon circle of consternations and affrights, did these inscrutable creatures at the center freely and fearlessly indulge in all peaceful concernments; yea, serenely revelled in dalliance and delight. But even so, amid the tornadoed Atlantic of my being; I do myself still forever centrally disport in mute calm; and while ponderous planets of unwaning woe revolve round me, deep down and deep inland there I still bathe me in eternal mildness of joy.[15]

Through active visioning through American free verse, Ishmael arrives at his center: the feminine symbol of the self, the Shekinah, and it is this vision of delight in the midst of unwaning woe that he takes onto his rescue ship, the *Rachel.* Joy is the transforming emotion that comes to those who follow the way of Spiritual Democracy.

In their upward-gazing and approach toward the boat, the infant whales and their mothers, as seen by Ishmael's inward-gazing eyes, allow the self—the hidden feminine God-image in the monotheisms—to experience its own transformation by becoming manifest. Through acts of human affection toward the feminine symbol of the self we, too, are permitted to peer into the transparent depths of the collective psyche, where the animals of the deep reflect their own inner light back to us via human-divine reflection. Through the poet's soul-gaze both human consciousness and the animal psyche undergo a transformation of spiritual essences and the two—the human and the inhuman God—become one. The human and animal world exchange glances in the temporal/nontemporal moment that transcends all dualities of gender, space, and time. Both participants—the human and the divine—enter an eternal and temporal act of creation where "touch" of the animal by Queequeg's human hand is equivalent to being "touched" by God—and vice versa. This is shaman-ism, where the trickster (Ishmael) is being made increasingly self-realized as an image of wholeness in all of us. The animal and the human dimensions of the self are one in the American psyche, not separate but the same: anima mundi. This is a blissful vision to behold.

Here Melville has seen through the very impulse of the hunter myth that launched his epic story to the very depths of divinity: God united with the femi-nine in the human psyche. The anima, Rachel, also partakes of this union when Ishmael boards her "devious" cruise ship. The quaternity of "sames" being enacted here becomes increasingly self-realized as an image of wholeness in all of us. Ishmael and Queequeg form a marriage at the surface level in the boat above the waters, while the deeper union of whale mothers with whale sisters appears beneath the surface in the depths of the collective psyche below. The "anima function" Queequeg provides for Ishmael is a transcendent or meta-physical one, because it enables him to bring pairs of opposites in his masculine-feminine nature—love and violence, good and evil, male and female—together into a same-sex union that enables Ishmael to experience delight, ecstasy, or joy. By leading the boat to the center of the whale herd, Queequeg leads in the men to the nursing mothers and their "whale-sisters" unite in a circular image of the feminine selfhood. Through this image, Melville's women readers, too, are invited to undergo transformation by entering the sacred precincts of the female-female marriage, a concentric circle of pregnant mothers swimming delightfully together.

Ahab never "touches" the feminine side of the "living God" so he can there-fore never experience the delight of following in God's ways. Yet Queequeg and Ishmael feel and see the image of the feminine deity, which proves to be the way of the world's salvation aboard the *Rachel*. Through a same-sex coniunctio between the whale "Mothers" and "sisters" with their ancestral "grandmoth-ers" and "great grandmothers" Melville is able to revive our feelings for the deep-feminine that draws us onward. This is an important psychological fact and a symbol for Spiritual Democracy, for unlike the twin heroes of myth who "struggle" against the Great Mother[16] like Gilgamesh killing Humbaba, the new Gilgamesh-Enkidu pair, Ishmael-Queequeg, is called to rebirth the mother as a symbol for the self just as same-sex female and male couples are incubating matriarchal consciousness when the planet needs to rescue itself from masculine hero archetypes.

Thus, through transformations wrought in the human-divine realm Melville broke through the humanized notion of the anima to the very depths of the objective psyche. In his later poetry, Clarel, he achieved a "Pocahontas-wedding / Of contraries": a union of extreme opposites in the cultural psyche. In *Moby Dick*, this breakthrough and resurrection in Ishmael is taken aboard the whale ship the *Rachel*—the Hebrew "marriage bride." Melville draws on this later to depict a union of opposites in the feminine symbol of the rose in his poem "The Rose Farmer." The marriage of opposites between the "Handsome Sailor" and the Shekinah is also evident in the final words of Melville's posthumously published novel *Billy Budd*: "Billy ascended; and ascending, took the full rose of the dawn."[17] The rose, like Father Mapple's delight, is also a biblical allegory found in the Song of Solomon 2:1 and Isaiah 35:1 in reference to "the rose of Sharon." But the primary symbolism of the rose is Sufi and may be traced to the Islamic poet Yoomy in *Mardi*, derived from Melville's reading of the poet Hafiz.

Melville appears to have worked out the problem of tickster integration symbolically in *Moby Dick*. He took the Hebrew-Christian-Islamic dispensation of God further on American shores by tracing the lineage of Spiritual Democracy to Pocahontas. As a marriage symbol for the compassionate matrix of the mythopoetic imagination in the United States, Pocahontas (1595 to 1617) is one of the best-known figures for transcultural peace between whites and Native Americans in early U.S. and British history, and as such, she points the way toward a potential worldwide harmony among all people. As the daughter of an important Algonquin chief, Powhatan, the young Pocahontas became very helpful in establishing permanent peacemaking between her tribe and early settlers of Southern Maryland and Virginia. Pocahontas was taught Christian doctrine as a young girl and was baptized as "Rebecca," the appellation of Rachel's mother in the Hebrew Bible. Thus, Pocahontas is historically a name of a matriarch in the American cultural unconscious, for, like Melville, the early colonists were deeply steeped in Hebrew-Christian lore. Like Hiawatha, then, who brought the Great Law of Peace to warring Native American tribes, Pocahontas-as-Rachel carried the torch of Spiritual Democracy even farther, as a lasting peacetime-keeper between Native Americans and some early settlers of the U.S. colonies. More, her marriage to the colonist John Rolfe, who introduced the cultivation of tobacco in Virginia, reveals her priceless significance as a female peacemaker, bridging warring nations through her transmission of a once-thought-to-be healing herb: tobacco. This original sacred crop of her people, tobacco, is persistent in Melville's story during the symbolic smoking of the tomahawk pipe by Queequeg and Ishmael, just before they jump into bed together and are ritually "married" in a compassionating embrace, as husband and wife.

Melville's image of male-male coniunctio obliterates nineteenth-century cultural stereotypes of marriage as exclusively heterosexual. Beyond that, he gives a representative-image of a Satan-driven America (Ahab), which, like America herself, was not aware of her shadow, cunning, or evil. To conjure up both the trickster (the White Whale, and also Ishmael himself) and also the homoerotic imagination to do battle with evil was a magisterial effort on Melville's part to magnify our consciousness at a symbolic level and bring about a transformation of our God-consciousness. Melville's male *hierosgamos,* or "holy marriage," image includes the body, evil, and the feminine.

What can this symbol of delight mean for the United States and the world in an age of Spiritual Democracy? Melville was attempting to bring a new image of an American self into the consciousness of Puritan America in order to transform our religious attitudes by making us all equals. His use of the image of Rachel weeping for her lost children suggests that integration of the trickster can ultimately lead us to an experience of healing the anima mundi.

Whether Melville himself—a married man with children—was homosexual, bisexual, or heterosexual is a question that will never be answered definitively because, as we've seen in our analysis of Whitman, the shamanic archetype transgresses all sexual orientations. It can simply be termed *bi-erotic.* The poet-shaman builds a bridge to the new democracy of the American self that is transnational and transcendent of gender. By maintaining a dual attitude toward sex, where the boundaries between homosexuality, homoeros, and homospirituality are dissolved, Melville forges an image of "marriage" that holds sway for all people regardless of gender or sexual orientation, and thereby unites us, so that neither light nor dark sides of the self are left out.

To achieve a hierosgamos through same-sex union with the friend of the soul (the "twin") and then to unite with the feminine symbol of the Shekinah aboard the *Rachel,* representative of the traditional Jewish Sabbath bride, is truly a mystical path. Anticipating this final union as the goal of the later stage of his individuation, four years before *Moby Dick* was published, Melville wrote in *Mardi:* "Sphere in sphere, it burned:—the one Shekinah!"[18]

The goal of this movement toward reconciliation between Judaism and mystical Islam depends on the revitalization of the marriage archetype in the collective psyche of humanity moving toward a bi-erotic image that's inclusive of all people. It's in fact a revitalization movement, following the integration of the shadow (homosexuality) of the Hebrew-Christian-Islamic dispensation that we see taking place in parts of world culture today. Melville constructs a political, economic, and religious meaning for the evolution of American society as a whole and for the worldwide movement toward Spiritual Democracy.

By confronting the collective illness of homophobia, Indian-hating, and denigration of the feminine in the personal and cultural unconscious, Melville, like Whitman, served a shamanic function of healing for all people. He started down this sacred path of healing the world through writing in solitude, in nature, in the peaceful atmosphere of anima-consciousness at Arrowhead, his home in the Berkshires of Massachusetts. The poet-shaman entered the realm of imaginatio in order to free the anima, the same-sex archetype, and the positive sides of the self from evil (Ahab-Fedallah), from power intrusions, and from possession by the banished sons of darkness (Satan, Devil, Ibliss).

Moby Dick speaks to a central religious problem of our times: how to live in accordance with our deepest vocation, our call from the self, to arrive at the fullest possible experience of our integrity and its accompanying feeling of delight. When a person stands for his or her "own inexorable self," Father Mapple-Melville tells us, it may lead us to this joyful inward state. Delight is a metaphor for the shamanic state of consciousness (ecstasy, bliss, joy), which comes from the conscious living out of one's vocation in space and time. The shadow (evil) that stands in the way to this delightful state of affairs in the United States and the world is symbolized by Ahab and his primary partner in crime, the Persian assassin Fedallah. Even though Ahab speaks in an ecstatic post-Shakespearean language, giving us an impression that he may be the carrier of the new conscious value of emotional and ethical awareness, he's only endowed with the "gift" for "high perception" and is never able to experience the "low enjoying power"—the humanizing factor of human eros, love, and delight: "This lovely light, it lights not me; all loveliness is anguish to me, since I can ne'er enjoy. Gifted with the high perception, I lack the low, enjoying power; damned, most subtly and most malignantly! Damned in the midst of Paradise!"[19]

Ahab's message to humanity is not Father Mapple's message of individuation and delight. Instead it's a message of resentment, unconscious anger, manic rage, and unhealing woe. However, it's this image of Ahab that carries these projections into consciousness so that transformation may occur. Ahab, it seems, is a necessary evil needed to bring about positive change.

The accent of the shamanic poem, or novel, is, upon the cosmic experience of resurrection through symbolic death, on the death and rebirth of religion. In the Gothic literature category to which *Moby Dick* belongs, there is no reconciliation or rebirth of religion that takes place between science and art, thinking and emotion, no conjunction with the rose, no union, no delight. However, the shamanic genre looks forward to the principle of individuation, where the experience of delight and conjunction of sames and opposites can be potentially realized by anyone. The shamanic genre points to the integration of evil and the self-realization of the Shekinah or rose, the anima mundi as the integrative matrix of all the arts and sciences. The goal of this movement is nothing less than revitalization of the world soul.

20

AFTERWORD
A Bi-Erotic Libido Model
for the Way Forward

The groundbreaking psychotherapists Sigmund Freud and Carl Jung were undoubtedly at least partly responsible for biases in our society's current attitudes about homosexuality and same-sex marriage. They couldn't possibly have foreseen this situation, but their influential model of libido was based on the heterosexual bias of European culture, a bias they inherited from the Judeo-Christian values they grew up with, in which man-woman pairings were the norm and same-sex pairings were seen as abominations—if they were even seen at all.

Today more and more citizens in our society are asking for democracy to be put into practice and for all people to experience equality. There are, of course, encouraging developments in the realm of gay rights. In recent years, California has been a particularly active battleground. On October 11, 2011, Governor Jerry Brown signed into legislation a bill prohibiting the bullying of gay and lesbian kids at school, which was a courageous move on his part. More recently, on June 26, 2013, the U.S. Supreme Court ruled that the sponsors of the state's ban on same-sex marriages, Proposition 8, had no legal right to interfere with unity and social justice. Gays and lesbians, whose marriages were prohibited by the voters in 2008 after a bitter and corrupt campaign, were suddenly free to marry in the state. In this instance, compassion won out over prejudice, religious bigotry, and evil, with cheers erupting joyously across much of the nation. The enormously powerful language of the Supreme Court struck down the federal Defense of Marriage Act and paved the way to topple same-sex marriage bans in many more states, creating what is likely to be seen as a domino effect across the United States and perhaps in many other countries. This progress reflects the democratic spirit that Herman Melville and Walt Whitman stood for in their political uprightness. Married gay and lesbian couples in several states now have full equality in a stunning legal victory under Barack Obama's watch. He will be remembered as the first president in history who, after experiencing an "evolution" in conscience, came out in full support of Spiritual Democracy—with pride.

Early Jungian scholars tended to miss the profound significance of the male-male "marriage" as a living symbol for Spiritual Democracy, which now, in light of the triumph of marriage equality in California, is all quite obvious. In addition to such legal protection, a more comprehensive theory of psychic energy and marriage is needed to replace the prior model provided by Freud and Jung, whose work was tarnished by Eurocentric and heterosexual-centric prejudices. As we've seen, the poetry and prose of Whitman and Melville provide fresh ground for a new vision.

Whitman chants for the "Great Idea" of Spiritual Democracy as a universal "law of successions."[1] His call is to "give the modern meaning of things."[2] Hence, the meaning of the modern becomes the main focus in Whitman's Spiritual Democracy. Meaning cannot be made. Meaning *happens*. All world religions convey a similar message: the way of God, Dao, enlightenment, Sufism, all such ways to truth, all spiritual paths, are also ways to democratic freedom, or meaning, in a transpersonal sense. In chapter 25 of the *Daodejing*, the philosopher Laozi refrains from naming Dao with any words other than "Meaning"—and the M is capitalized, which recalls Jung's reciting of the ancient sage's words: "I do not know its name. / But I call it 'Meaning.'"[3] Meaning transcends the God-images of history in Jung's view, as in Whitman's and Melville's, because it sees the name-giving one assigns to God as many manifestations of the "One Supreme."

Whitman asks in this context, "Why has it been taught that there is only one Supreme?—I say that there are and must be myriads of Supremes."[4] Meaning, then, is ultimately transcendent of any religious creed. And as Whitman made clear, the supreme meaning is always a cosmic meaning. The way of Jung is also cosmic: cosmic relatedness and connectedness to all that is. Spiritual Democracy, therefore, is your meaning, my meaning, whatever one's individual meaning might be. Meaning is found in the equality of the sexes, genders, races, religions, which is, at its primitive root, the place of Spiritual Democracy.

Spiritual Democracy, as we've seen, places all religions on an equal footing. It is situated in the present need of civilization for a new global myth that is not biased toward any one religion over another, or sees any one faith as a superior faith, but views all religions and their belief systems as equals. It is counter to fundamentalism in any form—we need no more Ahabs as would-be world-rulers.

"Produce great Persons," Whitman says, "the rest follows."[5] The task begins here, now, in one's own person, at home. "Some keep the Sabbath going to Church" says Emily Dickinson, "I keep it, staying at Home—"[6] Whitman never presumed to know what the future of democracy is or will be, nor did Melville when he let Ahab pronounce his fulminations regarding the "gaseous Fata Morgana"—mirage—of the American ship gone down in the whirling vortex of the Pacific.[7] These American writers merely vocalized it as a possibility. "How can I pierce the impenetrable blank of the future?" Whitman asks. Then, he adds prophetically, as Melville did as well: "I feel thy ominous greatness evil as well as good."[8]

As Jung says "evil needs to be pondered just as much as good."[9] If we are to arrive at true Spiritual Democracy across the globe, "good and evil" will indeed need to be considered to be "closer than identical twins!"[10] The most compendious of the alchemical writers Jung read was Gerhard Dorn, a thinker who captured the idea of Spiritual Democracy in a simple image: the unus mundus, "one world," a paradoxical unitary ecosphere beyond microcosm and macrocosm. The "consummation of the *mysterium coniunctionis*" was, Jung says, the spiritual aim of every "adept," a person who performed alchemical operations of producing the philosopher's stone, gold, or panacea.[11]

We turned to Melville's *Moby Dick* for a vision of evil that can truly heal us by leading us to reflect on these twins in the current clash between Islam and the West. What Melville illuminated for us is the shadow side of world's religions. In chapter 44 of *Moby Dick*, Ahab's charts were said to be "wrinkled" like the White Whale, who has a "wrinkled brow;" and similarly, Ahab's has "lines" imprinted on the "deeply marked chart of his forehead."[12] Thus, Ahab's charts of the four oceans of the world are marked on his forehead's brow, which means that he is a marked man, and God will take aim at him. All the world's charts are imprinted on his forehead, the area of his obsessive thinking. Ahab cannot see these charts, but the narrator Ishmael, who feels and sees, can see them. Safe aboard the rescuing ship, the *Rachel*, Ishmael remembers them and holds them in his heart.

Ishmael also recalls that Ahab suffered from "intolerably vivid dreams of the night." Because he lacks a reflecting consciousness with which to feel and thus to see into his dream's meanings, Ahab cannot reflect and therefore cannot integrate his nightmares of death and destruction into consciousness. The "spiritual throes" of Ahab's sleep-disturbances are the effects of living in a hell of a post-Gothic psyche. Divorced from sexuality, the hearth, the green shore, and the emotion of delight, there can be no integration of homoeros for Ahab, nor a reemergence of the feminine. Consequently there can be no marriage with Starbuck, nor love for his "wife and child" back home. Ishmael recalls that Ahab had been lying on a hammock, under which "forked flames and lightning shot up," as out of a "chasm"—a hell of his own making.

Like Gothic authors, such as Mary Shelley, Bram Stoker, and Robert Louis Stevenson, Melville knew that sleeplessness and restlessness were symptoms of the technological age. He had an acute awareness of the problem of the Gothic psyche, as is made self-evident in Ahab's searing pathos: the "gash" in his soul, the lack of love and the unrelatedness to his fellow men, and his intense homophobia, masculine rage, and agony. Ahab displayed a complete disregard for his wife, or anima, on the mainland, a marked disconnect from nature (whales, buffalo, stars), and from the feminine rose of the Sufi poet Hafiz and of the Biblical Sharon. All of these disconnects make up one dissociated brain, one that is more fundamentalist-driven than that any of the world's religious fanatics.

Melville took the problem posited by the Gothic psyche to a far greater depth than the other Gothic writers by pointing to the intensifying "agent" (God) as the source of Gothic "horror," as an "eternal, living principal" that terrifies all men. He traced our night terrors to their source. In sleep, Ishmael writes, the dissociation of the "characterizing mind" becomes so distracted from its intensifying agent (Nature's God) that the mind is said to be "no longer an integral" with the soul. The mind (thinking) becomes divorced from the soul (feeling as a mystical path) and with reckless will, forces itself against the instincts, into a "self-assumed, independent being of its own."[13] This is an accurate diagnosis of the power-psychology of Ahab's "dictatorship" aboard the *Pequod*. "God help thee, old man," says Ishmael, "thy thoughts have created a creature in thee; and he whose intense thinking thus makes him a Prometheus; a vulture feeds upon the heart forever; that vulture the very creature he creates."[14] Here we see a stark contrast between the intense thinking of religious fundamentalism and thinking-with-the-heart. As Melville told Nathaniel Hawthorne, "I stand for the heart, to the dogs with the head."

Until Melville read the work of William Shakespeare and Hafiz in 1849, the poet in him could not speak truly. For Melville, the Sufi poets in particular played a pivotal role in the rediscovery of his path with a heart. Reading Shakespeare enabled Melville to dive more deeply into the roots of Spiritual Democracy than ever before, to reach "bottom," and to see and feel the mystical meaningful poetry of the great Sufi masters. During his reading of Shakespeare and Hafiz, all of Melville's shamanic powers were in a state of excitement, a trancelike exultation. He complained in a letter that the "vile small print" of his Shakespeare volumes were "unendurable to my eyes which are as tender as young sperms."[15] This direct association between his eyes and the eyes of the sperm whale suggest that as one of the world's greatest thought-divers, Shakespeare enabled Melville to see at a depth miles below the surface of the sea, the collective psyche, into the inscrutable mysteries of the self. Through Melville's shamanic transport, the reader may have begun to hear, see, and feel the prose falling off by degrees, like a snake shedding its skin, such as when the Ishmael referred to the whale Moby Dick as celestial: "some plumed and glistening god uprising from the sea."[16] In such luminous passages, Melville placed the radiance of Spiritual Democracy into our hands, and showed us that we too are the center of the universe. Thus, Melville lends us eyes and heart so that we might begin to see and to feel into what we are doing to the wild God of Nature. He opened our eyes so that we might be healed of our blindness.

In Melville's copy of Shakespeare's *King Lear*, after the tragic scene of the blinding of the character Gloucester (which moved Melville to write in his marginalia the comment "Terrific!"), he underscored Shakespeare's words: "That slaves your ordinance, that will not see / Because he does not feel."[17] Feeling and seeing are keys, therefore, to understanding Melville's art. Feeling leads readers to experience emotional truths of the archetypal world, and seeing helps audiences understand them. Blinding, moreover, is a metaphor for religious fundamentalism, and Melville makes good use of this in *Moby Dick*. Melville capitalized on the metaphor of blinding, when a whale of "Ethiopian" hue suffers its eyes being put out by the pricking-lance of the first mate, Flask. In such a scene, Melville wounds us through feeling, so that we might begin to see into the destruction we are doing to the environment, to indigenous peoples, to African American slaves in the South, and to the shamanistic foundation which forms the heart and soul of Spiritual Democracy in America and the world.

When the White Whale begins to thrash in its fury, seeing and feeling are all. The feeling of the sperm whale is large, oceanic, like the Pacific: God-feeling. Moby Dick hates Ahab more than he hates any other whale hunter. Through Melville's reading Shakespeare and Hafiz, the author was enabled to establish a link with his feeling function, to love and to hate like he had never loved and hated before. Melville let the power of the Ethiopian whale spurt thick blood and spout gore through him, revealing a psychological law at work: through industry, science, technology, and religious fundamentalism, our collective souls are violated.

We all have a splintered part within us, a wounded-fundamentalist Ahab, who needs embracing, loving, and healing. The Ethiopian whale, on the other hand, is pure innocence. Ahab represents religious fundamentalism, which is intolerant of Spiritual Democracy, while the Ethiopian whale represents the equality of all things. As master initiators into the art of telling the truth, Hafiz and Shakespeare wounded Melville; they opened a vein in his emotional body, so that the blood of the grape, Dionysus, and Didymus (Hafiz), could flow through: "My lord Hafiz, priest of bowers" who "lauds the grape of Shiraz."[18]

As Melville wrote to Hawthorne in May of 1851: "I read Solomon more and more, and every time see deeper and deeper unspeakable meanings in him. I did not think of Fame, a year ago, as I do now."[19] Moby Dick the whale wounded Melville, and made a man of him. All men conspire to suppress their emotional truths of fear, hatred, rage, delight, and divine laughter, yet, in *Moby Dick*, Melville broke that pattern of silence that keeps men overly civilized in relation to their fellow men.

We cannot overlook the concomitant increase in homoerotic feelings of love and warmth expressed toward his mentor Nathaniel Hawthorne during Melville's reading of Hafiz and Shakespeare. God willed it. It was his fate, and it was through his writing of *The Whale* that Melville learned love. This was a spiritual love that filled him with a feminine light of the godhead. Writing with eyes as tender as those of young sperm whales, and seeing and feeling his fate clearly, he wrote to Hawthorne: "Though I wrote the Gospels in this century, I should die in the gutter."[20]

Melville's famous letter to Hawthorne, a declaration of his love, was perhaps the greatest meditation on homoeros since Plato in classical Greece. Yet, like Whitman, he went far beyond Platonic philosophy, Sufism, and Shakespeare to give birth to a new notion of same-sex marriage: a cornerstone of Spiritual Democracy. By deepening his commitment to the political, economic, and religious dimensions of democracy, Melville broke through the indigenous foundation to the "Great God Absolute."

Blind Ahab blasphemed against the God of Spiritual Democracy and for this sacrilege against God, his intensifying agent, the White Whale's fury was magnified. Because of the book's unprecedented accent on homosexuality, pantheism, violence, the feminine, and evil, it would take nearly one hundred fifty years before scholars would uncover all its "hidden" meanings. Melville wrote a "wicked," complicated book, and not one to be digested at a single reading. Its full effect can only be integrated if readers are willing to endure the wounding, or symbolic crucifixion required for its assimilation.

Melville cooked and broiled the book in blood and hellfire in an effort to make the dark side of the monotheistic God-image conscious in us, and in this way, he was attempting to further the Christian message of caritas, not spread a "Gospel" of Ahabian hate. He calls for the end of all "dictatorships" and fundamentalist creeds. His text predicts a possible end to religious fundamentalism.

Only Pip connects Ahab momentarily to the holiness and love of his fellow man: Pip, the African American; Pip, the negro boy. Only after Ahab expresses love for Pip does he ask God to bless Pip, and bless the captain of the *Rachel*, and to crucify his fundamentalist brain: "God! God! God! Stave my brain!" In this magnificent scene, Ahab momentary regains his capacity to see. As Olsen says, "Shakespeare gave him [Melville] a bag of tricks."[21]

Ahab is an exponent of a "black art" in America, which goes down with the "witch-hunters" ship *Pequod* in the Pacific, with Ahab and Fedallah at its head. Ishmael, the lover of men, the man of right feeling and heart, survives the encounter with the White Whale to become a signifier of an unprejudiced, feminist, and nonhomophobic America that sees the way ahead: Spiritual Democracy.

Melville's genius is that, like Ralph Waldo Emerson and Walt Whitman, he took time to study the Koran and the poetry of Hafiz. Melville's "voice" in the novel is the multireligious narrator Ishmael, who observes Ramadan with Queequeg, performs the Arabic gesture of respect, the *salaam*, three times before the pagan idol Yojo, and worships in a true Hindu fashion. Ishmael knows that the aim of Muhammad and of "the Friend"—whether in Sufism, Islam, Judaism, or Christianity—is love. Thus, by being America's first champion of Spiritual Democracy, Melville knew he was standing completely alone with his whale. In Melville's view, it was heretical, but necessary for him to write about homosexuality, Islamophobia, Indian-hating, the evils of slavery, religious fundamentalism, and the reemergence of the feminine across all religions dispensations. Melville understood the story's potential to provide healing to audiences in a psychological age. Sigmund Freud—the "doctor of sex"—was born in 1856, five years after the publication of *Moby Dick*, and one year after the first printing of *Leaves of Grass*, which makes these two American shaman-poets forerunners of the psychological age by a half century.

As Jung showed with his theory of synchronicity, all events in the cosmos are linked together by a common thread of meaning.[22] Whitman, too, understood this: "I hear not the volumes of sound merely, I am moved by the exquisite meanings."[23]

The archetype of Spiritual Democracy is more than symbolic. As we saw in our analysis of *Moby Dick*, modern real-life events mirror those in the novel.

Currently, God's "fury" is an active force of potential destruction. Violence continues to flare in nations surrounding the Persian Gulf and elsewhere in the Middle East and Northern Africa. The extremist groups including the Taliban, Hamas, and Hezbollah continue the destructive ways, while the United States, Britain, and Israel are viewed as "Great Satans" by the people of many countries.

As this unholy confrontation of clashing nations becomes more and more chaotic and presents an increasingly serious threat to the safety of all humans, we must ask what we can do as citizens of the planet to address such problems. Given the increasing "fires" ignited from splits in the monotheistic God-images in many parts of the world today, we need to find psychological answers to the problem of the evil of God's shadow to avert approaching tides of war. Jung's answer, as we have seen, is that we must learn to shoot "The arrow of the Lord's deliverance" (Psalm 38:2) at the object of limitation within our own conceptions of what God appears to be, by taking careful aim, spiritually and psychologically.

The solution lies through a radiant burning fire in the human heart, and throbbing in everything in the universe like a beating drum, a fierce emotion that does not split the opposites between love and hate, peace and violence, but is integrated at a higher moral level through sacred activism. The way through to an acceptance of God's shadow appears to be through the assimilation of our fear, our vulnerability, and our modesty before God, whatever our conception of "God" may be, channeled into a calling, or sacred vocation to heal our earth and air and sea and rescue them—and ourselves—from dire peril. If Spiritual Democracy is to emerge in the current age of globalization, we will each be required to make our inner evil conscious, lest we be thrown into another war, and destroy ourselves and many other species. The stakes are high, and so far, in the West, political and economic democracy has led the way. It's time for us to enter the next stage.

We'll end with some final words from Walt Whitman, whose grand idea, Spiritual Democracy, lights our way forward. Let Whitman speak:

> Poem incarnating the mind of an old man, whose life has been magnificently developed—the wildest and most exuberant joy—the utterance of hope and floods of anticipation—faith in whatever—but all enfolded in Joy Joy Joy, which underlies and overtops the whole effusion.[24]

These notebook entries became reminders in prose of the great poem he wanted to write on the importance of joy as the crowning emotion of his work. And sure enough, following the call of his vocation, he did just that. Whitman wrote in his 1860 poem "A Song of Joys," a poem Melville surely would have delighted in:

O the whaleman's joys!

. . . .

O ripen'd joy of womanhood!

. . . .

O the orator's joys!

. . . .

O the joy of manly self-hood![25]

And in his poem "Excelsior" Whitman continued with this shamanistic theme: "I am glad with devouring ecstasy to make joyous hymns for the whole earth."[26] Now he was figuratively on fire, as any reader can clearly see. The theme of Spiritual Democracy was gaining rapidly upon him as he wrote out the meaning of his life. Then, in the seminal year, 1871, when he put forth his notion of Spiritual Democracy in his prose work "Democratic Vistas," he wrote the following lines in his great masterpiece "Passage to India":

We too take ship O soul,
Joyous we too launch out on trackless seas,
Fearless for unknown shores on waves of ecstasy we sail,

. . . .

Ah more than any priest O soul we too believe in God

. . . .

O my brave soul!
O farther farther sail!
O daring joy, but safe! are they not all the seas of God?
O farther, farther, farther sail![27]

Finally, in a seven-line poem from 1871, Whitman extends the metaphor of the ship's voyage further in this beautiful poem, "Joy, Shipmate, Joy!"

Joy, shipmate, joy!
(Pleas'd to my soul at death I cry,)
Our life is closed, our life begins,
The long, long anchorage we leave,
The ship is clear at last, she leaps!
She swiftly courses from the shore,
Joy, shipmate, joy.[28]

Part Three

TEN WAYS TO PRACTICE
SPIRITUAL DEMOCRACY

Spiritual Democracy begins at home. We can all take action in our personal lives to find peace within ourselves and stimulate positive change in the world.

1. *Follow your conscience.* If we had one religious text as the basis of our Constitution of the United States of America, where would our religious freedom be? Do you listen to your spiritual conscience? Or, do you listen to a priest, a rabbi, an imam, a guru, a therapist, a professor, a relative, a friend? It's good to learn from the different teachers in our lives, but it's equally good to experience growth by following your own conscience. This process is what Jung calls "individuation." The indwelling of "the self" in each person as a democratic idea, for we are each recipients of the divine. We owe it to ourselves to heed our own inner voice and calling.

2. *Immerse in nature.* Being in nature can facilitate your connection to the earth and the cosmos. Honing an awareness of natural forms and processes helps you develop and realize a democratic relationship to the earth and everything around you, where humanity, other species, and the world's forests, rivers, and seas are all experienced as equals. Take trips into the wilderness, climb a mountain, camp out under the stars, or walk on the seashore to experience a communion with the planet.

3. *Practice vocalism.* Walt Whitman was an advocate of the technique of "vocalism," the divine power to speak words in the open air. Let

yourself go, surrender to language through automatic writing, which is the uncensored freedom of written expression, by just starting to write without judging your thoughts. Buy a journal and an attractive pen to evoke the muse. Whether you write poetry, memories, or stray observations, frequent writing can help you to see your own beliefs, values, and visions taking form.

4. *Watch your dreams.* Notice images, figures, and feelings that express these judgments and projections. For example, latent anti-Semitism might be revealed in a dream in which an image of a Jewish person is contaminated with strong, negative emotions. Consider keeping careful track of your dreams in your journal, as dreams can reveal some of our innermost and "buried" thoughts. Bring these thoughts to the surface.

5. *Practice tolerance.* Work diligently on the task of confronting your shadow and evil and transform yourself by a change of heart. Practice religious tolerance and learn more about different religions. Appreciate the variety and value that each religion brings to various people in different cultures across the globe. Bring this mindfulness practice into actions through intentional awareness of the thoughts, feelings, and images that arise for you as you go through your everyday habits of life. Take time to journal and write your experiences down.

6. *Be mindful of judgments.* Bring to mind a person who is familiar to you and has a different belief than your own about a specific topic, such as same-sex marriage, religion, or abortion. Notice judgments that come to mind as you think about this person and see if you can open up to their different perspective, while holding the value of the principle of Spiritual Democracy in your heart. Be mindful of your judgments about others who have different attitudes, values, and beliefs different than or contrary to your own. If possible, engage in a live conversation about this issue with someone you know.

7. *Beware of projections.* It's essential to the practice of Spiritual Democracy to pay very careful attention to your projections. Projections are shadow complexes, which are simply ways we demonize others or pronounce others wrong or evil when we cannot own and integrate such negative characteristics in ourselves. Projections tend to be stronger and more toxic than judgments and are potentially destructive. Examples of projections are homophobia, Islamophobia, racism, and sexism. One exercise to work with these projectiles is to be mindful of the areas

of shadow projection obstructing compassion. Reflect, journal, and discuss your process of self-scrutiny with a friend or confidante.

8. *Consider a change in cultural attitudes.* Reflect on the way in which a change in cultural attitudes can be conducive to Spiritual Democracy, and how a change in one of these attitudes may affect others in movement toward global transformation. These ten attitudes are: aesthetic, philosophical, social, religious, psychological, environmental, political, economic, scientific, and ethical. An example of a need for change in attitude might be the debate of whether same-sex couples adopting, conceiving, and parenting children should have equal rights with heterosexual families. This could require a change in psychological understanding, which shows that same-sex couples can provide the maternal and paternal parenting functions in a way that facilitates a child's development in a way that is equal with heterosexual parenting. Another example of a change in attitude might be the open acceptance by the Roman Catholic Church of women into the priesthood. Now, reflect on a change in these ten cultural attitudes about an issue that you feel is meaningful to you and how this change in attitude could facilitate more harmony between nations, races, genders, families and religious groups.

9. *Speak up.* Spiritual Democracy does not only mean tolerance, but also taking on tough issues and staying in dialogue with people without resorting to ill will, animosity, or violence. Speak up politically, religiously, and nonviolently for what you value and believe, and do it out of your deepest conscience, integrity, and joy. Use the technique of active imagination to work with dreams that are numinous in nature. Be compassionate. Develop your heart.

10. *Introduce others to Spiritual Democracy.* Bring all of these practices into your everyday life, relationships, and work. Find ways to practice and embody Spiritual Democracy, and raise awareness of it in others. For example, talk to people about the notion of religious equality with friends, family, children, mentors, therapists, religious teachers, and others in your social network. Bring playfulness, creativity, and laughter into your experience.

BIBLIOGRAPHY

Allan, G. and E. Folsom. *Walt Whitman & The World*. Iowa City: University of Iowa, 1995.

Aurobindo, S. *The Future Poetry*. Pondicherry: Sri Aurobindo Ashram, 1994.

Beebe, J. "The Trickster in the Arts." *The San Francisco Jung Institute Library Journal* 2 (Winter 1981): no. 2, pp. 22–54.

Beebe, J. "Toward an Image of Male Partnership," cited in Hopcke, R., K. Carrington, & S. Wirth. *Same-Sex Love and the Path to Wholeness*. Boston: Shambhala Publications, 1993.

———. *Integrity in Depth*. New York: Fromm International, 1995.

Bercovitch, S. *The Puritan Origins of the American Self*. New Haven, CT: Yale, 1975.

Bloom, H. *Modern Critical Views: Walt Whitman*. New York: Chelsea House, 1985.

Bly, R. *American Poetry: Wildness and Domesticity*, New York: Harper & Row, 1990.

Brown. J. *The Sacred Pipe: Black Elk's Account of the Seven Rites of the Oglala Sioux*. New York: Penguin, 1971.

Bucke, R. M. *Cosmic Consciousness*. London: Arkana, 1901.

Chai, L. *The Romantic Foundations of the American Renaissance*. Ithaca, NY: Cornell, 1987.

Crain, C. *American Sympathy: Men, Friendship, and Literature in the New Nation*. New Haven, CT: Yale, 2001.

Davis, D. *Religion and the Continental Congress 1774–1776*. New York: Oxford University Press, 2000.

Dickinson, E. *The Complete Poems of Emily Dickinson*. Edited by Thomas Johnson. New York: Little, Brown and Company, 1951.

Dimock, W. *Empire for Liberty: Melville and the Politics of Individualism*. Princeton, NJ: Princeton University Press, 1989.

Douglas, C. *Translate this Darkness: The Life of Christiana Morgan*. New York: Simon & Schuster, 1993.

Dumas, M. *Jefferson the Virginian*. Boston: Little, Brown and Company, 1948.

Edinger, E. *Ego and Archetype*. New York: Penguin, 1972.

———. *Melville's Moby-Dick: An American Nekyia*. Toronto: Inner City Books, 1995.

Eliade, M. *Shamanism: Archaic Techniques of Ecstasy*. Translated by W. Trask. Princeton, NJ: Bollingen, 1951/1964.

Ellenberger, H. *The Discovery of the Unconscious: The History and Evolution of Dynamic Psychiatry*. New York: Basic Books, 1970.

Emerson, R. W. *Essays and Lectures*. New York: Library of America, 1983.

Erkkila, B. *Whitman: The Political Poet*. New York: Oxford University Press, 1989.

Everson, W. *Robinson Jeffers: Fragments of an Older Fury*. Berkeley, CA: Oyez, 1968.

———. *Archetype West: The West Coast as a Literary Region*. Berkeley, CA: Oyez, 1976.

Fakhry, M. *An Interpretation of the* Qur'an: *English Translation of the Meanings*. New York: New York University Press, 2002.

Fiedler, L. *Love and Death in the American Novel*. Champaign, IL: Dalkey Archive Press, 1960.

Finkelstein, D. *Melville's Orienda*. New York: Octagon, 1971.

Folsom, E. *Walt Whitman's Native Representations*. Cambridge: Cambridge University Press, 1994.

———. "Whitman's Calamus Photos," *Breaking Bounds: Whitman & American Cultural Studies*. New York: Oxford University Press, 1996.

Fox, M. *Confessions: The Making of a Post-Denominational Priest*. San Francisco: Harper, 1996.

———. *The Hidden Spirituality of Men: Ten Metaphors to Awaken the Sacred Masculine*. Novato, CA: New World Library, 2008.

Friedman, M. *Problematic Rebel*. Chicago: University of Chicago Press, 1970.

Frost, R. *The Robert Frost Reader: Poetry and Prose*. New York: Henry Holt & Co., 1972.

Goldman, S. *Melville's Protest Theism: The Hidden and Silent God in Clarel*. DeKalb, IL: Northern Illinois University Press, 1993.

Halifax, J. *Shaman: The Wounded Healer*. London: Thames & Hudson, 1982.

Hardwick, E. *Herman Melville*. New York: Penguin, 2000.

Harned, T. *The Letters of Anne Gilchrist and Walt Whitman*. New York: Haskell House, 1973.

Henderson, J. *The Wisdom of the Serpent: The Myths of Death, Rebirth, and Resurrection*. Princeton, NJ: Princeton University Press, 1963.

———. *Thresholds of Initiation*. Middletown, CT: Wesleyan University Press, 1967.

———. *Cultural Attitudes in Psychological Perspective*. Toronto: Inner City Books, 1980.

———. *Shadow and Self*. Wilmette: Chiron, 1990.

Herrmann, S. "A Conversation with William Everson: Shamanism, American Poetry, and the Vision Quest," *The San Francisco Jung Institute Library Journal* 24, no. 4 (2005): 70–88.

———. "Colloquy with the Inner Friend: Jung's Religious Feeling for Islam," *Jung Journal: Culture & Psyche* 3, no. 4 (2009): 123–132.

———. "The Cultural Complex in Walt Whitman," *The San Francisco Jung Institute Library Journal* no. 4 (2004): 34–61.

————. "Donald Kalsched: The Inner World of Trauma," *The San Francisco Jung Institute Library Journal* 19, no. 2 (2000): 51–71.

————. "Donald Sandner: The Shamanic Archetype," *The San Francisco Jung Institute Library Journal* 21, no. 2 (2002): 23–42.

————. "Emergence of the Bipolar Cultural Complex in Walt Whitman," *The Journal of Analytical Psychology* 52, no. 4 (2007): 463–478.

————. "Letters to the Editor," *The San Francisco Jung Institute Library Journal* 21, no. 4 (2003): 5–11.

————. "Melville's Portrait of Same-Sex Marriage in *Moby-Dick*," *Jung Journal: Culture & Psyche* 4, no. 3 (2010): 65–89.

————. "Melville's Vision of Evil," *The San Francisco Jung Institute Library Journal* 22, no. 3 (2003): 15–56.

————. "Murray Stein: The Transformative Image," *The San Francisco Jung Institute Library Journal* 17, no. 1 (1998): 17–39.

————. "The Emergence of Moby Dick in the Dreams of a Five-Year-Old Boy," *Cultures and Identities in Transition: Jungian Perspectives*. New York: Routledge, 2010.

————. "The Visionary Artist: A Problem for Jungian Literary Criticism," *The San Francisco Jung Institute Library Journal* 16, no. 1 (1997): 35–68.

————. "Walt Whitman and the Homoerotic Imagination," *Jung Journal: Culture and Psyche* 1, no. 2 (2007): 16–47.

————. "Whitman, Dickinson and Melville—American Poet-Shamans: Forerunners of Poetry Therapy," *Journal of Poetry Therapy* 16, no. 1 (2003): 19–27.

————. *Walt Whitman: Shamanism, Spiritual Democracy, and the World Soul*. Durham: Eloquent Books, 2010.

————. *William Everson: The Shaman's Call*. New York: Eloquent Books, 2009.

Hesse, H. *Siddhartha*. New York: New Directions, 1951.

Hillway, T. and L. Mansfield. *Moby-Dick: Centennial Essays*. Dallas: Southern Methodist University, 1953.

————. *Herman Melville*. New York: Twayne, 1963.

Hopcke, R., K. Carrington, and S. Wirth. *Same-Sex Love and the Path to Wholeness*. Boston: Shambhala Publications, 1993.

Hutchinson, G. *The Ecstatic Whitman: Literary Shamanism & the Crisis of the Union*. Columbus, OH: Ohio State University Press, 1986.

Jaffe, A. *The Myth of Meaning: Jung and the Expansion of Consciousness*. New York: Penguin, 1971.

James, W. *The Varieties of Religious Experience*. New York: Image, 1978.

Jerusalem Bible. Garden City, NY: Doubleday & Co, 1966.

Johansen, B. *Forgotten Founders: How the American Indian Helped Shape Democracy*. Boston, MA: The Harvard Common Press, 1982

Jung, C. G. *C. G. Jung Analytical Psychology: Notes of the Seminars Given in 1925*. Edited by William McGuire. Bollingen Series. Princeton, NJ: Princeton University Press, 1989.

————. *C. G. Jung Letters*. Edited by Gerhard Adler. 2 vols. Bollingen Series. Princeton, NJ: Princeton University Press, 1953.

————. *C. G. Jung Speaking: Interviews and Encounters.* R. F. C. Hull (ed.). Bollingen Series. Princeton, NJ: Princeton University Press, 1977.

————. *Collected Works of C. G. Jung.* Edited by William McGuire. 20 vols. Bollingen Series. Princeton, NJ: Princeton University Press, 1974.

————. *Dream Analysis: Notes of the Seminar Given in 1928–1930.* Bollingen Series. Princeton, NJ: Princeton University Press, 1984.

————. *Nietzsche's Zarathustra: Notes of the Seminars Given in 1934–1939.* Edited by James Garrett. 2 vols. Bollingen Series. Princeton, NJ: Princeton University Press, 1988.

————. *Memories, Dreams, Reflections.* A. Jaffe & R. and C. Winston (trans. and eds.). New York: Vintage, 1961.

————. *The Freud/Jung Letters.* Bollingen Series. Princeton, NJ: Princeton University Press, 1974.

————. *The Red Book.* Edited and with an Introduction by Sonu Shamdasani. New York: Norton, 2009.

————. *The Visions Seminars.* 2 vols. Zurich: Spring Publications, 1976.

Kaplan, J. *Walt Whitman: A Life.* New York: Simon & Schuster, 1980.

Kerényi. C. *Dionysos: Archetypal Image of Indestructible Life.* Bollingen Series. Princeton, NJ: Princeton University Press, 1976.

Kimbles, S. "The Cultural Complex and the Myth of Invisibility," *The Vision Thing: Myth, Politics, and Psyche in the World.* London: Routledge, 2000.

Kirsch. J. "The Problem of Dictatorship as represented in *Moby-Dick*," *Current Trends in Analytical Psychology.* London: Tavistock, 1961.

————. "Herman Melville in Search of the Self: Moby Dick," *Psychological Perspectives* 7, no. 1 (1976): 54–74.

Klammer, M. *Whitman, Slavery, and the Emergence of Leaves of Grass,* Pennsylvania State University Press, 1995.

Kuebrich, D. *Minor Prophecy: Walt Whitman's New American Religion.* Indianapolis: Indiana, 1989.

Ladinsky. D. *The Gift: Poems by Hafiz the Great Sufi Master.* New York: Penguin, 1999.

Lawrence, D. H. *Studies in Classic American Literature,* New York: Viking, 1961.

Levine, R. S. *The Cambridge Companion to Herman Melville.* Cambridge: Cambridge University Press, 1998.

Lowenfels, W. *Walt Whitman's Civil War.* New York: Alfred A. Knopf, 1971.

Martin, R. *Hero, Captain, and Stranger.* Chapel Hill: University of North Carolina, 1986.

Matheissen, W. O. *American Renaissance: Art and Expression in the Age of Emerson and Whitman.* New York: Oxford University Press, 1941.

Melville, H. *Clarel: A Poem and Pilgrimage in the Holy Land.* Vol. 12, *The Writings of Herman Melville.* Evanston: Northwestern-Newberry, 1991.

————. *Correspondence.* Vol. 14, *The Writings of Herman Melville.* Evanston: Northwestern-Newberry, 1993.

————. *Hawthorne and His Mosses.* Vol. 9, *The Writings of Herman Melville.* Evanston: Northwestern-Newberry, 1856/1984.

————. *Mardi and a Voyage Thither.* New York: The Library of America, 1846/1982.

————. *Moby-Dick.* New York: Penguin, 1992.

———. *Omoo: A Narrative of Adventures in the South Seas*. New York: The Library of America, 1846/1982.

———. *Pierre or The Ambiguities*. Edited and with an introduction by Henry A. Murray. New York: Hendricks House, 1962.

———. *Redburn*. Vol. 4, *The Writings of Herman Melville*. Evanston: Northwestern-Newberry, 1849/1969.

———. *The Confidence-Man*. Vol. 10, *The Writings of Herman Melville*. Evanston: Northwestern-Newberry, 1856/1984.

———. *Typee: A Peep at Polynesian Life*. Vol. 1, *The Writings of Herman Melville*. Evanston: Northwestern-Newberry, 1846/1968.

———. *White Jacket*. Vol. 5, *The Writings of Herman Melville*. Evanston: Northwestern-Newberry, 1849/1982.

Monick, E. *Phallos: Sacred Image of the Masculine*. Toronto: Inner City, 1987.

Moyne, J. and C. Barks. *Open Secret: Versions of Rumi*. Putney, Vermont: Threshold, 1884.

Neihardt, J. *Black Elk Speaks*. Lincoln: University of Nebraska Press, 1961.

Neumann, E. *The Origins and History of Consciousness*. Bollingen Series. Princeton, NJ: Princeton University Press, 1954.

———. *The Great Mother*. Bollingen Series. Princeton, NJ: Princeton University Press, 1963.

Nolan, J. *Poet-Chief: The Native American Poetics of Walt Whitman and Pablo Neruda*. Albuquerque: University of New Mexico Press, 1994.

Noll, R. *The Jung Cult: The Origins of a Charismatic Movement*. Princeton, NJ: Princeton University Press, 1994.

Olson, C. *Call Me Ishmael*. Baltimore: The Johns Hopkins University Press, 1947.

Otto, R. *The Idea of the Holy*. New York: Oxford University Press, 1950.

Parker, H. *Herman Melville: A Biography*. Baltimore: The Johns Hopkins University Press, 1996.

Philbrick, N. *In the Heart of the Sea: The Tragedy of the Whaleship Essex*. New York: Penguin, 2000.

Radin, P. *The Trickster: A Study in American Indian Mythology*. New York: Schocken, 1956.

Rajasekharaiah, T. R. *The Roots of Whitman's Grass*. Rutherford: Fairleigh Dickinson University Press, 1970.

Rank, O. *Art and Artist: Creative Urge and Personality Development*. New York: Alfred A. Knopf, 1932.

Reynolds, D. *Walt Whitman's America: A Cultural Biography*. New York: Vintage, 1995.

Richardson, R. *Emerson: The Mind on Fire*. Berkeley, CA: University of California Press, 1995.

Robertson-Lorant, L. *Melville: A Biography*. New York: Clarkson Potter, 1996.

Robertson, M. *Worshiping Walt: The Whitman Disciples*. Princeton: Princeton University Press, 2008.

Rupke, N. *Alexander von Humboldt: A Metabiography*. Chicago: University of Chicago Press, 2005.

Ryce-Menuhin, J. *Jung and the Monotheisms: Judaism, Christianity, and Islam*. London: Routledge, 1994.

Safransky, R. *Schopenhauer and the Wild Years of Philosophy*. Cambridge, MA: Harvard University Press, 1987.

Schmidgall, G. *Walt Whitman: A Gay Life*. New York: Dutton, 1997.

Shelly, P. *A Library of Poetical Literature in Thirty-Two Volumes*. Introduction by Edward Dowden, Vol. 1. New York: Co-Operative Publication Society, 1949.

Sewall, R. *The Life of Emily Dickinson*. Cambridge, MA: Harvard University Press, 1980.

Singer, T, and S. Kimbles. *The Cultural Complex: Contemporary Jungian Perspectives on Psyche and Society*. New York: Brunner-Routledge, 2004.

Slotkin, R. *Regeneration through Violence*. New York: HarperPerennial, 1973.

Stein, M. "'Divinity Expresses the Self' . . . An Investigation," *Journal of Analytical Psychology* 53 (2008): 305–327.

———. *In Midlife*. Dallas, TX: Spring, 1983.

———. *Jung's Treatment of Christianity*. Wilmette: Chiron, 1985.

———. *Solar Conscience Lunar Conscience*. Wilmette: Chiron, 1993.

———. *Transformation: Emergence of the Self*, College Station, TX: Texas A & M University Press, 1998.

Stone, D. *Spiritual Democracy: Restoring the Heart of America*. Friday Harbor, WA: Nutshell Books, 2010.

Stuckey, S. *African Culture and Melville's Art*. New York: Oxford University Press, 2009.

Sugg, R. *Jungian Literary Criticism*. Evanston, IL: Northwestern University Press, 1992.

Sutton, W. *American Free Verse*. New York: New Directions, 1973.

Symonds, J. *Walt Whitman: A Study*. New York: AMS Press, 1968.

Taylor, E. *William James on Exceptional Mental States: The 1896 Lowell Lectures*. Portsmouth, NH: Jetty House, 2010.

Thompson, L. *Melville's Quarrel with God*. Princeton, NJ: Princeton University Press, 1952.

Thoreau, H. D. *A Week On the Concord and Merrimac Rivers*. Boston, MA: Houghton, Mifflin & Co., 1891.

Traubel, H. *With Walt Whitman in Camden*. Carbondale, IL: Southern Illinois University Press, 1953/1992.

Van Cromphout, G. *Emerson's Modernity and the Example of Goethe*. Columbia, MO: University of Missouri, 1990.

Van Gennep, A. *The Rites of Passage*. Chicago, IL: The University of Chicago Press, 1960.

Vivekananda, S. *The Complete Works of Swami Vivekananda*. Published in Nine Volumes by Swami Bodhasarananda. Mayavati Memorial Edition. Kolkata: Advaita Ashrama, 2007.

Von Humboldt, A. *Cosmos: A Sketch of the Physical Description of the Universe*. Vol. 1. Baltimore, MD: The John Hopkins University Press, 1997.

———. *Cosmos: A Sketch of the Physical Description of the Universe*. Vol. 2. Baltimore, MD: The John Hopkins University Press, 1997.

Von Franz, M. L. "The Inferior Function," *Jung's Typology*. Dallas, TX: Spring, 1971.

———. *C. G. Jung: His Myth in Our Time*. Translated by W. Kennedy. Boston: Little, Brown and Company, 1975.

————. *On Divinization and Synchronicity.* Toronto, Canada: Inner City Books, 1980.

————. *Projection and Re-collection in Jungian Psychology.* La Salle: Open Court, 1980.

Wadlington, W. *The Confidence Game in American Literature.* Princeton, NJ: Princeton University Press, 1975.

Walls, L. D. *The Passage to Cosmos: Alexander Von Humboldt and the Shaping of America.* Chicago, IL: The University of Chicago Press, 2009.

Warren, J. *Walt Whitman's Language Experiment.* University Park and London: Pennsylvania State University Press, 1990.

Whitman, W. *American Bard: The Original Preface to Leaves of Grass Arranged in Verse by William Everson.* New York: Viking, 1981.

————. *Leaves of Grass: The 150th Anniversary Edition.* Edited by Jason Stacy. Iowa City, IA: Iowa University Press, 1860/2010.

————. *Leaves of Grass.* New York: Library of America/Vintage, 1992.

————. *Notebooks and Unpublished Prose Manuscripts.* Edited by Edward F. Grier. 6 vols. New York: New York University Press, 1984.

————. *Notes and Fragments.* Edited by Richard Maurice Bucke. Ontario: A. Talbot & Co., 1899.

————. *Notes and Fragments.* Edited by Richard Maurice Bucke. Folcroft, PA: Folcroft Library Editions, 1899/1972.

————. *Prose Works 1892.* Edited by Floyd Stovall. 2 vols. New York: New York University Press, 1963–1964.

————. *The Correspondence.* Edited by Edwin Haviland Miller. 6 vols. New York: New York University Press, 1961–1977.

————. *Walt Whitman: Complete Poetry and Collected Prose.* New York: Library of America, 1982.

Wiencek, H. *An Imperfect God: George Washington, his Slaves and the Creation of America.* New York: Farrar, Straus and Giroux, 2003.

Wilder, T. *American Characteristics.* New York: Harper & Row, 1979.

Wilson, J. *The Hawthorne and Melville Friendship.* London: McFarland, 1991.

Zeller, M. "The Task of the Analyst," *Psychological Perspectives* 6 (1975): 75.

ENDNOTES

Principal Sources

Notes are divided into seven principal sources: 1) The Poetry, Prose and Conversations of Walt Whitman & Walt Whitman Encyclopedia, 2) The Writings of Herman Melville, *Moby Dick*, and *Mardi*, 3) The *Complete Poetry* of Emily Dickinson, with # representing the poem's number in the Johnson edition, 4) *Collected Works* of C. G. Jung, with ¶ representing the paragraph number as in standard English use in all Jungian journals published internationally, 5) Volumes 1 and 2 of Alexander von Humboldt's book *Cosmos*, 6) William James's *Varieties of Religious Experience,* and 7) Derek H. Davis's *Religion and the Continental Congress 1774–1789.* All seven of these principal sources may be quickly identified under the following list of abbreviations.

Abbreviations

CP . . . . Dickinson, E. *The Complete Poems of Emily Dickinson.* Thomas Johnson, Ed., New York: Little, Brown and Company, 1951.

CS1 . . . . Von Humboldt, A. *Cosmos: A Sketch of the Physical Description of the Universe.* Vol. 1. Baltimore, MD: The John Hopkins University Press, 1997.

CS2 . . . . Von Humboldt, A. *Cosmos: A Sketch of the Physical Description of the Universe.* Vol. 2. Baltimore, MD: The John Hopkins University Press, 1997.

348 Spiritual Democracy

CW . . . . *Collected Works of C. G. Jung*. Edited by William McGuire. 20 vols. Bollingen Series. Princeton, NJ: Princeton University Press, 1956–1990.

DBN . . . . *Daybooks and Notebooks of Walt Whitman*. Edited by William White. 3 vols. New York: New York University Press, 1978.

LG . . . . Whitman, W. *Leaves of Grass*. New York: Library of America/Vintage, 1992.

LG, 1860 . . . . Whitman, W. *Leaves of Grass: The 150th Anniversary Edition*. Edited by Jason Stacy. Iowa City, IA: Iowa University Press, 1860.

MD . . . . Melville, H. *Moby-Dick*. New York: Penguin, 1992.

MVT . . . . Melville, H. *Mardi and a Voyage Thither*. New York: Library of America, 1982.

NNE . . . . *The Writings of Herman Melville, The Northwestern-Newberry Edition* (1993). 14 vols. Chicago, IL: Northwestern University Press, 1968-1993.

NUPM . . . . *Notebooks and Unpublished Prose Manuscripts*. Edited by Edward F. Grier. 6 vols. New York: New York University Press, 1984.

PP . . . . *Walt Whitman: Complete Poetry and Collected Prose*. New York: Library of America, 1982.

RCC . . . . Davis, D. *Religion and the Continental Congress 1774–1776*. New York: Oxford University Press, 2000.

TCWSV . . . . *The Complete Works of Swami Vivekananda*. Published in Nine Volumes by Swami Bodhasarananda. Mayavati Memorial Edition. Kolkata: Advaita Ashrama, 2007.

VRE . . . . James, W. *The Varieties of Religious Experience*. New York: Image, 1978.

WWC . . . . Traubel, H. *With Walt Whitman in Camden*. Published in Nine Volumes by Southern Illinois University Press, 1953/1992.

WWE . . . . *Walt Whitman an Encyclopedia*. Edited by J.R. LeMaster and D. D. Kummings. New York: Garland Publishing, 1998.

INTRODUCTION

1. Only in America could a book like *Leaves of Grass* have been written. In the U.S. Constitution, we find the central principle of Spiritual Democracy enshrined in the Religion Clauses, where, according to Derek H. Davis, "the framers' central purpose in both clauses was to protect religious liberty, to prohibit the coercion of religious practice or conscience, a goal that remains paramount today." *RCC*, 9. The emergence of the religious clauses paved the way for the conception of a new liberated God-notion in American society free and unfettered from any dogmas of scripture. The supreme authority for the Constitution's framers is not the Bible, or any other religious volume, but the God of Nature as the author of our individuality. James Madison, one of the chief architects of the Constitution fought courageously to prohibit the emergence of a "national religion" by insisting on the "full and legal rights of conscience," which he believed should not be infringed upon by any judicial or governing body. *RCC*, 17. Thus, the Declaration of Independence emphasizes

the individual's right to determine his or her own religious beliefs and act freely and without coercion upon such beliefs with right *conscience*. Never before in the history of the world was the selfhood of humanity granted such broad religious freedoms from arcane morals and laws and religious faiths that may be outgrown through individual acts of conscience. The accent on freedom, liberty, and equality opened up the possibility of personal and collective wholeness, where Spiritual Democracy can now be made possible for each person by means of a sacred calling, or vocation. As far as I am aware, the first time the term Spiritual Democracy was used in America was by Henry Alonzo Myers in his paper "Whitman's Conception of the Spiritual Democracy, 1855-1856," published in 1934 in American Literature 6. While Walt Whitman did not coin the term Spiritual Democracy, he did define "Religious Democracy" and foresaw that an evolution would take place transnationally from the "core" of our New World "democracy" to the "spiritual" (*PP* 949) strata, which has and will continue to emerge out of the "national, archetypes of literature" (*PP* 972) to transform and revolutionize the world. Whitman intuited that "a sublime and serious Religious Democracy" will eventually take command, reconstructing, democratizing society" (*PP* 977) out of the self-knowledge in each and every person who is disciplined enough to achieve self-consciousness.

2. While Cotton Mather and the early Puritans of America placed special emphasis on the notion of a "summons to a social" or "spiritual vocation," or a "calling" as a way to attempt to encompass the whole man (Bercovitch, S. *The Puritan Origins of the American Self*. New Haven, CT: Yale University Press, 1975: 6), I mean it in the way that accords with Whitman's, Herman Melville's, Emily Dickinson's, and Ralph Waldo Emerson's views on the *call* or *vocation*. In a journal entry, Emerson wrote, for instance, "Until he can communicate himself to others in his full stature and proportion, he does not yet find his vocation. . . . Every man has his own vocation. The talent is the call. . . . He inclines to do something which is . . . good when it is done, but which no other man can do. He has no rival. For the more truly he consults his own powers, the more difference will his work exhibit from the work of any other." (Emerson, Ralph Waldo. *Essays and Lectures*. New York: Library of America, 1983: 310–311). Emerson was fully aware that his vocation was as a lecturer and writer of prose, not as the poetic "genius" he said would arise in America, the timely man with his eye opened to a vision of the "new religion," the "reconciler" upon "whom all things await."

3. For a discussion of the mythopoetic function of the unconscious, see Ellenberger, H. *The Discovery of the Unconscious: The History and Evolution of Dynamic Psychiatry*, New York: Basic Books, 1970: 318.

4. Three of the framers of the U.S. Constitution, Benjamin Franklin, John Adams, and Thomas Jefferson, were brought together by Congress to design a permanent insignia to enshrine the values of the new nation and this is the great seal of the United States. In this great seal the God-in-Nature speaks in Latin words *e pluribus unum*. This emblematized motto in the seal was originally intended to express the union of the first thirteen states, but its symbolism goes much deeper than that, to the very impulse that led the colonists to leave Europe: the quest for religious liberty. *RCC*, 137–139.

5. For a full overview of the idea of the self in Puritanism, see Sacvan Bercovitch, S. *The*

Puritan Origins of the American Self. New Haven, CT: Yale University Press, 1975. Although the idea of the self may be found in American Puritanism, it was not until after the writing of the Constitution that the concept began to take on a wholesome possibility for everyone that culminates in Ralph Waldo Emerson's lectures, where the aim and drive of each person is to arrive at his or her own "unattained but attainable self." Robert D. Richardson. *Emerson: The Mind on Fire.* Berkeley, CA: University of California Press, 1995: 311.

6. Johansen, B. *Forgotten Founders: How the American Indian Helped Shape Democracy.* Boston, MA: The Harvard Common Press, 1982: 22.

7. Religious liberty was viewed by the framers as a natural human right. "In the eighteenth century as never before," writes Davis, "'nature' had stepped in between God and man so that there was no longer any way to know God's will except by discovering the 'laws' of nature, which of course would be the laws of 'Nature's God' (The Declaration's wording)." *RCC,* 102. The use of the wording "Nature's God" made plenty of room for the equal celebration of any person's religion.

8. *LG,* 245.

9. By science, we mean the empirical validity of God made possible in American art-speech through 1) "free-verse," or "vocalism;" Whitman calls this the "divine power to speak words;" and 2) pragmatism or analytical depth-psychology, the study of direct religions experience, discovered by William James and Carl G. Jung.

10. The framers' original intent in the Religious Clauses is located in the affirmation of the Constitution's architect, James Madison, who, according to Davis, solemnly declared that "any alliance or coalition between Government and Religion . . . cannot be too carefully guarded against." *RCC,* 229. While the aim of the founding fathers was to guard against religious and governmental coalitions, the God-notion they conceived in the wording "Nature's God" was still in a state of incubation when the Religious Clauses were drafted. This is to say that they were merely pregnant with a new idea that had not fully come to birth. The new spirit that might inform not only the American government but world governance across all nations, finds its fullest voice and fruit in the poetry and prose works of Walt Whitman.

11. *PP,* 960.

12. Vocation may sound like a pretentious word to some readers. I learned early in my career from the Santa Cruz poet William Everson, while I had the honor to serve as his teaching assistant at the University of California, Santa Cruz (UCSC), between 1980 and 1981, that a person's vocation is a calling from the inner voice to engage in sacred work in relationship to the Self and the community; such a vocation generates a connection to others, provides one with a sense of meaning, and creates forms of action that have a spiritual basis, in harmony with Nature, God, and the social world. Everson believed that every vocation is controlled by a designated group of archetypal symbols. These symbols, according to Everson, orient us toward our proper forms of work in the world, work that corresponds with our psyche, purpose, and personality. Like Emerson and Whitman, Everson saw his calling as a teacher of American poets and writers. He had a way of evoking the vocational archetype in whomever he was moved to instruct. In this sense he was much like Whitman,

in chant #30 of the "Calamus" poem cluster of Whitman's mature years, where Whitman offered his "promise to California" to "teach robust American love." Whitman famously said: "I know very well that I and robust love belong among you, inland, and along the Western Sea, / For these States tend inland, and toward the Western Sea—and I will also" (*LG, 1860,* 371). William Everson was a passionate man who touched others by infusing insight and a hunger for self-discovery in the manner of a shaman-poet. If ever a California bard fulfilled Whitman's promise to be an active teacher of writers, printers, and poets on the Pacific Coast, it was William Everson. Moreover, he was a great Jungian literary critic. Everson recognized my knowledge in this area as a young man and asked me to teach C. G. Jung's theories, as well as his own extension of Jung's 1932 essay "The Development of the Personality," as it had become known in America, through a theory of the vocational archetype. As "vocation" means to be called and is derived from voice, *vocare,* it is worth noting that Jung's original German title for this 1932 lecture given at the Kulturbund, Vienna, was "Die Stimme Des Innern" (The Inner Voice). Our objectives in the course were not to call poets into being as his course title Birth of a Poet might have suggested, but to birth personalities to their ability to read the poetry of their own existence, as evidenced in their dreams and inner imaginings. We were aware of the problem that vocation presents in the development of anyone's personality, whether or not literary practice is in that person's future. "True personality," wrote Jung "is always a vocation and puts its trust in it as in God, despite its being, as the ordinary man would say, only a personal feeling. But vocation acts like a law of God from which there is no escape" (*CW* 17: ¶ 300). I have since learned that in "Birth of a Poet" Everson was articulating the central principle of Whitman's 1860 call to the "Poets to Come," to embrace his notion of Spiritual Democracy. This was a sacred vocation in which all could join. In "Birth of a Poet," many students and I felt that we were "touched" personally and led to that vision by one of the totemic figures of American poetry, part of a shamanic transmission from a father of which he was but a recent avatar in a very old, perhaps 40,000- to 70,000-year-old tradition. I would like to say a special thanks to Bill Everson for helping to launch my vocation as a writer. For further reading on the subject of vocation, see Herrmann, S. *William Everson: The Shaman's Call.* New York: Eloquent Books, 2009.

13. An important influence on the rehabilitation of the feeling function in central Europe was the thirteenth-century German mystic Meister Eckhart. C. G. Jung quotes Eckhart in *Psychological Types* as saying: "He that is right in his feeling is right in any place and in any company, but if he is wrong he finds nothing right whatever or with whom he may be. For a man of right feeling has God with him" (*CW* 6:¶ 417).

1. Cosmos

1. Emerson's Essays, "The Poet."
2. In 1832, Emerson referred to the transformative significance of a science of the cosmos on the modification of all religions in a sermon on astronomy, where he declared in awe: "Astronomy irresistibly modifies all religion. . . . Let us express our

astonishment before we are swallowed up in the yeast of the abyss. I will lift up my hands and say Kosmos." Richardson, Robert D. *Emerson: The Mind on Fire,* Berkeley, CA: University of California Press, 1996: 5.

3.   *CS1,* 56, 57.
4.   *CS1, 49.*
5.   *CS1,* 25.
6.   *CS1,* 25.
7.   *CS1,* 59.
8.   *CS1,* 358.
9.   *LG,* 174.
10. *CW* 13:¶ 335.
11. Herrmann, S. "Melville's Vision of Evil," *The San Francisco Jung Institute Library Journal* 22, no. 3. (2003): 15–56.
12. Whitman never uses the term Spiritual Democracy in print, although he does refer to the "spiritualization" of democracy when he proposed "a sublime and serious Religious Democracy sternly taking command, dissolving the old, sloughing off surfaces, and from its own interior and vital principles, reconstructing, democratizing society." See *PP,* 997.
13. Jung, C. G. *C. G. Jung Speaking: Interviews and Encounters.* Edited by William McGuire and R. F. C. Hull. Bollingen Series XCVII. Princeton, NJ: Princeton University Press, 1977: 68.
14. *CS1,* 68.
15. *CS1,* 149.
16. *CS2,* 98.
17. *LG,* 192.
18. *CS2,* 19.
19. *CS2,* 20.
20. *CS2,* 26–27.
21. *CS2,* 30.
22. *NUPM,* 5:1888.
23. *CS2,* 57.
24. *CS2,* 58.
25. *CS2,* 42.
26. *CS2,* 199.
27. *CS2,* 302.
28. *LG,* 400.
29. *LG,* 540.
30. *LG,* 169.
31. *LG,* 169.
32. *LG,* 533.
33. *LG,* 538.
34. *LG,* 618.
35. *LG,* 244.
36. *LG,* 217.
37. *NUPM,* 1:55.

38. *CS1*, 24.

39. *NUPM*, 1:72.

40. In *Wandlüngen und Symbole der Libido*, C. G. Jung says that "Burckhardt seems to have glimpsed this truth, when he said that every Greek of the classical period carries in himself a little bit of Oedipus, and every German a little bit of Faust" (*CW* 5:¶ 45). So too might we say that every American carries in himself or herself a little bit of Ishmael, and a little bit of Ahab, and by extension, this intuition also applies to the world.

2. Spiritual Democracy as a Science of God

1. Rupke, N. *Alexander von Humboldt: A Metabiography*. Chicago, IL: University of Chicago Press, 2005: xxiii.

2. Jung, C. G. *Jung Speaking*, 98.

3. "As a Swiss," wrote Jung, "I am an inveterate democrat, yet I recognize that Nature is aristocratic and, what is even more, esoteric." *CW* 11:¶ 537.

4. Indeed, there is something about Whitman's faith in Spiritual Democracy that is complementary to Jung's criticisms of the unconscious side of religious belief, and this is why, I feel, he is so refreshing today: he reflects hope in the world's youth to embody the idealism of America's most enduring values.

5. *CW* 6:¶ 407–433.

6. *PP*, 659.

7. *PP*, 980.

8. *PP*, 960.

9. *PP*, 976–977.

10. *LG*, 233.

11. Herrmann, S. *Walt Whitman: Shamanism, Spiritual Democracy, and the World Soul*. Durham, NC: Eloquent Books, 2010.

12. *CP* #1102.

13. *CW* 6:¶ 417.

14. *LG*, 296.

15. *PP*, 962.

16. *PP*, 938.

17. *PP*, 981.

18. *PP*, 970.

19. *PP*, 937.

20. *PP*, 990.

21. *PP*, 990.

3. From Humboldt to Jung

1. *CS1*, 346.

2. *CS1*, 351–352.

3. *CS1*, 352.

4. Rupke, *Alexander von Humboldt: A Metabiography*. Chicago: University of Chicago Press, 2005.

5. *CS1*, 358.

6. *CS1*, 359.

7. Richardson. *Emerson: The Mind on Fire*, 115.

8. Richardson. *Emerson: The Mind on Fire*, 407.

9. Chai, L. *The Romantic Foundations of the American Renaissance*. Ithaca: Cornell University Press, 1987: 248–251.

10. *NNE*, 14:121.

11. Van Cromphout, G. *Emerson's Modernity and the Example of Goethe*. MO and London: University of Missouri, 1990: 41.

12. Matheissen, W. O. *American Renaissance: Art and Expression in the Age of Emerson and Whitman*. London, Oxford, and New York: Oxford University Press, 1941: 185.

13. Matheissen, *American Renaissance*, 181.

14. Of the ten cultural attitudes I cite in this book, the scientific attitude was central to Whitman's vision of Spiritual Democracy. At the center of Whitman's vocation was his calling to heal the national complexes around slavery and race. In rebellion against the evils of slavery, Whitman became the fiercest bard of the American Civil War. Such a scientific attitude of worldwide healing was something Whitman had great faith in: the unity of humankind made possible through the upcoming science of God. Such a science, of the body and the soul and the spirit, as equal in everyone, was foreseen by the poet as a way to promote transcultural healing, and his best symbol for this unity, in poetry and prose, is interracial intermarriage.

15. A few further facts must be added here. Like James, Vivekananda read *Leaves of Grass*, including "Passage to India," and Whitman's prose work "Democratic Vistas" was included in those readings. From Vivekananda's admiring reference to Whitman as "the Sannyasin of America," it is clear that he saw Whitman as a true brother in spirit. Hence, when Vivekananda introduced Vedanta to the heart and soul of America, he promoted religious unity as a way to speak up for and equalize all faiths; his vocation to teach religious unity on American soil also made a lasting impact on what is now commonly referred to as the Inter-faith movement. James met Vivekananda in 1894 and again in 1896, when Vivekananda lectured at Harvard University. But Vivekananda's message of Spiritual Democracy was made most translucent in his talk "Buddha's Message to the World," delivered in San Francisco, California, on March 18, 1900, a year before James's Gifford Lectures began: "Men must have education. They speak of democracy, of the equality of all men, these days. But how will man know he is equal with all? He . . . must pierce through . . . to the pure truth that is in his inmost Self . . . When he realizes this he becomes free that moment, he achieves equality . . . He abandons the idea that there was ever any man who was lower than himself. Then he can talk of equality; not until then" (*TCWSV* 8: 94). Six months before he died, Vivekananda was planning a visit to California and in ill-health he wrote finally to Sister Christine: "This is to pay your 'Passage to India' if you accept Mrs. Sevier's invitation" (*TCWSV* 9: 174). The fact that the Swami placed the title of Whitman's poem "Passage to India" in quotes in this letter is clear indication of the love and comradeship he felt for Whitman.

16. *VRE,* 17.

17. *VRE,* 101.

18. *VRE,* 66–67.

19. *VRE,* 245.

20. *VRE,* 419.

21. *VRE,* 421.

22. *VRE,* 440.

23. *VRE,* 442. Note how crucial feeling is to this endeavor: Feeling values experience and facts over doctrines and dogmas that dictate morals in absolutist terms. Feeling gives freedom to people to make personal decisions in matters of conscience with compassion and courage.

24. *VRE,* 471–472.

25. *VRE,* 483.

26. *VRE,* 495.

27. *VRE,* 498.

28. *VRE,* 470.

29. Jung, C. G. *C. G. Jung Letters.* Edited by Gerhard Adler. Vol. 1, 1906–1950. Bollingen Series. Princeton, NJ: Princeton University Press, 1953: 531.

30. Jung, C. G. *C. G. Jung Letters.* Vol. 2: 1951–1961. 1953: 330.

31. *VRE,* 434.

32. Jung, C. G. *Nietzsche's Zarathustra: Notes of the Seminars Given in 1934–1939.* Edited by James Garrett. Vol. 2. Bollingen Series. Princeton, NJ: Princeton University Press, 1988: 1176.

33. Ellenberger, *The Discovery of the Unconscious,* 314.

34. Sugg, R. *Jungian Literary Criticism.* Evanston, IL: Northwestern University Press, 1992: 42.

35. *CW* 5:xxv.

36. *CW* 5:¶ 45.

37. *CW* 5:¶ 474.

38. *CW* 5:¶ 474.

39. In Jungian analyst Murray Stein's brilliant book *Transformation: Emergence of the Self,* the author describes how transformations take place in people during periods of deep structural change, and he applies Jung's concept to artists, writers, and people of all kinds. This book had a profound impact on my understanding of global change as a social and cultural phenomenon. Stein covers the issue in post-Jungian thought about the self and its apparent relations to the Divine in an equally enlightening way. According to Stein, Jung's self-concept creates the basis for a linkage between analytical psychology and spiritual ideas of transcendence. Divinity, Divinization, Divineness, or *die Göttlichkeit* "forms and shapes *(ausdrückt)* the self as a *coincidentia oppositorum* . . . The self mirrors the Divinity (at least to some degree)." Divineness and the self are not identical, in Stein's view, but as the ground of all human images and ideas of Deity, the self, appears to be "grounded in and fused with Divinity" (cited in Stein. M. "'Divinity Expresses the self' . . . An Investigation," *Journal of Analytical Psychology* 53 (2008): 309, 316), and at certain times of transition in life the psychological and religious realms may indeed be inseparable. In some intricate way

the self, Divineness, and psyche are inextricably intertwined in the transparency of the reflecting mind. See especially Stein, M. *Transformation: Emergence of the Self*, College Station, TX: Texas A & M University Press, 1988 and Herrmann, S. "Murray Stein: The Transformative Image." *The San Francisco Jung Institute Library Journal* 17, no. 1 (1998).

40. *CW* 5:¶ 477.
41. *CW* 5:¶ 478.
42. *CW* 5:¶ 481.
43. Johansen, *Forgotten Founders*, 84.
44. Johansen, *Forgotten Founders*, 29.
45. Johansen, *Forgotten Founders*, 89.
46. Stone, D. *Spiritual Democracy: Restoring the Heart of America*. Friday Harbor, WA: Nutshell Books, 2010: 66–67.
47. *CW* 18:¶ 1390.
48. Jung, C. G. *C. G. Jung Analytical Psychology: Notes of the Seminars Given in 1925*. Edited by William McGuire. Bollingen Series. Princeton, NJ: Princeton University Press, 1989: 28.
49. Jung, *C. G. Jung Analytical Psychology*, 27.
50. Jung, *C. G. Jung Analytical Psychology*, 27.
51. Jung, *C. G. Jung Analytical Psychology*, 31.
52. Jung, C. G. *Psychology of the Unconscious: A Study of the Transformations and Symbols of the Libido*. Supplementary Vol. B, *The Collected Works of C. G. Jung*. Bollingen Series. Princeton, NJ: Princeton University Press, 1916/1991: 28.
53. I would like to thank Jungian analysts Thomas Singer and Samuel Kimbles for their important extensions of Jung's notion of the national complex to areas of politics, international relations, and civil and legal domains. Each, in their own distinct ways, has taken the concept of the national complex far beyond Jung's original usage, into areas of ethnic, racial, and group strife, across many cultures and nationalities. For further reading see Singer, T, & S. Kimbles. *The Cultural Complex: Contemporary Jungian Perspectives on Psyche and Society.* New York: Brunner-Routledge, 2004. Also Herrmann, S. "The Cultural Complex in Walt Whitman," *The San Francisco Jung Institute Library Journal* 23, no. 4 (2007); Herrmann, S. "Emergence of the Bipolar Cultural Complex in Walt Whitman," *The Journal of Analytical Psychology* 52, no. 4 (2007): 463–478. What I am taking aboard here, in this chapter, is Whitman's unique way of transcending cultural complexes in U.S. society through the ten cultural attitudes I am positing, to touch a transnational, transcultural dimension in the world soul, or *anima mundi*, and may be applied to the common humanity inside each of us. Whitman does this beautifully by penetrating to the nuclear core of Spiritual Democracy, the common root of all ethic and elementary beliefs, via a world-equalizing and world-embracing poetry that is inclusive of all faiths, to liberate the science of religious liberty that forms and informs the essential lifeway of the American self and its global mythos.
54. A second might have been the psychoanalyst Christiana Morgan, whose visions he analyzed in a seminar in the 1930s.

55. *CW* 5:¶ 521.
56. *CW* 5:¶ 523.
57. Herrmann, S. "Whitman, Dickinson and Melville—American Poet-Shamans: Forerunners of Poetry Therapy," *Journal of Poetry Therapy* 16, no. 1 (2003).
58. *NUPM*, 1:73.

4. JUNG ON SPIRITUAL DEMOCRACY

1.   *CW* 18:¶ 1569.
2.   *CW* 18:¶ 1573.
3.   *CW* 18:¶ 1624.
4.   *LG*, 480.
5.   *LG*, 482.
6.   Lowenfels, W. *Walt Whitman's Civil War*. New York: Alfred A. Knopf, 1971: 14–15.
7.   *LG*, 469.
8.   *CW* 13:¶ 335.
9.   *CW* 18:¶ 1661.
10. *CW* 11:¶ 758.
11. *CW* 18:¶ 1390.
12. Jung, *C. G. Jung Speaking*, 98.
13. Jung quotes liberally from the Book of Isaiah and the Gospels in the opening lines of his *Red Book*.
14. *CW* 18:¶ 1398.
15. *CW* 18:¶ 1396.
16. Jung, *C. G. Jung Speaking*, 95, 98.
17. *CW* 11:¶ 9.
18. *CW* 11:¶ 6.
19. *CW* 11:¶ 9.
20. *CW* 18:¶ 1392.
21. *CW* 11:¶ 10.
22. Jung, *Psychology of the Unconscious*, Footnote 42, ¶ 353.
23. Jung, *Psychology of the Unconscious*, ¶ 227.
24. *CW* 18:¶ 1381.
25. *CW* 18:¶ 1378, 1380.
26. *CW* 18:¶ 1398.
27. Jung, *C. G. Jung Speaking*, 98.
28. *CW* 10:¶ 588.
29. *CW* 10:¶ 386.
30. *CW* 10:¶ 388.
31. While it is not generally recognized that Eckhart is post-Christian in his religious attitude, Jung recognized by 1921 that his concepts of the feminine dimension of divinity and evil were sufficiently developed to advance a new God-concept of the self that is purely psychological. Nevertheless, from a theological standpoint, Eckhart was still working within a Christian tradition as a Dominican mystic and preacher,

and while he has been widely regarded as a major bridge to Hinduism and Buddhism, especially Zen, for the East and West, his evolution of an image of evil in human relationships, national conflicts, and war was, quite understandably, not as evolved as Melville's or Whitman's or Jung's. Thus, while Eckhart certainly lived during the era of the Christian mystics, his God-concept was on the way toward breaking free beyond the traditional Christian understanding toward what Whitman calls Spiritual Democracy. Spiritual Democracy begins in the Christian West with Eckhart, since it was Eckhart who prayed God to rid himself of all traditional images of God for a final leave-taking from creedal or orthodox interpretations of divinity into an unformed "fourth" and ever-fertile ground of the feminine godhead.

32. *CW* 10:¶ 397.
33. *CW* 10:¶ 138.
34. One possible exception of this is the chance that Jung read a chapter on Whitman by William James in *Varieties of Religious Experience*. Nonetheless, James's view of Whitman is not representative of his views on Spiritual Democracy, nor is it inclusive of his vision of evil.
35. *CW* 18:¶ 1637.
36. *CW* 18:¶ 1638.
37. *CW* 18:¶ 1643.
38. *CW* 18:¶ 1649.
39. *CW* 18:¶ 1666.
40. *CW* 18:¶ 1669.
41. *CW* 18:¶ 1669.
42. *CW* 18:¶ 1672.
43. Jung, *Nietzsche's Zarathustra*, 1:5.
44. Jung, C. G. *The Red Book*. Edited with an Introduction by Sonu Shamdasani. New York: Norton, 2009: 229.
45. Jung, C. G. *Dream Analysis: Notes of the Seminar Given in 1928–1930*. Bollingen Series. Princeton, NJ: Princeton University Press, 1984: 513.
46. *LG*, 1984: 247.
47. Jung, *Dream Analysis*, 336.
48. Jung, *Dream Analysis*, 337.
49. Jung, *Dream Analysis*, 513.
50. Fakhry, M. *An Interpretation of the* Qur'an: *English Translation of the Meanings*. New York: New York University Press, 2002.
51. Fakhry, *An Interpretation of the* Qur'an.
52. *CW* 18:¶ 1580.
53. Jung, *The Red Book*, 211.
54. Jung, *The Red Book*, 211.
55. *CW* 11:¶ 758.
56. Jung, *The Red Book*, 213.
57. Jung, C. G. *Jung Analytical Psychology: Notes of the Seminars Given in 1925*, 25.
58. Jung, C. G. *Memories, Dreams, Reflections*. A. Jaffe & R. and C. Winston (trans. and eds.). New York: Vintage, 1961: 171.

59. Jung, *Memories, Dreams, Reflections,* xxiv.

60. Jung, *Nietzsche's Zarathustra,* 1: 214–215.

61. Jung, *The Red Book,* 272.

62. Jung, *The Red Book,* 213.

63. Jung, *The Red Book,* 229.

64. Jung, *The Red Book,* 254.

65. Jung, *Nietzsche's Zarathustra,* 2: 795.

5. HEALING THE NATIONAL COMPLEX

1. This chapter is an edited version of my paper "The Emergence of the Cultural Complex in Walt Whitman" given at The North American Conference of Jungian Analysts & Candidates in Chicago on September 23, 2005.

2. *LG,* 376.

3. Henderson, J. *Cultural Attitudes in Psychological Perspective.* Toronto: Inner City Books, 1980.

4. I am indebted to Steven Joseph for his suggestion that I include the economic attitude in my talk. Luigi Zoja, whose books I reviewed, has written about the depth-psychological implications of economics in his *Growth and Guilt;* Andrew Samuels has suggested that there is an Economic Psyche; and Betty Sue Flowers has written about the Economic Myth as the myth of our time (Flowers, Betty S. "Practicing Politics in the Economic Myth," *The San Francisco Jung Institute Library Journal* 18, no. 4 (2000). Outside of psychology, Aldo Leopold in his seminal book, *A Sand County Almanac,* may have been the best formulator of the environmental attitude; and more recently, Hester Solomon has spoken in the pages of *The Journal of Analytical Psychology* about the ethical attitude as a developmental achievement fostered by analysis.

5. Wiencek, H. *An Imperfect God: George Washington, His Slaves and the Creation of America.* New York: Farrar, Straus and Giroux, 2003: 41, 274.

6. Wiencek, *An Imperfect God,* 361.

7. Whitman, W. *American Bard:* The Original Preface to Leaves of Grass Arranged in Verse by William Everson. New York: Viking, 1981: 13.

8. Wiencek, *An Imperfect God,* 362.

9. *LG,* 113.

10. Kaplan, J. *Walt Whitman: A Life.* New York: Simon and Schuster, 1980: 69.

11. Folsom, E. "Whitman's Calamus Photos," in *Breaking Bounds: Whitman & American Cultural Studies,* New York: Oxford University Press, 1996: 71.

12. *WWE,* 112, 113.

13. *WWE,* 91.

14. Erkkila, B. *Whitman: The Political Poet.* New York: Oxford University Press, 1989: 101.

15. Whitman, *American Bard,* 11.

16. Erkkila, Whitman: The Political Poet, 240.

17. "The world exists, as I understand it, to teach the science of liberty," Emerson wrote, which suggests that the vocation of the world is to teach the lessons of such a science

that is, in fact, at the heart of American political life. No one teaches this science of Spiritual Democracy as well as Whitman's does. As Emerson wrote about *Leaves of Grass*, to Secretary of State Seward, they "are more deeply American, democratic, and in the interests of political liberty, than those of any other poet." Richardson. *Emerson: The Mind on Fire*, 503, 528.

18. Folsom, E. *Walt Whitman's Native Representations*. Cambridge: Cambridge University Press, 1994: 72.

19. Traubel, H. *With Walt Whitman in Camden*. Carbondale, IL: Southern Illinois Press, Vol. 2: July 16–October 31, 1888. 1953/1992: 283.

20. Traubel, *With Walt Whitman in Camden*, 2:317.

21. Traubel, *With Walt Whitman in Camden*, 2:35.

22. Traubel, *With Walt Whitman in Camden*, 2:53.

23. *NUPM*, 4:1312.

24. Traubel, *With Walt Whitman in Camden*, 2:472.

25. Traubel, *With Walt Whitman in Camden*, 3:69.

26. Traubel, *With Walt Whitman in Camden*, 2:88.

27. *LG*, 597, 598.

6. Whitman's "New Bible": The Foundation of a Religious Vision

1. The idea of "original intent" is at the center of the debate surrounding the issue of same-sex marriage in America: What did the framers of the Declaration of Independence intend when they drafted the Constitution and the Bill of Rights? Must the U.S. Supreme Court justices be committed to the Constitution's meanings of original intent in setting a framework for law and public policy in the nation? If so, what is the meaning of religion in America? What is the meaning of what God intends? (See *RCC*, x–xi).

2. The heart of this chapter comes from a presentation given as an informal talk to the Washington Friends of Walt Whitman, on the border of Rock Creek Park at the home of Neil Richardson, on September 10, 2010.

3. *NUPM*, 6:2046.

4. *PP*, 1001.

5. *NUPM*, 1:353.

6. *PP*, 1142.

7. *LG*, 245.

8. He had shown some of them his *Liber Novus*, which we know today as *The Red Book*.

9. *LG*, 665.

10. *LG*, *1860*, 414.

11. *LG*, 296.

12. *LG*, 538.

13. Rajasekharaiah, T. R. *The Roots of Whitman's Grass*. Rutherford: Fairleigh Dickinson University Press, 1970: 33.

14. *PP*, 1141.

15. *LG, 1860,* 105.
16. *LG, 1860,* 108, 114, 122.
17. *PP,* 1010.
18. *LG,* 306.
19. *LG, 1860,* 111.
20. *NUPM,* 1:81.
21. *NUPM,* 1:66.
22. *LG, 1860,* 125.
23. *LG,* 98.
24. *LG, 1860,* 189.
25. *LG,* 51.
26. Robertson, M. *Worshiping Walt: The Whitman Disciples.* Princeton, NJ: Princeton University Press, 2008: 21.
27. Robertson, *Worshiping Walt,* 122.
28. Robertson, *Worshiping Walt,* 252.
29. *LG, 1860,* 188.
30. *NUPM,* 6:2049.
31. *LG,* 570.
32. *PP,* 1002.
33. *PP,* 1001.
34. *PP,* 1003.
35. *PP,* 1001.
36. *LG,* 573.
37. *LG,* 256.
38. *LG, 1860,* 167, 169.
39. Symonds, J. *Walt Whitman: A Study.* New York: AMS Press, 1968: 19.
40. The first sixteen words of the First Amendment to the U.S. Constitution read: "Congress shall make no law respecting an establishment of religion, or prohibiting the free exercise thereof." *RCC,*9.
41. *LG,* 509.
42. Symonds, *Walt Whitman: A Study,* 22.
43. *LG,* 377.
44. *LG,* 376.
45. *LG,* 376.
46. *PP,* 1024, 1025.

7. Walt Whitman's Global Vision

1. The first section of this chapter comes in part from a talk I gave with the Anglican priest Matthew Fox on February 6, 2011, at the Berkeley Unitarian-Universalist Church in Kensington entitled "How Walt Whitman Speaks to Unitarians."
2. *NUPM,* 1:57.
3. *NUPM,* 1:71.
4. *NUPM,* 1:79.

5. Whitman, *American Bard*, 33.
6. *NUPM*, 6:2089.
7. *LG*, 236.
8. *WWE*, 616.
9. *PP*, 1003.
10. Thoreau, H. D. *A Week On the Concord and Merrimac Rivers*. Boston, MA: Houghton, Mifflin & Co., 1891: 153.
11. Whitman, *American Bard*, 33.
12. Fox, M. *Confessions: The Making of a Post-Denominational* Priest. San Francisco: Harper, 1996.
13. *NUPM*, 6:2095.
14. *LG*, 246.
15. *NUPM*, 1:112.
16. Folsom, "Whitman's Calamus Photos."
17. *LG*, 307.
18. Herrmann, *Walt Whitman: Shamanism, Spiritual Democracy, and the World Soul*.
19. Traubel, *With Walt Whitman in Camden*, 6:342.
20. *PP*, 955.
21. *LG*, 170.
22. *LG*, 169.
23. Eliade (1951) says that the shaman "invents" his own technique for inducing ecstasy, which involves a very specific technology—sometimes pharmacological, sometimes musical (including the use of instruments of his own making, like rattles or drums, or his voice, as when the Navajo healer sings his cure), sometimes psychological (a tradition continued in the psychoanalytic schools of today with each their "technical innovations"), but he does not specifically name "vocalism" as I describe it here, following Whitman among these techniques. Nevertheless, the way Whitman develops this technique as a basis for what he wants to do as a poet seems to me characteristically shamanic.
24. Bucke, R. M. *Cosmic Consciousness*. London: Arkana, 1901.
25. The second section of this chapter comes from a talk I gave at the International House (I-House) at University of California, Berkeley, on February 10, 2011.
26. *LG*, 288.
27. Whitman, Walt. *Prose Works 1892*. Edited by Floyd Stovall. Vol 2, *Collected Writings of Walt Whitman*. New York: New York University Press, 1963–1964: 512.
28. *NUPM*, 6:2089.
29. *NUPM*, 1:79.
30. Whitman, *American Bard*, 33.
31. *LG*, 237.
32. *LG*, 236.
33. Jung, *Memories, Dreams, Reflections*, 297.
34. *NUPM*, 6: 2089.
35. Whitman, *American Bard*, 22.
36. Whitman, *Prose Works 1892*, 2: 512.

37. Whitman, W. *The Correspondence*. Edited by Edwin Haviland Miller. Vol. 3. Iowa Whitman Series. New York: New York University Press, 1961–1977: 369.
38. Whitman, *American Bard*, 22.
39. *LG*, 296.
40. *LG*, 359.
41. *LG*, 534.
42. *PP*, 1003.
43. *PP*, 1326.
44. Symonds, J. *Walt Whitman: A Study*. New York: AMS Press, 1968: xxvi.
45. *NUPM*, 1:73.
46. *LG*, 180.
47. *LG*, 181.
48. *LG*, 236.
49. *LG*, 292.
50. *NUPM*, 6:2097.
51. *LG*, 239.
52. *LG*, 239.
53. Whitman, *American Bard*, 22.
54. *LG*, 296.
55. *PP*, 977.
56. *PP*, 980.
57. *NUPM*, 1:64.
58. The first careful reader to comment in a celebratory way on Whitman's transcendent achievement as a "Buddhist poet" in the United States was Emerson. In a letter Emerson wrote that *Leaves of Grass* is "the best piece of American Buddhism that anyone has had strength to write. American to the bone." Cited in Richardson, *Emerson: The Mind on Fire*, 527.
59. *CS2*, 198–199.
60. *CS2*, 199.
61. *LG*, 223.
62. *PP*, 947.
63. Symonds, *Walt Whitman: A Study*, 44.
64. Whitman, *American Bard*, 14.
65. *LG*, 652.
66. Traubel, *With Walt Whitman in Camden*, 1:10.
67. Traubel, *With Walt Whitman in Camden*, 1:398.
68. *NUPM*, 1:57.
69. *NUPM*, 1:63.
70. *LG*, 47.
71. Traubel, *With Walt Whitman in Camden*, 3:453.
72. *LG*, 192–194.
73. Traubel, *With Walt Whitman in Camden*, 7:358–360.
74. Whitman, *American Bard*, 14.
75. Whitman. W. *Notes and Fragments*. Edited by Richard Maurice Bucke. Ontario: A.

Talbot & Co., 1899: 33.

76. *LG*, 287.

77. *LG*, 289–292.

78. *LG*, 294–297.

79. *LG*, 246.

80. Aurobindo, S. *The Future Poetry*. Pondicherry: Sri Aurobindo Ashram, 1994: 173.

8. THE BI-EROTIC AS TRANSCENDENT SEXUALITY

1. *LG*, 294.

2. *LG, 1860*, 287.

3. *LG, 1860*, 288–289.

4. *LG*, 253.

5. *LG, 1860*, 290.

6. *LG, 1860*, 290.

7. *LG, 1860*, 291.

8. Erkkila, B. *Whitman: The Political Poet*. New York: Oxford University Press, 1989: 262.

9. *LG*, 490.

10. Erkkila, *Whitman: The Political Poet*, 308.

11. *LG*, 490.

12. *LG, 1856*, 276.

13. *LG, 1860*, 295.

14. *LG, 1860*, 295.

15. *LG, 1860*, 296.

16. *LG, 1860*, 299.

17. *LG, 1860*, 297.

18. *LG, 1860*, 299.

19. *LG, 1860*, 299.

20. *LG, 1860*, 295.

21. *LG, 1860*, 303.

22. Whitman, *American Bard*, 22.

23. *LG, 1860*, 304.

24. *LG, 1860*, 303.

25. *LG, 1860*, 305.

26. *LG, 1860*, 308.

27. *LG, 1860*, 306.

28. *LG, 1860*, 309.

29. *LG, 1860*, 311.

30. *LG, 1860*, 314.

31. *NUPM*, 1:67.

32. *LG*, 452.

33. *CP*, # 442.

34. *PP*, 930.

35. *LG, 1860*, 309.
36. *LG, 1860*, 310.
37. *PP*, 915.
38. Erkkila, *Whitman: The Political Poet*, 308.
39. *CW* 8:¶ 398.
40. *CW* 8:¶ 382.
41. *CW* 8:¶ 417.
42. *LG, 1860*, 6, 12.
43. *LG*, 188.
44. *LG*, 246.
45. *LG, 1860*, 341.
46. *CW* 8: ¶805.
47. *LG, 1860*, 342.
48. *LG, 1860*, 356.
49. *LG, 1860*, 342.
50. *LG, 1860*, 343.
51. *LG, 1860*, 343.
52. *LG, 1860*, 344.
53. *LG, 1860*, 345.
54. *CW* 8:¶ 800.
55. *CW* 8:¶ 808.
56. *LG, 1860*, 353.
57. *LG, 1860*, 355.
58. *LG, 1860*, 355.
59. *LG, 1860*, 356.
60. *LG, 1860*, 356.
61. *LG, 1860*, 357.
62. *LG, 1860*, 358.
63. *LG, 1860*, 362.
64. *LG, 1860*, 368.
65. *LG, 1860*, 370.
66. *LG, 1860*, 371.
67. *LG, 1860*, 375.
68. *LG, 1860*, 375.
69. Erkkila, *Whitman: The Political Poet*, 308.
70. *LG, 1860*, 376.
71. *LG, 1860*, 376.
72. *LG, 1860*, 377.
73. *LG, 1860*, 377.
74. I am sure the Muslim nations would have no problem with Whitman's "Calamus" poems. Certainly Rumi and Hafiz and Saadi would all have no problem with Whitman's metaphors of same-sex love, as it cannot be doubted that Rumi's love for Shams of Tabriz, and Hafiz's love for Attar, was homoerotic and homospiritual at its core. Roman Catholicism and Orthodox Judaism, moreover, are going to have

to work out the problem of what to do with homosexuality in their own religious cultures too. Yet the young people in Rome and Israel and Cairo have already moved beyond the priests and rabbis and imams, and the clerics in Islam are going to be challenged by the young people of Iran, Saudi Arabia, and Afghanistan too. All nations will be called to open up to a greater human equality; it is only, in my view, a matter of time.

75. *LG, 1860,* 349.

76. Whitman, *American Bard,* 15.

77. Whitman, *American Bard,* 17.

9. Shamanism and Spiritual Democracy: A Post-Humboldtian Notion of the Cosmos

1. Halifax, J. *Shaman: The Wounded Healer.* London: Thames and Hudson, 1982: 1.

2. Herrmann, S. "Donald Sandner: The Shamanic Archetype." *The San Francisco Jung Institute Library Journal* 21, no. 2 (2002).

3. *CP,* # 986.

4. *CP,* # 632.

5. Rank, O. *Art and Artist: Creative Urge and Personality Development.* New York: W. W. Norton & Co., 1932: 12.

6. Rank, *Art and Artist,* 57.

7. *LG,* 50.

8. *LG,* 210.

9. Whitman, *American Bard,* 33.

10. Whitman, *American Bard,* 33.

11. *CP,* # 1545.

12. Only in the United States could a book like *Moby Dick* have been brought to birth. For in its early chapters we see him using the free exercise portion of the religious clauses of the First Amendment to the U.S. Constitution articulated clearly in the worlds of Ishmael, who says about his night with Queequeg in the Spouter Inn: "we undressed and went to bed, at peace with our own consciences and all the world" (*MD,* 58). The emergence of the Religion Clauses represents the birth of a new American God-image of religious liberty free and unfettered from the dogma of scripture, for the authority among the Deists was no longer the Bible but the Supreme Being as the author of Nature. It was James Madison who fought most valiantly to prohibit the emergence of a national religion in America by insisting on the "full and legal rights of conscience," which he believed must never be infringed upon by any judicial or governing body (*RCC,* 17).

13. Whitman, *American Bard,* 33.

14. In the margin of an 1849 magazine article Whitman wrote, "Humboldt, in his Kosmos, citing Schiller, has observed of the Greeks: 'With them the landscape is always the mere background, of a picture, in the foreground of which human figures are moving'" (cited in Reynolds, D. *Walt Whitman's America: A Cultural Biography.* New York: Vintage, 1995: 245); Whitman may have read earlier passages from

Humboldt in Emerson, who for a time he claimed as his "Master." Emerson was reading Humboldt's *Personal Narrative of a Voyage to the Equinoctical Regions*, his amazing account of his journey to South America, in December of 1830, and he began reading the first volume of Humboldt's ambitious *Kosmos* in September of 1845, when it was first translated into English (Richardson, *Emerson: The Mind on Fire*, 101, 406).

15. *LG*, 219.
16. *CS1*, 23, 33.
17. Walls, *The Passage to Cosmos*, 75.
18. Walls, *The Passage to Cosmos*, 183.
19. Whitman, *American Bard*, 14, 18, 22, 26
20. Stein, M. *In Midlife*. Dallas, TX: Spring, 1983.
21. *LG*, 395.
22. Henderson, J. *Thresholds of Initiation*. Middletown, CT: Wesleyan University Press, 1967: 152.
23. *NUPM*, 5:1651.
24. *LG*, 354.
25. *NUPM*, 5:1653.
26. *NUPM*, 5:1654.
27. *NUPM*, 5:1657.
28. *NUPM*, 5:1660.
29. *RCC*, 25.
30. *RCC*, 65.
31. *LG*, 355.
32. *RCC*, 97.
33. *RCC*, 137–149.
34. *RCC*, 151.
35. *RCC*, 209.
36. *RCC*, 218.
37. Walls, *The Passage to Cosmos*, 99.
38. Rupke, N. *Alexander von Humboldt: A Metabiography*. Chicago: University of Chicago Press, 2005: xxiii.
39. *NUPM*, 5:1651.
40. *LG*, 354.
41. *NUPM*, 5:1661–1662.
42. *NUPM*, 1:65.
43. Contemporary psychotherapy offers a practical way to realize this possibility, and many have availed themselves of it for just the reason Whitman gives for doing so.
44. *LG*, 367.
45. *PP*, 985.
46. Eliade, M. *Shamanism: Archaic Techniques of Ecstasy*. Translated by W. Trask. Bollingen Series. Princeton, NJ: Princeton University Press, 1951/1964: 510–511.
47. *PP*, 985.
48. *LG*, 399.
49. *LG*, 539.

50. *LG*, 561.
51. *LG*, *1860*, 1.
52. *LG*,*1860*, 183–184.
53. *LG*, 560, 561.
54. *CS1*, 24.
55. *LG*, 561.
56. *LG*, *1860*, 187.
57. *LG*, *1860*, 335.
58. *LG*, *1860*, 187.
59. *LG*, *1860*, 187.
60. *CS1*, 79.
61. *LG*, *1860*, 184.
62. *LG*, *1860*, 326.
63. *LG*, *1860*, 326–328.
64. *LG*, *1860*, 330.
65. *LG*, 219. For further discussion see Griffith, James D. "The Pregnant Muse: Language and Birth in 'A song of the Rolling Earth.'" *Walt Whitman Quarterly Review* 1 (1983): 1–8.
66. *LG*, *1860*, 329.
67. *LG*, *1860*, 329.
68. *LG*, *1860*, 330.
69. *LG*, *1860*, 331.
70. *LG*, *1860*, 332.
71. *LG*, 219.
72. *LG*, *1860*, 331.
73. *LG*, *1860*, 332.
74. *LG*, *1860*, 333.
75. *LG*, *1860*, 334.
76. *LG*, *1860*, 334.
77. *LG*, *1860*, 335.
78. *LG*, *1860*, 336.
79. *LG*, *1860*, 336.
80. *LG*, *1860*, 336.
81. *LG*, *1860*, 336.
82. *CS1*, 359.
83. *LG*, *1860*, 330.
84. *LG*, *1860*, 336.
85. *LG*, *1860*, 335.
86. *PP*, 833.
87. *LG*, *1860*, 415.
88. *LG*, 238.
89. *LG*, 344.

10. Whitman as Preserver of the Psychic Integrity of the Community

1. Eliade, *Shamanism*, 508.
2. Beebe, J. *Integrity in Depth*. New York: Fromm International, 1995: 16.
3. Beebe, *Integrity*, 10.
4. Beebe, *Integrity*, 106–107.
5. Beebe, *Integrity*, 107.
6. *PP,* 656.
7. To be sure, the early support Whitman received from Emerson was a major light in sustaining his sense of self-confidence throughout his long career as a poet. Horace Traubel reports that Emerson told Whitman: "You have a great pack howling at your heels always, Mr. Whitman; I hope you show them all a proper contempt; they deserve no more than your heels." Cited in Richardson, *Emerson: The Mind on Fire*, 530.
8. Beebe, *Integrity*, 20.
9. *LG, 1860,* 345.
10. Bercovitch, *The Puritan Origins of the American Self*, 172.
11. *PP,* 1335.
12. *PP,* 915.
13. *PP,* 660.
14. *PP,* 659.
15. *LG,* 535.
16. Traubel, *With Walt Whitman in Camden,* 1:351.
17. Beebe, *Integrity*, 19.
18. Beebe, *Integrity*, 91–92.
19. Stein, Murray. *Solar Conscience Lunar Conscience*. Wilmette: Chiron, 1993.
20. *PP,* 915.
21. *LG,* 534–535.
22. *CW* 14:¶ 634.
23. *PP,* 669.
24. *PP,* 658.
25. *PP,* 664. This is precisely what Whitman said everybody was so fascinated by when they encountered Emerson's personality: "His usual manner carried something with it and sweet beyond description. There is in some men an indefinable something which flows out and over you like a flood of light, as if they possessed it illimitably, that their whole being suffused with it. Being, in fact that is precisely the word. Emerson's whole attitude shed forth such an impression . . . never a face more gifted with the power to express, fascinate, maintain." Richardson, *Emerson: The Mind on Fire*, 530–531.
26. *LG,* 535.
27. *LG,* 336.
28. *CP,* # 303.
29. *LG,* 210.
30. *LG,* 482.
31. In another conversation with Traubel, we learn that Whitman believed that Emerson

had predicted correctly that he was in fact the American bard the new nation had been calling for: "I remember Emerson said to me in one of our talks: 'You have won far more plaudits, have many more friends, Mr. Whitman, that you are aware of; you will be patient I know; the world will come to your way in the end because you have put it in your debt and such obligations are always acknowledged and met.' The gentle Emerson. He would lay his hand on my coat sleeve when he was about to say something; touch me sort of half-apologetically as if saying, if I may be permitted!" Traubel, *With Walt Whitman in Camden*, 4: 413. Quoted in: Richardson, *Emerson: The Mind on Fire*, 530.

32. *PP,* 659.
33. *LG,* 483.
34. *LG,* 248. It was established earlier that Spiritual Democracy is based on the quaternity, not the trinity. Trinitas here refers to Whitman's three stages of democracy: political, economic, and religious.
35. *LG,* 275.
36. *PP,* 949.
37. *NUPM,* 4:1555.
38. *LG,* 483.
39. *LG,* 482.
40. *LG,* 390.
41. *LG,* 388.
42. *PP,* 932.
43. *PP,* 962.
44. *PP,* 964.
45. *PP,* 970.
46. *PP,* 980.
47. *PP,* 981.
48. *PP,* 982.
49. *PP,* 983.
50. *PP,* 1003.
51. *NUPM,* 6:2097.
52. *PP,* 661.
53. *PP,* 657.
54. Schmidgall, G. *Walt Whitman: A Gay Life.* New York: Dutton, 1997: 79.
55. Beebe, *Integrity*, 32.
56. Beebe, *Integrity*, 17.

11. *Moby Dick:*
The Evolution of a New Myth for our Times

1. This chapter comes from a talk given to the Personal Theology group at the Universalist-Unitarian Church of Kensington, California, on January 8, 2012. Martha Helming was moderator.
2. Sometimes such myths are described as archetypal, implying that they have achieved a level of collective significance that transcends the cultures from which they emerged.

3. *MD*, 7.
4. *MD*, 53–54.
5. In his 1855 preface to Leaves of Grass Walt Whitman wrote: "THE AMERICANS, of all nations at any time upon the earth probably have the fullest poetical nature" (*American Bard*, 9–10). I would like to suggest that Whitman's and Melville's visions are as vital today as they were during the Civil War, and will continue to be in the future, because of the particular focus in the present world situation right now on democracy: the need for new unifying myths during a time of cultural crisis and call for worldwide change. By 1861, both Melville and Whitman had found their voices as poets of religious Democracy. I've explored what Whitman means by Spiritual Democracy in Drum Taps in part 1 of this book, and the same could be done by examining Melville's meanings in *Battle Pieces and Aspects of the War*, to show how relevant his notions are in that book and demonstrating how his visions of Spiritual Democracy may be applied to current sociopolitical and cultural issues, such as the notions of religious equality, Nature's God, and same-sex marriage during the war. I can only suggest here that Melville and Whitman both found their callings as poets during the Civil War, and hint at how the Succession War became the umbilicus, the center, around which their entire works turned, for my aim in what follows will be limited to the task of trying out the meanings of *Moby Dick*.
6. *MD*, 496–497.
7. *MD*, 497.
8. *MD*, 498.
9. *MD*, 498.
10. *MD*, 499.
11. *MD*, 498.
12. *MD*, 596.
13. *MD*, 499.
14. Taylor, E. *William James on Exceptional Mental States: The 1896 Lowell Lectures.* Portsmouth, NH: Jetty House, 2010: 117.
15. Taylor, *William James on Exceptional Mental States*, 118.
16. Taylor, *William James on Exceptional Mental States*, 129.
17. *MD*, 183.
18. Stuckey, S. *African Culture and Melville's Art.* New York: Oxford University Press, 2009: 81.
19. *MD*, 6.
20. *MD*, 549.
21. *MD*, 551.
22. *MD*, 551.
23. *MD*, 550.
24. *MD*, 551.

12. HERMAN MELVILLE: THE QUEST FOR YILLAH

1. *Correspondence*, Vol. 14: 106.
2. Taylor, *William James;* Jung, *CW* 14:¶ 780.

3. *CW* 14:¶ 781.
4. Finkelstein, D. *Melville's Orienda*. New York: Octagon, 1971: 204.
5. Melville, H. *Correspondence*, Vol. 14: 106.
6. *MVT*, 663.
7. *CW* 14:¶ 769.
8. *CW* 14:¶ 769.
9. *MVT*, 1252.
10. *CW* 14:¶ 768.
11. *CW* 14:¶ 770.
12. Stuckey, *African Culture and Melville's Art*, 18.
13. Herrmann, S. "Colloquy with the Inner Friend: Jung's Religious Feeling for Islam." *Jung Journal: Culture & Psyche* 3, no. 4 (2009): 123–132.
14. Jung, *Memories, Dreams, Reflections*, 238–244.
15. *MVT*, 859.
16. Melville, H. *Correspondence*, Vol. 14: 106.
17. Melville, H. *Correspondence*, Vol. 14: 106.
18. *MVT*, 1022, 1023.
19. Finkelstein, *Melville's Orienda*, 219.
20. *MVT*, 1256.
21. *MVT*, 1213.
22. *MVT*, 1214.
23. *MVT*, 1215–1216.
24. *MVT*, 1094.
25. *CW* 14:¶ 778.
26. *CW* 14:¶ 778.
27. *CW* 14:¶ 782.
28. *CW* 14:¶ 785.
29. *CW* 14:¶ 787.
30. *CW* 14:¶ 788.
31. *MVT*, 1256.
32. *MVT*, 1257.
33. *MVT*, 1257, 1258.
34. *MVT*, 1282.
35. *MVT*, 1291.
36. *MVT*, 1291.
37. *MVT*, 1291–1292.
38. *MVT*, 1298.

13. Toward a Hypothesis of the Bi-Erotic

1. Melville, "Hawthorne and His Mosses," Vol. 9: 239–240.
2. Melville, "Hawthorne and His Mosses," Vol. 9: 239.
3. Melville, "Hawthorne and His Mosses," Vol. 9: 241.
4. Melville, "Hawthorne and His Mosses," Vol. 9: 243.

5.   Melville, "Hawthorne and His Mosses," Vol. 9: 244.

6.   Melville, "Hawthorne and His Mosses," Vol. 9: 244.

7.   Melville, "Hawthorne and His Mosses," Vol. 9: 247.

8.   Melville, "Hawthorne and His Mosses," Vol. 9: 247–248. Let it be clear to the reader that I am not trying to position America's poet-shamans as superior to Shakespeare, or any other national poet of stature; my point is that Melville, Whitman, and Dickinson all knew they were onto something "new" in the realm of spiritual ideas, and this was the source of their literary genius: their vocations to transmit to the world of letters a notion of Spiritual Democracy as a vein of pure gold that can potentially change the world, if it can be translated transnationally, into a One-World dispensation of the unity of all races, in a language of the human heart.

9.   Melville, "Hawthorne and His Mosses," Vol. 9: 248.

10. Melville, "Hawthorne and His Mosses," Vol. 9: 248.

11. Melville, "Hawthorne and His Mosses," Vol. 9: 249.

12. Melville, "Hawthorne and His Mosses," Vol. 9: 252.

13. *MVT,*

14. *MVT,* 1203.

15. *MVT,* 1203.

16. *MVT,* 1258.

17. Safransky, R. *Schopenhauer and the Wild Years of Philosophy,* Cambridge, MA: Harvard University Press, 1987: 198.

18. Safransky, *Schopenhauer and the Wild Years of Philosophy,* 132.

19. Melville, H. *Redburn,* Vol. 4: 225.

20. Melville, H. *Redburn,* Vol. 4: 339–340.

21. *MVT,* Vol. 9: 593.

22. Fiedler, L. *Love and Death in the American Novel.* Illinois State University: Dalkey Archive Press, 1960: 382.

23. *MD,* 470.

24. Melville, H. *Correspondence,* Vol. 14: 212.

25. Walls, *The Passage to Cosmos,* 29.

26. For an in-depth analysis of the homoerotic imagination, see Herrmann, S. "Walt Whitman and the Homoerotic Imagination," *Jung Journal: Culture and Psyche* 1, no. 2 (2007): 16–47. *Culture and Psyche,* Vol. 1, No. 2, pp. 16–47.

27. Ellenberger, *The Discovery of the Unconscious,* 447.

28. Ellenberger, *The Discovery of the Unconscious,* 466, 467, 460.

29. Ellenberger, *The Discovery of the Unconscious,* 447.

30. Ellenberger, *The Discovery of the Unconscious,* 450.

31. Ellenberger, *The Discovery of the Unconscious,* 447, 448.

32. Olson, C. *Call Me Ishmael.* Baltimore, MD: The Johns Hopkins University Press, 1947: 39, italics mine.

33. Ellenberger, *The Discovery of the Unconscious,* 448.

34. In my book *Walt Whitman: Shamanism, Spiritual Democracy, and the World Soul,* I hypothesized two coniunctios that constitute a bi-erotic structure of human wholeness in the world soul; each may be inclusive of "lower" and "higher" copulation imagery.

These combinations are made possible by Whitman's breakthrough to the psychoid dimension of human sexuality in 1860, even if he does not state them explicitly: 1) male-female/female-male coniunctio: heteroerotic; and 2) male-male/female-female *coniunctio:* homoerotic. I suggested further that bi-erotic marriage symbolism is an archetypal-developmental phenomenon of experience belonging to the individuation of all people, and it is the poet's job to make these marriage possibilities known by means of amplification through metaphorical imagery. As further evidence for this hypothesis, I discuss the "portraits" of same-sex marriage that were brought to light by Ed Folsom in his essay "Whitman's Calamus Photographs." These photos (fourteen in total) contain what Folsom refers to as images of Whitman with four different young men in a "wedding pose." These photographs were all kept well hidden by Whitman and his closest friends to protect him from accusations of homosexuality. In each of the portraits with the four friends—Peter Doyle, Harry Stafford, Bill Duckett, and Warren Fritzinger—Whitman is said to be "cross-posing" in "traditional wedding poses of an old man/bride/groom" married to a "young man/groom/bride." Folsom, E. "Whitman's Calamus Photos," in *Breaking Bounds: Whitman & American Cultural Studies,* New York: Oxford University Press, 1996: 205. In my view, the bi-erotic includes all dimensions of relatedness along the spectrum defined by the poles of spirit and sex and does not preclude the presence of love in all of them. The difference, then, is between lust and love.

35. Melville. H. *Pierre or The Ambiguities.* Edited and with an introduction by Henry A. Murray. New York: Hendricks House, 1962: 254.

36. Parker, H. *Herman Melville: A Biography.* Baltimore, MD: The Johns Hopkins University, 1996: 846, 847.

37. Olson, *Call Me Ishmael,* 52.

38. Melville, *Correspondence,* Vol. 14: 213.

39. Melville, *Redburn,* Vol. 4: 225.

40. Melville, H. *Clarel: A Poem and Pilgrimage in the Holy Land,* Vol. 12, The Writings of Herman Melville The Northwestern-Newberry Edition. Evanston, IL: Northwestern University Press, 1991: 225.

41. Melville, *Clarel,* Vol. 12: 226, 227.

42. This letter has been lost to history.

43. Seelye cited in Wilson, J. *The Hawthorne and Melville Friendship.* London: McFarland, 1991: 193–194.

44. *MVT,* 1022, 1023.

45. Kerényi. C. *Dionysos: Archetypal Image of Indestructible Life.* Bollingen Series. Princeton, NJ: Princeton University Press, 1976: 75.

46. Melville, *Correspondence,* Vol. 14: 212–213.

47. Kerényi, *Dionysos,* 277.

48. *CW* 16:¶ 454.

49. Wilson, *The Hawthorne and Melville Friendship,* 19.

50. Wilson, *The Hawthorne and Melville Friendship,* 21.

51. Wilson, *The Hawthorne and Melville Friendship,* 38.

52. Melville, "Hawthorne and His Mosses," Vol. 9: 240.

53. Melville, "Hawthorne and His Mosses," Vol. 9: 240.
54. Seelye cited in Wilson, *The Hawthorne and Melville Friendship*, 198.
55. *Correspondence*, Vol. 14: 212–213.
56. Wilson, *The Hawthorne and Melville Friendship*, 172.
57. Wilson, *The Hawthorne and Melville Friendship*, 184.
58. Wilson, *The Hawthorne and Melville Friendship*, 29–30.
59. Melville, *Clarel*, Vol. 12: 313–473.

14. *MOBY DICK* AND THE TRICKSTER

1. Jung, *CW* 18:¶ 563.
2. Radin, P. *The Trickster: A Study in American Indian Mythology.* New York: Schocken, 1956: xxiii–xxiv.
3. Radin, *The Trickster*, 164.
4. Radin, *The Trickster*, 165.
5. Radin, *The Trickster*, 166.
6. *MD*, 499.
7. *MD*, 500.
8. Radin, *The Trickster*, 168.
9. Van Gennep, A. *The Rites of Passage.* Chicago, IL: The University of Chicago Press, 1960: 130–139.
0. Melville, H. *White Jacket.* Vol. 5, *The Writings of Herman Melville.*Evanston, IL: Northwestern University Press, 1849/1970: 395.
11. *MD*, 455–456.
12. *MD*, 57.
13. *MD*, 58.
14. *MD*, 200–201.
15. *MD*, 459–460.
16. Eliade, *Shamanism*, 153.
17. Olson, *Call Me Ishmael*, 46.
18. "Flowers in such a world as ours? / Who is the god of all these flowers, ? / Signor Didymus, who knows? / None the less I take repose, / Believe, and worship here with wine / In vaulted chapel of the vine / Before the alter of the rose." Melville, *Clarel*, Vol. 12: 313.
19. *LG*, 246.
20. Ryce-Menuhin, J. *Jung and the Monotheisms: Judaism, Christianity, and Islam.* London: Routledge, 1994: 1, 90.
21. Jung, C. G. *Nietzsche's Zarathustra.* Vol. 1, *Notes of the Seminars Given in 1934–1939.* Edited by James Garrett. Bollingen Series. Princeton, NJ: Princeton University Press, 1988: 493.
22. Herrmann, S. "Colloquy with the Inner Friend: Jung's Religious Feeling for Islam." *Jung Journal: Culture & Psyche* 3, no. 4 (2009): 123–132.
23. Melville, H. *White Jacket.* Vol. 5, *The Writings of Herman Melville.*Evanston, IL: Northwestern University Press, 1849/1970: 151.

24. Paul Giles; cited in Levine, R. S. *The Cambridge Companion to Herman Melville*. Cambridge, UK: Cambridge University Press, 1998: 235.
25. Herrmann, S. "The Visionary Artist: A Problem for Jungian Literary Criticism." *The San Francisco Jung Institute Library Journal* 16, no. 1, 1997.
26. *MD*, 126.
27. Ladinsky, D. *The Gift: Poems by Hafiz the Great Sufi Master*. New York: Penguin, 1999: 1.
28. Ladinsky, *The Gift*, 33.
29. Ladinsky, *The Gift*, 57.
30. Ladinsky, *The Gift*, 36.
31. Ladinsky, *The Gift*, 39.
32. Ladinsky, *The Gift*, 57.
33. Ladinsky, *The Gift*, 65.
34. *MD*, 4.
35. *CW* 11:¶ 392.
36. *MD*, 478, italics mine.
37. *CW* 9.1:¶ 267.
38. *CW* 9.1:¶ 256.
39. *CW* 11:¶ 395.
40. *MD*, 481, italics mine.
41. *MD*, 7.

15. The Marriage of Sames: "A Bosom Friend"

1. *MD*, 10.
2. Finkelstein, *Melville's Orienda*, 94.
3. *MD*, 14.
4. *MD*, 15.
5. *MD*, 16–18.
6. *MD*, 20.
7. Finkelstein, *Melville's Orienda*, 94.
8. *MD*, 23.
9. *MD*, 24.
10. *MD*, 469–470.
11. Fakhry, *An Interpretation of the* Qur'an, 1–2.
12. *MD*, 498.
13. *MD*, 499.
14. *MD*, 498.
15. *MD*, 25.
16. Philbrick, N. *In the Heart of the Sea: The Tragedy of the Whaleship Essex*. New York: Penguin, 2000.
17. *MD*, 56.
18. *RCC*, 90.
19. *RCC*, 95.

20. *RCC*, 17.
21. *RCC*, 208.
22. *RCC*, 102.
23. *RCC*, 109.
24. *MD*, 28.
25. *MD*, 28–29.
26. *MD*, 30.
27. *MD*, 31.
28. *MD*, 122.
29. *MD*, 6.
30. *MD*, 7.
31. *NUPM*, 1:73.
32. Herrmann, S. "Melville's Portrait of Same-Sex Marriage in *Moby-Dick*." *Jung Journal: Culture & Psyche* 4, no. 3 (2010): 65–89.
33. *CW* 9.1¶ 256.
34. *MD*, 21.
35. Melville, *White Jacket*, Vol. 5:151.
36. Personal communication from Beebe, 2000.
37. Wilson, *The Hawthorne and Melville Friendship*, 38.
38. Ladinsky, *The Gift*, 46.

16. *Moby Dick:* The Characters Behind the Names

1. *MD*, 3.
2. *MD*, 118–119.
3. Melville, *White Jacket*, Vol. 5:267.
4. *MD*, 122.
5. Melville, *White Jacket*, Vol. 5:169.
6. Finkelstein, *Melville's Orienda*, 232.
7. *CW* 11:¶ 713.
8. *MD*, 62.
9. *MD*, 90.
10. Richardson, *Emerson: The Mind on Fire*, 4.
11. *PP*, 1144, 1145.
12. James, *The Varieties of Religious Experience*, 280.
13. Richardson, *Emerson: The Mind on Fire*, 96.
14. Richardson, *Emerson: The Mind on Fire*, 5.
15. Richardson, *Emerson: The Mind on Fire*, 406, 407.
16. Richardson, *Emerson: The Mind on Fire*, 423, 424.
17. Richardson, *Emerson: The Mind on Fire*, 493
18. Finkelstein, *Melville's Orienda*, 164.
19. Lawrence, D. H. *Studies in Classic American Literature*, New York: Viking, 1961: 171.
20. *MD*, 43.
21. *MD*, 47.

22. *MD*, 340.
23. *MD*, 53–54.
24. *MD*, 461.
25. Parker, *Herman Melville: A Biography*, 817.
26. *MD*, 54.
27. *MD*, 51.
28. *CW* 5: 654.
29. *MD*, 88.
30. *MD*, 135.
31. Matheissen, *American Renaissance*, 443.
32. *MD*, 108.
33. *MD*, 101.
34. *MD*, 239.
35. Melville, *The Confidence-Man*, Vol. 10. Evanston, IL: Northwestern University Press, 1856/1984: 140.
36. Melville, *The Confidence-Man*, Vol. 10, 142.
37. Melville, *The Confidence-Man*, Vol. 10, 144–150.
38. *MD*, 89.
39. *MD*, 88.
40. *MD*, 147.
41. *MD*, 203.
42. *MD*, 625.
43. *MD*, 121.
44. *CW* 15:¶ 88.
45. Jung, C. G. *C. G. Jung Letters*. Edited by Gerhard Adler. Vol. 2, 1951–1961. Bollingen Series. Princeton, NJ: Princeton University Press, 1953: 17–18.
46. Melville, *Correspondence*, Vol. 14: 196.
47. Thompson, *Melville's Quarrel with God*, 20, 21.
48. Eliade, *Shamanism*, 68.
49. *MD*, 219.
50. *MD*, 475.
51. *MD*, 135.
52. *MD*, 88.
53. *MD*, 236.
54. *MD*, 78.
55. Finkelstein, *Melville's Orienda*, 230.
56. *MD*, 236.
57. *MD*, 482.
58. *MD*, 611.
59. *MD*, 7.
60. Dimock, W. *Empire for Liberty: Melville and the Politics of Individualism*. Princeton, NJ: Princeton University Press, 1989: 117.
61. Finkelstein, *Melville's Orienda*, 152.
62. *MD*, 236.
63. Finkelstein, Melville's Orienda, 230.
64. Finkelstein, Melville's Orienda, 94.
65. Olson, Call Me Ishmael, 39.

17. The Fall of the Dictatorships
as Portrayed in *Moby Dick*

1.   *CW* 18: 1661.
2.   *MD*, 135.
3.   *MD*, 182.
4.   *MD*, 237.
5.   *MD*, 471.
6.   *CS1*, 23, 33.
7.   *MD*, 471.
8.   *RCC*, 9.
9.   *MD*, 58.
10. *CW* 6: 325.
11. *LG*, 639.
12. *LG*, 540–542.
13. Jung, C. G. and S. Freud. *The Freud/Jung Letters*. Bollingen Series. Princeton, NJ: Princeton University Press, 1974: 293.
14. Jung, *The Freud/Jung Letters*, 294.
15. Jung, *The Freud/Jung Letters*, 294.
16. Melville, Hawthorne and His Mosses," Vol. 9:248.
17. *MD*, 58.
18. Melville, *Correspondence*, Vol. 14:192.
19. Friedman, M. *Problematic Rebel*. Chicago, IL: University of Chicago Press, 1970: 52.
20. *MD*, 542.
21. Joseph Henderson, personal communication, January 10, 2004.
22. *MD*, 237.
23. *CW* 11:¶ 9.
24. *CW* 11:¶ 6.
25. *CW* 11:¶ 9.
26. *CW* 11:¶ 10.
27. *CW* 11:¶ 11.
28. *CW* 11:¶ 44.
29. *CW* 10:¶ 386.
30. *CW* 10:¶ 388.
31. *CW* 10:¶ 397.
32. *CW* 10:¶ 138.
33. Dimock, *Empire for Liberty*, 117.
34. *MD*, 126, 127.
35. *CW* 5:¶ 45.
36. *CW* 5:¶ 45.
37. *MD*, 7.
38. *MD*, 520.
39. *MD*, 159.
40. *MD*, 541.
41. *MD*, 542.
42. *MD*, 550, 551.

43. *MD*, 584, 585.
44. *CW* 8:¶ 493.
45. *MD*, 584.
46. Goldman, S. *Melville's Protest Theism: The Hidden and Silent God in Clarel.* DeKalb, IL: Northern Illinois University Press, 1993: 175.
47. *MD*, 570.
48. *MD*, 618.
49. *MD*, 618.

18. Metamorphosis of the Gods

1. *CW* 5:¶ 129–130, 170.
2. *CW* 6:¶ 412.
3. *CW* 10:¶ 585.
4. *MD*, 551.
5. *MD*, 551.
6. Finkelstein, *Melville's Orienda*, 232.
7. *CW* 6:¶ 432.
8. *CW* 6:¶ 828.
9. Olson, *Call Me Ishmael*, 52.
10. Olson, *Call Me Ishmael*, 56.
11. *MD*, 590.
12. *MD*, 590.
13. *MD*, 592.
14. *MD*, 590.
15. *MD*, 183.
16. *MD*, 591.
17. *MD*, 281.
18. *MD*, 122.
19. *MD*, 591.
20. Friedman, *Problematic Rebel*, 81.
21. *MD*, 611.
22. *MD*, 593.
23. Friedman, *Problematic Rebel*, 79.

19. The Re-Emergence of the Feminine

1. *MD*, 623.
2. Finkelstein, *Melville's Orienda*, 232.
3. *MD*, 625.
4. Neumann, E. *The Great Mother.* Bollingen Series. Princeton, NJ: Princeton University Press, 1963: 330.
5. Friedman, *Problematic Rebel*, 81.
6. *MD*, 201–202.

7. Islamic men who were more or less homoerotic and who Melville read (Rumi, Saadi, and Hafiz) "invented" the *anima* according to de Rougemont in *Love and the Western World*.
8. *MD*, 349.
9. *MD*, 349.
10. Jung extends his otherwise limiting notions about homosexuality by speaking of the potential "greater personality" that matures by calling him "that inner friend of the soul into whom Nature herself would like to change us—that other person who we also are and yet never can attain to completely" (C. G. Jung, *CW* 9.1:¶ 235). ". . . [T]hat "inner friend so often seems to be our enemy" (C. G. Jung, *CW* 9.1:¶ 237, 238, 258), Jung continues. Now, perhaps more than at any other time in history the inner friend of the imagination is making his presence felt in society as homosexual, as a comrade and lover of world culture, and the twin of democracy. Jung cautions about the projection of the archetype of friendship onto many friends. The Self is man's friend he says "inasmuch as this man is alone; inasmuch as this man projects the self into many friends, the self is never a friend, but an archenemy" (Carl Jung, *Nietzsche's Zarathustra*, I, 699).
11. *Webster's*, 1085.
12. Melville, *Correspondence*, Vol. 14: 141, 160.
13. *MD*, 422.
14. *MD*, 422–424.
15. *MD*, 422–424.
16. Neumann, *The Great Mother*, 90–101.
17. Melville, H. *Billy Budd, Sailor*. New York: Library of America, 1984: 1427.
18. *MVT*, 636.
19. *MD*, 183.

20. Afterword:
A Bi-Erotic Libido Model for the Way Forward

1. *PP*, 792.
2. *PP*, 1352.
3. *CW* 8:¶ 918.
4. *NUPM*, 6:2043.
5. *LG*, 470.
6. *CP*, # 324.
7. *MD*, 623.
8. *LG*, 571.
9. *CW* 12:¶ 36.
10. *CW* 12:¶ 24.
11. *CW* 14:¶ 767.
12. *MD*, 215.
13. *MD*, 219.
14. *MD*, 220.

15. Olson, *Call Me Ishmael*, 39.

16. *MD*, 523.

17. Olson, *Call Me Ishmael*, 50.

18. Melville, *Clarel: A Poem and Pilgrimage in the Holy Land*, Vol. 12, 313, 473.

19. Parker, *Herman Melville*, 817.

20. Parker, *Herman Melville*, 842, 843.

21. Olson, *Call Me Ishmael*, 61, 62, 65.

22. As Dimock has argued in *Empire for Liberty*, Melville displayed a *cultural identity within historical process* and sought, by way of corrective and compensatory social symbols, to confront the worldwide epidemic of "empire building" (Dimock 1989: 5). As I have myself shown in three earlier essays, moreover, Melville attempted to heal the complexes within nations and actually provide through his imaginative writings *solutions* for problems of war and violence between ethnic, political, and religious groups. Given an archetypal reading, and seeing Ishmael as a peacemaker between nations in this book, *Moby Dick* is clearly a myth whose time has come. Let me provide one final example of this. When a five-year-old patient of mine told me that he was having recurrent nightmares about whaling, shortly after September 11, 2001, where the submerged body of Moby Dick and other whales were emerging repeatedly from the sea in his dreams, and how, being instructed by Ahab in hunting whales, he continuously thrust imaginary harpoons into the terrifying apparitions, I was simply flabbergasted and also anguished, by what I was seeing. At the time he came to see me, I was already engaged in writing this manuscript on American poetry that included Melville's works. It was a true synchrony that reminded me that a mythologem like *Moby Dick* is no respecter of age, or even time. It is an archetype that by its very nature is transgressive of such categories. Still, I had to rub my eyes a little to make sure what I was experiencing was true. In my twenty-five years of psychotherapy practice with children, I have never met a child of five or younger other than Jacob who has seen the movie *Moby Dick*. Apparently he had viewed the newest version of the film starring Patrick Stewart as Captain Ahab, at a friend's house. His entrance into my practice occurred in 2002. It was also the year after 9/11, when America was deeply preoccupied with images of titanic inflation. My patient had seen the film shortly after the Twin Towers were destroyed. For a full discussion, see Herrmann, S. "The Emergence of Moby Dick in the Dreams of a Five-Year-Old Boy." *Cultures and Identities in Transition: Jungian Perspectives*. New York: Routledge, 2010.

23. *LG*, 564.

24. *NUPM*, 1:102.

25. *LG*, 322–328.

26. *LG*, 589.

27. *LG*, 537, 539, 540.

28. *LG*, 60

INDEX

M

ABOUT THE AUTHOR

Steven Herrmann's writing is recognized nationally and internationally. He has published over thirty papers and two books, *William Everson: The Shaman's Call* (2009) and *Walt Whitman: Shamanism, Spiritual Democracy, and the World Soul* (2010). He has taught on the subjects of Whitman and Melville at the C. G. Jung Institutes of San Francisco, Chicago, and Zurich, as well as at the Washington Friends of Walt Whitman, UC Berkeley and UC Santa Cruz. Herrmann's expertise in Jungian Literary Criticism makes him one of the seminal thinkers in the international field, and a foremost authority on Whitman and Melville in post-Jungian studies. Herrmann, a poet and Jungian psychotherapist, has a clinical practice in Oakland, California.

SACRED ACTIVISM SERIES

SACRED
ACTIVISM SERIES

Heart in Action

When the joy of compassionate service is combined with the pragmatic drive to transform all existing economic, social, and political institutions, a radical divine force is born: Sacred Activism. The Sacred Activism Series, published by North Atlantic Books, presents leading voices that embody the tenets of Sacred Activism—compassion, service, and sacred consciousness—while addressing the crucial issues of our time and inspiring radical action.

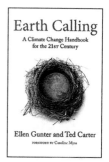

The More Beautiful World Our Hearts Know Is Possible

Charles Eisenstein

Collapsing Consciously

Carolyn Baker

Earth Calling

Ellen Gunter and Ted Carter

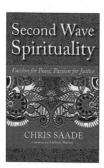

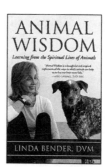

Second Wave Spirituality

Chris Saade

Animal Wisdom

Linda Bender

Pioneering the Possible

Scilla Elworthy

OCTOBER, 2014

The Sacred Activism Series was cocreated by Andrew Harvey, visionary, spiritual teacher, and founder of the Institute for Sacred Activism, and Douglas Reil, associate publisher and managing director of North Atlantic Books. Harvey serves as the series editor and drives outreach efforts worldwide.